Stewart   32.⁰⁰

UNDERSTANDING
BLACK AFRICA

UNDERSTANDING BLACK AFRICA

Data and Analysis of Social Change and Nation Building

Donald George Morrison

with Robert Cameron Mitchell
and John Naber Paden

A WASHINGTON INSTITUTE BOOK

PARAGON HOUSE
NEW YORK

IRVINGTON PUBLISHERS, INC.
NEW YORK

Co-Published in the United States and Canada by

Paragon House   Irvington Publishers, Inc.
90 Fifth Avenue   740 Broadway
New York, NY 10011   New York, NY 10003

For distribution outside the U.S. and Canada, write to Third World Publishing,
151 Stratford Rd, Birmingham Warwickshire, B11 1RD England.

A Washington Institute Book

Library of Congress Cataloging-in-Publication Data

Morrison, Donald George.
    Understanding Black Africa.

    Bibliography: p.
    1. Africa, Sub-Saharan. I. Mitchell, Robert Cameron.
II. Paden, John N. III. Title.
DT352.5.M67 1989   967   88-33052
ISBN 0-88702-043-7

UNDERSTANDING BLACK AFRICA was formerly announced as
ISBN 0-8290-2228-7 (Cloth edition) and ISBN 0-8290-1371-7 (Paperback edition).

10 9 8 7 6 5 4 3 2 1

Cover design: The Bramble Company, Ashley Falls, Massachusetts
Cover graphics: Continuous design applied on Benin bronze sculpture, Nigeria

Printed in the United States of America

Abbreviated Table of Contents

Detailed Table of Contents

Independent Black Africa; land and people of Africa; physical features; peoples of Africa; cultural patterns; historic continuities; early kingdoms and states; the era of Western contact; colonialism; nationalism and independence; social change and nation-building; social change; modernization; patterns of social change; three models of social change; patterns of nation-building; nation-building; three models of nation-building; international issues; pan-Africanism and inter-African relationships; liberation movements in Southern Africa; neocolonialism; U.S. policy in Africa.

Introduction; an example of a cross-national study; a critique of Finer's findings; a re-analysis of the question; how to do a cross-national study; operationalizations; testing

Bibliography; area; population; population growth; Europeans

Bibliography; speakers of dominant language; language density

Bibliography; literacy; primary, secondary and third-level enrollment; rates of change in enrollment; educational expenditures

Bibliography; urbanization rates; capital primacy

Bibliography; radios; newspapers; telephones; commercial vehicles

Bibliography; religious identifiers (traditional, Christian, Muslim); affiliates; independent Christian churches; mission density

Bibliography; parties; voting turnout; independence election; elite and communal instability; armed forces; defense budget

List of Figures and Tables

Preface

This book is the third of a set of three which the authors as directors of the African National Integration Project determined to publish in order to present data on social, political, and economic development in Africa and an analysis of political development using that data. The first book, *Black Africa: A Comparative Handbook* was published in 1972. A second enlarged edition will be published at the same time as this book. Another book, by Morrison, *Conflict and Violence: An Empirical Test of a Theory of Political Learning in African States,* is also forthcoming. This book completes that set and is intended to be of use as a general reference for those interested in Africa and as a supplementary text suitable for undergraduate and graduate courses on contemporary Africa.

As we noted in *Black Africa,* a list of the number of people who have played a role in this work is very long, and we will not enumerate all the contributors to the original project again. But there have been other people and resources made available to us subsequent to the publication of *Black Africa,* first edition. Additional funding has come from a Rockefeller Foundation grant to Donald Morrison at the University of Ibadan. Resources have also been generously provided by the Political Science Department and Computing Centre at Ibadan University, Nigeria—as well as the support of the Institute for Behavioral Research and Computing Centre at York University in Toronto and the Department of Sociology and the Liberal Arts College Fund for Research at the Pennsylvania State University. Further support for Morrison has come from the Political Science Department and the Center for International Studies at M.I.T., the Center for Social Science Computation and Research, and the Department of Sociology at the University of Washington.

Our colleagues have given us support in these various endeavors. The late Prof. B. J. Dudley at Ibadan was of particular help in facilitating work on the manuscript, as were our various colleagues in African studies through their comments on our earlier works.

We have been fortunate in having able research assistants. At Ibadan these were Judy Burdin Asuni, Godfrey Onwaukaife and Emanuel Eboh; at M.I.T., Ann Fryling; at the University of Washington, Douglas Adams—who did much of the art work and pasted up the galleys. Richard de Canio, a doctoral candidate in English who, not familiar with computers, nevertheless mastered a computerized typesetting system and made possible much of the complex typesetting incorporated in this book and *Black Africa,* Hoa Diep Le, Binh Tchau, and Ticha Veoung were of particular importance in the work at the University of Washington. At York University, Samuel Ifejeka; and at Penn State, Patricia Wilson and Linda Wolfe played important roles. Special thanks go to Judith Pullan, Cathy Boccio and Marilyn McIntyre for their very able editorial work and to Diane Boulais and Zenda Krape for typing an earlier "final" draft.

While we feel that the data and discussions in this book are of great importance to building an understanding of the current developments in sub-Saharan Africa, they are not intended to be specifically attuned to day-to-day events. For example, the recurrent droughts in various parts of Africa have dominated the headlines of the world's newspapers and broadcast journalism, as well. The droughts and the associated ecological disasters, much of it permanent, have been a recurrent feature of life in the Sahel, eastern Africa and some other parts of the continent. They have claimed tens of thousands of lives, destroyed much of the social fabric of traditional life in these areas and, concentrated the attention of the world on the horrors that many of Africa's people encounter daily. To the extent that data and analysis of such momentous issues can be handled with data of the type included in this volume, it is to analyze the character and capabilities of African political systems to deal with challenges to the societies of Africa to survive and master their environment. Many analysts argue that resource constraints are only one element in the explanation of the effects of social and environmental change in Africa today. To that extent, this data is oriented towards the explanation and understanding of the social and political systems in these countries and their abilities to deal with such challenge.

The book presents data for a period of about two decades of independent history for most of these countries. More recent data may be gathered by individuals with respect to issues of interest. The journals and other publications cited in the appendices facilitate this process. In addition, more recent volumes in series that were used as sources for the data tables can also be accessed. In general, requirements for closure in order to go through the long writing and publications process meant data was gathered for the period up to about 1981 for events data and one to two years before that for aggregate data. The emphasis is on historic processes, therefore. Some events of particular importance were added beyond those closure dates where it was thought essential to give an accurate picture. Nevertheless, no matter what our cut-off date, it will need augmentation for some research questions and not for others.

xiii

Introduction

In 1972 we published the first edition of *Black Africa: A Comparative Handbook*. *Black Africa* presented for the first time in a single source several hundred social, economic and political aspects of comparative data on 32 independent Black African countries. This large (and expensive) book was intended primarily as a reference work for libraries and as a source of comparative data for scholars. It was apparent to us when we were preparing *Black Africa* that there was also a need for a relatively inexpensive comparative handbook for students of Africa. We envisioned a book which would contain a selection of the data from *Black Africa* (updated whenever possible and now for 41 independent Black African states) along with interpretive essays, maps, and bibliography. Such a book, we felt, would also serve a wider audience than *Black Africa* and be an ideal supplementary text book for Africa-related courses. This book is the result.

In order to achieve these objectives we have divided the book into five parts: (I) Introductory overview of social change and nation-building; (II) Introduction to cross-national analysis; (III) Comparative data profiles; (IV) Introduction to case-study methods; and (V) Country profiles. We also present appendices on other general sources of information and a correlation matrix for the data in Part III. Besides these sections we have interspersed throughout the text a considerable number of maps to illustrate both contemporary and historical phenomena which will hopefully aid the reader's appreciation of Africa. While introductions precede Parts III and V we would in the following like to present an overview of the sections of the book and a guide on how to use them.

The first section, *Part I*, is intended to give a brief overview of contemporary Africa, the historical developments leading up to the present time, and a review of the conceptual framework around which the book is organized. This is not intended as a substitute for the book-length works that cover various aspects of these areas, but as a brief summary of such works. We present various maps in this section to illustrate historical events and trends that are discussed. However, we eschew footnotes and detailed sources, leaving the bibliographic detail to Parts III and V. This essay could profitably be read by any user of the book.

Part II is an introduction to the use of simple quantitative cross-national research techniques. Careful reading of this essay will prepare the reader to use the comparative data profiles in Part III to test ideas the reader may have about how the variables relate to each other (hypothesis testing). For example, are Muslim countries more developed than non-Muslim countries; does a rapid increase in education promote political instability? The cross-national methodology is briefly described and illustrated through a summary and critique of S.E. Finer's study of one-party regimes in Africa. The second section of the essay addresses itself directly to the reader who wishes to test a hypothesis using the data presented in this book. It suggests sources of hypotheses and outlines the steps that are followed in such a study. For a number of readers, Part II will be the most demanding (and perhaps the most rewarding) section of the book and might be deferred until the reader has familiarized himself or herself with the remaining sections.

Part III, Comparative Data profiles, contains overviews, bibliographies, and data on various substantive topics relevant to social change and nation-building. This section is divided into an introduction to the section and nine chapters. The chapters cover: (1) land and population; (2) language; (3) education; (4) urbanization; (5) communication; (6) religion; (7) political development and the military; (8) economic development; and (9) foreign relations. Each of these chapters has a common format. *First*, we present an overview of the subject (e.g., economic development) both conceptual and empirical for Africa. This is only a brief introduction. *Second*, a bibliographic essay sets out the various works on the subject which the reader should consult. This is a key aspect of the section both for an increased understanding of Africa and to familiarize one with the relevant concepts and issues. While these bibliographic essays try to present the most important works, we generally do not report country studies unless they are outstanding examples. Such references can be found in the bibliographies of a later section of the book, Part V.

The *third* section of each chapter in Part III is a presentation of selected variables appropriate to the chapter. Each variable is presented for forty-one countries (or fewer, if data is not available on them all), and definitions, sources, and a short discussion of the data are added. As we note, brevity requires a representative selection, and more data and discussion can be found in *Black Africa: A Comparative Handbook*, second edition, as well as in the sources noted in Appendices I and IV. In some of the tables we provide a variable or measure for different time periods (e.g., 1966 and 1971) so that changes can be observed over time as well as differences across countries. Some users will analyze this data in the format of procedures described in Part II, but others will only be interested in a particular country's value or will use them in a manner discussed in Part IV to choose appropriate case studies. It is hoped that this section will stimulate the appreciation of the changes going on in

Black Africa as well as provide insights into the effects of different approaches to nation-building and mechanisms of social change.

In *Part IV*'s essay we describe another approach to the study of social change and nation-building, the case study. Case studies of one type or another are the most common type of study undertaken by students for term papers as well as by scholars who write books and articles on Africa. In this essay we present a brief review of the various types of case studies, including their advantages and disadvantages and some of the procedures and examples of doing each type. It is important to emphasize that the most satisfactory types of case study involve *comparisons*. Therefore, the methodological considerations presented in the essay on cross-national research in Part II are an indispensable background to the case study research strategy. Readers who have some experience in doing research may wish to skip this chapter.

The last part of the book, *Part V*, provides selected information on each of the countries reviewed in this book. There are four headings under which data is presented. Some of the data which had already appeared in an aggregate form in Part III is presented here in detailed form. More detailed information is available in the second edition of *Black Africa*. The four headings are:

I. Basic Information (size, population, exports, etc.)
II. Elite Political Instability Patterns
III. Country Features Worthy of Special Study
IV. Selected Bibliography

Guide to the Use of the Book

Since this book is designed as a guide and resource for the study of Black Africa, it is not intended that it be read from cover to cover, but to be consulted as relevant. Most readers could read the overview of Part I with profit and should familiarize themselves with the general structure of the book. A review of the section on the case study, Part IV, could precede reference to specific country chapters in Part V, although this is not necessary. Part V can be directly consulted for information or bibliographic citations on specific countries. Individual data points for countries can also be found in Part III, Comparative Data Profiles.

For those interested in full comparative studies, a study of the material in Part II should be undertaken. Part III can then be read in areas of interest. Typically, a reader might refer to a particular chapter in Part III, such as urbanization or political development, for bibliographic citations, data, or the brief introduction to each chapter. It is envisaged that references to particular countries or subjects will be the most common reference to the book.

The other major use will be to refer to the maps that are throughout the book. Either a particular country's map, or a map related to the substantive areas referred to in Part III, or some of the historical maps of Part I may prove of considerable use to readers.

While the data and bibliographies are the latest available as of the writing of this book they will become less useful as time goes on. However, much of the data sources used are published periodically, so a variable of interest often can be updated by reference to later editions of the source of the original data. The major journals as listed in Appendix IV have book review sections which can be referred to for the most recent publications.

About The Authors

Donald George Morrison holds a joint appointment in the Harvard University Office of Information Technology and the Boston University African Studies Center. He has held faculty appointments at M.I.T., Northwestern University and York University, Canada, where he was Director of the Methods & Analysis Section, Institute of Behavioural Research. He was also Director of the Center for Social Science Computation Research at the University of Washington and was Director of the Computing Center at the University of Ibadan, Nigeria. He received his Ph.D. in Political Science from M.I.T.

Robert Cameron Mitchell is Senior Staff Sociologist at Resources for the Future. He has held faculty positions at Northwestern University and Swarthmore College. He received his Ph.D. in Sociology from Northwestern University.

John Naber Paden is Clarence J. Robinson Professor of International Studies at George Mason University. He was previously Director of the Program of African Studies and Professor of Political Science at Northwestern University. He received his Ph.D. in Political Science from Harvard University.

PART I

AN INTRODUCTION TO SOCIAL CHANGE AND NATION-BUILDING IN BLACK AFRICA

The major topics around which this book is organized are the broad and fundamental ones of social change and nation-building. Social change refers to the processes whereby the basic institutions, values, and behavioral patterns of a society are reoriented in new directions. Nation-building involves the creation of political order, the creation of economic, social and political linkages within a state, and the growth of a common sense of national identity and culture by its population. After an introduction to the concept of Independent Black Africa this chapter presents a brief overview of the geography, culture, and history of the continent. This is an essential background to the consideration of change and nation-building which forms the remainder of the chapter.

INDEPENDENT BLACK AFRICA

As of now, over fifty states on the continent of Africa are members of the United Nations. This does not include Namibia. Of the African member states of the United Nations, we have excluded from this book the Arab states of North Africa (Morocco, Algeria, Tunisia, Libya, and Egypt), the white-dominated Republic of South Africa, and the island states of Cape Verde, Mauritius, Sao Tomé, and Comoros. The reason why the states of northern Africa are omitted from our comparison here is primarily because they have had very different pat-

terns of historical development from the states of independent Black Africa and also because data have been more generally available on these areas than on Black Africa. The Republic of South Africa is omitted because the Black peoples of this country have yet to become independent, and we have restricted our comparison to independent states except for the inclusion of Namibia which is illegally occupied by South Africa. The 41 states which remain comprise the complete list of independent Black African continental states plus Madagascar. This is what we mean by independent Black Africa or Black Africa throughout this book.

The timing of Black Africa's independence is of importance in comparative analysis. In 1956 the Anglo-Egyptian Sudan became independent. In 1957 Ghana became the first all-black state to achieve independence. In 1958 Guinea became the first state in French Africa to demand and achieve independence. Most of the other states in West and Equatorial Africa, including the Belgian Congo (now Zaire), became independent in 1960 while most of the states in English-speaking East and Central Africa followed suit in the first six years of the 1960's. The delay of independence in East and Central Africa was due to the presence of European settlers in several of the states, and to the unsuccessful attempt to coordinate the timing of independence so as to encourage greater political unity among the East and Central African states. Thus,

1

Figure 1.1   Political Map of Black Africa

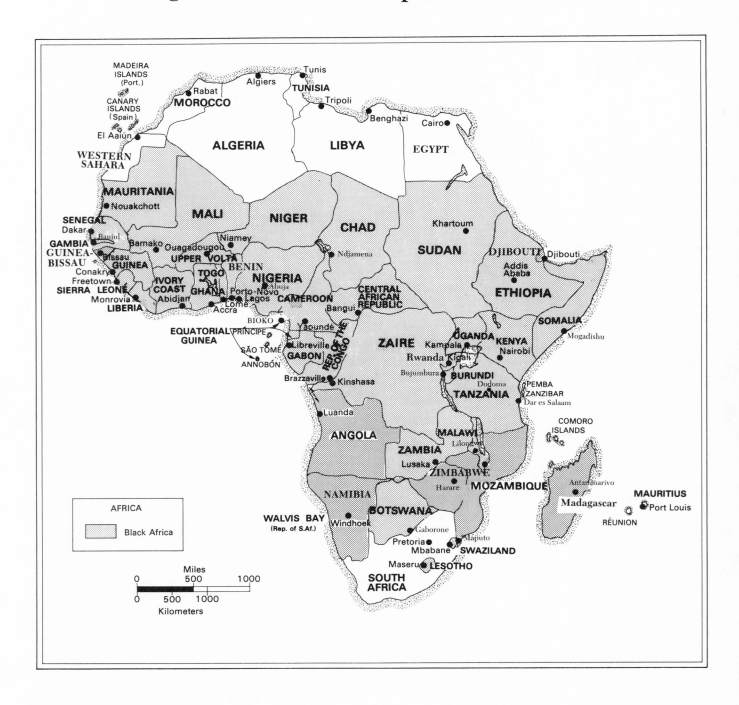

during the decade of 1956 to 1966, 30 states in Black Africa became independent. Significantly, two states were never formal colonies: Ethiopia and Liberia. The remaining states became independent in the years 1968-1980. The criterion of "independence" is regarded as significant not merely in a legal sense, but because whatever the arguments for neo-colonial influence and continued economic dependency, the fact of sovereignty has produced demonstrable changes in political, economic, and social organization and development within African states.

LAND AND PEOPLE OF AFRICA

The continent of Africa has an area of about 11.5 million square miles. This is almost as much as the land mass of China and the Soviet Union combined. The continent is compact, with relatively few natural harbors. The map in Figure 5.1 shows the large river systems of the Niger (West Africa), the Zaire (formerly the Congo in West-Central Africa), the Nile (North-East Africa) and the Zambezi (East-Central Africa) which give Africa the greatest water power potential in the world. Figure 1.2 shows how much of the continent is a plateau surrounded by a narrow lowland strip along the coast.

Figure 1.2   Relief

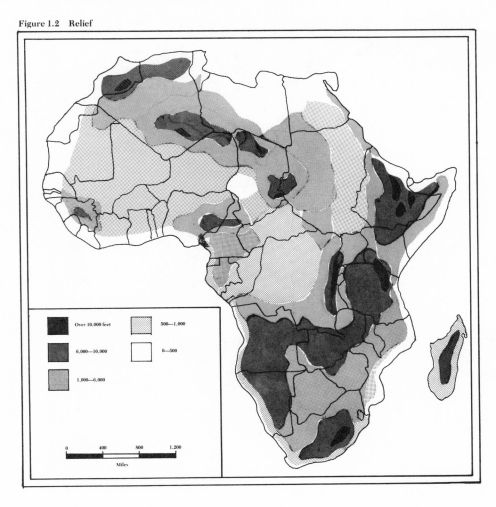

Over 10,000 feet

6,000—10,000

1,000—6,000

500—1,000

0—500

0   400   800   1,200

Miles

Figure 1.3   Major Vegetation Zones of Africa

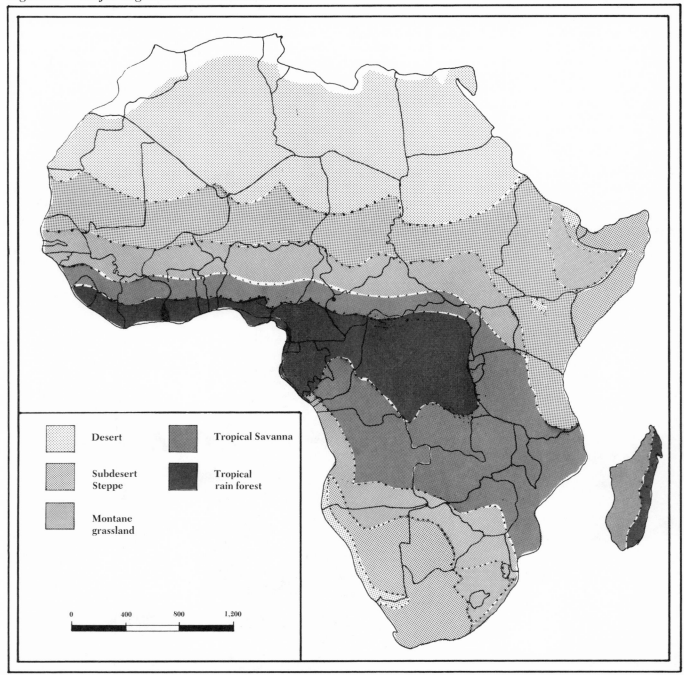

Desert

Subdesert
Steppe

Montane
grassland

Tropical Savanna

Tropical
rain forest

0   400   800   1,200

There are five major ecological zones in Africa. The most widespread of these zones is the grassland savanna which includes wooded areas and open plains. Most of inland West Africa, East Africa and South Africa consist of savannaland. Second, is the rain forest zone. In these areas there is a high annual rainfall and heavy tropical growth. The major tropical rain forest in Africa extends from Southern Nigeria through Zaire to the East African highlands. Rain forests are a relatively small portion of the total continent, but it has been this area which has often been used to stereotype Africa as "a land of jungles." To some extent this stereotype is perpetuated by the fact that along the coastal rim of much of West Africa there is a thin stretch of rain forest vegetation. Since many of the capital cities of West Africa are on the coast, this may give the visitor an impression of dense vegetation which is, in fact, not typical of West Africa. See Figure 1.3.

The desert zones are the third major ecological zone. Most prominent is the Sahara Desert between the savanna in West Africa and the Mediterranean zone in North Africa, but in addition there is the Namib Desert in South-West Africa and the Kalahari Desert in south-ern Africa. Beginning in 1970 and lasting to 1974, successive years of drought struck the savanna belt which stretches 4,000 miles across West to East Africa. Figure 1.4 shows the affected area. Besides threatening millions of people with starvation, the delicate ecological balance of the area has been severely altered. As a consequence, the Sahara Desert has marched southward (up to 60 miles in 1973 according to one source) into the marginal area known as the Sahel, from the Arabic word meaning shore; huge Lake Chad was divided into four ponds; and vast areas became deforested. Similar phenomena have occurred around the world on the same latitude suggesting to meteorologists that a basic shift in the world's weather patterns, perhaps the result of a slight cooling of the earth, may be the cause. If this is so, what appears to be a serious but temporary catastrophe may involve a major permanent ecological change which will require significant adaptive changes in a number of what are already among the poorest countries in Black Africa. While the rains did return, the area as well as other parts of the continent have been affected by variable weather patterns throughout the last decade.

**Figure 1.4   The Sahara, Sahel
and the Area of the African Drought**

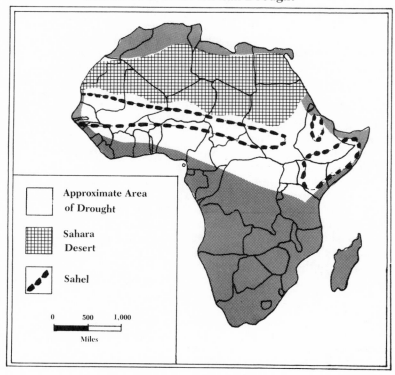

Fourth, is the Mediterranean zone which includes both the north and south tips of Africa. Temperatures here are cooler than in the savanna zones although the vegetation is similar. Fifth, are the highlands of Africa, including portions of Ethiopia, Uganda, and most of Lesotho. In these areas, the climate is cool, and the altitude may average between 8,000 and 12,000 feet. Overall, therefore, most of Africa is savanna grassland, with a rain forest belt extending through the middle of the continent, with deserts in both northern and southern Africa, with Mediterranean zones on the coastal areas of northern and southern Africa, and with occasional highlands in eastern and southern Africa.

Archeologists have found skeletal remains in East Africa which seem to indicate that the ancestors of modern man were dwelling in that area approximately two million or more years ago. The evolution of these human-like beings is subject to much speculation but it is clear that Africa may be regarded as one of the cradles of mankind. The uniquely human mode of adaptation to environmental situations was the use of culture or learned behavior such as tool making and language. Human beings as we know them today probably began to emerge at least as early as 35,000 years ago and the physical features of contemporary populations in the world probably evolved during this fairly recent period.

The question of physical features has always had both scientific and political implications. From a scientific point of view, race is a *biological* concept in which genetic inheritance is determined by selective adaptation to environment and by cross-fertilization of gene pools. From a political point of view, physical differences have often become cultural symbols of community differences, especially where such physical differences are preserved by in-group marriage patterns.

Modern geneticists do not divide people into categories such as white, brown, yellow, or black. Rather, given the fact that each individual carries approximately 100,000 distinct genetic traits, geneticists are more interested in the statistical distribution of combinations of these gene traits. It is social differences, and often prejudices, which select certain of these traits and attach social, economic, or political significance to them. Whatever scientific or popular racial categories may emerge, there is *no evidence* to indicate that any particular racial category is superior to any other in the ability to generate and maintain cultural systems.

In Africa there have been a number of physical adaptations to the environment. A prevailing feature throughout the continent is dark skin color, which seems to be an adaptation to high temperatures. Thus, dark skin encourages cooling and prevents oversynthesis of vitamin D. Within Africa, however, there is a wide range of differences in skin color and most populations in North Africa have brown rather than black skins. The two basic patterns in Africa in terms of stature and build include: (1) shorter, stockier persons, usually characteristic of the rain forest ecological zones; (2) taller, slimmer, more narrow-featured individuals, characteristic of the savannalands and deserts. In both cases, these features may be regarded as adaptations to environment.

With regard to cross-fertilization of genetic traits in Africa, the Nile Valley corridor, on a north-south axis, and the Sudanic Belt corridor, on the east-west axis, have been melting pots of human populations for as far back as human history bears evidence. In eastern Africa, particularly in island or coastal areas, there seems to have been considerable contact with both the Mediterranean world and the Far East. The people of Madagascar, for example, are clearly a mixture of south Asian and African backgrounds.

As far as the political and social significance of physical characteristics in Africa goes, the prevailing pattern is one in which *cultural* and *language* boundaries are *far more significant* than racial boundaries. This pattern changed to some extent during the period of European incursion into Africa, since many of the European cultures brought with them, or rapidly evolved, theories of racial distinctiveness. Partly for this reason, the social and political implications of race are more clearly seen in southern Africa and parts of East Africa, where there were large populations of European settlers, rather than in West Africa where there have been relatively few European communities of any size. The Portuguese experience in Africa, however, has been different from most of the other European communities in that the Portuguese actively encouraged racial intermarriage, while at the same time they enforced cultural distinctiveness.

Peoples of Africa

The peoples of Africa historically have been organized in societies possessing a common sense of identity and sharing a common culture. There are more than one thousand language groups in Africa (see Part III., Chapter 2, and Fig. III, 2.1 for a further discussion of language) and many but not all of these language groups have had some form of internal social cohesion and identity and are therefore ethnic groups as well. Some ethnic groups in Africa are very large, for example the Hausa, Yoruba and Ibo peoples of Nigeria, each with a population of more than ten million. On the other hand, many of the ethnic societies in Africa are very small, some with memberships of less than 10,000.

The term 'ethnic' refers to a type of group identification which is viewed as fundamental in establishing 'we-they' relations, and within which kinship metaphors are often used to describe the nature of the relationships, which are diffuse rather than specific. Since ethnicity is an identity based on social definitions, it is important to note that it may, and does, change over time, or according to situation.

Figure 1.5   Distribution of Ethnic Groups in Southern and Eastern Africa

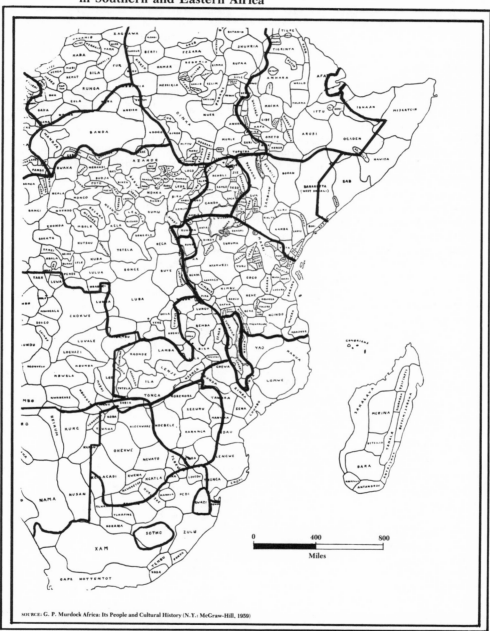

SOURCE: G. P. Murdock Africa: Its People and Cultural History (N.Y.: McGraw-Hill, 1959)

In the past, the ethnic societies of Africa were commonly referred to as "tribes." We prefer to substitute "ethnic group" for "tribe" because tribe has come in popular usage to connote the pejorative notion of "primitive," and to imply a static rather than dynamic view of these societies. Because social definitions vary according to time and to context, it is impossible to produce the authoritative "map" of the ethnic societies of Africa. A useful attempt at mapping by George Peter Murdock, however, is contained in a partial version in Fig. 1.5.

Since in traditional (defined as pre-colonial for convenience) society some ethnic identity groups lived in close proximity to each other, and may even have shared a common economic system, the concept of 'pluralism,' which refers to the existence of two or more ethnic groups which interact within a defined context, may be applied. This is especially true of the great kingdoms and empires which were based on ethnic pluralism. In such situations, there is a division of labor between ethnic groups, and often social stratification will follow ethnic lines. Overall, the prevailing mode of inter-ethnic interaction in Africa was cooperative rather than conflictful, except in the slave-trade areas. Colonial systems were pluralistic, of course, and modern African nations are complexly stratified in terms of both ethnicity and class.

Cultural Patterns

Ethnic societies in Africa are often distinctive in terms of their cultural patterns. This includes not only style factors, such as mode of dress, but more basic patterns of organized social life, such as patterns of marriage and succession, political authority, and economic specialization. Thus, some groups such as the Akan of Ghana, who practice matrilineal descent, regard women rather than men as the basic actors in society, especially with reference to marriage, kinship, and succession. Other groups, such as the Ibo of Nigeria, regard men and women to be equal in many aspects of life. Still other groups, such as the Hausa of Nigeria, regard men to be the primary units of social linkage. (See Fig. 1.6 for distribution of rules of descent in Africa.)

There are wide variations in the forms of political authority and structure in Black Africa. Some societies such as the Tiv of Nigeria, traditionally do not recognize any centralized authority. Other groups, such as the Tutsi of Rwanda and Burundi, the Amhara of Ethiopia, and many other African societies, have highly centralized political systems. In between these two extremes of centralization and decentralization are societies such as the Yoruba of Nigeria which combine principles of chieftancy with

Figure 1.6   Distribution of Rules of Descent

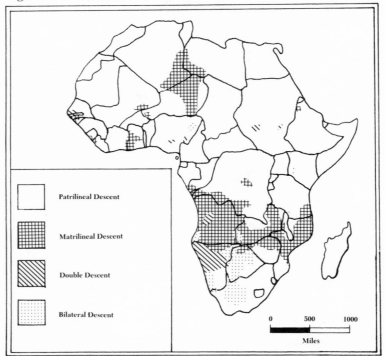

Patrilineal Descent

Matrilineal Descent

Double Descent

Bilateral Descent

0   500   1000

Miles

principles of representative democracy, notably elected councils.

With regard to economic specialization, a minority of African societies have concentrated on animal husbandry, particularly cattle raising, moving nomadically with seasonal changes. The Masai of Kenya and the Bororo Fulani of West Africa are two prime examples of this pattern. Most African traditional societies are identified with particular types of settled agricultural activities and live in villages. Still other groups, like the Yoruba, have come to be identified with urban life, and in many cases, with the occupations of trading and commerce.

The above observations on cultural variation within African ethnic society on matters of social, political, and economic organization should not mask the fact that there are underlying similarities as well as differences. The focus on family life and kinship, the close relationship in most cases of leaders to citizens, the lack of a written language, and the pre-industrial nature of economic specialization characterized most of the traditional societies of Africa. Most African peoples (the Amhara of Ethiopia are a notable exception) were at the tribal rather than the peasant level of social organization.

The significance of traditional cultural variation and similarity and the history of ethnic interaction, both cooperative and conflictful, are very much related to the contemporary problems of social change and nation-building in Black Africa. All of the states we examine are plural societies with the exception of Botswana, Lesotho, Swaziland, and Somalia. The average number of *major* ethnic cultural groupings per country is at least four. Problems of nation-building ranging from language policy in schools and mass media, to threats of civil war are often related to patterns of ethnic pluralism and competition within the new state.

HISTORIC CONTINUITIES

Early Kingdoms and States

The earliest known states in Africa were located in the Nile Valley. In about 3200 BC the Pharaoh Menes united lower and upper Egypt and the period of pharaonic rule began. One of the vassal states in the middle Nile region of Nubia revolted during the eighth century BC and established the kingdom of Kush, which conquered Egypt and ruled the pharaonic empire for about one hundred years. In the seventh century BC, Egypt was conquered by the Assyrians and the Kushitic kingdom shifted far to the south to near present day Khartoum and established a capital called Merowe. The Kushites maintained a flourishing culture and state system until they were conquered in about 325 AD by the Ethiopian kingdom of Axum.

The kingdom of Axum began to flourish in about 100 AD in the northern Ethiopian highlands. This kingdom has continued in an unbroken line of succession until the present day, and forms the nucleus of the modern state of Ethiopia. In about 325 AD the rulers of Axum converted to Coptic Christianity and much of the culture of present day Ethiopia derives from this cultural influence.

The kingdoms and empires of North and West Africa began to emerge on a large scale after the spread of Islamic culture in northern Africa during the seventh and eighth centuries AD. One of the earliest large scale West African kingdoms, however, predated the Islamic era. The empire of Ghana probably arose in the eighth century AD and was not conquered by Muslim invaders from North Africa until the middle of the eleventh century. This conquest of Ghana by the North African Berbers facilitated trans-Saharan trade which was to become so vital to the growth of empires in both North and West Africa. (See Fig. 1.7 for a map of the trans-Saharan trade routes.)

The empire of Ghana began to decline in the twelfth century and was finally taken over by another West African kingdom which conquered Ghana and located their Muslim empire in the middle Niger River region. The two Malian cities of Tombouctou and Jenne were well known as centers of learning and as terminals for the trans-Saharan caravan trade.

During the fourteenth and fifteenth centuries, however, the empire of Mali began to decline and was replaced by another Muslim empire located in the middle Niger region. The Songhai empire, with its capital at Gao, ruled very large areas until about 1600 AD when the Songhai empire was invaded by the kingdom of Morocco.

The three West African kingdoms of Ghana, Mali and Songhai were all based on central authority and large scale bureaucratic systems. The culture and literary life of these kingdoms were based on Arab and Islamic legacies, although all of them incorporated pre-existing West African cultural patterns into their state systems. From about the tenth century until the conquest of the western and central Sudan regions by Britain and France in the early twentieth century, there have been a series of city-state kingdoms and large scale empires in this area. Most of these kingdoms and empires eventually came to identify with Islamic civilization and this legacy persists into the present time. In what is now northern Nigeria, Hausa city-states such as Kano, Katsina, and Zaria have maintained large scale political systems and complex cultural patterns. All of these kingdoms were characterized

Figure 1.7   Trans-Saharan Trade Routes

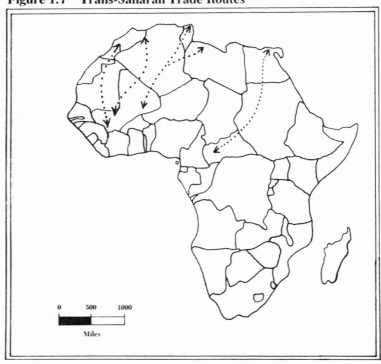

by horse cultures and were located in the savanna land area between the coastal rain forests and the Sahara Desert.

The growth of city states and kingdoms in coastal West Africa probably occurred at a later period. Thus, for example, the Ashanti, of modern Ghana, rose to power in the late seventeenth century. The kingdoms of Benin, Oyo, Dahomey and many others all flourished primarily after the sixteenth century, although in some cases their historical origins are still unknown.

Although there were fewer large scale kingdoms in East and Central Africa than in North East, North and West Africa, these portions of Africa did have significant examples of early kingdoms. In the lake region of present-day Uganda, there were a sequence of kingdoms of considerable importance. Kitara flourished from about 1200 to 1500 AD; Bunyoro, emerged in about 1500 and is today one of the important regions of Uganda; and the kingdom of Buganda emerged in about 1600 and is the largest and perhaps most influential of the present-day kingdoms in Uganda.

In contemporary Zaire, there were important kingdoms which emerged in the fifteenth century including, the Kongo kingdom (1400-1600); the Luba kingdom (1400-1600); and the Lunda kingdom (1450-1700).

Along the coast of East Africa there have been important city-states since about the tenth century. Such states include Lamu, Malindi, Mombasa, Zanzibar, Kilwa, and Sofala. Many of these city-states were based on or influenced by Islamic culture borne by Arab traders.

During this period, many of the remaining portions of Africa were either uninhabited or populated by ethnolinguistic communities of relatively small scale. These small scale, community-oriented societies may have been the predominant feature in this pre-Western era, but little is known at this time about the history of such peoples. (See Fig. 1.8 for the locations of these early kingdoms).

Figure 1.8   Nineteenth Century Africa Before the Colonial Partition

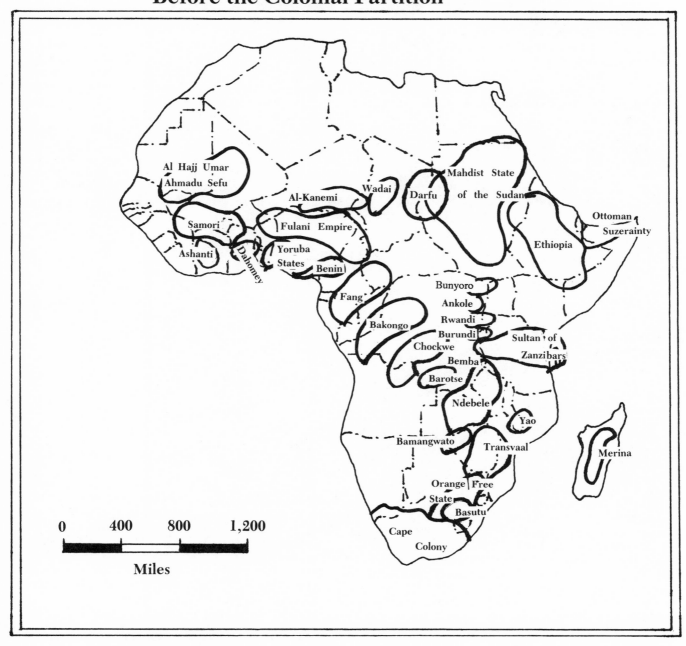

Al Hajj Umar
Ahmadu Sefu
Al-Kanemi
Wadai
Mahdist State
Darfu   of the Sudan
Ottoman
Suzerainty
Samori
Fulani Empire
Ethiopia
Ashanti
Dahomey
Yoruba States
Benin
Fang
Bunyoro
Ankole
Bakongo
Rwandi
Burundi
Sultan of Zanzibars
Chockwe
Bemba
Barotse
Ndebele
Yao
Bamangwato
Transvaal
Merina
Orange Free State
Basutu
Cape Colony

0   400   800   1,200

Miles

The Era of Western Contact

European contact with Africa may by roughly dated from the middle of the fifteenth century, although the Mediterranean world was clearly in contact with parts of coastal Africa from a much earlier period. Portugal was the first European country to embark on the systematic exploration of coastal Africa. In 1487, Portuguese ships rounded the Cape of Good Hope and began to establish trading posts along the East African coast. The period 1600 to 1800 saw most of the other European powers attempt to establish trading posts along the African coast.

During this same two century period, the nature of the trading contacts came to center heavily on slaves. The development of plantation agriculture in the New World had created a heavy demand for labor and the so-called 'triangle trade' emerged whereby slaves were brought to the New World, exchanged for raw materials

such as sugar and cotton, which were then shipped to Europe for processing, and then European manufactured goods were often used in exchange for more slaves in West Africa. (See Fig. 1.9 for the flows in the world slave trade.)

During the nineteenth century, the anti-slave trade movement developed in Europe and America and by about 1850 it was illegal in almost every European and American country to transport slaves across the Atlantic. The enforcement of these new regulations was partly responsible for the emergence of colonialism, in its formal twentieth century sense. British traders hoped to expand their sphere of influence and "legitimate" trade into the interior regions of Africa. In order to do this, expeditionary forces were often required to subdue peoples and to create the "peace" necessary for trade in areas which had been torn by internecine warfare, stimulated by the slave trade.

Figure 1.9   Slave Trade Routes in Seventeenth and Eighteenth Centuries

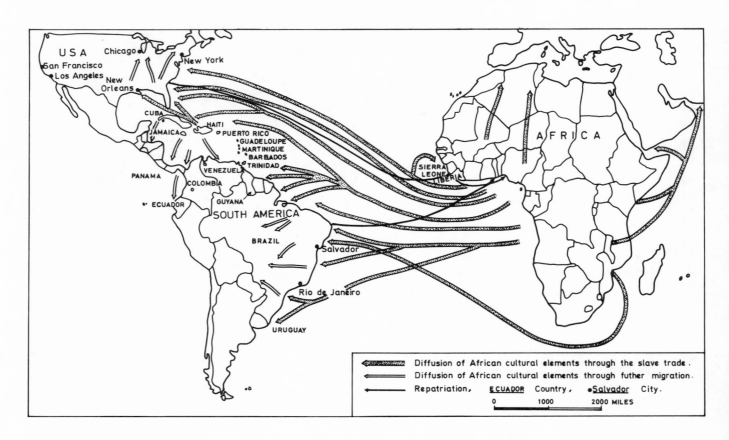

Colonialism

With the industrialization of Europe in the nineteenth century and the emergence of modern nation states, a new importance was attached to Africa in European capitals. Africa was seen to be an area of raw materials, and was a potential market for European goods. It was also seen to be strategically important in the global system of power alliances which was emerging. By 1884, at the Congress of Berlin, most of the European states came together and agreed on the ground rules for dividing up Africa.

During the period 1885 to 1914 the 'scramble for Africa' occurred, and international boundaries were drawn which form much of the present state system in Africa. As a consequence of this scramble, administrative systems were established in the various territories which may be described as 'colonial'. The two major European powers to establish colonial systems in Africa were Britain and France. After World War I, the limited amount of German territory in Africa was redistributed, in most cases to either France or Britain, as 'mandated' territories under the League of Nations.

The period of formal European colonialism in Africa may be dated from about 1900, when most of the interterritorial boundaries were formed, to about 1960, when most of the African states received independence. The impact of this colonial era is still being felt, but scholars are divided as to whether it fundamentally changed the pattern of African life or rather was a surface phenomenon whose impact did not extend beyond a small group of educated elites. (See Fig. 1.10 for a picture of the developing colonial structure from 1830 to 1924.)

The colonial legacy, however, has affected social change and nation-building in several direct ways. At the risk of over-simplifying it is possible to say that British policy was identified with *indirect* rule, in which British governors and residents worked through traditional authorities with regard to taxation, law, succession to leadership, and community boundaries. This system had the effect of encouraging ethnic particularism and traditional cultures, and produced an indigenous elite with strong roots in their home areas. French policy was based on *direct* rule, which established administrative units which cut across traditional boundaries, created a trans-ethnic elite, and used the French language at all levels of administration. Belgian policy was initially one of *company* rule, with private companies responsible for areas of administration, but was later changed to *direct* rule. The Belgians tried *not* to produce national elites; education was limited to the primary level and was geared entirely to semi-skilled occupational training.

Another major difference in colonial policies was with regard to *land*. In most of West Africa, the French and British refused to allocate land to European settlers or companies. By contrast, in parts of British East and Central Africa, plus the Belgian Congo, land was sold to European settlers and companies, causing a number of political problems in the nationalist era.

Nationalism and Independence

In both French and British areas of Africa, Africans were participating in some form of local government from the early decades of the twentieth century. In the 1920's, there developed in British West Africa some reform movements which are probably the earliest nationalist movements in Africa. These movements were based in the coastal cities and were primarily concerned with abuses of the colonial system but partly stimulated by opposition to colonial rule in other areas such as India. Not until World War II, did the idea of national political parties take hold in Africa, and the idea of independence from colonial rule began to gather momentum. In the post-war era, parties emerged in all parts of Africa, but the strongest parties were clearly in West Africa where there was no European settler-class to block demands. During the period 1945 to 1960, African nationalist parties consolidated their support, won local elections, and kept up pressure for more and more Africanization of the governments of their areas. Ghana set the standard in the independence process: by 1951, Dr. Nkrumah had organized the Convention Peoples Party and had won the national elections which paved the way for 'self-rule' and finally independence in 1957. The independence of Ghana stimulated nationalist movements in all parts of Africa. In 1958, the French Fifth Republic was established by General de Gaulle and a referendum was held to determine whether African states wanted independence, or a loose commonwealth type of association with France. Only Guinea voted for complete independence, but the example was powerful, and by 1960 all of the other French colonies in Africa had opted for complete independence.

Until the collapse of the Portuguese empire in 1975, in only one Black African colony, Kenya, was there widespread violence leading to independence. The alienation of land in Kenya, particularly in the Kikuyu areas, had begun to cause problems as early as the 1920's. In 1952, a state of emergency was declared when "Mau Mau" nationalists began sporadic attacks. In 1963, Kenya became independent under the leadership of Jomo Kenyatta, whom the British had detained in prison during most of

Figure 1.10   The Development of Colonial Africa, 1830—1950

1830

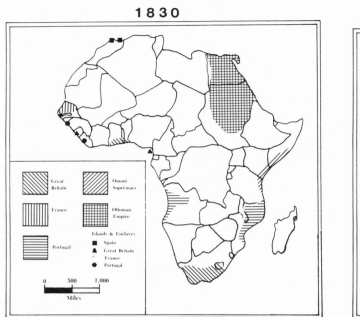

1885

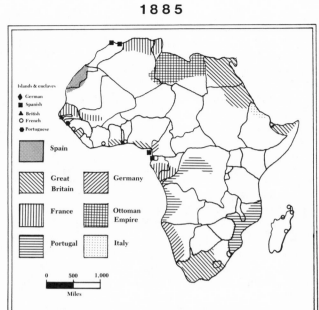

1914

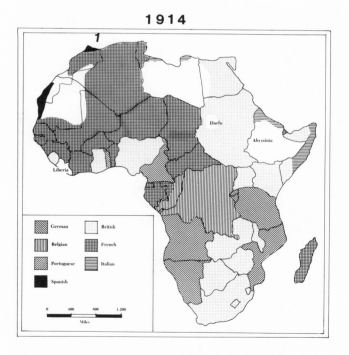

1950

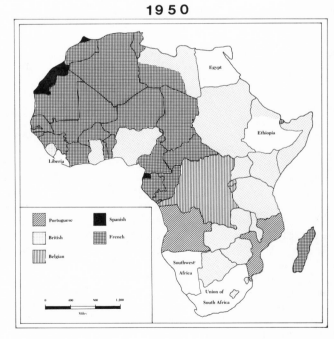

the emergency period on the grounds that he was primarily responsible for Mau Mau.

During the nationalist era, 1945-60, important developments occurred in the growth of party systems, usually multiparty until the time of independence, in the Africanization of the civil service, and the general mobilization of African peoples. The Belgian Congo (now Zaire) is an exception to this, since no preparations were made for independence. When independence came to the Congo in 1960, the state immediately collapsed because of the lack of preparation.

SOCIAL CHANGE AND NATION-BUILDING

Social Change

Social change refers to a difference in a social structure occurring over time. Social structures involve constellations of roles or patterned expectations of behavior about how the occupant of the role (e.g. father) should act toward others (e.g. son). One aspect of a matrilineal descent structure, to give an example, is the expectation that the person who has the role of the maternal uncle to a child will assume certain responsibilities for the child's well-being that the child's father assumes in other types of descent structures. It would be a social change if the maternal uncles in a society came to deny their responsibilities for their sister's children in favor of their own children. Such a change happens in Africa today where peoples having matrilineal structures are converted to Islam which defines the father as the key provider for his children. In this example it is the *nature* of the role being enacted that changes, with behavior eventually reflecting the new set of expectations or norms. Social change may also involve changes in *access* to roles, as where higher educational qualifications are required to become a soldier or a clerk or where women are permitted to become telephone linepeople when previously only men were hired for this occupation. A third type of change involves the creation of *new* roles such as member of parliament or factory lathe operator in a society where these roles did not exist before.

The examples of change that are given above involve particular roles. These roles are found within constellations of roles or social structures. The family, government, civil service, army, corporation are all social structures. Sometimes the word institution is used to refer to these kinds of social structures. Specific role changes have repercussions throughout their institutional context and must be studied as part of a larger whole.

It will be apparent that social change is a general term

that refers to an extremely wide range of behavior. Contrary to some stereotypes of "eternal Africa," African traditional societies have always been experiencing change. Colonialism and independence simply introduced new and powerful factors that have produced new directions of change or accelerated already existing propensities to change. Three general trends of change that have resulted in Africa and the Third World today are the increases in scale, in occupational specialization, and in control over the natural environment.

Increase in scale refers to cooperative behavior or social relations between individuals or systems of individuals, to the point where such individuals or systems are interlinked and often interdependent. An obvious form of increase in scale is the growth of urban centers and urban networks. Urbanization refers to the growth of high density population areas and to the linkage of these urban centers into overall systems of interaction. Within urban centers, individuals may specialize in particular occupations and hence, are dependent on other individuals through exchange or redistribution mechanisms for most goods and services. Often there is also a division of labor between cities. Thus, an inland city may be a railhead for distribution of imported goods and a collection center for agricultural produce, while a port city will serve as a point of entry for imported goods and a point of exit for exported agricultural produce and other goods. The two cities are linked into a single overall system of interdependence. To accommodate such interdependence and linkage, communication systems and transportation systems must be developed which are appropriate to the degree of complexity of the specialization and increase in scale. Such communications might take written or electronic forms, or consist of personal exchanges. Many traditional African societies were relatively isolated although some, such as the kingdoms of Mali and Kongo had extensive linkages across the Sahara in the first case and overseas with Portugal in the fifteenth and sixteenth centuries in the second case.

An increase in occupational specialization usually allows for more efficient production and distribution of goods and services. The ideal type of an efficient system of occupational specialization such as a bureaucracy or assembly line tends to recruit individuals into occupational roles on the basis of merit (universalism) rather than on the basis of family ties (particularism), although in some cases family traditions of specialization have clearly produced individuals who excel in or dominate their occupational endeavors. Limited occupational specialization was found in traditional Africa generally, and to a fairly developed extent in certain societies such as the Yoruba, but nowhere near as much as in contemporary Western countries.

An increase in control over the natural environment requires, as an important threshold, that nature be regarded in terms of cause and effect rather than in terms of supernatural irrationality. This 'scientific' approach is translated into control by means of technology, which is the ability to manipulate natural elements and principles to desired ends. Some degree of technological complexity is necessary to any form of urbanization and increase in scale or occupational specialization. Technology may be associated with economic production, with communications networks, with means of political control, including warfare, and in fact in all aspects of societal life. The education or training required for the effective utilization of modern technology includes not only an understanding of scientific or technological principles, but also principles of social organization which are necessary to accommodate large and complex systems of human interdependence. At the same time, such education should also stress adaptability and innovation since technological change is an on-going process in which learned principles are always being modified to meet new situations. Traditional African societies had achieved iron age technology for thousands of years before the colonial impact although the wheel was not in general use. The introduction of Western education is one of the most important of the changes instituted by the Western impact on Black Africa.

Modernization

The term 'modernization' is widely used as an overall term to refer to the set of social changes currently taking place in the developing nations. Until this point we have deliberately refrained from using this term, however, because it has been so widely misused to oversimplify and distort the experience of the Third World. Before indicating the proper use of modernization as an 'ideal type' we will discuss two of its major misuses.

The first problem with the popular use of the term modernization concerns the role of 'tradition.' Modernization involves the shift from 'tradition' to 'modernity,' of course, but the oversimplified model of modernization assumed that *all* tradition as such was inimical to modernity and therefore had to be 'broken' and discarded in order for modernity to triumph. As scholars have studied the changes in the developing nations during the past several decades, however, there is an increasing consensus that this view is a distortion of a far more complex reality. In fact, although some aspects of tradition do hinder modernity, other aspects do not, and some may positively foster changes towards modernity. Furthermore, there may be different effects of the same element of tra-

dition, such as the extended family, depending on the particular context.

The confusion of modernization with 'westernization' is another serious misuse of the term. Just because the West is modern should not necessarily mean that a) developing nations have to recapitulate the same steps of becoming modern that the West did, nor b) that developing nations have to become like Western nations as they approach modernity. To be sure, the industrialization achieved by the West is a crucial part of modernization but are laissez-faire capitalism, the Western mode of factory organization, the Western form of urbanization, and the nuclear family all necessary marks of modernity? It seems not, especially since contemporary developed nations can import technology which is already developed instead of rediscovering it and can learn from the past mistakes made by the West. It is likely, therefore, that nations can become modern by following relatively differing paths with different resulting types of organization.

This does not mean that modernization and modernity cannot be used in the discussion of the changes taking place in Black Africa. They can but only if they are used as *ideal types*. An ideal type is a concept which deliberately exaggerates some aspect of reality in order to promote an understanding of that reality. Weber's concept of bureaucracy is such an ideal type. He put it forth as an exaggeration or pure type of the form of business and government organization he saw emerging in the nineteenth century in contrast to the previously existing administrative organization by personal retainers which he called patrimonialism. Thus, as an overall summary statement of long term change, one can refer to the shift from patrimonial to bureaucratic forms of administration. Actual organizations, however, are only *more or less* bureaucratic insofar as they approximate the several characteristics which Weber identified as comprising his ideal type. Bureaucracy as an ideal type is a deliberate oversimplification, therefore, whose value is as a summary of long term change and as a yardstick by which to measure the more complex forms which actual administrative organizations take.

In a similar way, modernity as contrasted with tradition is an exaggeration of reality which provides a statement of long term change and a model against which to compare the situation of particular nations. As the sociologist Reinhard Bendix has pointed out, a basic element in the definition of modernization is that it refers to a type of social change that has taken place in the West since the French and Industrial Revolutions of the eighteenth century and involves the notion of leading and following societies. *In this sense* it is appropriate to look to Western nations as exemplars of modernity, and in fact they do serve as more or less explicit models of desirable end states for many developing nations. But the use of modernity as an ideal type makes *no assumptions* about the necessity of imitating the Western nations, nor does it bear implications regarding the necessity of breaking tradition. The analyst using the terms as ideal types is, in fact, most interested in the *differences* between the units he is analyzing and the ideal types. Thus, instead of assuming that the nuclear family is a necessary part of modernity and that societies with extended family patterns must make this change if they hope to become modern, the analyst carefully examines the way the family pattern in the society he is studying helps or hinders aspects of modernization such as consumption, savings and factory labor.

Patterns of Social Change

There are several broad patterns of social change in Africa, determined to some extent by the traditional socio-economic patterns. Unlike Latin America, there has been very little feudalism in Africa (Ethiopia is the major exception), and large scale absentee-landlord farms are virtually non-existent. Unlike India, there is no real caste system. The structure of society in Africa is such that innovations have generally been accepted quickly, and there has been a receptivity to the more universalistic, as distinct from particularistic, forms of culture. The rapid spread of Christianity and Islam are perhaps indicators of this. The preliterate nature of most African societies is sufficient cause in itself for small scale organization, but with independence, the literacy rates have increased dramatically, as has the scale of social organizations.

Rather than being a block to rapid social change, it can be argued that the family structure of African society has facilitated change in many ways. At present, Africa has one of the highest rates of urbanization in the world. (See Fig. 4.1, part III, for a map of urban centers.) Family linkages are important in helping adjust to the city and in providing a social insurance against misfortune. In many areas, voluntary associations have served some of these family functions, but have not replaced the family as the prime unit of social organization.

Industrialization in Africa is proceeding in many areas, especially in coastal cities where processing plants, light industry, and large assembly plants are often located; but overall the level of industrialization is still low and Black Africa currently has an agriculturally-based economy. Most African factory-workers belong to trade unions, which are in many ways similar to those in Europe.

Economic development in the post-independence era has not been as rapid as many African statesmen would like. Economic development entails an assessment of resources, rational planning, building economic and infrastructural bases for development, providing the education necessary to mobilizing populations and facilitating communications (see Fig. 3.1 in Part III for a view of educational development) and increasing productivity to accommodate urbanization.

The differences between particular countries with regard to socio-economic change is partly a matter of government policy, and partly a matter of historic experiences and orientations. This is a further reason why a single model of modernization cannot be applied to Africa. In some countries, such as Guinea, all aspects of socio-economic change are regarded as subject to control by the state. In other states, such as Kenya, there is very little state control. In between are the "mixed" systems, such as Ghana. A close look at these three countries may illustrate some of the differences in approaches to socio-economic change.

Three Models of Social Change

In Guinea, which regards itself as a socialist country, the emphasis has been on general mobilization of the people to involvement in development, less concern with rates of growth than with control of growth, including investment and ownership of the means of production, strict control of education and even urbanization (migration into the capital city is forbidden without a work permit), and a strong emphasis on autonomy rather than dependence on the international economic system. Because of the trade union orientation of the national leadership, most of the occupations in the country are organized, and in a real sense, occupational groups are the basic form of mobilization. Because of the concern with controlled investment, many of the mineral resources of the country, especially aluminum, remain only partly tapped, and investment capital has not been available for rapid economic development.

In Kenya, by contrast, a sort of laissez-faire capitalism has emerged, which does not try to control socio-economic growth, but rather to coordinate it. There is no concerted mobilization of the people, yet urbanization growth rates are extremely high, and in the capital city, several large squatter communities have grown up in the past few years. Large infusions of European capital resulted in rapid economic growth, but such growth is unevenly distributed throughout the country and may not continue into the future even after the world recession of the early 1980s is over. Perhaps more than in any other African country, a working class, a middle class, and a political ruling class are emerging in almost classic terms. One attempt by the government to encourage and control development is the land resettlement policy, whereby land which formerly belonged to white settlers is being leased or sold to African farmers. The net result, however, is to break up large scale agricultural production units, with a resultant loss of efficiency, and without the mobilization of the African farmers. Henry Bienen, in a study of Kenya, does not find the loss of efficiency to be serious, however.

The state of Ghana may be regarded as a "mixed" economy, although during the Nkrumah era it was closer to the Guinea model, and during the Busia era, it was closer to the Kenya model. A composite style emerged in which there were balanced efforts at public and private development. For example, during the Nkrumah era, there was heavy reliance on the Kaiser Aluminum Company to help develop the country's bauxite and hydroelectric resources.

Despite one of the highest levels of education and urbanization, the chaos in the Ghanaian polity over the last two decades has made it one of the sickest economies in Africa and Ghanaians have emigrated in large numbers to other countries.

Patterns of Nation-Building

The young states of Black Africa contain an almost unprecedented number of ethnic and language groups. Adding to these the religious and ecological differences which characterize a number of the countries, and the fact that under colonialism some ethnic groups benefitted from educational and occupational opportunities far more than others, it is not surprising that some African states have had difficulty in establishing political order, national linkages and national identity.

Nation-Building

Nation-building refers to the processes whereby diverse societies, regions and groups within a country are linked into a national state-system. It is a special kind of social change. The process of nation-building in Africa differs from many other areas in so far as national state boundaries were inherited and were often arbitrary. In all cases, however, nation-building involves the establishment of sovereign authority within territorially-defined boundaries. Given the international state system which has emerged in the twentieth century, sovereign national states differ from other political organizations and units such as cities and regions, in being able to control access and egress to the territorial unit, maintain ultimate control over the allocation of resources within the unit, conduct relations with other states, and to support armed forces. Some states may perform these functions through coercive means and some may rely more on the consensus of the citizens. The process of nation-building usually includes at least three components: the establishment of political order, the creation of national linkages, and the growth of a sense of national identity among the population.

The establishment of political order is often taken for granted in functioning nation-states. In pre-integrated states, however, where national linkages and national identity have not yet developed, various sub-national groups may attempt to break away from the nation-state, or may resist the extension of national authority into their areas. Such resistance can take violent forms such as civil war, revolution, rebellion, irredentism, strikes, and riots.

Civil war refers to a situation where one territorial portion of a country or a particular ethnic group attempts to break off completely from the national state or to take over political power in the country. *Revolution* refers to a situation in which a major segment of society tries to replace the existing national authority and take over control of the existing state. *Rebellion* refers to the efforts of a sub-national group to resist the imposition of national authority, but without any necessary plans for separatism. *Irredentism* refers to a situation in which an international boundary divides a homogeneous group and the two or more resulting segments try to reunite in one way or another. A *general strike* refers to a situation where most of the wage and salary earners refuse to work as a protest against specific policies of the national authorities. *Riots* refer to situations which are usually spontaneous and often urban based, in which violence occurs for limited periods of time usually over a specific issue. In all of the above-mentioned forms of political disorder, it is assumed that significant social groups within the country are involved. Such groups may be ethnically based, etc., but all are related to social cleavage and stratification of the national society as a whole. For more detailed definitions of these events see *Black Africa*, second edition, Part I, Chapter 5.

Another form of political disorder has less to do with the society as a whole but rather is concentrated within the national elite itself. An elite group may try to replace those in power through extra-legal means. The *coup d'etat*, or military take-over, is the most common form of inter-elite conflict, although sometimes military take-overs reflect general disorder in the country as much as inter-elite conflict. Disorder at the elite level, however, can jeopardize the existence of the nation state, whether such disorder is caused by political assassination, by coup, or simply by breakdown in relations between national leaders.

The question of political order and disorder is complicated when it comes to moral evaluations. Often a coup against a despotic regime may be regarded with great relief within a country. In some situations it may be that revolution or even secession will result in the greatest good for the greatest number of people. It is empirically clear, however, that during periods of political disorder the survival of the nation-state itself is often at stake, and that nation-building at some point requires the establishment of agreed-upon rules for effecting change without violence or the threat of violence. Thus, while short-term political disorder may be beneficial in terms of political justice, or even nation-building, it is not functional to nation-building if continued over long periods.

The *second* dimension of nation-building is perhaps the most important: the establishment of national institutions and linkages, including political institutions, economic infra-structure, and communications networks. The essence of *'integration'* in any system, is effective interaction of sub-units. When such interaction is institutionalized, that is, put on a regular basis of expected behavioral patterns, a system may be regarded as fully integrated. Even in cases where sub-units retain their identities and even their cultural values, they may agree upon modes of cooperation and interdependence. The idea of interdependence is especially important, as mentioned above with regard to modernization, in the increase in scale of political, economic or social units. The establishment of national linkages implies some coordination of economic, social and political institutions, and this coordination is usually done by the national government, which is often based on a party system, but which may also include military or other forms of non-party rule. (In certain traditional systems, monarchies served this function.)†

The *third* aspect of nation-building is perhaps the most elusive to observe; i.e. the growth of *national identity*. Presumably political order may result from coercive techniques and national institutions may be established by bureaucrats and political elites, without a sense of common destiny being extended into the people at large. National identity does not necessarily entail giving up other forms of social identity (such as allegiance to an ethnic group), but does require a recognition that an individual is a citizen of a particular country and shares a destiny with that country which transcends his more localized loyalties. In a situation where national boundaries are inherited from colonial regimes rather than evolved, the extent of national identity at independence is often limited. National education efforts. including propaganda and use of mass media, are often necessary to instill a sense of national identity. In many cases, national identity increases as a result of external threats or external warfare.

Seven of the Black African states have experienced civil wars in the post-colonial era. In Zaire, formerly the Congo-Kinshasa, civil war broke out almost immediately after independence in 1960 when the Katanga province tried to break away and form an independent state. In Nigeria, the Eastern Region declared a secession in 1967 and adopted the name Biafra. For the next three years (until January 1970), Nigeria was involved in a civil war of major proportions. In the Sudan, the three southern provinces, which are non-Muslim and non-Arabic, were engaged in a protracted struggle for over 16 years to establish some kind of separate state or more autonomoy for the region. In Ethiopia, the Eritrean region began to engage in active separatism after it lost its federal status in the early 1960's. In Chad, the northern Muslim groups were originally disaffected for political reasons, and moved from sporadic instances of rebellion to civil war which only recently has subsided although with continuing conflict from outside sources. The situation in Burundi in about 1965 might more accurately be characterized as a revolution rather than a civil war, since the previously disenfranchised Hutu populations attempted to overthrow the Tutsi ruling elite. The resultant bloodshed, however, had many of the characteristics of a civil war. (See Part III, Fig. 7.2, for a pictorial summary of communal instability from independence through 1982.) The last of the civil wars is the conflict in post-independence Angola between the MPLA party and the UNITA party. This war is unique in the open involvement of the United States and Russia and the combat role played by South African and Cuban soldiers.

The instances of irredentism in Africa have been relatively few, considering the fact that nearly 150 major ethnic groups have been cut by international boundaries. The most problematic irredentism has been the Somali populations in Ethiopia and Kenya who have been in almost open warfare for the last two decades. Most instances of rebellion have been limited, or have been put down successfully. One significant example, however, was the Tiv rebellion in Nigeria from 1960 to 1966.

At the elite level, there have been more than 50 successful coups in over two dozen independent Black African states from their independence through 1982. In some cases, military leaders returned power to civilian governments, in other cases the military has governed through martial law. Some countries have experienced a disproportionate number of successful coups d'etat, including Congo (1963, 1968), Zaire (1960, 1965), Benin (1963, 1965, 1967, 1969, 1972), Ghana (1966, 1972, 1979, 1981), Nigeria (January 1966, July 1966, 1975), Sierra Leone (1967, 1968), Sudan (1958, 1969), Togo (1963, 1967), and Uganda (1966, 1971). The bulk of coups, however, occurred between 1964 and 1968 and may have been a reflection of a breakdown in inherited political systems which may be regarded as marking a transition to more appropriate forms of African government. (See Part III, Fig. 7.5 for the development of military regimes and Fig. 7.4 for a chart of political leadership changes.)

The overwhelming party pattern in the African states has been to establish single party systems. By the end of 1982, only seven of the 41 African states had multi-party systems, fifteen military regimes, and nineteen single-party systems. Some of the one-party systems were veiled military regimes. As recently as 1974, Ethiopia was a monarchy without a party system. It now is a military government without formal parties. (See Part III, Fig. 7.1, for a map of party systems.) Even in multi-party systems, one party has usually dominated. In short, during the independence period there has been an overwhelming tendency toward centralized institutionalized authority. In cases where this centralized authority has been unable to meet demands for economic welfare and political justice, such political institutions have often experienced the kind of instability mentioned above. It is clear, however, that attempts were made to establish national political institutions in most African states. It has been more difficult to establish national economic and social linkages since in most cases this meant a complete reorientation of the socio-economic structures. The experience of the first two decades after independence seems to indicate that the military will continue to play a significant role in the creation and coordination of national linkages.

Three Models of Nation-Building

There have been three different models or strategies of nation-building in Black Africa. These strategies may be seen as follows: (1) those states which regard themselves as multi-national and hence do not try to suppress cultural pluralism; (2) those states which are trying to achieve an amalgamation of peoples into a homogeneous national population; and, (3) those states which accept the fact of cultural pluralism but mediate it organizationally through occupational interest groups.

The nineteen-state system of Nigeria, while not based on ethnic categories, does reflect a sense of cultural pluralism and multi-nationalism within which Nigerian identity may be only one of several important identities. To some extent, citizenship in a particular state has become a substitute identity for ethnic identities, but at the same time it is quite clear that a person from Kano State in Nigeria is Hausa-Fulani, a person from Oyo State is Yoruba, and a person from Imo State is Ibo. Each of the states has a high degree of autonomy, although issues which affect the nation as a whole, including the issue of interethnic relations, are reserved to the federal government. Because Nigeria is a federation with most resources generated by oil revenues to the central government, the principles of centralization and decentralization are arranged in a manner which is less common in other federations. With regard to language policy, although English continues to be the national language, radio broadcasts are made in at least nine African languages and within the various states, a local language may even have official status.

In Tanzania, by contrast, the policy of imposing Swahili as a national language and the explicit prohibition of any kind of ethnic politics or representation clearly indicates a strategy of building Tanzanian identity which transcends any sub-national identity. A former military regime equivalent to the Tanzanian model is Zaire where President Mobutu has developed a vigorous personal style of leadership comparable in many ways to Nyerere in Tanzania. He has encouraged Lingala as a national language, has prohibited any reference to ethnicity in politics, has mobilized people for national political purposes through the single party system, and has tried to create symbols of African identity throughout the country, including changing the names of most towns and even of the country itself.

Ivory Coast represents the third strategy. There, French continues to be the national language and very close linkages are maintained with Paris. The whole idea of a national identity is regarded as less significant than participation in a world society and the needs of economic development. The single-party system is organized at its grass roots level around ethnic or kinship groups but at the national level the major de facto units of representation and power are economic or occupational interest groups. Thus, ethnic identity is not suppressed but it has been replaced with economic identities. The national leadership in Ivory Coast, symbolized by the president, Houphouet-Boigny, is more elitist than in

Tanzania or Nigeria and is typical of many former French colonies in Africa in having developed strongly entrenched national elites who have relatively few linkages with their original culture and languages. At the same time, Ivory Coast is working towards a larger regional unit through its involvement with the *Entente* and it may be that the lack of emphasis on a national identity will facilitate cooperation and perhaps eventually a union with the other *Entente* states: Benin, Togo, Niger, and Upper Volta.

INTERNATIONAL ISSUES

Although the emphasis in this book is on social change and nation-building within each of the particular African states, it is clear that international patterns are very important in these processes. Such international relationships may also be 'issues' in the sense that they are controversial and have a potential for international crisis. Such issues include pan-Africanism and inter-African relations, the problem of liberation in southern Africa, relations with former colonial powers (often described as 'neo-colonialism'), and the issue of U.S. policy in Africa.

Pan-Africanism and Inter-African Relationships

Throughout most of the twentieth century, up until the time of independence, there were small but significant groups of Africans, usually outside of the continent, who were dedicated to the unity of the African continent as a whole. In the nationalist era, prior to independence, much of this pan-Africanist thought was translated into the nationalist movements within the respective countries. After independence, a new era in African political thought and relations may be identified: the rise of national self-interest. Many of the larger federations which had existed during the colonial era, such as the French West African Federation, the French Equatorial African Federation, the Central African Federation, and the East African High Commission, were dissolved into their respective components. At the same time, there was a renewed concern for reorienting the infra structural relations within and between African states to allow for the same kind of linkages which have been discussed above with regard to nation-building. A number of economic unions were formed, including the Afro-Malagasy Joint Organization (OCAM), which included most of the French-speaking African states; the West African Economic and Customs Union; the Entente Council (Ivory Coast, Upper Volta, Togo, Benin, and Niger); the Central African Economic and Customs Union; the Union of

Central African States; and the East African Community. These economic unions were intended to reduce trade barriers and to encourage the free flow of resources.

In 1963 a major political event occurred in the history of pan-Africanism, with the establishment of the Organization of African Unity (OAU). All of the African states became members, and the OAU set up a number of communication channels to discuss problems common to each of the states. The OAU states also affirmed in 1964 their respect for the international boundaries which they had inherited, and they began to express their concern about the decolonizaion of those portions of Africa which were still under European domination. While the OAU continues to be a coordinating body, and hence does not have any real strength independent of its component members, it has continued to aid in the planning of political cooperation and institutional linkages between the various African states, has attempted to mediate in cases where political order has broken down, and has served to foster an African identity. In 1982, however, serious rifts threatened the continued existence of the OAU.

Liberation Movements in Southern Africa

The liberation committee of the OAU has had relatively little direct impact on the national liberation movements in southern Africa although it has served to legitimize and encourage them. The two remaining problem areas as of 1983 are Namibia and the white-dominated state of South Africa. Zimbabwe (formerly Rhodesia) was a major site of a liberation movement until 1980.

The issue of Rhodesia was complicated, partly because of its colonial status. From 1923 until 1965, Southern Rhodesia was a "self-governing" British colony, dominated by local white settlers. In November 1965 the majority party of the white settlers declared Rhodesia to be sovereign and independent from all British control. Unfortunately, such a unilateral declaration of independence left the majority of citizens in the country, i.e., the Africans, in a situation which appeared to be one of permanent domination. Of a total population of about five million, only 250,000 were Europeans. Thus, more than four million Africans were left wihout any significant political representation. The issue of Southern Rhodesia, or Zimbabwe as it is now called, was an a major international issue and was debated in the United Nations, where most of the countries of the world agreed to voluntary economic sanctions against the white-settler regime. Military force, however, was not used, despite the urgings of many African states, and the white-settler regime survived until 1980, aided to a large extent by South Africa and until 1975 by Portugal. There were two Zimbabwean liberation movements, but the one led by Robert Mugabe won the independence election. The other led by Joshua Nkomo is in opposition as of early 1983 and the possibility of civil war exists.

The Republic of South Africa is by far the most overwhelming problem in southern Africa and the most difficult to deal with. The Republic of South Africa has a population of about 28.5 million of which about 68% are African, about 19% are European, and the remainder are Asiatic, mainly Indian, or "Coloreds," i.e. racially mixed. The European community is divided into two major groups: the Afrikaners, of Dutch descent, and the English. The Afrikaners, who are the largest portion of the European community, began to emigrate to South Africa in the middle of the seventeenth century and regard themselves as having a legitimate claim to being located where they are. The Afrikaners, who regard themselves neither as European nor African but distinctive in their own right, have developed a fierce nationalism which is reinforced by their language, their fundamentalist religious beliefs, their status in society, and their cultural patterns.

The political problem in South Africa centers around the fact that the Africans have been disenfranchised and subjected to a harsh set of controls which makes the Republic of South Africa such a totalitarian regime. All movement by Africans within the country is rigidly controlled through pass laws, and most interaction between Africans and Europeans is forbidden. A new development in this policy of *apartheid*, or "separate development," has been the policy of setting aside homelands for each of the distinctive African ethnic groups with the eventual goal of political independence. In some ways these homelands are comparable to the early Indian reservations in the United States and because of their isolation and lack of resources, have little hope of development.

All political resistance movements in South Africa have been suppressed, and the few groups in exile have very little access to political activity in South Africa. A system of informers within the African community makes it extremely difficult for nationalist or liberationist movements to get a foothold within the country. It is partly for this reason that African nationalists place a high priority on liberating the buffer areas between independent Black Africa and the Republic of South Africa as a preliminary to any confrontation with South Africa. During 1971-1972, however, the Republic of South Africa began to recognize its tenuous relations with independent Black African states and also recognized its need to expand its markets to the north. As a result, the government of South Africa began to engage in "dialogue" with some of the independent Black African states including Malawi, Ivory Coast, and Uganda in the hopes of improving relations. It also pressured Rhodesia to negotiate

with its nationalist leaders. Such "dialogue" was dismissed by most of the liberation movements as an attempt to disguise the situation in South Africa and as a way of avoiding a direct confrontation with Black African states. It remains to be seen what effect the South African involvement in the Angolan civil war will have on "dialogue."

Neo-colonialism

The most significant external relations of independent Black African states are not with other African states, nor are they with the problem area of South Africa, but rather they are with the economically developed countries of Europe and North America. Within this latter category, African relations with former colonial powers are clearly most important. Thus, most English-speaking African states are linked up with the sterling zone, and continue to maintain linkages with the "Commonwealth," most French-speaking states continue to remain in the franc zone and maintain very close relations with Paris. Most of the aid and trade of African countries is dependent on the former colonial powers. Within this situation, some of the East-West cold war alliances have been transferred to Africa, and in certain countries, especially Guinea, Nigeria, Zaire, Egypt, and Ethiopia, American and Soviet aid has been competitive in the same way in which it is competitive in the periphery zones of the Communist world. (See Part III, Fig. 9.1, for aid patterns.) While this book will not explore the nature of these international linkages in any detail except in the chapter on foreign relations, it is clear that external linkages are important to the internal processes of social change and nation-building within independent African states. Thus, external aid may very much influence whether infra-structures could be built which would begin to link up other regions within a country. International trade patterns may determine the kinds of agricultural produce or mineral resources, including petroleum, which are taken out of a country, and hence may determine the relative level of modernization within a country, including disparities of economic development within different regions, and also the direction of transportation development, and hence in a very real sense, the development of an interurban system. Those who wish to explore the impact of international relations on internal development are encouraged to pursue the reading in Chapter 8 and 9 in Part III.

U.S. Policy in Africa

Perhaps the most important aspect of U.S. policy in Africa as it affects the process of nation-building, is support for the 1964 OAU resolution affirming the present international boundary system in Africa. At the same time, U.S. policy has encouraged larger regional integration among African states since it was clear that economic development depended in most cases on such economies of scale. U.S. policy in Africa, however, is a relatively recent development since prior to independence all African affairs were handled through the respective European country desks. Perhaps because Africa was not directly involved in cold war activities and because there was relatively little U.S. economic investment in Africa, the general posture of American policy has been to maintain minimal contact and minimal obligations. One significant exception to this during the mid-1960s was the Peace Corp program and the other exception was the U.S. involvement in the Angolan civil war.

There are four pressures which tend to pull the United States into a more active concern with Africa: (1) the opportunities for investment in economic development are great and U.S. business, particularly through the multi-national corporations, is involved in African economic development; (2) major instances of instability in African states sometimes lead to international involvement of the sort which was evident in the Zairean crisis in the early 1960s, the Nigerian civil war, and, most recently and dramatically, in the Angolan civil war; (3) about one-tenth of the population of the U.S. is of African descent and the cultural linkages between North America and Africa will probably increase; (4) the problems of liberation in southern Africa are of such magnitude as to involve virtually all world powers. It is clear that with regard to the issue of South Africa, some Black American groups are becoming increasingly concerned about the situation in southern Africa and have set as a priority the liberation of those areas. As Black-American organizations become more influential in the determination of U.S. foreign policy, important domestic pressure may be brought to bear on both the Senate Foreign Relations Committee and the White House itself. The United States government has participated in the general arms embargo to South Africa. At the same time, many U.S. companies have important investments in the Republic of South Africa. Whether these companies, under pressure from political groups in the U.S., will take an active role in social or political change within South Africa remains to be seen.

PART II

CROSS-NATIONAL RESEARCH:

An Introduction to a Methodology

Introduction

The nine chapters of Part III provide the reader with general introductions to the ecology, demography, cultural complexity, social change, economic and political development, and international relations of contemporary Black African states. These introductions attempt to generalize about the major problems and the outstanding characteristics of these countries. Verbal discussion in each chapter is supplemented by (1) annotated bibliographical information which it is hoped will guide the reader to the most helpful contemporary literature on these subjects, and (2) by 41 tables showing the rank order on each of these variables for each of forty-one Black African countries, and their individual values on a wide variety of variables selected and updated from the larger collection in *Black Africa*, second edition. The purpose of this chapter is to introduce the reader to the methodology of cross-national research,[1] and by so doing, to indicate some of the ways the generalizations stated in this and other books on Africa may be evaluated, and some of the ways data of the kind given in the following section may be used in such evaluations.

Cross-national research, in simple terms, may be defined as the application of scientific methodology for establishing generalizations about human experience on the basis of the systematic comparison of countries as units of analysis. While cross-national research is a somewhat esoteric intellectual activity,[2] and one which may be legitimately criticized from a number of perspectives,[3] as we shall discuss later, it is an appropriate and useful technique if used with adequate caution. We may think that the USA is more democratic than the USSR;

we are told that democratic nations are more stable than non-democratic nations, that more economically developed nations are more democratic than underdeveloped nations, and that ideological differences between countries become less noticeable as they become more economically advanced, etc. Cross-national research is simply a systematic way of assessing the truth value of statements such as these.

Our brief introduction to the method consists of two parts. We first illustrate the method by examining one section of a published article by S.E. Finer and subjecting it to a careful critique. In this exercise we show how the steps of theory, operationalization or measurement, and testing are employed by Finer. We then show how to correct some of the weaknesses in Finer's analysis and use some of the data contained in the *Black Africa* book to retest his hypothesis and to refute Finer's conclusion about the relationship of one party regimes and political instability. The second part of this introduction to the method is a necessarily simplified step by step guide to doing a cross-national study using the kind of data contained in this book. Our expectation is that careful study of this introduction to cross-national analysis will sufficiently equip the novice to go ahead and use the data in this book to test some hypotheses of his or her own.

An Example of a Cross-National Study

In an article entitled "The One-Party Regimes in Africa: Reconsiderations," *Government and Opposition* (1967), p. 491-508, S.E. Finer examines the question of whether or not the establishment of single or single-dominant political parties contributes to the political and economic development of the new countries of Africa. His analysis is a useful example of relatively simple cross-national research procedures and its weaknesses highlight some important aspects of the method.

Finer deals first with the *theory* underlying the arguments of those who propose that single party regimes are advantageous to the development of African states. He points out that advocates of this proposition suggest that the single party regime (1) increases economic development, (2) follows the natural inclinations of the populations of African states, (3) increases the chances of building unified countries, and (4) increases the chances of avoiding political instability. Then Finer attempts to refute each of these propositions in relation to the Black African experience. For the most part he cites only a few specific examples in support of his analysis, but his examination of the last proposition, concerning the relationship between single party regimes and the avoidance of political instability, approximates the standards of scientific hypothesis testing using cross-national comparisons. We will rephrase his analysis of this last proposition to indicate the logic of cross-national research more clearly.

Let us suppose that instead of trying to dismiss the argument about the advantages of single-party regimes in maintaining political stability, *in toto*, Finer had looked first simply at the adequacy of the implicit theory underlying this argument in strictly logical terms. That theory might be formulated as follows:

Axiom 1.   The greater the number of political parties in a country, the greater the amount of economic resources devoted to sustaining political activity in political parties.

Axiom 2.   The greater the amount of economic resources devoted to sustaining political parties the less the amount of economic resources devoted to other activities such as economic development. (Hence a shift of resources from investment to consumption.)

Axiom 3.   The greater the number of political parties in a country, the greater the degree of conflict in the country over the goals of the different political parties.

Axiom 4.   The greater the economic development in countries, the less the ideological division and conflict between different political parties.

Axiom 5.   The greater the conflict between political parties in the country, the greater the likelihood of political instability in the country.

Hypothesis: The greater the number of political parties, the greater the likelihood of political instability.

The rationale for this hypothesis is that multi-party systems not only directly encourage conflict, but they also decrease the probability of economic development and the consequent moderation of inter-party conflict. Now, *if* we felt that this theory was adequate, i.e., we were satisfied about the logical propriety of moving from axioms to the hypothesis, and about the *a priori* truth of the axioms, how would we decide whether or not the hypothesis was true in the observable experience of African countries?

Finer's analysis of this question is based on an *operationalization* or measurement of the variables in the hypothesis as follows. African states are classified according to two nominal, dichotomous variables—(1) whether or not they had experienced a coup d'etat within a specified time period (a measure of political instability), and (2) whether or not they had only one political party at the time of the occurrence of a coup d'état, or at the time of the analysis in the case of countries not experiencing coups d'etat (a measure of a single party state).

Finer then adopts the following *testing*·procedure: if there is a more or less equal probability of experiencing coups d'etat, or of not experiencing coups d'etat, for single and multi-party regimes, then the hypothesis is refuted. Finer asks us to agree that 20 African states were single party regimes either at the time he wrote or at the time they experienced a coup d'etat, and that 15 were multi-party or no-party regimes. He further asks us to agree that 17 of these 35 states had experienced coups d'etat, and that 18 had not. Unfortunately Finer does not specifically name all the 35 countries that he was dealing with, because there were more than 35 countries that he might have selected to deal with from the African continent. We have to take his classification of the countries on his measures by faith. Nevertheless, we can so arrange his data as shown in Table 2.1.

From this data Finer concludes: "The chances that a multi-party state will experience a military coup are just over fifty-fifty; for a single-party state, just under fifty-fifty! In view of the small numbers involved there is nothing between them. So the claim that the single-party state provides greater stability than the multi-party state is. . . false." (p.506)[4]

A Critique of Finer's Study

Now, we may ask, what confidence can we place in Finer's conclusion that there is no empirical reason to

Table 2.1   Party Type and Political Instability for 35 African Nations

	No Coup	Coup d'Etat	Total
Multi-party States	46% (7)	54% (8)	100% (5)
Single-Party States	55% (11)	45% (9)	100% (20)
			(35)

maintain the proposition that single-party states provide greater stability than the multi-party state? Does Finer conclusively refute this particular propostion, and can we conclude more generally that there is no relationship between party systems and political instability? In order to evaluate this question, or any other piece of cross-national research, we have to consider the three cornerstones of the scientific method—theory, operationalization and testing—and evaluate their application in the research before us.

Consider first, the question of *theoretical adequacy.* While Finer is not generally concerned with the theoretical argument, and confines himself to the empirical evaluation of the ideas of advocates of the single-party thesis in its different forms, we may object that his statement of the proposition is too over-simplified to be theoretically adequate. As he himself is at pains to point out, there are no hard and fast lines between single and multi-party states which make much sense. There is at least the African case of the no-party state like Ethiopia, which Finer does mention, and the distinction between two-party states and multi-party states, which Finer does not mention, but which Duverger, one of the principal students of political parties, considers to be the critical distinction in the analysis of the impact of parties on the political stability of states.[5] Furthermore, we might argue, an adequate theory of the relationship between party systems and political development must consider historical evolution of party systems. There is a difference between states which have always had single parties, and those which have had multiple parties superceded later by a single party; and there is a difference between multi-party systems which have had historically insignificant parties with a single dominant party and those which have had numerous significant independent parties. Theoretically, that is, if it is argued that one-party states increase the likelihood of political stability because they reduce the conflict between organized political interests in the society, we must distinguish somehow between multi-party systems that are more or less conflictful .

These questions about the theoretical adequacy of the proposition which Finer investigates relate intimately to considerations of the adequacy of Finer's *operationalization* or measurement. The adequacy of operationaliza-

tions in social scientific research are customarily evaluated in terms of their *validity* and *reliability*. The validity of an operationalization is the degree to which the experience it refers to is the experience symbolized in a proposition. The reliability of an operationalization is the degree to which the experience it refers to is capable of similar description by more than one observer.

With regard to the reliability[7] of Finer's operationalizations we may have little quarrel.[8] It seems reasonable that we will not disagree often as to whether or not a particular state has experienced military intervention in a coup d'etat,[9] or as to whether it has one or more than one political party. The validity of Finer's operationalizations are more suspect, especially if we are not satisfied with the theoretical status of the proposition he chooses to test.

Finer's conclusions and his proposition have to do with the stability-instability of national political systems, and he operationalizes political instability as the experience of military intervention in the form of a coup d'etat which clearly has something to do with political instability. However, can we be satisfied with an operationalization that confines the meaning of political instability solely to the experience of a coup d'etat? Must we agree that all states which have not experienced a successful coup d'etat are stable? Surely it would be fair to insist that unsuccessful coups, plots to overthrow governments by coup d'etat, civil wars, rebellions, revolutions and a host of other possible instances of the breakdown of normal political relationships in a country should also be included as evidence of political instability, and that we need an operationalization which will more adequately reflect the variance among countries in the *degree of instability* of these different kinds and intensities that they experience. And if we call upon Finer to make his theoretical justification of the proposition more adequate by referring to the number of political parties, and the relative distribution of power among political partites, then we shall of course, question the validity of the operationalization of party systems as either single or multi-party nations.[10]

What of Finer's method of testing? Given the operationalization of the proposition, there can be no argument against his procedure. Cross-tabulation is a simple, and appealing procedure for evaluating data to test propositions which we will describe in more detail in a later section of this chapter. While Finer does not need to use them, there are also a number of statistical techniques we can use to systematically assess whether or not a given relationship is greater than would be expected by chance.[11] But although the method of cross-tabulation Finer uses is appropriate to the operationalization of his proposition, there are other ways of operationalizing and testing similar propositions which we can discuss briefly.

A Re-analysis of the Question

We have criticized the over-simplistic nature of Finer's operationalization of political instability. Suppose then that we re-state the proposition to say that *the greater the dispersion of power in the party system of a nation the greater the likelihood of political instability in that nation* and try to test this hypothesis using more adequate measures.

First, let us operationalize the dispersion of power in the party system in terms of three variables:[12] (a) the number of legal political parties in existence in a nation during the period 1957-1969; (b) the proportion of the popular vote received by the ruling party in the election preceding the acquisition of independence in a nation; and (c) the legislative fractionalization in a country which is equal to one minus the sum of the squared proportions of legislative seats held by each party.[13] Data on the first and second of these variables is available in this book and the third variable is in *Black Africa*. Each of these variables gives us an interval measure permitting a wide range of variation between countries. Secondly, let us re-conceptualize political instability as elite instability and communal instability, as we have suggested elsewhere,[14] and use the operationalizations for these variables given in Part III, chapter seven of this book. These operationalizations also give us interval distinctions between the incidence of political instability in different states, based on a detailed accounting of their historical experience be-

tween their dates of independence and 1969.

If we agree that these operationalizations are adequate[15] for an examination of our proposition (and the reader should note that their reliability is likely to be less than Finer's measures, a typical trade-off when more complex measures are used),[16] then we can use the Pearson product-moment correlation as a measure of the relationship between two interval scales. This statistic cannot be explained here,[17] but the reader who is unfamiliar with it should accept for the moment that when the value of this statistic is 1.00 there is a perfect linear relationship between two variables such that the position of a country with respect to one variable can be perfectly predicted from its position on the other, and that when the value of the statistic is zero, there is no predictable relationship between the two variables.[18] When the value of the statistic is positive, we conclude that higher values on one variable predict to higher value on the other and vice versa (a positive relationship), and when the value of the statistic is negative we conclude that higher values on one variable predict to lower values on the other and vice versa (a negative relationship). For our present purposes, we wish to see the degree to which the relationships between each of our operationalizations of the dispersion of power among political parties and each of our operationalizations of political instability are positive and greater than zero. The relevant data is given in Table 2.2.

The data here indicate that there is a consistently positive relationship between these variables, as predicted by our proposition; that is, for example, the greater the number of parties the greater the instability. The data further show that the *strength* of the relationships is moderate but nevertheless not negligible, by the standards of social science, especially when we have allowed a number of possible zero magnitude correlations as tests of our proposition.[19] Figure 2.1 shows one of the relationships graphically. Each dot represents one of the countries. We might conclude, therefore, that there is reason to support the hypothesis that one-party systems promote political stability, and to disagree with Finer's conclusion. We leave to the student the exercise of pointing out further rival hypotheses[20] about the relationship between parties and political instability, and of indicating the deficiencies in the operationalization and testing of three proposition we have just discussed.

How to Do a Cross-National Study

We conclude this section by presenting a very simple summary of the steps a researcher can adopt to carry out his or her own comparative study and an example of such a study using the data available in Parts III and V of this Handbook as well as data from other sources.

Table 2.2   Political Instability Independence to 1969

	Elite Instability	Communal Instability
Number of Political Parties 1957-1969	.46	.35
Legislative Fractional- ization at Independence	.38	.34
Percent Vote Gained by Ruling Party at Independence	-.55	-.62

Figure 2.1   Relationship Between Number of Parties and Elite Instability for 32 African States.

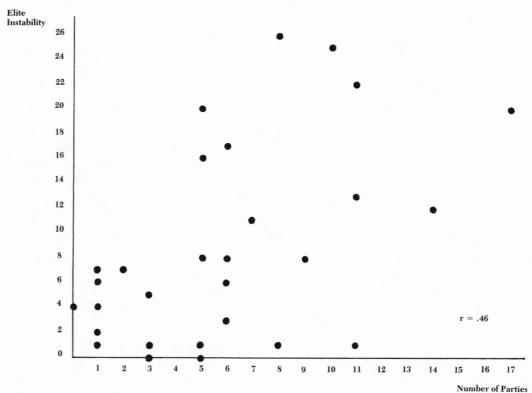

Table 2.3   Summary of Steps in Cross-National Analysis

I.   Theory

a.)Develop propositions that relate two or more variables with each other. These may come from the literature or be based on personal *a priori* expectations.

b.)Try to state the assumptions and propositions to be tested as clearly as possible.

c.)Gather evidence of previous studies on the propostions.

d.)Decide which alternative explanations may be plausible and state them as clearly as possible.

II.   Operationalization

a.)Decide on an appropriate measure or measures for the variables under consideration.

b.)Review sources of data and if they are insufficient, reconsider point IIa for possible alternative measures.

c.)Review possible sources of error in the data.

d.)Collect data.

III.   Testing

a.)Decide on an appropriate statistical method to test the theoretical propositions of Part I above. (e.g., cross-tabulation, correlations, regression, path analysis etc.)

b.)Where possible, utilize multiple operationalizations to assess converging evidence with regard to the propositions.

c.)Carry out statistical evaluations to assess whether the propositions are supported.

d.)Interpret the meaning of the data patterns paying special attention to the cases that do not fit the hypothesized pattern.

Table 2.3 summarizes the steps involved in carrying out a cross-national analysis. The following notes briefly amplify the summary and are directed to those without quantitative research experience who wish to undertake their own comparative study using the data presented in this book and/or other data.

Theory. In deciding on a proposition to test using cross-national analysis the researcher has to draw upon his or her own knowledge of the subject area and/or the published writings on the subject. A certain amount of ingenuity is required in using the existing literature, however, because it is rather rare to find generalizations already in acceptable proposition form even in scholarly books and journal articles. What the researcher sometimes needs to do is to take the implicit assumptions of the author and make them explicit. Perhaps a writer of an article on the impact of colonialism assumes without ever really saying it that colonialism hindered economic development. By making his assumption explicit in the form: the greater the colonial impact on an African country the less economically developed it will be, it is made into a testable proposition.

Another procedure along this line is to take broad or qualified generalizations and make them as specific and logically integrated as possible. Consider the following quote from an article on the relationship between education and modernization:

It has been shown, for instance, that in some post-colonial African societies educational processes generated new aspirations and expectations which could not be fulfilled in the existing social frameworks and consequently, led to frustration, alienation and disruptive oppositionism.[21]

It is possible to develop a set of propositions from this statement such as:

Axiom 1.   In a modernizing country, the more education a person has, the greater his aspirations and expectations.

Axiom 2.   The slower the economic growth of a country, the less the aspirations and expectations of its more educated citizens will be met.

Axiom 3.   The less a person's aspirations and expectations are met, the more frustrated, alienated, and opposed to the existing social order he becomes.

Axiom 4.   The greater the number of frustrated, alienated, and opposition-oriented people in a state, the greater the political instability of that state.

Hypothesis: The greater the imbalance between the educational expansion and economic development of a country, the greater the likelihood of political instability in that country.

With practice the reader will find that it is possible to derive propositions from many different types of scholarly literature. The trick is to draw out the implications of statements and to make them explicit. Since the object is to test the statement to see if it holds up for a given body of data, the statement must be expressed in such a way that it is possible for it to be *falsified*. Therefore, in one sense the task may be viewed as making "extreme" or "unqualified" statements. This does not mean that cross-national hypotheses are necessarily simple minded—the proposition form also permits us to take the complexity of a situation into account. In the example given above the hypothesis might have stated simply that the greater the expansion of education the greater the political instability. But a further variable was added "opportunity" and the hypothesis was stated in terms of the imbalance between educational expansion and economic development. In the end, however, the hypothesis is stated in such a way that it is unequivocal and can be falsified providing, of course, that its variables can be quantified or operationalized.

The notion of alternative explanations is very important. Often a researcher does not consider alternative explanations until he or she finds that the hypothesis is not confirmed and he or she wants to develop another possible explanation. It is better to consider possible alternatives at the time of planning the research paper so that the relevant data can be gathered to test the alternative too, if at all possible.

Consider the following hypothesis: the greater the exposure of African peoples to the influence of Christian missionaries, the greater their economic development. Since Christian missionaries were very active in educational work, an alternative explanation of economic development would involve the growth of education. Other possible alternative explanations of economic development are the number of Europeans resident in a country before World War II and/or the country's resources.[22]

As far as drawing on his or her own knowledge of the subject area goes, even if the researcher has only a limited knowledge of the field it should not be hard to make up some personal *a priori* propositions which can be usefully tested with the existing data. The exploration of such propositions can be an excellent way to learn more about the subject area. In thinking up such propositions the reader should not hesitate to include propositions which seem to be "obviously" true because all too often what seems to be obvious turns out to be problematic when the data are actually examined. And even if the proposition does turn out to be true there may be some interesting cases of countries that do not fit the predictions of the hypothesis as the rest do. These countries are good candidates for the other form of analysis, case studies, which we discuss in a later section of this book. Examples of possible *a priori* propositions are: the longer the effective colonial rule, the greater the economic development of African states; Christian African countries are more developed economically than Muslim African countries; for African states, the greater the struggle for independence, the greater the likelihood of one party rule; the greater the cultural homogeneity of African states, the greater their political stability; and the greater the economic growth of African countries, the greater their rate of urbanization.

Operationalizations. The questions of reliability and validity discussed earlier in our analysis of Finer's article must be taken into account when the concepts in any proposition are measured. Again, ingenuity is needed to devise or discover those measures which: a) satisfactorily measure the concept (have validity), b) are as free from error as possible (have reliability), and c) for which data is available in some form. There are trade-offs involved here. If existing data are used rather than data gathered especially for the specific study that is being undertaken, the validity is likely to be lowered but at a considerable saving in time. Perfection is rarely possible in social research without unlimited funds. What is important is that the researcher recognize the limitations of his or her study and interpret the results with appropriate caution.

For a cross-national study of African nations, there are several sources of existing data available to the researcher where the data is *arranged by variable* for most of the African nations. This book is one such source and a much larger selection of variables is contained in *Black Africa*, first and second editions. The *AID Economic Data Books*, the *UN Demographic* and *Statistical Yearbooks* and the *World Bank Atlas* also contain such data, some of which is contained in *Black Africa*.

A second form in which data on African nations is available is in books which provide reasonably comparable data arranged by country. *Africa 1971*, etc., *Africa Contemporary Record*, *AID Economic Data Book*, *Africa South of the Sahara*, *Europa Yearbook*, *Statesman's Yearbook*, and *The World Christian Encyclopedia* are reference works of this type and most are published in annual editions.

Existing data may be used as is or the researcher may wish to create from the existing data new variables which are more appropriate to the concepts he or she wishes to measure. One obvious example of this is the calculation of a *per capita* measure by dividing a variable such as acres of arable land or GNP by a second variable, the population of the nation. A more sophisticated example would be the operationalization of the imbalance concept in the education and political instability hypothesis. The transformation of a theoretical concept like this into a measure involves a number of decisions, often arbitrary, by the researcher.

In order to operationalize the education/economic development imbalance concept mentioned above, for example, two variables must be combined: a measure of educational expansion and a measure of economic development. Educational expansion, e.g., itself requires the combination of two educational measures at different points in time. The researcher first needs to make a decision as to what level of education--primary, secondary or university--he or she wants to measure. This decision should be based on which level is most relevant to the substance of the proposition, in this case which level would be thought to most affect aspirations and expectations. University level education would probably be the most valid measure if comparable data for two time periods could be found; failing this, secondary level data would probably be adequate. In Part III of this book Table 3.4 gives data for secondary school enrollment per 10,000 population taken from the *U.N. Statistical Yearbook*. Using earlier editions of the *U.N. Statistical Yearbook* a change variable could be calculated. But Table 5.11, in Black Africa, (first edition) presents a change variable which is already calculated: Percent Change in Secondary School Enrollment per Capita 1962-1966. The researcher could either calculate the new variable or use this existing variable for the earlier time, which is a period when many African countries were rapidly expanding educational opportunities in the immediate post-independence period. The researcher could also use *both* measures to see how sensitive the result is to a specific set of measurements, a procedure called multi-operationalization and which we strongly recommend.

For measures of economic development this book, in Part III, presents, in Tables 8.2 and 8.4, Per Capita Energy Consumption and Per Capita GDP among possible measures. If we suppose that a choice is made to use change in secondary school enrollment for 1960-1970 as the educational variable, the GNP 1977 variable would be a suitable measure. In the example below, however, the 1962-1966 variable from *Black Africa* is used out of convenience to illustrate the calculation of the imbalance measure.

We next need to decide how to calculate the imbalance measure. There are a number of ways to do this, but one simple way would be to take the rank order of each country on the GDP variable and to subtract it from the rank order of that country on the enrollment change variable. For example, looking just at the 32 countries considered in the first edition of *Black Africa*, a country like

Gabon which has a rank order of 1 on GDP and a rank order of 20 (rounded off from 19.5) on enrollment change would get an imbalance score of 19, whereas a country like Mauritania which is 1 on enrollment change but 11 (of the 32 countries) in rank on GDP gets a -10. The greater the negative value, it is hypothesized, the greater the imbalance.

Testing. Once having developed the proposition and the measures of its concepts, the remaining task is to arrange the data in the appropriate way to see whether the proposition is supported or not. The techniques used by a beginning researcher for this purpose will depend on the level of training he or she has had in methods and statistics. Competent use of the full range of statistical techniques is highly desirable for sophisticated data analysis, but even if a student has not had statistical training the use of simple cross-tabulations may be used with profit to examine data, and this can be done without the use of a computer because the number of cases involved here (no more than 41 countries) is small. The next several paragraphs are directed to the researcher who has never done data analysis using cross-tabulations and who does not have computer skills.

Table 2.4 takes two tables from the first edition of *Black Africa* and shows how a variable for education and a variable for GNP may be trichotomized for cross-tabulation. Each variable was arbitrarily divided into three categories. As the distribution for primary enrollment is relatively smooth, the 32 countries for which data is available are divided into three approximately equal sized groups. The distribution on per capita GNP was a little different. Looking at the data on GNP we notice that there is a gap between Senegal and Sierra Leone of twenty dollars which suggests a "natural" breaking point between the "high" and the "medium" countries which was used as the dividing line even though it meant that the "medium" and "low" categories have slightly more cases in them than the "high" GNP nations.

A cross-tabulation presents the data on two variables jointly. Therefore, looking at the cross-tabulation in Table 2.5, we see that the top left hand cell contains those five countries which are high on both of the variables while the bottom right hand cell has the six countries which are low on both with the rest of the cells containing the countries which fall into the remaining joint categories. Usually a cross-tabulation table simply shows the numbers of the cases, but in this case, in order to illustrate how the table is constructed, the names of the countries are entered as well. This practice is also useful in that it shows the names of the deviant cases such as

TABLE 2.4 Data Examples from *Black Africa*

TABLE 5.5 Primary School Enrollment per 1000 Population and Total Primary Enrollment, 1966

RANGE = 210.00
MEAN = 81.25
STANDARD DEVIATION = 53.11

POPULATION PERCENT	CUM. COUNTRY	RANK	COUNTRY NAME	VALUE	RANGE DECILE	TOTAL
0.4	0.4	1.0	CONGO (BRA)	221	1	186544
0.8	0.4	2.0	LESOTHO	195	2	167169
1.0	0.2	3.0	GABON	169	3	79162
4.8	3.8	4.0	GHANA	163		1292213
7.3	2.5	5.0	CAMEROON	133	5	713557
16.4	9.1	6.0	ZAIRE	130		1995000
16.7	0.3	7.5	BOTSWANA	124		71557
18.5	1.8	7.5	ZAMBIA	124		473432
19.2	0.7	9.5	CAR	105		148845
24.0	4.8	9.5	KENYA	105	6	1010889
24.5	0.5	11.0	LIBERIA	101		110251
26.4	1.9	12.0	IVORY COAST	98		381452
27.2	0.8	13.0	TOGO	94	7	157548
31.4	4.2	14.0	UGANDA	73	8	564190
33.3	1.9	15.0	MALAWI	71		286753
39.0	5.7	16.0	TANZANIA	63		740991
40.7	1.7	17.0	SENEGAL	61		218795
42.2	1.5	18.5	BURUNDI	57		183366
43.7	1.5	18.5	RWANDA	57		176176
44.9	1.2	20.0	DAHOMEY	55		132690
46.0	1.1	21.0	SIERRA LEONE	52	9	125943
47.6	1.6	22.5	CHAD	51		172485
72.6	25.0	22.5	NIGERIA	51		3025981
74.3	1.7	24.0	GUINEA	46		164119
74.5	0.2	25.0	GAMBIA	42		14218
76.7	2.2	26.5	MALI	35		161605
83.4	6.7	26.5	SUDAN	35		492085
85.7	2.3	28.0	UPPER VOLTA	22	10	107588
87.4	1.7	29.0	NIGER	21		70656
87.9	0.5	30.0	MAURITANIA	19		20000
98.8	10.9	31.0	ETHIOPIA	16		378750
100.0	1.2	32.0	SOMALIA	11		28890

SOURCE: *UNESCO Statistical Yearbook 1968*, Table 2.7. *Rwanda:* 1963 data; *Gambia, Guinea, Mauritania, Senegal, Sudan, Upper Volta:* 1965; *Botswana, Malawi:* 1967.

TABLE 4.4 Per Capita GNP in U.S. Dollars, 1968

RANGE = 260.00
MEAN = 120.63
STANDARD DEVIATION = 65.43

POPULATION PERCENT	CUM. COUNTRY	RANK	COUNTRY NAME	VALUE	RANGE DECILE	
0.2	0.2	1.0	GABON	310	1	HIGH
2.1	1.9	2.0	IVORY COAST	260	2	
2.5	0.4	3.0	CONGO (BRA)	230	4	
4.3	1.8	4.0	ZAMBIA	220		
4.8	0.5	5.0	LIBERIA	210		
5.3	0.5	6.0	MAURITANIA	180	6	
9.1	3.8	7.5	GHANA	170		
10.8	1.7	7.5	SENEGAL	170	7	
11.9	1.1	9.0	SIERRA LEONE	150		
14.4	2.5	10.0	CAMEROON	140		
19.2	4.8	11.0	KENYA	130		
19.9	0.7	12.0	CAR	120	8	
24.1	4.2	13.0	UGANDA	110		MEDIUM
24.4	0.3	15.5	BOTSWANA	100	9	
24.6	0.2	15.5	GAMBIA	100		
31.3	6.7	15.5	SUDAN	100		
32.1	0.8	15.5	TOGO	100		
41.2	9.1	19.0	ZAIRE	90		
42.9	1.7	19.0	GUINEA	90		
45.1	2.2	19.0	MALI	90		
46.3	1.2	22.0	DAHOMEY	80		
46.7	0.4	22.0	LESOTHO	80		
52.4	5.7	22.0	TANZANIA	80		
63.3	10.9	25.5	ETHIOPIA	70	10	LOW
65.0	1.7	25.5	NIGER	70		
90.0	25.0	25.5	NIGERIA	70		
91.5	1.5	25.5	RWANDA	70		
93.1	1.6	28.5	CHAD	60		
94.3	1.2	28.5	SOMALIA	60		
95.8	1.5	31.0	BURUNDI	50		
97.7	1.9	31.0	MALAWI	50		
100.0	2.3	31.0	UPPER VOLTA	50		

SOURCE: *World Bank Atlas 1970. Botswana, Gambia, Lesotho, Rwanda, Somalia:* Estimates are tentative.

Table 2.5   Primary Enrollment by Per Capita GNP for Thirty-two African Countries.

Primary Enrollment per 1,000 population, 1966

Per Capita GNP ca. 1968	HIGH	MEDIUM	LOW	TOTAL
HIGH ($310-170)	*Gabon* 56% *Congo* Zambia **(5)** Ghana Liberia	*Ivory Coast* 33% *Togo* *Senegal* (3)	*Mauritania* 11% (1)	100% (9)
MEDIUM ($150-90)	*Cameroon* 46% *Central African* *Republic* Kenya (5) Botswana Zaire	Uganda 18% Sierra Leone (2)	*Guinea* 36% *Mali* Gambia (4) Sudan	100% (11)
LOW ($80-50)	Lesotho 8% (1)	*Benin* 42% Tanzania Rwanda (5) Burundi Malawi	*Niger* 50% *Upper Volta* *Chad* (6) Ethiopia Somalia Nigeria	100% (12)

Note: italicized countries are former French colonies.

BLACK AFRICA, First Edition (1972).

Lesotho which, contrary to our prediction, is low on GNP but high on primary enrollment. A search may be made for the special circumstances which resulted in this situation.

Once having tabulated the numbers of countries in each category, the next step is to calculate the percentages[23] following the rule of *percentaging in the direction of hypothesized causation*. If the assumption is that wealth permits high expenditures on education one would percent across the rows as is done in this table. Naturally, GNP in 1968 cannot really cause educational enrollments in 1966 but the assumption might be made that ranking on GNP is relatively stable and because 1968 data are the only data available it can stand as an approximation for earlier GNP data. It is much preferred to have the causal variable for an earlier time period if at all possible. In this case the reverse causal assumption might be made—that the educational attainment of nations leads to their economic development. Since ranking on educational data changes fairly rapidly, an adequate test of this hypothesis would definitely require earlier data.

Having the data in a table, the next step is to interpret the data pattern to see if the proposition is supported. Just looking at the distribution of the cases in Table 2.5 suggests that countries high on per capita GNP are also high or medium on enrollment whereas those low on GNP tend to be medium or low on enrollment. The countries that are medium on GNP are split: some are high and an equal number are low on enrollment. If the relationship between the two variables was a strong one, we would expect the majority of the countries that are medium on GNP to be medium on enrollment. The simplest interpretation of this data pattern is that at the extremes, GNP does affect education. If there were more cases it would be possible to make a statistical evaluation of the relationship using statistics such as Chi Square to see how many times out of a hundred one would find this data pattern by chance.

The cross-tabulation in Table 2.5 is a bivariate one. An important aspect of the cross-tabulation method is that it permits the introduction of third (or more, if there are enough cases) variables to see how they influence the original relationship. In this way the researcher can explore the findings to see how alternative hypotheses affect the original relationship. Tables 2.6, a and b, provide an example of this. The question is, is there any difference between the former French and the former British African countries in the relationship of GNP to primary enrollment? In Table 2.5 the former French countries are italicized for ease of identification and Table 2.6a presents the data for them alone. Percentages are given but the number of cases is so small that they should be treated with caution. Comparison of Tables 2.6 a and 2.6 b suggest that there is no real difference between the two sets of countries in the relationship of GNP and primary enrollment; the pattern of the percentages *roughly* duplicates the overall pattern in Table 2.5. Because the number of countries is so small the best procedure in doing third-order cross tabulations is to dichotomize the variables so each cell will have as many possible entries as possible.

Table 2.6a   Primary Enrollment by GNP for Former French Africa.

		Enrollment per 1,000 Population, 1966				
		HIGH	MEDIUM	LOW	TOTAL	
GNP per Capita, ca. 1968	HIGH	(2) 33%	(3) 50%	(1) 17%	101%	(6)
	MEDIUM	(2) 50%	(0) 0%	(2) 50%	100%	(4)
	LOW	(0) 0%	(1) 25%	(3) 75%	100%	(4)
						(14)

Table 2.6b   Primary Enrollment by GNP for former British Africa.

Enrollment Per 1,000 Population, 1966

		HIGH	MEDIUM	LOW	TOTAL
	HIGH	(2) 100%	(0)	(0)	100% (2)
GNP per Capita, ca. 1968	MEDIUM	(2) 33%	(1) 17%	(3) 50%	101% (6)
	LOW	(1) 20%	(2) 40%	(2) 40%	100% (5)
					(13)

Table 2.7   Hypothetical Example of Third Order Cross- Tabulation

	Low Primary Enrollment 1960			High Primary Enrollment 1960	
	GNP 1970			GNP 1970	
	HIGH	LOW		HIGH	LOW
HIGH			HIGH		
Missionary Presence 1930					
LOW			LOW		

The use of third variables enables the researcher to explore a number of competing hypotheses. In an earlier example we mentioned that for the hypothesis, "the greater the exposure to Christian missionaries, the greater the economic development of African countries," the growth of education is an alternative hypothesis. This possibility would be tested, using a third order cross-tabulation, and dichotomous variables. How the data would be ordered in a table is shown in Table 2.7. If missionaries and GNP were equally correlated in countries with high and low levels of primary education in 1960, we would have to reject the alternative hypothesis and conclude that it was the activities of the non-educational missionaries which somehow promoted economic development. The use of third variables is limited only by the research imagination of the researcher and the available data.

Footnotes

[1] We will use the term cross-national in our discussions but all that follows can also be used in the comparative study of other social or political aggregates, or units of analysis, such as regions, cultural or ethnic groups, trade unions, political parties, etc.

[2] For a more complete treatment of cross-national analysis than can be given in this essay see Ted R. Gurr, *Politimetrics* (Englewood Cliffs, N.Y.: Prentice-Hall, 1972) and the essays in Volume I of *Black Africa* second edition.

[3] For a critical discussion of the problems of this method see, Oran Young, "Professor Russett: Industrious Tailor to a Naked Emperor," *World Politics* 21 (April 1969): 468-511, and our discussion in Section A of *Black Africa* second edition. Also see the review article by R. Burrowes, 'Theory Si, Data No!' *World Politics* 24 (October 1972): 120-144.

[4] The reader should note that this information for the entire independence period is available in Part V of this book. A useful exercise would be to evaluate the proposition at different points in time (e.g., 1964, 1968, 1972) or using different bench-marks in time, such as six years after independence; proximity to elections; or recency of coups in other countries.

[5] P. Duverger, *Political Parties* (London: Methuen, 1969).

[6] See Part V for charts of the changes in political party structure for each country from 1957 to 1980.

[7] For a discussion of reliability see Volume I of *Black Africa* second edition, and the books mentioned in Appendix 3 of this book, particularly those works on measurement and scaling.

[8] This is partly because we do not know what they are!

[9] Nevertheless, there will be cases such as Gabon in 1964 or Ethiopia in 1960 where it is not clear how to code the results of the events.

[10] Of course, more complex patterns may be observed, such as a relation that depends on certain temporal lags before a one-party state shows the instability that more open systems might show earlier. Hence, a one-party system might be stable initially but later suffer severe instability because of a failure to accomplish the functions of a party system.

[11] Still, even in the case of Table 2.1 it would be useful to have a summary statistical measure to present. The student who is interested in statistical explanations of propositions operationalized in terms of nominal or ordinal variables—i.e., variables for which quantitative symbols do not indicate the precise numerical difference in the value of the variable--should consult the very useful introductory text by Linton G. Freeman, *Elementary Applied Statistics* (New York: Wiley, 1965). Other major sources are S. Siegel, *Non-Parametric Statistics* (New York: McGraw-Hill, 1956) and D. Hildebrand, J. Laing and H. Rosenthal, *Prediction Analysis* (New York: Wiley, 1977).

[12] For a seminal statement on the use of multiple operationalizations see D. Campbell and D. Fiske, "Convergent and Discriminant Validation using the Multitrait-Multimethod Matrix," *Psychological Bulletin* 56 (1959): 81-105.

[13] The formula is $1 - \Sigma p_i^2$ where p_i is the proportion of seats held by the ith party and N is the number of parties.

[14] See D. G. Morrison and H. M. Stevenson, "Cultural Pluralism, Modernization and Conflict," *Canadian Journal of Political Science* V (March 1972): 82-103, D. G. Morrison and H. M. Stevenson, "Political Instability in Independent Black Africa: More Dimensions of Conflict Behavior Within Nations," *Journal of Conflict Resolution* (Sept. 1971), and D. G. Morrison *Political Learning in African States*, forthcoming.

[15] That is, that these variables possess *face validity* since they appear to relate to the concepts being investigated.

[16] This occurs because more coder judgements are required, and therefore the possibility of error in coding increases. Note that increased validity often is gained at the cost of decreased reliability. See Campbell and Fiske *op. cit.* for a discussion of this problem.

[17] For treatments of statistics useful to social scientists see, among other textbooks, H. M. Blalock, *Social Statistics* (New York: McGraw-Hill, 1979) and D. J. Palumbo, *Statistics in Political and Behavioral Sciences* (New York: Appleton-Century-Crofts, 1969).

[18] See Fig. 2.1 for a graphic illustration of such relationships as well as T. Gurr *op. cit.*.

[19] The reader may be interested to know that, although assessments of statistical significance are not strictly appropriate to data that is not derived from a random sample of nations, if we could consider these 32 African nations to be a sample of all future African nations, then the chances of randomly obtaining correlations that are larger than .30 is

only five in a hundred. The chances, therefore, that the evidence in this table is a fallacious confirmation of our hypotheses are small.

[20] The concept of rival, alternative, or competing hypotheses relates to the common existence of several competing explanations for a particular social phenomena. It is the role of empirical research in part to investigate such conflicts and attempt to resolve such rival explanations.

[21] Lydia Aran, S. N. Eisenstadt and Chaim Adler, "The Effectiveness of Educational Systems in the Processes of Modernization," *Comparative Education Review* 16 (February 1972), p. 31.

[22] For a cross-national analysis of this topic see Raymond F. Hopkins, "Christianity and Sociopolitical Change in Sub-Saharan Africa,"

Social Forces 44 (1966): 555-562 and Robert Cameron Mitchell and Donald George Morrison, "On Christianity and Sociopolitical Change," *Social Forces* 48 (1970): 397-408. The second article is a methodological critique of the first article and includes a reanalysis of the original data. These articles consider a number of the topics covered in this chapter in more detail than is possible here.

[23] If a computer is used, both the table and the calculation of statistics like percentages and tests of significance are done automatically and with great speed. Existing "package" programs like SPSS, SAS or BMDP are relatively easy to learn to use and do not require specialized statistical or computing knowledge.

Part III
COMPARATIVE DATA PROFILES

Introduction

Part Three presents data on 41 variables in a form appropriate to the type of analysis outlined in the essay in Part II. The tables are grouped by category and can be used to test hypotheses about the relations between the social, political and economic characteristics of nation-states. These table can also be used for general informational purposes, of course, and the essay in Part IV explains their relevance to case studies. We include maps in each section to aid in the appreciation of the numeric data.

These 41 variables have been carefully selected and updated from the much larger collection of variables which are contained in the second edition of *Black Africa*. Readers who need more data than are contained in this volume should consult *Black Africa*, the second edition.

The measures (or variables) presented here are grouped into nine chapter topics. Each chapter has; (a) a short outline of the subject; (b) an annotated bibliography for further study; and (c) several tables illustrative of data relevant to the topic and from which hypotheses could be generated or tested. In the short outline we present a brief sketch of the concepts and issues relevant to that chapter heading. We avoid footnotes, leaving the question of sources to the bibliography. The purpose of these sketches is to give an overview of the concepts, issues, and experience in Africa of the subject of that chapter. In the annotated bibliography important sources on the subject are presented. The reader then can pursue further reading using the references contained in the works cited and by reference to *Black Africa* second edition.

The data are presented in the 41 tables which are reproduced from computer printout. We have designed these tables to be easy to read, yet to contain a variety of useful information. For each variable the countries are ordered in terms of their position on that variable from high to low. The reader who wants the simplest information from the table merely needs to read the title and definition and then to look at the column under A to either find a specific country or to see how the 41 countries compare on that variable.

However, the other information given in the tables will be useful to many readers. In Figure 3.1 a sample table is reprinted. Each element of the table is labeled and an explanation of these elements is given below.

Figure 3.A   Sample Table (Table 6.3)

A **Table 6.3 Estimated Percent Identifiers with Christianity, 1980 (A), 1970 (B), and 1966 (C).**

B *Definition:* Estimated percent of the population who identify with Christianity. This is different from the churches' official membership figures which are lower.

C *Comments:* The major Christian types are the Ethiopian Orthodox church (an ancient form of Christianity found only in Ethiopia), the Roman Catholic Church, the various Protestant denominations, and the African independent Churches (see Table 6.4). This variable includes all these Christians.

Christianity is growing rapidly in many African countries, especially in Central and East Africa, and some argue that its growth rate for Black Africa exceeds Islam's. Roman Catholicism is strongest in the former French colonies and the former Belgian Congo, although two-thirds of Zambia's Christians are Roman Catholic and Lesotho, Nigeria, and Tanzania have large Catholic minorities. Protestant churches have evolved from the status of foreign-controlled mission churches to the status of national churches under the control of indigenous pastors and laity.

I Range =   96.00
Mean =   47.59
Standard Deviation = **K**   33.13   **L**

Population Percent							
Cum.	Country	Rank	Country Name	A	Range Decile	B	C
.16	.16	1.5	Gabon	96	1	96	75
.45	.29	1.5	Namibia	96		95	89
8.74	8.29	3.0	Zaire	95		90	65
9.19	.45	4.5	Congo	93		92	64
9.57	.38	4.5	Lesotho	93		86	81
11.52	1.95	6.0	Angola	90		83	55
11.62	.10	7.0	Equatorial Guinea	89		88	89
12.90	1.28	8.0	Burundi	86	2	74	64
13.48	.58	9.0	Central African R	84		77	47
17.43	3.95	10.0	Uganda	78		69	60
17.59	.16	11.0	Swaziland	77		70	60
22.19	4.60	12.5	Kenya	73	3	64	58
23.55	1.36	12.5	Rwanda	73		62	42
25.20	1.65	14.0	Zambia	72		65	30
26.86	1.66	15.0	Malawi	65	4	59	42
30.37	3.51	16.0	Ghana	63		53	46
32.63	2.26	17.0	Zimbabwe	58		52	45
42.34	9.71	18.0	Ethiopia	57	5	55	37
44.75	2.41	19.0	Cameroon	56		47	49
47.23	2.48	20.0	Madagascar	51		49	38
47.46	.23	21.0	Botswana	50		43	29
68.46	21.00	22.0	Nigeria	49		45	35
73.62	5.16	23.0	Tanzania	44	6	36	40
76.61	2.99	24.0	Mozambique	40		30	21
77.36	.75	25.0	Togo	37	7	30	28
77.89	.53	26.0	Liberia	35		31	25
79.23	1.34	27.0	Chad	33		31	10
81.45	2.22	28.0	Ivory Coast	32		28	18
82.45	1.00	29.0	Benin	23	8	19	18
84.42	1.97	30.0	Upper Volta	12	9	10	6
84.61	.19	31.0	Guinea-Bissau	10		13	9
84.71	.10	33.0	Djibouti	9	10	13	10
85.70	.99	33.0	Sierra Leone	9		8	7
91.94	6.24	33.0	Sudan	9		7	4
93.58	1.64	35.0	Senegal	6		6	4
93.75	.27	36.0	Gambia	3		3	4
95.62	1.87	37.0	Mali	2		2	1
97.19	1.57	39.0	Guinea	1		1	1
97.65	.46	39.0	Mauritania	1		1	0
98.98	1.33	39.0	Niger	1		1	1
100.00	1.03	41.0	Somalia	0		0	0

(Labels in figure: **H** Population Percent, **F** Country Name, **J** Range Decile, **N**, **M**, **D** SOURCES: *Black Africa* second edition., **E**)

D SOURCES: *Black Africa* second edition.

(A) = *Title*: The table title describes the variable and the year. In this case the variable is the estimated percent of the population who identify with Christianity in the years 1980, 1970 and 1966.

(B) = *Definition*: When it is necessary to define the variable more precisely and less ambiguously, additional information is given here.

(C) = *Comments*: These are brief interpretative and/or explanatory remarks about the data pattern. They are meant to be suggestive rather than comprehensive or authoritative.

(D) = *Sources*: The source is given as *Black Africa* second edition, where all these tables can be found. Full details about the sources for these data are presented there.

(E) = *Data Not Available*: Whenever data is unavailable for any of the countries covered in this book, the names of the missing countries are listed here. In this example, estimates are available for all countries.

(F) = *Value*: The data in this column are the values for the variable for each country. The 96 opposite Gabon indicates that 96 percent of Gabon's population identified themselves as Christians in about 1980.

(G) = *Total*: For some of the tables in this book we give the total for that variable for each country as well as the per capita figure. The units for the total are given in the definition, e.g. millions of US dollars for Gross Domestic Product in Table 8.4.

(H) = *Rank*: The countries are listed in the table in rank order from those which have the highest value on the variable to those which have the lowest value. This column gives the rank of every country on the variable. It shows Gabon first, Ghana sixteenth and Upper Volta thirtieth out of 41 countries in percent of population who identify as Christians. Countries which are *tied* at the same value, such as Kenya and Rwanda which both have a value of 73 percent, are given the same rank. This is calculated as the average of the ranks which they cover. In the case of Kenya and Rwanda these ranks are 12 and 13. The average is 12.5 which is the rank given to each.

The next four statistics provide a simple summary of some aspects of the distribution of the values for the 41 countries in the table. They are all expressed in the original measurement units, in this case percentages.

(I) = *Range*: This is the distance between the highest and the lowest value of the variable and shows the limits within which all measurements fall. In this case the distance between Gabon's 96 percent and Somalia's 0 gives a range of 96.

(J) = *Range Decile*: The numbers in this column show which countries fall into which decile (or tenth) of the range. In this case the range is 96 so each decile is 9.6. Every country in Table 6.3 whose value lies between 96 (highest value) and 86.4 (lowest value within one decile

of the highest value) is in the first decile of the range. Thus Gabon (value 96), Namibia (value 96), Zaire (value 95), Congo (value 93), Lesotho (value 93), Angola (value 90), and Equatorial Guinea (value 89) are in the first decile. Burundi, Central African Republic, Uganda and Swaziland are in the second decile while three countries are in the third decile, etc. A glance at the range decile column will show how evenly or unevenly the countries are distributed across the range. For instance, when the country having the highest value is in decile 1 and the country with the next highest value is in decile 8, the distribution across the range is highly uneven. In the case of this table, the distribution across the range is mainly at the two extremes of the distribution with many of the countries being principally either Christian or Muslim. There are a number of countries for which this is not the case, however, and they represent some interesting cases for the study of culturally plural societies.

(K) = *Mean*: The mean may be thought of as the central tendency of the distribution. It is that score about which deviations in one direction equal deviations in the other. It is calculated by taking the sum of all the values (in column E) and dividing them by the total number of values (in this case by 41). The mean for Table 6.3 is 47.59. In cases where the distribution is skewed, the countries with values closest to the mean will be closer either to the top or the bottom of the rank ordered countries.

(L) = *Standard Deviation*: This is an index of variability or how the values depart from the central tendency or the mean of a distribution. It is the square root of the variance for a distribution. For Table 6.3 the standard deviation is 33.13. The higher the standard deviation, the greater all the countries' dissimilarity as a whole.

As an aid in interpreting the data, the remaining two sets of figures give information about the size of each country relative to the other countries covered by this book.

(M) = *Country Population Percent*: The figures in this column give the percent each country's population is of the total population for all 41 countries. The figures in this column show that Congo's 1980 population of 1,500,000 comprises about one half of one percent of the total (.45), while Nigeria's 72,600,000 people comprise 21.0 percent of the total. A glance at this column will show such things as whether the smaller countries are grouped at the top or the bottom of a distribution. In the case of Table 6.3 the distribution by size of country is fairly even, although the lower values tend to be held in greater proportion by small countries. The country population percent is also a useful reminder of absolute values. In a table presented in Chapter 5, "Telephones per 10,000 Population," Congo has a much higher value than Nigeria. Nigeria has a larger number of telephones,

121,000 to Congo's 12,000, but Nigeria's telephones are spread across a much larger population.

(N) = *Cumulative Population Percent*: The figures in this column give the country population percent (K) in a cumulative fashion beginning with the population percent of the country with the highest value. At every point in the distribution of the value it shows the percentage of the total 41-country population accounted for by those countries which hold that value or a higher one. For example, the 23 countries that have a value of 44 or higher account for 73.6 percent of the total population of all 41 countries. The figure of 100 opposite Somalia in this column shows that the 41 countries for which data were available on this variable account for 100 percent of the total population. If there were missing data, fewer countries (i.e., less than 41) would appear and the percentage would be less than 100%.

Chapter 1

Land and Population

The continent of Africa, second largest after Asia, comprises over 22% of the world's land area and about 9% of its population. Tropical Africa has been described by William Hance as a plateau continent, possessing few good natural harbors, with narrow coastal plains, two-fifths of which is steppe or desert and one-fifth savanna. Nevertheless, this land mass embraces a considerable variety of ecological areas from arid deserts to dense jungle, from snow-capped mountains to hot coastal cities and from temperate zones to some of the hottest areas known to man. This diversity is also a characteristic of its population distribution (see Figure 1.1) where both some of the sparsest as well as some of the most densely-populated areas in the world can be found. In this chapter we present some basic information about the land-area and population of the forty-one countries that are reviewed in this book.

Agriculture and herding remain the principal pursuits of the vast majority of Africans. About three-fifths of the cultivated area of tropical Africa is devoted to subsistence farming. However the soils, particularly in the rain forest and savanna, are poorly structured with little top-soil and require careful cultivation if they are to remain usable. The much publicized droughts of the 1970's stem, in part, from the overuse, particularly overgrazing, of such land. Neither land nor solar radiation are lacking, however, and only inadequacies in technique and deficiencies in rainfall stand in the way of greater agricultural productivity. Slow progress is being made in developing a scientifically advanced agriculture suitable for the tropics. The forests, of which Africa possesses 17% of the world total, represent an important and valuable resource which has only been modestly exploited to date. Cattle and African wildlife also form a considerable resource as does the rapidly expanding fisheries industry.

The mineral potential and the availability of energy resources vary widely from country to country, but overall Africa has great mineral wealth. For instance, iron ore is mined in Mauritania, Angola, Guinea, Sierra Leone, Liberia and Swaziland, and coal is found in at least six of the countries discussed in this book. Other important mineral sources include copper (Zambia, Zaire, Uganda) and diamonds (Angola, Sierra Leone, Liberia, Central African Republic, Tanzania, Lesotho and Botswana). According to a United Nations survey in 1970, Africa as a whole produced the following percentage of the world's minerals: cobalt, 66; copper, 21; diamonds, 76; gold, 81; phosphates, 24; tin, 11; chromium, 29; and petroleum, 13. Since there are considerable areas which have not had thorough geological surveys, important new discoveries are constantly being made.

Africa is considered to have the greatest water power potential of any continent. This potential added to the considerable reserves of uranium ore (Gabon and Niger) to fuel nuclear power plants, low sulphur petroleum deposits (Nigeria, Cameroon, Gabon, Angola, and Zaire), and natural gas (Nigeria) present a promising energy picture for economic development. Except for the unequal distribution of such resources as well as the lack of some minerals, most prominently coking coal for an iron and steel industry, Africa has most of the natural resources required for rapid and sustained economic development.

In 1980 the 41 African countries which we consider in this book had a total population of about 350 million and constituted about seven percent of the world's population. In terms of their traditional culture, these peoples may be grouped into as many as 2,000 ethnic groups with separate languages, cultures, and senses of identity. Inhabiting a great diversity of habitats, from deserts to rain forests, the vast majority of these people are still cultivators and herders.

It is thought that Black Africa's population size remained relatively stable for the three or four centuries preceeding this one. One factor which contributed to this stability was undoubtedly the slave trade which, over five centuries, removed an estimated 10-15 million young Africans from the continent. Since 1900 the slow introduction of modern medicine and health measures have begun the process of lowering the death rate. The result is the present growth rate of about 2.7% or higher

4 1

Figure 1.1 Population Density

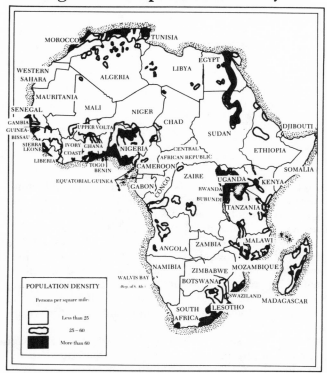

POPULATION DENSITY

Persons per square mile:

Less than 25

25 – 60

More than 60

(annual growth) which is among the highest growth rates for the world. At this rate of growth Black Africa will double its population in about a quarter century.

The prospects are for a further increase in the growth rate in the next decades, however, which would shorten even further the number of years required to double the population. Africa has the highest death rates and the highest birth rates of all the world's regions. Since African peoples traditionally value children highly and since Black Africa has the lowest level of literacy and of family planning activity in the world, reduction in the birth rate is very likely to come about slowly. In the meantime health measures continue to spread, ensuring a drop in the death rates. If African women continue to have six to seven babies on the average, and more of these babies live, the implications for population growth are dramatic. One of the results of this population situation is the youthfulness of the population. In most African countries, as with many Asian and South American countries, nearly half the people are under 15 years of age (compared with 25% in the United States).

At present, very few African countries have active family planning programs. Kenya was the first, in 1966, to adopt an official population policy and program. By the mid-1970s Ghana and Botswana had joined Kenya in im-

plementing such a program. Several African countries were critical of such programs during the 1974 World Population Conference in Bucharest, viewing them as low in priority when compared with the need to stimulate economic development. According to a 1975 annual review of family planning programs by the Population Council, there is a gradual trend towards greater acceptance of family planning as a health measure in Africa. But, as that report points out:

> Rapid population growth is not perceived as a major problem in most (sub-Saharan) countries. Some African leaders, especially in Francophone countries, feel that the international aid community has tried to impose antinatalist policies on them, at the expense of more fundamental development issues.[1]

[1]Walter B. Watson and Robert J. Lapham (eds.), "Family Programs: World Review 1974," *Studies in Family Planning* 6 (August 1975): 301.

BIBLIOGRAPHY

Useful introductions to the geography and population of tropical Africa include R. J. Harrison Church, et. al., *Africa and the Islands* (New York: Wiley, 1965); William A. Hance, *The Geography of Modern Africa*, third edition (New York: Columbia University Press, 1980); and George T. Kimble, *Tropical Africa*, 2 vols. (New York: Twentieth Century Fund, 1960); and *Economic Atlas—Africa* (Oxford: Oxford University Press, 1965). Other recent works are: L. Dudley Stamp, *Africa: A Study in Tropical Development* 3rd ed. (New York: Wiley, 1972), and R. Manswell Prothero (ed.) *People and Land in Africa South of the Sahara* (New York: Oxford University Press, 1972) and John C. Caldwell, ed., *Population Growth and Socioeconomic Change in West Africa* (New York: Columbia University Press, 1975). It is clear, however, that these will be in need of revision or replacement as the recent censuses, changes in knowledge of minerals, and advances in economic development continue.

Two major technical works on African demography are J. D. Caldwell and C. Okonjo (eds.) *The Population of Tropical Africa* (New York: Longmans, 1968) and William Brass, et. al., *The Demography of Tropical Africa* (Princeton, N.J.: Princeton University Press, 1968). Also see R. B. Tabbarah "Toward a Theory of Demographic Development," *Economic Development and Cultural Change* 19, (1971):257—276. A useful and less technical discussion is Leon F. Bouvier, "Africa and Its Population Growth," *Population Bulletin* 30, No. 1 (1975).

The question of under what conditions Africa will undergo the "demographic transition" is an important one.

For a comprehensive review of the status of demographic transition theory see A. J. Coale, "The Demographic Transition" in *Proceedings of the IUSSP International Population Conference*, Vol. 1 (Liege: International Union for the Scientific Study of Population, 1973):53—72. Michael S. Teitelbaum in "Relevance of Demographic Transition Theory for Developing Countries" *Science* 188 (2 May 1975):420—425 suggests that the theory offers only a partial explanation of European trends and ambiguous advice for developing countries. John Caldwell reviews the role of family planning in "Family Planning in Continental Sub-Saharan Africa" in *The Politics of Family Planning in the Third World* (London: George Allen and Unwin, 1973).

Various census reports and summaries are often available and can be useful. Sources such as the *U.N. Demographic Yearbook* provide discussions on census reliabilities as do works cited in the previous paragraph. An important study of a controversial census is, I. I. Ekanem, *The 1963 Nigerian Census: A Critical Appraisal* (Benin: Ethiope, 1972).

Introduction to the physical, agricultural, and mineral resources of Africa can be found in the works cited in the first paragraph as well as in William A. Hance, *African Economic Development*, 2nd ed. (New York: Praeger, 1967); W. T. W. Morgan, ed. *East Africa: Its Peoples and Resources* (N.Y.: Oxford University Press, 1969); David Hapgood and Max F. Millikan *No Easy Harvest: The Dilemma of Agriculture in Underdeveloped Countries* (Boston: Little Brown, 1967); and William Allen, *The African Husbandman* (Edinburgh: Oliver and Boyd, 1965). An overview of the imporant research begun at the International Institute for Tropical Agriculture at Ibadan, Nigeria, is presented in D. J. Greenland, "Bringing the Green Revolution to the Shifting Cultivator," *Science* 190 (Nov. 28, 1975):841—844. Environmental questions have become a serious issue in the developed nations. For discussions which consider Africa see D. F. Owen, *Man's Environmental Predicament* (London: Oxford University Press, 1973), and M. F. Thomas and G. W. Whittington *Environment and Land Use in Africa* (New York: Harper and Row, 1972). W. E. Ormerod in "Ecological Effect of Control of African Trystosomiasis," *Science* 191 (27 February 1976):815—821, argues that a connection between the West African cattle industry and Sahelian drought is possible. Numerous country studies exist and Part V of this book should be consulted for country-specific studies.

For other studies which specifically relate geography and space to the problems of economic development see S. H. Ominde (ed.) *Studies in East African Geography and Development* (Berkeley: University of California Press, 1972); R. H. T. Smith (ed.) "Spatial Structure and Process in Tropical West Africa" *Economic Geography* (July 1972):229—235; A. M. O'Connor *The Geography of Tropical African Development* (New York: Pergammon, 1970); E. A. J. Johnson *The Organization of Space in Developing Countries* (Cambridge, Mass.: Harvard University Press, 1970); and A. Mabogunje "Manufacturing and the Geography of Development in Tropical Africa" *Economic Geography* 49 (January 1973):1—20.

TABLE 1.1   Area of Country in 1,000 Square Kilometers, 1980

Definition: Total area enclosed within the country's boundaries including that covered by water. The area is given in thousands of square kilometers. Area given in square miles can be found in Part V for each country.

Comments: As can be seen from the table, African nations vary considerably in land area, the largest being over 200 times the size of the smallest. It should be noted that these differences do not always indicate comparative amounts of usable land as many of the larger countries have considerable desert areas where virtually no one lives. The larger countries tend either to be land-locked or ones in which most of the population lives in the interior with only difficult access to the sea. Nigeria is, however, an exception to this general observation. A few countries have boundaries which are in dispute, such as Ethiopia and Somalia, and Mauritania, as well as those where the boundaries are not clearly delimited. The latter situation would only make a minor difference, however, in the data.

```
Range =        2495.00
Mean =          562.49
Standard Deviation =          587.81
```

Population Percent		Rank	Country Name	A	Range Decile
Cum.	Country				
6.24	6.24	1.0	Sudan	2506	1
14.53	8.29	2.0	Zaire	2345	
15.87	1.34	3.0	Chad	1284	5
17.20	1.33	4.0	Niger	1267	
19.15	1.95	5.0	Angola	1247	6
21.02	1.87	6.0	Mali	1240	
30.73	9.71	7.0	Ethiopia	1222	
31.19	.46	8.0	Mauritania	1031	
36.35	5.16	9.0	Tanzania	945	7
57.35	21.00	10.0	Nigeria	924	
57.64	.29	11.0	Namibia	824	
60.63	2.99	12.0	Mozambique	783	
62.28	1.65	13.0	Zambia	753	8
63.31	1.03	14.0	Somalia	638	
63.89	.58	15.0	Central African R	623	
64.12	.23	16.0	Botswana	600	
66.60	2.48	17.0	Madagascar	587	
71.20	4.60	18.0	Kenya	583	
73.61	2.41	19.0	Cameroon	475	9
75.87	2.26	20.0	Zimbabwe	391	
76.32	.45	21.0	Congo	342	
78.54	2.22	22.0	Ivory Coast	322	
80.51	1.97	23.0	Upper Volta	274	
80.67	.16	24.0	Gabon	268	
82.24	1.57	25.0	Guinea	246	10
85.75	3.51	26.0	Ghana	239	
89.70	3.95	27.0	Uganda	236	
91.34	1.64	28.0	Senegal	197	
93.00	1.66	29.0	Malawi	118	
94.00	1.00	30.0	Benin	113	
94.53	.53	31.0	Liberia	111	
95.52	.99	32.0	Sierra Leone	72	
96.27	.75	33.0	Togo	57	
96.46	.19	34.0	Guinea-Bissau	36	
96.84	.38	35.0	Lesotho	30	
98.12	1.28	36.5	Burundi	28	
98.22	.10	36.5	Equatorial Guinea	28	
99.58	1.36	38.0	Rwanda	26	
99.68	.10	39.0	Djibouti	23	
99.84	.16	40.0	Swaziland	17	
100.00	.17	41.0	Gambia	11	

SOURCE: *Black Africa* second edition

TABLE 1.2   Estimated Population in Millions, 1980 (A); Year of Latest Census (B)

Definition: Year of latest census includes year of sample survey if no census has been taken. It is zero if no census or survey of any kind has ever been carried out.

Comments: Most African countries now have had a complete census since the mid-1960s but national population figures must be regarded as estimates in many cases, especially that of Nigeria. As can be seen in the table there is considerable variation in population as well as in area for these African countries. The largest country (Nigeria) has over 200 people for every person in the smallest country. The *average* population for each country is less than ten million, but the *median* (the point where half of the countries have larger, and half smaller populations) is slightly more than half the average showing that the majority of these countries have relatively small populations.

```
Range =        72.30
Mean =          8.45
Standard Deviation =          12.54
```

Population Percent		Rank	Country Name	A	Range Decile	B
Cum.	Country					
21.00	21.00	1.0	Nigeria	72.6	1	
30.71	9.71	2.0	Ethiopia	33.6	6	
39.00	8.29	3.0	Zaire	28.7	7	70
45.24	6.24	4.0	Sudan	21.6	8	73
50.40	5.16	5.0	Tanzania	17.8		74
55.00	4.60	6.0	Kenya	15.9		69
58.95	3.95	7.0	Uganda	13.7	9	69
62.46	3.51	8.0	Ghana	12.1		70
65.45	2.99	9.0	Mozambique	10.3		80
67.93	2.48	10.0	Madagascar	8.6		75
70.34	2.41	11.0	Cameroon	8.3		76
72.60	2.26	12.0	Zimbabwe	7.8		69
74.82	2.22	13.0	Ivory Coast	7.6		75
76.77	1.95	14.5	Angola	6.8	10	70
78.74	1.97	14.5	Upper Volta	6.8		75
80.61	1.87	16.0	Mali	6.5		76
82.27	1.66	18.0	Malawi	5.7		77
83.91	1.64	18.0	Senegal	5.7		76
85.56	1.65	18.0	Zambia	5.7		69
87.13	1.57	20.0	Guinea	5.4		72
88.46	1.33	21.0	Niger	5.3		77
89.82	1.36	22.0	Rwanda	4.7		78
91.16	1.34	23.0	Chad	4.6		68
92.44	1.28	24.0	Burundi	4.4		71
93.47	1.03	25.0	Somalia	3.6		75
94.47	1.00	26.0	Benin	3.5		79
95.46	.99	27.0	Sierra Leone	3.4		74
96.21	.75	28.0	Togo	2.6		70
96.79	.58	29.0	Central African R	2.0		75
97.32	.53	30.0	Liberia	1.9		74
97.78	.46	31.0	Mauritania	1.7		77
98.23	.45	32.0	Congo	1.5		74
98.61	.38	33.0	Lesotho	1.3		76
98.90	.29	34.0	Namibia	1.0		70
99.13	.23	35.0	Botswana	.8		81
99.30	.17	37.0	Gambia	.6		73
99.49	.19	37.0	Guinea-Bissau	.6		79
99.65	.16	37.0	Swaziland	.6		76
99.81	.16	39.0	Gabon	.5		72
99.91	.10	40.5	Djibouti	.3		76
100.00	.10	40.5	Equatorial Guinea	.3		60

SOURCE: *Black Africa* second edition

Table1.3 Annual Percent of Population Increase, 1970—1980 (A) and 1960—1970 (B)

Definition: Population natural increase is the difference between the , birth rate and death rate. The net immigration rate is added to this figure to get the total value of population increase. The figure given is the average annual rate of increase for the years 1970 to 1980.

Comments: The rate of natural increase is difficult to calculate with accuracy in Africa since the registration of deaths and births are not required or enforced in most countries. Hence the estimates given should be regarded as very tentative and subject to considerable error margins. Nevertheless, the general pattern shown here is probably an accurate one. A few countries, such as Gabon have a nearly stagnant population while others, particularly in eastern Africa, have rapidly growing populations. In 1975 the average percent of population increase for the world was 1.9 and 2.7 for Latin America. As for most of the developing world, the reason for such an increase is not due to increased birth rates but to rapidly falling death rates caused by the introduction of modern medicine, improved public health facilities, and planning.

```
Range =          5.00
Mean =           2.64
Standard Deviation =         .75
```

Population Percent Cum.	Country	Rank	Country Name	A	Range Decile	B
2.22	2.22	1.0	Ivory Coast	6.0	1	3.8
6.82	4.60	2.0	Kenya	3.8	5	3.5
7.35	.53	3.0	Liberia	3.4	6	3.2
9.61	2.26	4.0	Zimbabwe	3.3		3.9
9.78	.17	5.5	Gambia	3.1		3.2
11.44	1.66	5.5	Malawi	3.1		2.8
14.95	3.51	9.0	Ghana	3.0	7	2.4
16.52	1.57	9.0	Guinea	3.0		2.9
21.68	5.16	9.0	Tanzania	3.0		2.7
25.63	3.95	9.0	Uganda	3.0		3.7
27.28	1.65	9.0	Zambia	3.0		2.8
28.28	1.00	13.0	Benin	2.9		2.6
28.57	.29	13.0	Namibia	2.9		2.0
29.93	1.36	13.0	Rwanda	2.9		2.6
31.26	1.33	15.0	Niger	2.8		3.3
31.71	.45	17.0	Congo	2.7		2.1
32.17	.46	17.0	Mauritania	2.7		2.5
40.46	8.29	17.0	Zaire	2.7		2.0
61.46	21.00	20.5	Nigeria	2.6		2.5
63.10	1.64	20.5	Senegal	2.6		2.5
69.34	6.24	20.5	Sudan	2.6		2.3
70.09	.75	20.5	Togo	2.6		2.7
79.80	9.71	25.5	Ethiopia	2.5	8	2.4
82.28	2.48	25.5	Madagascar	2.5		2.2
84.15	1.87	25.5	Mali	2.5		2.4
85.14	.99	25.5	Sierra Leone	2.5		2.2
86.17	1.03	25.5	Somalia	2.5		2.4
86.33	.16	25.5	Swaziland	2.5		2.2
86.71	.38	29.0	Lesotho	2.4		2.0
88.66	1.95	31.0	Angola	2.3		1.6
88.76	.10	31.0	Djibouti	2.3		2.0
91.75	2.99	31.0	Mozambique	2.3		2.4
94.16	2.41	34.0	Cameroon	2.2		1.8
94.74	.58	34.0	Central African R	2.2		2.2
96.08	1.34	34.0	Chad	2.2		1.9
96.31	.23	36.5	Botswana	1.9	9	1.9
97.59	1.28	36.5	Burundi	1.9		2.4
97.69	.10	38.0	Equatorial Guinea	1.7		1.4
99.66	1.97	39.0	Upper Volta	1.6		1.6
99.85	.19	40.0	Guinea-Bissau	1.5	10	-.6
100.00	.16	41.0	Gabon	1.0		.6

SOURCE: *Black Africa* second edition

Table 1.4 Percent European Population, ca. 1970 (A), 1960 (B), and ca. 1925 (C).

Definition: This figure includes all Europeans resident in the country. In some countries (especially West Africa) all non-Africans are represented in the figures while in other countries, especially East Africa, Asians and other non-Europeans are counted separately.

Comments: The influence of foreigners on the social and political life of a country can be significant. There have been major differences in the penetration of these countries by Europeans and such differences are often viewed as important to the continuing role of the ex-metropole in the country.

```
Range =          12.97
Mean =            1.35
Standard Deviation =           2.76
```

Population Percent Cum.	Country	Rank	Country Name	A	Range Decile	B	C
.29	.29	1.0	Namibia	13.00	1	14.10	1.14
.39	.10	2.0	Djibouti	11.70	2	14.10	
2.34	1.95	3.0	Angola	5.71	6	3.58	1.61
5.33	2.99	4.5	Mozambique	3.50	8	1.53	1.02
7.59	2.26	4.5	Zimbabwe	3.50		1.53	3.73
7.75	.16	6.0	Gabon	3.14		1.12	.17
7.91	.16	7.0	Swaziland	2.33	9	1.95	1.98
9.55	1.64	8.0	Senegal	1.22	10	2.00	.36
9.78	.23	9.0	Botswana	1.15		.80	.69
10.78	1.00	10.0	Benin	1.14		1.25	.06
11.23	.45	11.0	Congo	1.00		1.56	.13
13.45	2.22	12.0	Ivory Coast	.88		.56	.07
15.32	1.87	13.0	Mali	.76		.19	.06
19.92	4.60	14.0	Kenya	.73		.37	.34
20.50	.58	15.0	Central African R	.46		.40	.10
22.98	2.48	16.0	Madagascar	.45		1.50	.50
23.17	.19	17.5	Guinea-Bissau	.40		.50	.10
24.50	1.33	17.5	Niger	.40		.31	.02
24.60	.10	19.0	Equatorial Guinea	.37		2.87	.29
27.01	2.41	20.5	Cameroon	.34		.42	.07
30.96	3.95	20.5	Uganda	.34		.17	.05
31.49	.53	22.0	Liberia	.32		.20	.01
37.73	6.24	23.5	Sudan	.31		.27	.09
46.02	8.29	23.5	Zaire	.31		.84	.26
47.68	1.66	25.0	Malawi	.20		.17	.08
48.67	.99	26.0	Sierra Leone	.19		.09	.07
49.05	.38	27.0	Lesotho	.18		.28	.34
52.56	3.51	28.5	Ghana	.16		.16	.07
53.02	.46	28.5	Mauritania	.16		.21	.04
54.36	1.34	30.5	Chad	.13		.10	.03
75.36	21.00	30.5	Nigeria	.13		.10	.02
85.07	9.71	32.0	Ethiopia	.12		.13	.03
86.35	1.28	33.5	Burundi	.11		.07	.01
91.51	5.16	33.5	Tanzania	.11		.22	.13
93.08	1.57	35.0	Guinea	.10		.06	.10
93.25	.17	36.0	Gambia	.08		.33	.10
94.28	1.03	37.5	Somalia	.07		.24	.13
95.03	.75	37.5	Togo	.07		.14	.08
97.00	1.97	39.0	Upper Volta	.06		.09	.02
98.65	1.65	40.0	Zambia	.05		2.31	.54
100.00	1.36	41.0	Rwanda	.03		.15	.02

SOURCE: *Black Africa* second edition.

Chapter 2

Languages

There are more than a thousand indigenous languages spoken in the countries reviewed in this book. (Knappert 1965, page 95-105). Some linguists estimate the number to be as low as 800 (Alexandre, 1971) while others estimate over 1,200 distinct languages. One of the reasons that the number of languages in Africa is difficult to assess is the lack of agreement as to what constitutes a dialect as distinct from a language. In general, a dialect is differentiated from a distinct language in being intelligible, to some extent, to a speaker of the parent language.

While many of the languages in Africa are spoken by only a few people, that is, less than 10,000, several of the languages are understood by millions. The most widely spoken languages include Arabic (in northern Africa), Swahili (in central and eastern Africa), and Hausa (in western Africa). In addition to widespread use, many of the major languages have a significant tradition of written literature as well, including Yoruba (Nigeria), Amharic (Ethiopia), Zulu (South Africa), Luganda (Uganda) and Twi (Ghana).

Even though Africa has perhaps the largest number of languages per capita of any area in the world, it is possible to group these languages into language families. Linguists usually base their typologies either on word similarities (e.g. Greenberg, 1966 see chapter bibliography) or on historical relatedness (e.g. Guthrie, 1962). The Greenberg typology is perhaps the most widely accepted, and includes: (1) Congo-Kordofanian (including Benue-Congo which includes Bantu); (2) Nilo-Saharan (which includes such Sudanic languages as Kanuri); (3) Afro-Asiatic (including Hausa and Arabic); and (4) Kho-

isan (including the click languages such as the Bushman and Hottentot). See Figure 2.1, for the distribution of these language groupings, and *Black Africa*, Part 1, Chapter 2, for a fuller discussion of language measurements and typologies.

The number of languages, number of language speakers, and family group of languages, is important to the new African states. While most Africans are multilingual, the relative presence or absence of national languages of communication may be important to both economic development and the creation of national political structures. In most African countries French, English, or Arabic is the official national language. In some countries an indigenous language has become the official national language, e.g. Swahili in Tanzania and Kenya, Kinyaranda in Burundi, Somali in Somalia, Sango in Central African Republic, Setswana in Botswana, Sesotho in Lesotho, Chewa in Malawi, and Swati in Swaziland. After 1966 Arabic became the official language along with French in Mauritania. Two of the most critical areas of language use in the new states are in elementary education and radio broadcasting. Many of the African states use local vernaculars to serve these two functions.

While we do not present data on the subject, multilingualism is characteristic of large parts of Africa. In some areas a person may speak as many as four or five languages! To some extent the different languages spoken may be functionally differentiated, e.g., trading, official, education, family, and religious activities may each use a different language.

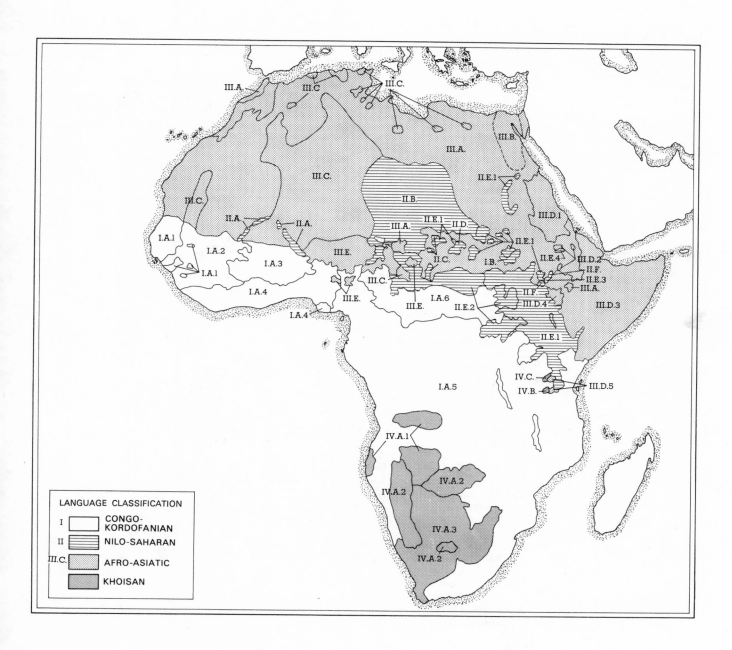

LANGUAGE CLASSIFICATION

I CONGO-KORDOFANIAN

II NILO-SAHARAN

III.C. AFRO-ASIATIC

KHOISAN

Figure 2.1   Language Families of Africa: Greenberg's 1963 Classification

Language Family (macro-phylum)	Major Sections (phyla/families)	Examples of individual languages or groups
I. Congo-Kordofanian	A. Niger-Congo	
	A-1. West Atlantic	Fulani, Wolof, Serer, Temme, Limba, Soninke, Malinké, Bambara, Kpellé,
	A-2. Mande	Senoufo, Mossi, Grusi, Kabré, Bargu, Kru, Bété, Bassa, Ewé, Akan, Yoruba,
	A-3. Voltaic (Gur)	Bantu family, Tiv, Ibibio, Basa, Mbum, Gbaya, Banda, Mbaka, Sango
	A-4. Kwa ("others")	
	A-5. Benue-Congo	
	A-6. Adamawa	
	B. Kordofanian	
	B-1. Koalib	Kanderma
	B-2. Tegali	Rashad
	B-3. Talodi	Lafofa
	B-4. Tumtum	Tuleshi
	B-5. Katla	Tima
II. Nilo-Saharan	A. Songhai	
	B. Saharan	Kanuri (Kanembu)
	C. Maban	Maba
	D. Fur	
	E. Chari-Nile	
	E-1. Eastern Sudanic	Nubian group, Nilotic family, (Acholi, Lango, Nuer)
	E-2. Central Sudanic	
	E-3. Berua	
	E-4. Kunama	
	F. Koman	Koma
III. Afro-Asiatic	A. Semitic	Arabic
	B. Egyptian	
	C. Berber	
	D. Cushitic	
	D-1. Northern Cushitic	Beja
	D-2. Central Cushitic	Bogo
	D-3. Eastern Cushitic	Saho-Afar, Somali, Galla
	D-4. Western Cushitic	Janjero
	D-5. Southern Cushitic	Burungi
	E. Chad	Hausa, Bana, Banana (Masa)
IV. Khoisan	A. South African Khoisan	(Not significant in the countries contained in this Handbook)
	A-1. Northern South African Khoisan	
	A-2. Central South African Khoisan	
	A-3. Southern South African Khoisan	
	B. Sandawe	
	C. Hatsa	

BIBLIOGRAPHY

A few authors have attempted to estimate language distribution for each of the African states. One of the earliest attempts was Duncan MacDougald, Jr., *The Language and Press of Africa* (Philadelphia: University of Pennsylvania Press, 1944) where most of his estimates were based on ethnic distribution data. Although many of these estimates have very questionable reliability and multi-lingualism and *lingua francas* were ignored, several contemporary studies such as I. Adelman and C. T. Morris, *Society, Politics, and Economic Development* (Baltimore, Md.: Johns Hopkins Press, 1967) and A. S. Banks and R. B. Textor, *Cross-Policy Survey* (Cambridge: Masachusetts Institute of Technology Press, 1963) have drawn on this source. Rustow's "Language, Modernization, and Nationhood—An Attempt at Typology," in Fishman, et. al., *Language Problems of the Developing Nations* (New York: Wiley, 1968) also draws on the earlier estimates and much of this material is unreliable. One contemporary linguist, Jan Knappert, in "Language Problems of the New Nations of Africa," *Africa Quarterly* 5 (1965): 95—105, has made estimates which we regard as relatively reliable and they provide the basis of the data in this chapter. A country by country discussion of these data sources and the derivation of our own estimates can be found in *Black Africa*.

For a general introduction see Edgar A. Gregersen, *Language in Africa: An Introductory Survey* (New York: Gordon and Breach, 1977). Two of the most useful anthologies on language use and policy in Africa are J. A. Fishman, C. A. Ferguson, and J. Das Gupta (eds.), *Language Problems of Developing Nations* (New York: Wiley, 1968) and W. H. Whiteley (ed.), *Language Use and Social Change: Problems of Multi-Lingualism with Special Reference to Eastern Africa* (New York: Oxford University Press, 1971). A review of these problems can be seen in *Africa Report's* review of the "politics of language" 18 (July—August 1973): 16—25. Also see T. P. Gorman (ed.), *Language in Education in Eastern Africa: Papers from the First Eastern Africa Conference on Language and Linguistics* (Nairobi: Oxford University Press, 1970) and J. H. Greenberg, *Language, Culture, and Commu-*

nication (Stanford, Calif.: Stanford University Press, 1971).

On the issue of language classification see J. H. Greenberg, *The Languages of Africa* Indiana University Research Center in Anthropology, Folklore and Linguistics Publ. No 25 (Bloomington, Ind: 1966), and footnote 6 in *Black Africa* first edition, for numerous articles discussing this seminal work. An older work still of interest is M. Guthrie, *The Classification of Bantu Languages* (London: Oxford University Press, 1948). In addition, the early work of D. Westerman and M. Bryan, *Languages of West Africa: Handbook of African Languages* (London: Oxford University Press, 1952) and the more recent work of C. F. and F. M. Voegelin, "Languages of the World: Africa Fascile One," *Anthropological Linguistics* 6 (1964): 1—339 should be consulted. Recent additions are: W. E. Welmers, *African Language Structures* (Berkeley: University of California Press, 1973); P. Alexandre, *An Introduction to Language and Languages in Africa* (London: Heinemann, 1972) and M. L. Bender, R. L. Cooper, and C. A. Ferguson, "Language in Ethiopia: Implications of a Survey for Sociolinguistic Theory and Method," *Language in Society* 1 (Oct. 1972): 215—234. The *Journal of African Languages* also provides more technical works on African languages. Also see J. Berry and J.H. Greenberg eds. *Linguistics in Sub-Saharan Africa* (The Hague: Mouton, 1971).

Other aspects of language can be reviewed in J. Berry, "Language Systems and Literature," in J. Paden and E. Soja (eds.), *The African Experience* (Evanston, Ill.: Northwestern University Press, 1970); O. Awolowo, *The People's Republic* (Ibadan: Oxford University Press, 1968); and D. Dalby (ed.), *Language and History in Africa* (New York: Africana, 1971). Pierre Alexandre's "Understanded of Which People," *Africa Report* 18 (July—August 1973): 16—22 presents an overview of African language policies with a special emphasis on Zaire.

TABLE 2.1 Percent Speaking Dominant Vernacular Language, ca. 1977

Definition: Percent of total population who speak the dominant vernacular language (including *lingua francas*) as a first or second language.

Comments: The question of language homogeneity within a country is perhaps the most important criterion in determining whether a state is multi-national or not. In seven of the countries reviewed in this book (Botswana, Lesotho, Somalia, Madagascar, Burundi, Rwanda, Swaziland) the vernacular of the major ethnic group in the country is spoken by 90 percent or more of the population, and these countries may be regarded as linguistically homogeneous. Tanzania is somewhat unique in having encouraged a *lingua franca* (Swahili) which is now spoken by most people in the country, although the language is not primarily associated with any particular ethnic group in the country. Mauritania is also somewhat unique among the 41 countries in this book in that it is part of the Arab-speaking world, with the exception of important but relatively small groups along the Senegal border. Sudan also has a large Arab-speaking population.

Range = 76.00
Mean = 61.80
Standard Deviation = 22.84

Population Percent Cum.	Country	Rank	Country Name	A	Range Decile
2.48	2.48	1.0	Madagascar	100	1
2.86	.38	2.0	Lesotho	99	
3.09	.23	3.5	Botswana	98	
4.45	1.36	3.5	Rwanda	98	
5.48	1.03	5.0	Somalia	97	
5.64	.16	6.5	Swaziland	95	
10.80	5.16	6.5	Tanzania	95	
12.08	1.28	8.5	Burundi	90	2
12.54	.46	8.5	Mauritania	90	
12.64	.10	10.5	Equatorial Guinea	85	
17.24	4.60	10.5	Kenya	85	
18.57	1.33	12.0	Niger	81	3
20.83	2.26	13.0	Zimbabwe	78	
22.47	1.64	14.0	Senegal	67	5
22.57	.10	15.5	Djibouti	65	
28.81	6.24	15.5	Sudan	65	
29.81	1.00	19.0	Benin	60	6
31.15	1.34	19.0	Chad	60	
31.32	.17	19.0	Gambia	60	
32.98	1.66	19.0	Malawi	60	
34.95	1.97	19.0	Upper Volta	60	
55.95	21.00	22.0	Nigeria	55	
56.40	.45	23.0	Congo	52	7
66.11	9.71	26.0	Ethiopia	50	
66.27	.16	26.0	Gabon	50	
68.14	1.87	26.0	Mali	50	
68.43	.29	26.0	Namibia	50	
69.18	.75	26.0	Togo	50	
70.75	1.57	29.0	Guinea	48	
71.74	.99	30.0	Sierra Leone	45	8
75.25	3.51	31.5	Ghana	44	
75.78	.53	31.5	Liberia	44	
79.73	3.95	33.0	Uganda	41	
81.68	1.95	35.0	Angola	40	
84.67	2.99	35.0	Mozambique	40	
92.96	8.29	35.0	Zaire	40	
94.61	1.65	37.0	Zambia	35	9
95.19	.58	38.0	Central African R	31	10
95.38	.19	39.0	Guinea-Bissau	30	
97.60	2.22	40.0	Ivory Coast	27	
100.00	2.41	41.0	Cameroon	24	

SOURCE: *Black Africa* (second edition)

TABLE 2.2 Number of Languages Per Million Population, 1977 (A) and Total Number of Languages (B)

Definition: The number of languages as reported in the right hand column, is divided by the population of the respective country.

Comments: This variable, "Number of languages per million population, 1977," takes into account the size difference between the Black African countries, showing how the absolute number of languages per country may be a misleading guide to the language complexity of the state.

In the countries with the highest number of languages per million, there has been widespread encouragement of a single national language (i.e., French in Gabon and Ivory Coast; Sango, an artificially created composite language, in Central African Republic; English in Liberia and Zambia). The language policies in large multi-national states, such as Nigeria and Sudan, have been directly related to the ethnic politics of those countries.

Range = 27.60
Mean = 6.53
Standard Deviation = 6.90

Population Percent Cum.	Country	Rank	Country Name	A	Range Decile	B
.75	.75	1.0	Togo	27.7	1	56
1.33	.58	2.0	Central African R	24.3	2	41
1.49	.16	3.0	Gabon	21.4	3	15
2.02	.53	4.0	Liberia	18.3	4	29
2.12	.10	5.0	Equatorial Guinea	17.0		5
3.77	1.65	6.0	Zambia	15.2	5	69
3.94	.17	7.5	Gambia	12.6	6	6
6.16	2.22	7.5	Ivory Coast	12.6		57
6.35	.19	9.5	Guinea-Bissau	12.0		6
12.59	6.24	9.5	Sudan	12.0		171
15.00	2.41	11.0	Cameroon	8.3	8	50
15.16	.16	12.0	Swaziland	7.0		3
16.50	1.34	13.0	Chad	5.9		22
16.95	.45	14.0	Congo	5.8		7
17.05	.10	15.0	Djibouti	5.5	9	6
18.62	1.57	16.0	Guinea	5.4		22
19.62	1.00	17.0	Benin	5.3		15
21.59	1.97	18.0	Upper Volta	4.8		27
23.54	1.95	19.0	Angola	4.2		25
27.05	3.51	20.0	Ghana	4.1		37
32.21	5.16	21.0	Tanzania	4.0		56
33.54	1.33	22.0	Niger	3.3		14
33.77	.23	23.0	Botswana	3.1		2
34.76	.99	24.0	Sierra Leone	2.9		8
36.63	1.87	25.0	Mali	2.8	10	15
44.92	8.29	26.0	Zaire	2.7		61
54.63	9.71	27.0	Ethiopia	2.4		63
58.58	3.95	28.0	Uganda	2.3		24
79.58	21.00	29.0	Nigeria	2.2		125
81.22	1.64	30.0	Senegal	2.0		8
81.60	.38	31.0	Lesotho	1.9		2
86.20	4.60	32.0	Kenya	1.8		22
86.66	.46	33.0	Mauritania	1.6		2
89.65	2.99	34.0	Mozambique	1.3		11
91.31	1.66	35.0	Malawi	1.1		5
91.60	.29	36.0	Namibia	.8		10
92.63	1.03	37.0	Somalia	.7		2
93.91	1.28	38.0	Burundi	.6		2
95.27	1.36	39.0	Rwanda	.5		2
97.53	2.26	40.0	Zimbabwe	.4		3
100.00	2.48	41.0	Madagascar	.1		1

SOURCE: *Black Africa*, (second edition)

Chapter 3

Education

The growth of formal education in Africa over the last three or four decades has been phenomenal. Rates of school attendance often increased by several hundred percent. Education in this sense, is defined as the more or less consciously pursued or programmatic phase of acculturation that is observed in all societies. The function of educational institutions is viewed by some as an essentially conservative force insuring the perpetuation of existing cultural patterns, value orientations and behavioral norms. This perspective, however, is not applicable to the Western-based educational systems in Africa, which have been key instruments of transition.

Four different aspects of the role of education in Africa can be examined. The first is the approach adopted by economic planners who view the educational systems as the developers and mobilizers of human capital for the modern sector of the economy. Those who take this approach view human capital formation as one of the several factors determining increased national production and consumption. There is a revisionist school, however, which believes that such schooling does not accomplish this task but insures an elite that is not 'work oriented.'

A second approach emphasizes the "mass mobilizing" aspect of education. From this point of view, education is an important transformer of traditional social values and norms and a stimulant to participation in modern institutions. In this sense, education is one of six major categories of indicators in the "auditing of modernization" sugested by Daniel Lerner. He compared elementary, vocational, teacher training and university enrollment rates for several Middle Eastern countries and observed that an important requisite for non-erratic social change and political stability was balanced growth among major categories of indicators and among indicators within one category (e.g. teacher training must keep pace with primary enrollment). S. N. Eisenstadt expressed similar views by describing development in the educational field as a basic characteristic of modernization although he has changed his view in recent work and only partially re-

flects this point of view now. A more direct, empirical study of the influence of early educational experience on the political system in terms of adult political participation was conducted by Gabriel Almond and Sidney Verba. They found a positive relationship between participation in decision-making in the house and classroom, and later political participation in adulthood.

In contrast to this, the third approach is the "elite formation" emphasis of scholars such as C. Arnold Anderson, Remi Clignet, and Phillip Foster. They examine the impact of education on the social structure of African countries and argue that while education has in fact accelerated individual social mobility along new paths, certain groups or categories of people in the population have greater opportunity for education than others. Most particularly, the educated elite's children enjoy an advantage when pursuing educational qualifications. Here scholars question whether schooling has much effect on the intensity of ethnic identification and inequalities based on such perceived identity. The importance of modern education in Africa is seen by this approach in terms of its "elite" effects rather than as a mass mobilizing process in which general psychological commitments are formed.

A fourth approach takes a particular aspect of modernization, the developing of a sense of national identification which transcends ethnic loyalties, and assesses the contribution made to this process by the modern educational system. While positive attitudes toward the national political system may be internalized in the early stages of the educational process, the effective transmission of such attitudes increases as education itself becomes accepted as a social value. This process is not without difficulties, however. Although education at the mass level continues to inculcate the national loyalties and participatory values necessary for the perpetuation of modern political systems, the danger remains that the somewhat less than universal access to modern education in new nations will accentuate a growing rift between tradi-

Figure 3.1   Secondary and University Education in Black Africa

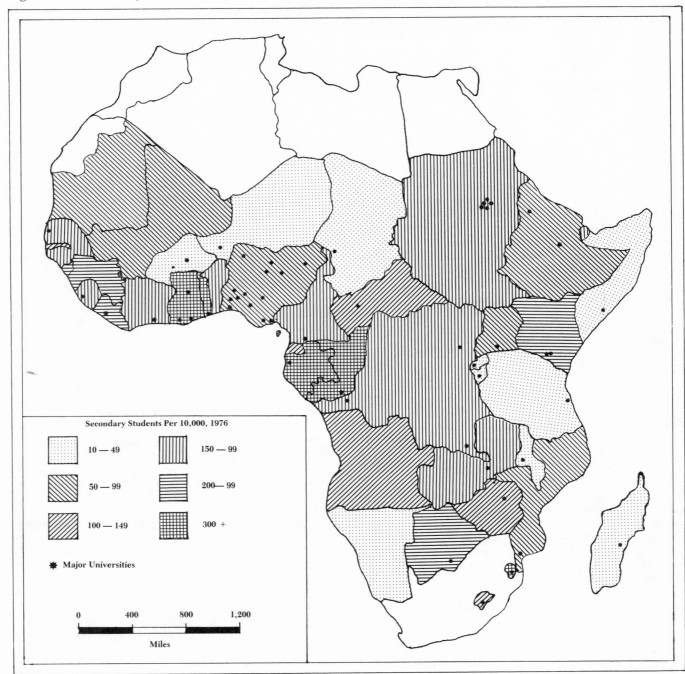

Secondary Students Per 10,000, 1976

10 — 49	150 — 99
50 — 99	200— 99
100 — 149	300 +

✳ Major Universities

0   400   800   1,200

Miles

*Namibia secondary education figures reflect 1966 data derived from E.C.A. Statistical Yearbook, 1972

tional and modern sectors of the population. And, as Coleman argues, inequalities in the distribution of education "may intensify divisions among different ethnic, regional, and parochial groups out of which nation-builders, partly through education, must forge a larger sense of national identity."

BIBLIOGRAPHY

For a statement on the educational problems and goals facing the newly independent African states, see UNESCO, *Conference of African States on the Development of Education in Africa: Final Report* (Paris: UNESCO, 1961). UNESCO has also published a series of volumes on educational facilities and programs for the world, including Africa, under the title, *World Survey of Education* Vol. 1 General (1955), Vol. 2, Primary (1958), Vol. 3, Secondary (1961) and Vol. 4, Higher Education (1966). Information from the UNESCO report about Africa can also be found in M. Sasnet and I. Sepmeyer, *Educational Systems of Africa* (Berkeley: University of California Press, 1966). For a discussion of the problems of cross-national comparisons see W. L. Kendall, *Statistics of Education in Developing Countries, and An Introduction to their Collection and Presentation* (Paris: UNESCO, 1968). For other general works on African education see D. G. Burns, *African Education* (London: Oxford University Press, 1965), Abdou Moumouni (translated by P. Ott), *Education in Africa* (New York: Praeger, 1968) and Godfrey Brown and Mervyn Hiskett, eds., *Conflict and Harmony in Education in Tropical Africa* (Cranbury, NJ: Fairleigh Dickinson University Press, 1976).

One of the major rationales for increased education is to provide a more efficient work force. For a general review of these arguments see F. Harbison and C. A. Myers, *Education, Manpower, and Economic Growth* (New York: McGraw-Hill, 1964). Also see R. de L. Loken, *Manpower Development in Africa* (New York: Praeger, 1969); F. Harbison, *A Human Resource Approach to the Development of African Nations* (Washington, D.C.: American Council on Education, 1971); and F. B. Waisanen and H. Kumata, "Education, Functional Literacy and Participation in Development," *International Journal of Comparative Sociology*, XIII (1972):21—35.

For reviews of the role of education in social and political development see L. G. Cowan, J. O'Connell, and D. G. Scanlon, *Education and Nation-Building in Africa*

(New York: Praeger, 1965) and R. Clignet and P. Foster, *The Fortunate Few* (Evanston, Ill.: Northwestern University Press, 1966) which is an important case study of secondary school students in the Ivory Coast that challenges some widely held views of the role of education in political development. Also see D. Kopf and G. Von der Muhill, "Political Socialization in Kenya and Tanzania," *Journal of Modern African Studies* 5 (May 1967):13—51, and A. Curle, *Educational Problems of Developing Societies* (New York: Praeger, 1969). See D. Lerner, *The Passing of Traditional Society* (New York: Free Press, 1958) for a major theoretical viewpoint as well as G. Almond and S. Verba, *The Civic Culture* (Boston: Little, Brown, 1963) and P. Reach, *Political Socialization in the New Nations of Africa* (New York: Teachers College Press, 1967). For an empirical study which raises questions about the effect of education see A. Peshkin, "Limitations of Schooling for Planned Political Socialization: Reflections on Nigeria," *Comparative Educational Review* (Sept. 1972):63—73. Also see D. R. Evans, *Teachers as Agents of National Development* (New York: Praeger, 1972) and K. Prewitt, *Education and Political Values* (Nairobi: East African Publishing House, 1973).

Education is not only important from the country's point of view as manpower generator and socializing agent, it is also the major vehicle for social mobility in most developing countries. Attempting to satisfy these demands often puts additional strains on the political system. For a review of these issues see D. Abernethy, *The Political Dilemma of Popular Education—An African Case* (Palo Alto, Calif.: Stanford University Press, 1969). Also see chapters in P. C. Lloyd, *The New Elites of Tropical Africa* (London: Oxford University Press, 1966). Other work on the effect of education as a modernizing agent includes: L. Aran, S. N. Eisenstadt, and C. Adler, "The Effectiveness of Educational Systems in the Process of Modernization," *Comparative Education Review* 16 (Feb. 1972):30—43; C. M. Coughenour, "Measures of

Individual Modernity: Review and Commentary," *International Journal of Comparative Sociology* XIII (1972):81—98; and M. Armer and R. Youtz, "Formal Education and Individual Modernity in an African Society," *American Journal of Sociology* (Jan. 1971):604—626.

A considerable literature on educational planning and policy has grown up. For an early statement in addition to the previously cited UNESCO works see G. N. Brown, "British Educational Policy in West and Central Africa," *Journal of Modern African Studies* 2 (1964):365—377 and K. Busia, *Purposeful Education for Africa* (The Hague: Mouton, 1964). Critiques of these approaches are : R. Jolly and C. Colclough, "African Manpower Plans in Evaluation," *International Labour Review* 106 (1972):207—264; M. Carnoy and H. Thias, "Educational Planning with Flexible Wages: A Kenyan Example," *Economic Development and Cultural Change* 20 (April 1972):438—473; and W. C. Cash, "A Critique of Manpower Planning in Africa," in M. Blaugh (ed.) *Economics of Education* (Harmondsworth: Penguin, 1969). For an evaluation of one particular educational policy see E. Stables, *Education Since Uhuru—The Schools of Kenya* (Middletown, Conn.: Wesleyan University Press, 1969). Other case studies are cited in Part V of this book.

For comparative studies of educational policy, see R. Jolly, *Education in Africa: Research and Action* (Nairobi: East African Publishing House, 1969); R. Clignet and P. Foster, "French and British Colonial Education in Africa" *Comparative Education Review* 8 (1964):191—198, and L. G. Cowan, "British and French Education in Africa: A Critical Appraisal" in D. Piper and T. Cole (eds.), *Post Primary Education and Political and Economic Development* (Durham, N.C.: Duke University Press, 1964).

Various case studies have evaluated different levels of education: primary, secondary, and higher. Some examples of these are I. Okechukwu (ed.), *Education in Nigeria* (New York: Praeger, 1965); T. Balogh, "Misconceived Educational Programmes in Africa" *Universities Quarterly* (June 1962); F. Harbison, "The African University and Human Resources Development," *Journal of Modern African Studies* 3 (1965):53—62. Others include E. Ashby, *African Universities and the Western Tradition* (Cambridge, Mass.: Harvard University Press, 1964); M. O. Beshir, *Educational Development in the Sudan* (New York: Oxford University Press, 1969) and P. Foster, *Education and Social Change in Ghana* (Chicago: University of Chicago Press, 1964). For a critical study of a Nigerian university by a sociologist see Pierre L. Van den Berghe, *Power and Privilege at an African University* (London: Routledge & Kegan Paul, 1973).

For a case study which reviews educational effects on integration see D. M. Kurtz II. "Education and Elite Integration in Nigeria," *Comparative Education Review* 17 (Feb. 1973):58—70 and for data sources on education see the UNESCO and UN *Statistical Yearbooks* and *Black Africa*. Michael Armer's comprehensive *African Social Psychology: A Review and Annotated Bibliography* (New York: Africana, 1975) is relevant to many education topics. The *West African Journal of Education* (London: Cambridge University Press) is also a useful ongoing source.

**TABLE 3.1 Estimated Percent of Population Literate, 1977 (A),
1972 (B), 1965 (C), and 1955 (D).**

Definitions: The United Nations recommended definition of literacy is
the ability both to read and write. A literate person must be able to read
with understanding, and to write a short statement on everyday life, in
any one language. We have assumed that the AID definition of literacy
is similar to that of the U.N.

Comments: Literacy is difficult to measure with accuracy and this data
must be regarded with caution. Literacy represents the cumulative effects of an educational system including adult literacy programs.
Hence, while two countries may have similar rates of primary attendance in 1966, there may still be a considerable difference in the overall
literacy rate at that time. This can come about if one country has had
higher levels of attendance in the past than another country thereby
cumulating a greater stock of literate persons. According to the data
some countries have moderately high literacy rates (principally Congo,
Lesotho, Madagascar, Somalia, Swaziland, and Tanzania). Another
thirteen countries have a moderate level while half of the countries
have a rate of twenty percent or less, which are among the lowest in the
world.

```
Range =          61.00
Mean  =          25.10
Standard Deviation =        16.29
```

Population Percent Cum.	Country	Rank	Country Name	A	Range Decile	B	C	D
5.16	5.16	1.0	Tanzania	66	1	18	15	8
5.32	.16	2.0	Swaziland	65		36	30	22
6.35	1.03	3.0	Somalia	60		5	5	1
6.73	.38	4.0	Lesotho	52	3	70	60	50
7.18	.45	5.5	Congo	50		30	23	3
9.66	2.48	5.5	Madagascar	50		40	40	35
14.26	4.60	7.0	Kenya	40	5	25	25	23
15.91	1.65	8.0	Zambia	39		40	40	23
16.14	.23	9.5	Botswana	35	6	33	30	23
18.55	2.41	9.5	Cameroon	35		15	10	7
26.84	8.29	11.0	Zaire	31		50	40	37
30.35	3.51	13.5	Ghana	30		30	30	23
30.88	.53	13.5	Liberia	30		12	10	8
34.83	3.95	13.5	Uganda	30		30	30	25
37.09	2.26	13.5	Zimbabwe	30		28	25	
38.37	1.28	17.0	Burundi	25	7	10	10	8
40.03	1.66	17.0	Malawi	25		15	10	8
61.03	21.00	17.0	Nigeria	25		25	20	12
62.39	1.36	19.0	Rwanda	23	8	10	10	8
63.96	1.57	21.5	Guinea	20		10	10	3
66.18	2.22	21.5	Ivory Coast	20		21	20	3
66.47	.29	21.5	Namibia	20		18	15	
72.71	6.24	21.5	Sudan	20		13	13	12
73.46	.75	24.0	Togo	18		10	10	8
73.92	.46	25.0	Mauritania	17	9	5	5	3
75.26	1.34	28.0	Chad	15		8	5	3
75.36	.10	28.0	Equatorial Guinea	15		30	25	20
85.07	9.71	28.0	Ethiopia	15		5	5	3
88.06	2.99	28.0	Mozambique	15		7	3	2
89.05	.99	28.0	Sierra Leone	15		10	10	8
89.21	.16	31.0	Gabon	13		15	13	3
91.16	1.95	32.0	Angola	12		13	8	5
92.16	1.00	33.0	Benin	11	10	15	5	3
92.33	.17	35.0	Gambia	10		10	10	7
94.20	1.87	35.0	Mali	10		5	5	3
95.84	1.64	35.0	Senegal	10		10	7	3
97.17	1.33	37.0	Niger	8		5	3	1
97.75	.58	38.5	Central African R	7		8	5	3
97.94	.19	38.5	Guinea-Bissau	7		5	3	1
98.04	.10	40.5	Djibouti	5		5	5	
100.00	1.97	40.5	Upper Volta	5		7	7	3

SOURCE: *Black Africa*, second edition.

TABLE 3.2   **Primary Enrollment per 1,000 Population, 1977 (A), 1972 (B), 1966 (C) and Total Primary Enrollment 1976 (D), and 1972 (E).**

Definition: Total enrollment in primary or first-level education (typically including the first six to eight years of education) in all schools, public and private, divided by the national population estimate for that year.

Comments: The countries at the top of the table such as Gabon, Kenya and Namibia have nearly universal primary attendance, while the countries at the bottom are primarily inland countries, just south of the Sahara which are largely poor, Islamic (excepting Upper Volta and, to a lesser extent, Ethiopia) and lacking basic social infrastructure and resources. While enormous progress is being made in many countries which is often building on the base started by the church-related schools, primary education is still received by a minority in most countries. Since most countries have been increasing their commitment to education it is to be expected that these rates of attendance will continue to climb in countries where attendance is still low.

```
Range =          224.00
Mean =           108.24
Standard Deviation =          55.01
```

Population Percent Cum.	Country	Rank	Country Name	A	Range Decile	B	C	D	E
.16	.16	1.0	Gabon	248	1	203	169	130398	105600
4.76	4.60	2.0	Kenya	210	2	144	105	2894617	1676000
5.05	.29	3.0	Namibia	206		186	122	181616	155036
5.21	.16	4.0	Swaziland	187	3	176	152	92721	76343
5.59	.38	5.0	Lesotho	182		181	195	222004	176404
7.24	1.65	6.0	Zambia	178	4	176	124	872392	777873
7.47	.23	7.0	Botswana	177		119	124	125588	81662
8.22	.75	8.0	Togo	170		123	94	395381	257877
16.51	8.29	9.0	Zaire	150	5	141	130	3429076	3219554
18.92	2.41	10.5	Cameroon	149		158	133	1146437	968000
21.40	2.48	10.5	Madagascar	149		137	108	1133013	1004447
21.59	.19	12.0	Guinea-Bissau	140		100	23	83781	48007
23.85	2.26	13.0	Zimbabwe	130	6	134	128	863059	798046
25.51	1.66	14.0	Malawi	128		104	71	663940	484676
26.09	.58	15.0	Central African R	124		109	105	221412	177924
31.25	5.16	16.0	Tanzania	123		72	63	1956320	1004000
34.76	3.51	17.0	Ghana	122		159	163	1213291	1447195
34.86	.10	18.0	Equatorial Guinea	120		109	107	35977	31600
36.22	1.36	19.0	Rwanda	104	7	108	57	434150	400000
38.44	2.22	20.5	Ivory Coast	100		119	98	672707	527615
38.97	.53	20.5	Liberia	100		112	101	157821	135000
39.97	1.00	22.5	Benin	92		65	55	293648	186000
40.07	.10	22.5	Djibouti	92		78	47	9764	7746
42.02	1.95	24.0	Angola	88	8	89	42	516131	516131
45.97	3.95	25.0	Uganda	87		75	73	1036920	786227
46.42	.45	26.0	Congo	83		267	221	319101	262000
67.42	21.00	27.0	Nigeria	82		68	51	4889857	3854539
68.41	.99	28.0	Sierra Leone	73		64	52	205910	174000
69.44	1.03	29.0	Somalia	71		21	11	229030	61000
72.43	2.99	30.0	Mozambique	68	9	63	66	577997	526962
74.00	1.57	31.0	Guinea	65		49	46	324165	191287
80.24	6.24	32.0	Sudan	64		60	35	1217510	961411
81.88	1.64	33.0	Senegal	63		66	61	311800	266383
83.22	1.34	34.0	Chad	50		49	51	210882	184020
83.68	.46	35.0	Mauritania	49		32	19	72932	38900
83.85	.17	36.0	Gambia	47		51	42	25513	19421
85.72	1.87	37.0	Mali	43	10	45	35	252393	229879
87.05	1.33	38.0	Niger	34		24	21	159515	100892
88.33	1.28	39.5	Burundi	33		50	57	130739	180000
98.04	9.71	39.5	Ethiopia	33		28	16	959272	716729
100.00	1.97	41.0	Upper Volta	24		19	22	149270	108000

SOURCE: *Black Africa* second edition.

TABLE 3.3   Average Annual Percent Change in Primary School Enrollment Per Capita, 1970-1977 (A), 1960-1972 (B), and 1953-1960 (C).

Definition: The total percent change in enrollment per capita for 1970 to 1977 divided by seven (i.e., the number of years) and so on.

Comments: For most of these countries the three time periods coincide with the immediate pre-independence period and the first two decades of independence. While most countries have had steadily increasing enrollments per capita, the greatest rates of increase have tended to come from countries that were farthest behind in enrollments. Ghana is an exception to this tendency. The table indicates that some countries have had negative growth in the 1970s.

```
Range =            68.00
Mean =              5.63
Standard Deviation =        10.41
```

Population Percent Cum. Country		Rank	Country Name	A	Range Decile	B	C
1.03	1.03	1.0	Somalia	59.3	1	7.6	11.9
22.03	21.00	2.0	Nigeria	20.7	6	2.2	17.9
27.19	5.16	3.0	Tanzania	17.7	7	4.4	8.1
27.42	.23	4.0	Botswana	12.3		5.8	8.4
30.93	3.51	5.0	Ghana	11.8		9.5	-1.4
35.53	4.60	6.0	Kenya	11.4	8	4.0	14.5
35.99	.46	7.0	Mauritania	10.9		13.9	20.0
37.32	1.33	8.0	Niger	10.2		16.7	23.8
37.42	.10	9.0	Equatorial Guinea	10.1		2.9	1.1
37.61	.19	10.0	Guinea-Bissau	10.0		31.3	35.7
38.36	.75	11.0	Togo	9.6		7.9	6.6
48.07	9.71	12.0	Ethiopia	9.5		20.1	14.3
49.07	1.00	13.0	Benin	8.3		4.0	3.7
50.64	1.57	14.0	Guinea	8.2		4.8	34.9
52.61	1.97	15.0	Upper Volta	6.6		3.8	16.7
54.27	1.66	16.0	Malawi	5.8		2.2	2.2
54.43	.16	17.0	Gabon	5.6		5.4	11.6
54.72	.29	18.0	Namibia	5.3		6.7	2.8
54.82	.10	19.0	Djibouti	4.5	9	9.7	8.0
58.77	3.95	20.0	Uganda	4.0		-.5	8.6
59.35	.58	21.0	Central African R	3.4		8.2	13.8
61.83	2.48	22.0	Madagascar	3.0		5.2	5.6
62.00	.17	23.0	Gambia	1.8		10.1	4.8
68.24	6.24	24.0	Sudan	1.7		10.9	8.9
68.40	.16	25.0	Swaziland	1.5		6.2	4.0
69.74	1.34	26.0	Chad	.5		5.8	30.0
71.39	1.65	27.0	Zambia	.3		5.0	5.7
71.77	.38	28.0	Lesotho	.1		-.4	3.6
73.72	1.95	31.0	Angola	0		25.4	64.3
74.17	.45	31.0	Congo	0		6.5	12.5
77.16	2.99	31.0	Mozambique	0		-.1	17.2
78.15	.99	31.0	Sierra Leone	0		6.5	10.2
86.44	8.29	31.0	Zaire	0		2.8	4.7
88.70	2.26	34.0	Zimbabwe	-.7		.4	6.2
91.11	2.41	35.0	Cameroon	-.9		6.0	12.0
92.47	1.36	36.0	Rwanda	-1.0		10.8	12.6
94.34	1.87	37.0	Mali	-1.4		15.1	11.1
95.98	1.64	38.0	Senegal	-1.7		6.5	15.1
96.51	.53	39.0	Liberia	-3.5	10	8.3	3.5
98.73	2.22	40.0	Ivory Coast	-5.2		6.9	43.8
100.00	1.28	41.0	Burundi	-8.7		.5	12.6

SOURCE: *Black Africa* second edition.

TABLE 3.4   Secondary School Enrollment per 10,000 Population, 1976 (A), 1972 (B), 1966 (C), and 1962 (D).

Definition: Enrollment in general secondary education, excluding teacher training and vocational enrollment, in all schools, public and private, divided by the national population.

Comments: While Congo and Ghana have the most intensely developed secondary school systems in Black Africa, a number of other countries are making recent progress in developing secondary education, particularly Gabon and Guinea-Bissau. There is strong positive correlation between per capita income and secondary school enrollment per capita (see Appendix 3). Hence the countries with the lowest figures in this table tend to be the poorest countries in Africa. A country like Guinea-Bissau is an obvious exception to this generalization, however.

```
Range =        734.00
Mean =         172.65
Standard Deviation =        155.53
```

Population Percent Cum.	Country	Rank	Country Name	A	Range Decile	B	C	D
.45	.45	1.0	Congo	756	1	296	151	21
3.96	3.51	2.0	Ghana	578	3	640	213	281
4.15	.19	3.0	Guinea-Bissau	464	4	86	19	29
4.31	.16	4.0	Gabon	447	5	184	101	84
5.06	.75	5.0	Togo	350	6	123	75	53
5.22	.16	6.0	Swaziland	300	7	253	104	64
6.79	1.57	7.0	Guinea	250		153	46	12
7.02	.23	8.0	Botswana	230	8	114	32	17
7.55	.53	9.0	Liberia	217		132	104	61
12.15	4.60	10.0	Kenya	209		134	51	35
12.25	.10	11.0	Djibouti	188		191	97	42
20.54	8.29	12.0	Zaire	185		99	33	51
22.76	2.22	13.0	Ivory Coast	178		171	83	57
23.76	1.00	14.5	Benin	172		65	43	29
30.00	6.24	14.5	Sudan	172		106	66	56
32.41	2.41	16.5	Cameroon	166	9	124	53	60
33.40	.99	16.5	Sierra Leone	166		127	57	51
35.05	1.65	18.0	Zambia	156		133	63	23
36.69	1.64	19.0	Senegal	150		150	72	60
37.07	.38	20.0	Lesotho	147		91	33	15
37.17	.10	21.0	Equatorial Guinea	146		179	79	16
37.34	.17	22.0	Gambia	139		110	110	89
39.29	1.95	23.5	Angola	134		89	29	17
39.87	.58	23.5	Central African R	134		116	33	24
42.13	2.26	25.0	Zimbabwe	118		115	52	16
44.00	1.87	26.5	Mali	95	10	70	20	12
65.00	21.00	26.5	Nigeria	95		61	39	43
65.46	.46	28.0	Mauritania	75		48	14	1
75.17	9.71	29.0	Ethiopia	68		54	22	7
78.16	2.99	30.0	Mozambique	64		23	12	6
82.11	3.95	31.0	Uganda	56		42	118	56
83.45	1.34	32.0	Chad	46		27	24	10
88.61	5.16	33.0	Tanzania	41		31	20	19
89.64	1.03	34.0	Somalia	38		93	28	24
90.92	1.28	35.0	Burundi	34		18	12	13
92.58	1.66	36.0	Malawi	33		29	17	12
93.94	1.36	37.0	Rwanda	30		19	9	12
95.91	1.97	38.0	Upper Volta	29		19	11	7
97.24	1.33	39.0	Niger	28		20	9	8
99.72	2.48	40.0	Madagascar	22		23	89	80

DATA NOT AVAILABLE OR NOT APPLICABLE
FOR THE FOLLOWING COUNTRIES

Namibia

SOURCE: *Black Africa* second edition.

TABLE 3.5   Educational Expenditure as a Percent of Total Government Expenditure, 1977 (A), 1972 (B), 1965 (C), and 1958 (D).

Comments: Since independence, African governments have tended to devote a considerable proportion of their expenditures to education in the expectation that this will spur economic development, social mobility, and national integration. The average country is putting nearly 20 percent of its budget into education while some go as high as 40 percent.

```
Range =         31.90
Mean =          19.89
Standard Deviation =        7.15
```

Population Percent Cum. Country		Rank	Country Name	A	Range Decile	B	C	D
1.00	1.00	1.0	Benin	40.0	1	28.3	16.5	24.6
3.22	2.22	2.0	Ivory Coast	37.0		23.5	16.7	19.0
5.09	1.87	3.0	Mali	30.6	3	19.0	12.9	24.6
6.08	.99	4.0	Sierra Leone	28.8	4	22.2	19.4	24.2
6.53	.45	5.0	Congo	28.0		25.3	20.3	26.2
27.53	21.00	6.0	Nigeria	27.3		14.8	16.0	38.8
32.13	4.60	7.0	Kenya	26.6	5	18.7	11.9	23.4
40.42	8.29	8.0	Zaire	26.5		14.8	21.4	17.3
41.78	1.36	9.0	Rwanda	24.0	6	25.7	20.5	21.7
44.26	2.48	10.5	Madagascar	23.0		9.5	5.5	9.7
46.23	1.97	10.5	Upper Volta	23.0		21.5	16.1	16.4
48.64	2.41	12.0	Cameroon	22.5		19.7	16.4	14.0
49.39	.75	13.0	Togo	22.0		19.9	17.9	16.6
49.77	.38	14.0	Lesotho	21.2		19.3	27.9	18.8
51.05	1.28	15.0	Burundi	20.8	7	23.5	23.0	21.7
56.21	5.16	16.0	Tanzania	20.2		14.4	17.8	33.8
57.85	1.64	17.0	Senegal	19.8		13.9	8.7	12.5
61.36	3.51	18.0	Ghana	19.4		25.5	20.9	21.9
61.52	.16	19.0	Swaziland	18.7		15.3	15.8	9.7
63.18	1.66	20.0	Malawi	18.3		13.4	15.0	20.4
64.52	1.34	21.0	Chad	17.2	8	14.5	18.5	11.5
64.68	.16	22.5	Gabon	17.1		16.0	12.1	19.6
66.01	1.33	22.5	Niger	17.1		12.9	12.2	12.3
66.59	.58	24.5	Central Afri. R	17.0		15.6	13.6	19.3
68.16	1.57	24.5	Guinea	17.0		20.8	30.1	15.6
68.39	.23	26.0	Botswana	16.8		6.9	16.2	15.1
68.58	.19	27.0	Guinea-Bissau	15.6		7.9		
69.04	.46	28.0	Mauritania	15.4		26.6	14.3	15.0
75.28	6.24	29.0	Sudan	14.7		5.7	20.1	9.7
76.31	1.03	30.5	Somalia	13.0	9	6.3	7.0	6.1
77.96	1.65	30.5	Zambia	13.0		12.8	10.6	13.1
87.67	9.71	32.0	Ethiopia	12.8		16.7	10.2	11.3
91.62	3.95	33.0	Uganda	12.6		18.6	10.8	21.4
93.88	2.26	34.0	Zimbabwe	12.0		21.1	14.5	
93.98	.10	35.0	Djibouti	9.6	10			
94.51	.53	36.0	Liberia	9.1		13.1	13.5	10.7
94.68	.17	37.0	Gambia	8.1		9.8	12.6	10.6

```
DATA NOT AVAILABLE OR NOT APPLICABLE
FOR THE FOLLOWING COUNTRIES

Angola      Equatorial Guinea  Mozambique   Namibia
```

SOURCE: *Black Africa* second edition.

Chapter 4

Urbanization

Africa is at once, the least urbanized and the fastest urbanizing, of the world's continents. According to United Nations data for the entire continent of Africa, the percent of the population residing in localities of 20,000 or more inhabitants in 1960 was 13 percent, as compared with Asia's 17 percent and Latin America's 32 percent. In terms of urban growth, however, African cities have been growing at a very high rate. One hundred years ago there were only two cities approaching 100,000 in population in the countries considered in this book, while by 1965 there were more than one hundred cities of this size or greater, and some eighteen million Black Africans resided in towns of 30,000 or larger. Africa has experienced a 30 percent increase in the percent of the population in localities of 20,000 or more (1950—1960) as compared with the world (19 %) and North America (14 %) and the rate of increase has grown larger in the following decade. Between 1957 and 1967 the rate of migration to Dar es Salaam, for example, increased at an annual rate of 3 per cent; between 1962 and 1969 that of Nairobi grew at an annual rate of 15 per cent. This process has generally accelerated in the 1970s despite the decline in economic growth for most African countries during that time.

The recency of the growth of large settlements should not obscure the fact that cities have been an important aspect of African history for a thousand years or more. Although relatively small by present day standards, cities such as Kano, Timbuktu, Gao, Oyo, Ibadan and Mombasa developed as important centers of trade and political power at various times from the eleventh through the nineteenth centuries. We cannot assume that urbanization in some form would not have continued without exogenous influences. Some difference of opinion exists, however, among scholars as to whether these population centers can qualify as "cities" since while the usual criteria of size and density were met, social heterogeneity and functional specialization were not characteristic of some, and unified political authority and common institutions were not present in others.

Contemporary urbanization in Africa is one of the key components of the modernization process and one thought to be an important aspect of political development. Normally cities require a societal level of agricultural production adequate to produce a surplus in order to feed the non-agricultural urban population. These cities are typically centers of trade, communication and local manufacture. The major or capital city may also stand both as a referent or symbol of national identity, and as a source of mass media dissemination which operates to instill nationalistic sentiments and values. There exists the possibility that "overurbanization" may outstrip industrial development with negative consequences for political development.

The city exerts its influence on and through its inhabitants. African urban residents, relatively independent as they are from the land and from their traditional social matrix, tend to acquire certain aspects of a new way of life and to gradually modify their traditional world-view. The effect of urban life on the society as a whole is multiplied by the close ties African city dwellers maintain with their villages or homesteads. Most African city dwellers have been first generation migrants who participate in urban associations made up of people from the same village or area, who return home regularly, and provide hospitality for fellow villagers who visit the city. Through these influences African cities exert an influence far beyond their administrative boundaries. As a larger part of the population becomes native urbanites these processes may change.

The effect of urban life upon city dwellers should not be exaggerated, however. In earlier writings on African urbanization there was a tendency to suppose that the change to urban living by tribesmen brought about an extreme individualism, a loss of tribal identity or detribalization, and thus a tendency to feel normless or rootless. For an example of this perspective see G. Malengrean, "Observations on the Orientations of Sociological Researches in African Urban Centers, with Reference to

Figure 4.1   Urbanization in Black Africa

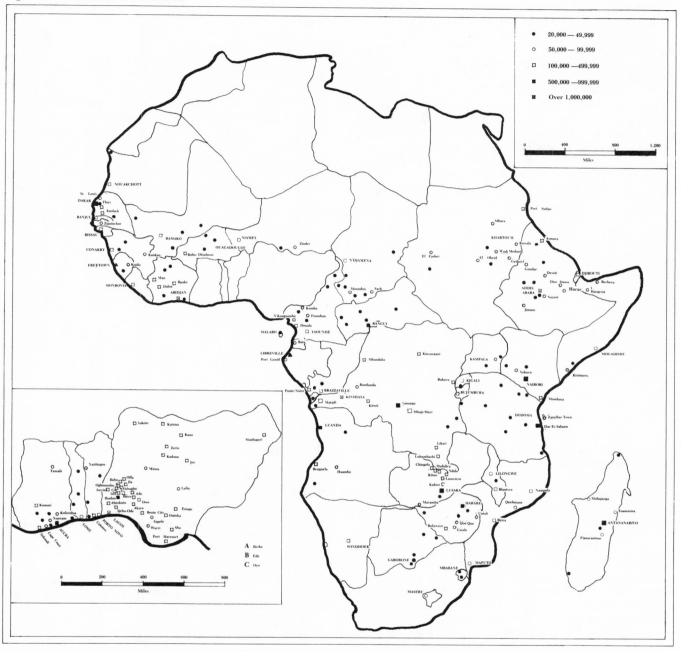

the Situation in the Belgian Congo," in *Social Implications of Industrialization and Urbanization in Africa South of the Sahara*, International African Institute, (Paris: UNESCO, 1956): pp. 624—638. Recent studies show that this analyis of the effects of urban living was distorted. There certainly are serious social problems in many overcrowded African cities and these will become more serious in the next decade as the ranks of the unemployed school leavers increase and concentrate in the cities. Nevertheless, the resiliency of African culture has led to the development of new forms of urban social organization, such as "friendly societies" and tribal associations, which mitigate the harshness of the new environment and relate the newcomers to their ethnic group in

significant new ways. The extended family, moreover, has tended to retain its importance despite the relative dispersions of its members both geographically and socially.

African cities may be differentiated in terms of function (administrative, mining, port, etc.), history (traditional, colonial, post-colonial), location (West Africa, East Africa, etc.), as well as size. The variables presented in this chapter treat all cities as alike, however, taking account only of size and that in a relatively limited manner. Nevertheless, the recency of foundation of most African cities and their general characteristic of serving as loci for rapidly expanding economic and/or political and administrative activities suggests that they share important underlying uniformities.

BIBLIOGRAPHY

A major attempt to synthesize the literature on African cities and urbanization is W. J. Hanna and J. L. Hanna's *Urban Dynamics in Black Africa: An Interdisciplinary Approach* second edition (New York: Aldine, 1981). The text provides useful summaries on present knowledge, especially on the topics of migration, urban conditions, urban ethnicity and urban politics and a bibliography. H. I. Ajaegbu's *African Urbanization: A Bibliography* (London International African Institute, 1972) has nearly 3,000 entries divided by country and city. More recent bibliographies are: Michael G. Schatzenberg, *Bibliography of Small Urban Centers in Rural Development in Africa* (African Studies Program, University of Wisconsin, 1979) and A. M. O'Connor, *Urbanization in Tropical Africa: An Annotated Bibliography* (Boston: G. K. Hall, 1981).

There are a number of general works on African urbanization. Especially recommended for an overview is the geographer W. A. Hance's *Population, Migration and Urbanization in Africa* (New York: Columbia University Press, 1970) and "Urbanization and Change" by Akin L. Mabogunje in J. N. Paden and E. W. Soja,

(eds.), *The African Experience V. 1, Essays* (Evanston, Ill.: Northwestern University Press, 1970), pp. 331-358. An important earlier volume which provides a good baseline for contemporary urbanization is Daryll Forde (ed.), *Social Implications of Industrialization and Urbanization in Africa South of the Sahara* (Paris: UNESCO, 1956). Three useful edited volumes are Hilda Kuper (ed.), *Urbanization and Migration in West Africa* (Berkeley: University of California Press, 1965), Horace M. Miner (ed.), *The City in Modern Africa* (New York: Praeger, 1967) and Kenneth L. Little (ed.) *Urbanization as a Social Process in Contemporary Africa* (London: Routledge and Kegan Paul, 1974). *African Urban Studies* published three times a year contains bibliography and notes on recent research. Also see J. Dutte (ed.), *The Urban Challenge in East Africa* (Nairobi: East African Publishing House, 1972).

The theory of primate cities is discussed in Arnold S. Linsky, "Some Generalizations Concerning Primate Cities," *Annals of the Association of American Geographers* 55 (1965):506—513 and Surrinder K. Mehta, "Some Demographic and Economic Correlates of Primate Cities: A Case for Re-evaluation," in Gerald Breese (ed.), *The City in Newly Developing Countries* (Englewood Cliffs, N.J.: Prentice-Hall, 1969), pp. 295—303. The Mehta paper in Breese's volume is somewhat expanded from its original published form in the journal, *Demography*. An analysis of urban primacy is Carol Owen and Ronald A. Witton, "National Division and Mobilization: A Reinterpretation of Primacy," *Economic Development and Cultural Change* 21 (Jan. 1973): 325—337.

Related to, but distinct from the primacy question is the notion of "overurbanization" (where higher proportions of a country's population live in urban areas than can be justified by the level of economic development). For a presentation of the concept see Philip Hauser, "The Social, Economic, and Technological Problems of Rapid Urbanization," in Bert F. Hoselitz and Wilbert E. Moore (eds.), *Industrialization and Society* (Paris: UNESCO and Mouton, 1963). Akin Mabogunje identifies Nigeria as overurbanized in "Urbanization in Nigeria: A Constraint on Economic Development," *Economic Development and Cultural Change* 13 (July 1965):413—438.

For discussions of traditional urbanism in Africa see Hilda Kuper (ed.), *Urbanization and Migration in West Africa* (Berkeley: University of California Press, 1965): pp / 1-22;) William Bascom, "Urbanization among the Yoruba," *American Journal of Sociology* 60 (1955): 445—454; Horace Miner, *The Primitive City of Timbuctoo* (Princeton, N.J.: Princeton University Press, 1953); "The Folk Urban Continuum," *American Sociological Review* 17 (1952):529—537; P. C. Lloyd, A. L. Mabogunje and B. Awe (eds.), *The City of Ibadan* (Cambridge: Cambridge University Press, 1967) and Eva Krapf-Askari, *Yoruba Towns and Cities* (Oxford: Clarendon Press, 1969).

The process of urbanization involves the increased mixing of groups from diverse ethnic, linguistic, ecological and social backgrounds. Some view the process as a continuation of rural life and ethnic distinctiveness such as the work by Abner Cohen in *Custom and Politics in Urban Africa: A Study of Hausa Migrants in Yoruba Towns* (London: Routledge & Kegan Paul, 1969) and the papers in the volume edited by him, *Urban Ethnicity* (London: Tavistock, 1974). Others view it as a process where ethnic boundaries are broken down and replaced by an increasing class formation and proletarianization of the migrants to the cites. An early example of this work is A. L. Epstein, "The Network and Urban Social Organization," *Human Problems in British Central Africa* 29 (1961):29—62; and "Urbanization and Social Change in Africa," *Current Anthropology* 8 (Oct. 1967):275—283.

For other statements on this subject see: J. C. Mitchell (ed.), *Social Networks in Urban Situations: Analyses of Personal Relationships in Central African Towns* (Manchester, Eng.: Manchester University Press, 1969);

and Kenneth Little, *African Women in Towns: An Aspect of Africa's Social Revolution* (New York: Cambridge University Press, 1973).

Several case studies of urban areas can be found in the country bibliographies of Part V. Examples are: J. S. La Fontaine, *City Politics: A Study of Leopoldville 1962—63* (New York: Cambridge University Press, 1970) and B. Williams and A. H. Walsh, *Urban Government for Metropolitan Lagos* (New York: Praeger, 1968).

The topic of urbanization and social change in Africa is the subject of a large number of articles. Among the best general discussions are: Peter C. W. Gutkind, "The African Urban Milieu: A Force in Rapid Change," *Civilisations* 12 (1962): 167—195; E. Franklin Frazier, "Urbanization and its Effects Upon the Task of Nation Building in Africa South of the Sahara," *Journal of Negro Education* 30 (1961):214—222; J. Clyde Mitchell, "Theoretical Orientations in African Urban Studies," in M. Banton (ed.), *The Social Anthropology of Complex Societies* (London: Tavistock, 1966). More recent attempts are R. Brandt, et. al., *The Industrial Town as Factor of Economic and Social Development* African Studies No. 77 (Munich: Welforum Verlag, 1975) and Josef Gugler and William Flanigan, *Urbanization and Social Change in West Africa* (New York: Cambridge University Press, 1978).

Two works by geographers on Nigeria and Kenya have important theoretical implications for the general study of urbanization. These are: Akin L. Mabogunje, *Urbanization in Nigeria* (New York: Africana Publishing, 1969) and Edward W. Soja, *The Geography of Modernization in Kenya* (Syracuse, N.Y.: Syracuse University Press, 1968). For review of the political problems of urbanization including an extensive bibliography see: Richard Stren, "Urban Policy in Africa: A Political Analysis," *African Studies Review* 15 (1972): 489—514. A major work on the growing problem of urban squatters is Marc Ross' study of Nairobi, *The Political Integration of Urban Squatters* (Evanston, Ill.: Northwestern University Press, 1973).

The literature on migration in Black Africa is closely related to the urban literature because many of the migrants are headed for the cities. Besides the works by the Hannas and Kuper noted above, several earlier studies worthy of mention are: J. C. Mitchell, "Wage Labor and African Population Movements in Central Africa," in Kenneth M. Barbour and R. M. Prothero (eds.), *Essays on African Population* (London: Routledge & Kegan Paul, 1961), pp. 193—248; S. U. Juiude, "Population Movements to the Main Urban Areas of Kenya," *Cahiers d'Études Africaines* 5 (1965):593—617; J. C. Caldwell, *African Rural-Urban Migration: The Movement to Ghana's Towns* (New York: Columbia University Press,

1969); Leonard Plotnicov, *Strangers to the City: Urban Man in Jos, Nigeria* (Pittsburgh, Pa.: Unviersity of Pittsburgh Press, 1967); and Eric W. Wood, "The Implications of Migrant Labour for Urban Social Systems in Africa," *Cahiers d'Études Africaines* 8 (1968):5—31. A recent work is S. Amin (ed.), *Modern Migrations in West Africa* (London: Oxford University Press, 1974).

The experience of the migrants in the cities and their relationship with their home towns has been studied in a number of African situations. *Conservatism and the Process of Urbanization in a South African City* (Cape Town: Oxford University Press, 1961) is an especially important work as is the work of Elliott P. Skinner on the Mossi of Upper Volta, "Labour Migration and its Relationship to Socio-Cultural Change in Mossi Society," *Africa* 30 (1960):375—401 and "Strangers in West African Societies," *Africa* 33 (1963):307—320.

Notable studies of special topics include the following. On family life: Peter Çutkind, "African Urban Family Life: Comment on and Analysis of Some Rural-Urban Differences," *Cahiers d'Études Africaines* 3 (1962):149—217; Peter Marris, *Family and Social Change in an African City* (London: Routledge & Kegan Paul, 1961); and Remi Clignet, *Many Wives, Many Powers: Authority and Power in Polygynous Families* (Evanston, Ill.: Northwestern University Press, 1970). On voluntary associations: Kenneth Little, *West African Urbanization: A Study of Voluntary Associations in Social Change* (Cambridge: Cambridge University Press, 1965) and David J. Parkin, "Urban Voluntary Associations as Institutions of Adaptation," *Man* 1 (1966):90-95. On urban unemployment: Peter C. W. Gutkind, "The Poor in Urban Africa: A Prolgoue to Modernization, Conflict, and the Unfinished Revolution," in W. Bloomberg, Jr. and H. J. Schmandt (eds.), *Power, Poverty and Urban Policy* (Beverly Hills, Calif.: Sage, 1968), pp. 355—396.

For a discussion of the pre-conditions for urbanization see Gideon Sjoberg, *The Pre-Industrial City* (New York: The Free Press, 1960); pp. 25—49. Two additional prerequisites cited by Sjoberg are a favorable ecological base and a complex social organization. Serious problems exist and may intensify in the next decade should the rate of urbanization outstrip the capacity of develping economies to absorb non-agricultural manpower. Useful case studies of urbanization are: C. Meillasoux's *Urbanization of an African Community: Voluntary Associations in Bamako* (Seattle: University of Washington Press, 1968); Valdo Pons, *Stanleyville, An African Urban Community under Belgian Administration* (London: Oxford University Press, 1969) and Harm J. de Bilg, *Mombassa: An African City* (Evanston, Ill.: Northwestern University Press, 1968).

TABLE 4.1   Estimated Percent Population in Cities of 20,000 or More ca. 1955

Definition: The populations of all towns over 20,000 population in 1955 are summed and divided by the country's total population for that year. It is not always clear whether the largest cities are urban agglomerations incorporating adjoining towns but presumably they are not.

Comments: In 1955 there were six countries with no towns over 20,000 (Botswana, Mauritania, Guinea-Bissau, Lesotho, Rwanda and Swaziland) and the highest urbanization level was 48% (Djibouti). The average level of urbanization was less than 6% in tropical Africa. There is a tendency for the coastal countries to have a higher urbanization level than the inland countries but this is far from a perfect relation. The reliability of data in this period tends to be much poorer than later information since it predates the modern censuses in Africa, for the most part, but it is clear that Africa was only beginning rapid urbanization in 1955.

```
(Range  =        48.40
Mean  =           5.77
Standard Deviation =            8.14
```

Population Percent Cum.	Country	Rank	Country Name	A	Range Decile
.10	.10	1.0	Djibouti	48.4	1
.55	.45	2.0	Congo	17.7	7
.65	.10	3.0	Equatorial Guinea	16.0	
2.29	1.64	4.0	Senegal	14.8	
4.55	2.26	5.0	Zimbabwe	14.0	8
6.20	1.65	6.0	Zambia	11.4	
27.20	21.00	7.0	Nigeria	9.4	9
27.37	.17	8.0	Gambia	8.3	
35.66	8.29	9.0	Zaire	8.0	
36.24	.58	10.0	Central African R	7.4	
39.75	3.51	11.0	Ghana	6.4	
42.23	2.48	12.0	Madagascar	6.2	
44.18	1.95	13.0	Angola	6.0	
44.47	.29	14.0	Namibia	5.8	
46.69	2.22	15.0	Ivory Coast	5.3	
52.93	6.24	16.0	Sudan	5.0	
55.34	2.41	17.5	Cameroon	4.7	10
55.50	.16	17.5	Gabon	4.7	
56.50	1.00	19.0	Benin	4.2	
57.53	1.03	20.0	Somalia	3.9	
62.13	4.60	21.0	Kenya	3.8	
63.12	.99	22.0	Sierra Leone	3.1	
63.87	.75	23.0	Togo	2.8	
66.86	2.99	24.0	Mozambique	2.4	
67.39	.53	25.5	Liberia	2.2	
69.26	1.87	25.5	Mali	2.2	
70.83	1.57	27.0	Guinea	2.1	
72.17	1.34	28.5	Chad	2.0	
74.14	1.97	28.5	Upper Volta	2.0	
83.85	9.71	30.0	Ethiopia	1.7	
89.01	5.16	31.0	Tanzania	1.5	
92.96	3.95	32.0	Uganda	.9	
94.29	1.33	33.0	Niger	.8	
95.57	1.28	34.0	Burundi	.7	
97.23	1.66	35.0	Malawi	.6	
97.46	.23	38.5	Botswana	0	
97.65	.19	38.5	Guinea-Bissau	0	
98.03	.38	38.5	Lesotho	0	
98.49	.46	38.5	Mauritania	0	
99.85	1.36	38.5	Rwanda	0	
100.00	.16	38.5	Swaziland	0	

SOURCE: *Black Africa* first edition, p. 162.

TABLE 4.2   Percent of Population in Cities of 20,000 or More, ca. 1977 (A), 1972 (B), and 1965 (C).

Definition: Largest cities' population is usually for the urban agglomeration. The data is either for the given year or represents an approximation for that year from the closest data available. Where a country has one or more cities slightly below 20,000, these cities were usually included in the calculation. For details on the list of cities, dates, and sources see the country by country reviews in Part V of this book.

Comments: As can be readily appreciated by comparing Tables 4.1 and 4.2, urban population is growing at a very rapid rate in tropical Africa. From 1955 to 1965, the average level of urbanization doubled. The process has continued and by 1977 the level of urbanization had increased to three times that of 1955. Every country has at least one town over 20,000 now. The most urbanized country remains Djibouti whose level of urbanization is now 50%.

```
Range  =        48.00
Mean  =          17.05
Standard Deviation =           10.76
```

Population Percent Cum.	Country	Rank	Country Name	A	Range Decile	B	C
.10	.10	1.0	Djibouti	50	1	53	81
.26	.16	2.0	Gabon	40	3	24	18
.71	.45	3.0	Congo	37		32	30
2.36	1.65	4.0	Zambia	36		30	20
2.94	.58	5.0	Central African R	31	4	22	18
3.97	1.03	6.0	Somalia	29	5	22	14
24.97	21.00	7.0	Nigeria	28		23	14
26.61	1.64	8.0	Senegal	27		27	24
28.83	2.22	9.0	Ivory Coast	26	6	21	14
28.93	.10	10.0	Equatorial Guinea	25		24	24
29.10	.17	11.5	Gambia	22		16	13
37.39	8.29	11.5	Zaire	22		17	12
40.90	3.51	13.0	Ghana	20	7	20	16
41.13	.23	14.0	Botswana	19		10	3
43.54	2.41	16.0	Cameroon	17		15	9
45.11	1.57	16.0	Guinea	17		15	7
47.37	2.26	16.0	Zimbabwe	17		10	8
48.36	.99	18.0	Sierra Leone	15	8	12	7
50.31	1.95	21.0	Angola	14		11	9
51.31	1.00	21.0	Benin	14		11	10
52.65	1.34	21.0	Chad	14		9	6
52.84	.19	21.0	Guinea-Bissau	14		14	10
53.30	.46	21.0	Mauritania	14		7	1
55.78	2.48	24.5	Madagascar	13		13	9
56.53	.75	24.5	Togo	13		14	8
57.06	.53	26.0	Liberia	12		9	9
58.93	1.87	28.5	Mali	11	9	6	6
65.17	6.24	28.5	Sudan	11		10	7
65.33	.16	28.5	Swaziland	11		11	6
67.30	1.97	28.5	Upper Volta	11		5	4
71.90	4.60	31.5	Kenya	10		9	7
74.89	2.99	31.5	Mozambique	10		8	6
75.18	.29	33.0	Namibia	9		9	8
80.34	5.16	34.0	Tanzania	8		6	5
90.05	9.71	35.5	Ethiopia	7		6	5
91.38	1.33	35.5	Niger	7		5	4
93.04	1.66	37.0	Malawi	6	10	4	3
94.32	1.28	38.5	Burundi	4		2	2
94.70	.38	38.5	Lesotho	4		3	2
96.06	1.36	40.5	Rwanda	2		1	1
100.00	3.95	40.5	Uganda	2		5	3

SOURCES: See Part V of this book and *Black Africa*, second edition.

TABLE 4.3   Primacy of Capital City, ca. 1977 (A), 1972 (B), and 1966 (C).

Definition: Population of the capital city divided by the sum of the population of the four largest cities (including the capital if it is one of the largest): or where fewer than four cities are 20,000 or above in population, by the population of the two or three largest cities. Where urban agglomeration data are available, it is used. In countries where only one or no cities were above 20,000 population, the index is arbitrarily given as 100. The higher the number the greater the primacy.

Comments: A score of over 50 indicates that the largest city is as large as the next three put together (or one or two if there are not three other cities). As can be seen in the table, thirty-four countries have a score of 50 or over and one other is in the range 44-49 with only six countries below this figure. This clearly illustrates the tendency in most of these countries for the capital to dominate the urban system at least in terms of population.

```
Range =          72.00
Mean =           68.27
Standard Deviation =          20.98
```

Population Percent							
Cum.	Country	Rank	Country Name	A	Range Decile	B	C
1.28	1.28	4.0	Burundi	100	1	100	100
1.38	.10	4.0	Djibouti	100		100	100
1.55	.17	4.0	Gambia	100		100	100
1.74	.19	4.0	Guinea-Bissau	100		100	100
2.12	.38	4.0	Lesotho	100		100	100
2.65	.53	4.0	Liberia	100		100	100
2.94	.29	4.0	Namibia	100		100	100
3.93	.99	8.0	Sierra Leone	91	2	61	85
5.50	1.57	9.0	Guinea	84	3	84	78
6.86	1.36	10.0	Rwanda	81		100	100
8.81	1.95	11.5	Angola	79		72	69
13.97	5.16	11.5	Tanzania	79		65	59
15.84	1.87	13.0	Mali	77	4	71	63
16.42	.58	15.5	Central African R	74		61	59
26.13	9.71	15.5	Ethiopia	74		71	69
28.35	2.22	15.5	Ivory Coast	74		75	66
29.10	.75	15.5	Togo	74		80	100
29.26	.16	18.5	Gabon	73		71	66
33.21	3.95	18.5	Uganda	73		70	75
34.85	1.64	20.5	Senegal	72		68	73
41.09	6.24	20.5	Sudan	72		73	69
42.43	1.34	22.0	Chad	68	5	62	56
42.89	.46	23.0	Mauritania	67		56	100
45.37	2.48	24.0	Madagascar	65		66	69
46.70	1.33	25.0	Niger	63	6	49	44
51.30	4.60	26.5	Kenya	62		63	58
54.29	2.99	26.5	Mozambique	62		59	62
62.58	8.29	28.0	Zaire	61		60	61
63.61	1.03	29.0	Somalia	59		57	55
84.61	21.00	30.0	Nigeria	58		50	43
88.12	3.51	31.0	Ghana	57		62	64
90.38	2.26	32.0	Zimbabwe	55	7	50	45
90.83	.45	33.0	Congo	54		60	60
90.99	.16	34.0	Swaziland	50		39	100
92.96	1.97	35.0	Upper Volta	49	8	44	46
94.61	1.65	36.0	Zambia	38	9	36	33
94.84	.23	37.0	Botswana	36		36	100
97.25	2.41	38.0	Cameroon	32	10	33	26
97.35	.10	39.5	Equatorial Guinea	29		32	50
99.01	1.66	39.5	Malawi	29		30	13
100.00	1.00	41.0	Benin	28		32	31

SOURCES: Data for these calculations taken from Part V of this book. Also see *Black Africa* second edition.

Chapter 5

COMMUNICATIONS   AND

TRANSPORT

The circulation and flow of information (communications) and the movement of physical goods and populations (transportation) have been emphasized in theories of economic and political development. In this chapter we present some data on mass communications and transportation. As can be seen from the tables, Black Africa has seen enormous growth in almost all areas of communications and transport in recent years. Nevertheless, there are considerable differences in the level and rates of growth among the countries reviewed in this book. Such variations partly account for, as well as reflect, differences in economic and socio-political development among these countries.

In terms of economic development, communications and transport play a critical role in facilitating economic growth and a rational allocation of resources over the entire economy. Such facilities can offer considerable economies of scale in facilitating other aspects of economic development. Care should be taken not to over-emphasize this aspect of development, however, since a balance in the creation of new investments seems required if development is to proceed in an orderly and continuous fashion.

In theories of political development, the growth of communications and transport systems is linked to the shift from traditional to modern society, the development of democratic decision-making structures, and the integration of national political communities. In the context of the frequently culturally-plural states of Africa, one of the critical problems facing the leaders is how to weld the population into one nation in terms of each individual's identification with the country as the basic political unit. This integrative process has been associated with, (1) the concept of *empathy*, that is the capacity of the individual to place himself in the role of others, and (2) *social mobilization*, where old patterns of interaction are broken down and people become aware of new life styles appropriate to urban and industrial society.

The consequences of such changes are not necessarily beneficial to individuals or countries since new demands which are put on the political system as a result of this process may not be met, and the all too frequent breakdown of social and political life may ensue.

Figure 5.1 Rivers, Major Roads and Railroads in Black Africa

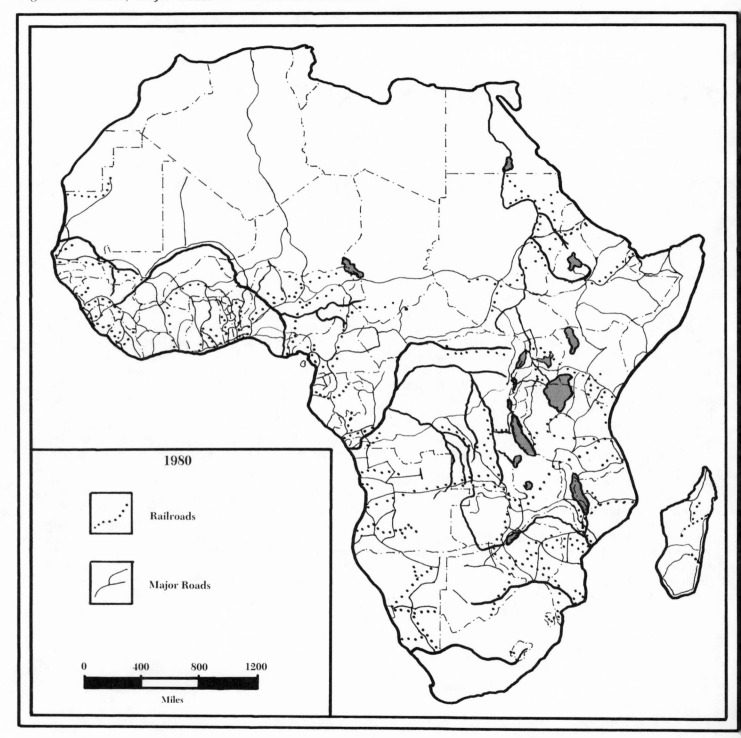

BIBLIOGRAPHY

For classic reviews of the theoretical aspects of communications see, for example, I. de Sola Pool (ed.), *Handbook of Communication* (Chicago: Rand McNally, 1973); L. Pye (ed.), *Communications and Political Development* (Princeton, N.J.: Princeton University Press, 1962); K. W. Deutsch, *Nationalism and Social Communications: An Inquiry into the Foundations of Nationalism* (New York: Massachusetts Institute of Technology Press and Wiley, 1953); P. Jacob and J. V. Toscano (eds.), *The Integration of Political Communities* (New York: J. B. Lippincott, 1964); D. Lerner, *The Passing of Traditional Society* (New York: Free Press, 1958); and E. Rogers, *Modernization Among Peasants: The Impact of Communications* (New York: Holt, Rinehart and Winston, 1969).

For communication's role in economic development see E. E. Hagen, *The Economics of Development* (Homewood, Ill.: Irwin, 1968) and S. Enke, *Economics for Development* (London: Dobson, 1963). The role of communications can be reviewed in various case studies such as L. Doob, *Communication in Africa: A Search for Boundaries* (New Haven, Conn.: Yale University Press, 1979); J. C. Condon, "Nation-Building and Image-Building in the Tanzanian Press," *Journal of Modern African Studies* 5 (1967):335—354; H. Mawlana, "Communications Media in Africa: A Critique in Retrospect and Prospect," in G. Carter and A. Paden (eds.), *Expanding Horizons in African Studies* (Evanston, Ill.: Northwestern University Press, 1969); and F. Barton, *The Press in Africa* (Nairobi: East African Publishing House, 1966). More recent works are, W. A. Hatchan, *Muffled Drums: The News Media in Africa* (Ames: Iowa State University Press, 1971); S. Olav (ed.), *Reporting Africa: In African and International Mass Media* (Uppsala: Scandanavian Institute of African Studies, 1971) and Dennis L. Wilcox, *Mass Media in Black Africa: Philosophy and Control* (New York: Praeger, 1975).

For reviews of the spatial aspects of transportation and communications see Lawrence Brown, *Diffusion* (New York: Methuen, 1981); E. M. Rogers, *Diffusion and Innovation*, 3rd ed. (New York: Free Press, 1983); P. Gould, "Tanzania 1920—1963: The Spatial Impress of the Modernization Process," *World Politics* 22 (1970):149—170; W. A. Hance, *African Economic Development* (New York: Praeger, 1975); B. Riddell, *The Spatial Dynamics of Modernization in Sierra Leone* (Evanston, Ill.: Northwestern University Press, 1970); and E. W. Soja, *The Geography of Modernization in Kenya* (Evanston, Ill.: Northwestern University Press, 1968).

Aspects of transportation analysis are discussed in E. J. Taafee, R. L. Morrill and P. Gould, "Transport Expansion in Underdeveloped Countries: A Comparative Analysis," *Geographical Review* 53 (Oct. 1963):503—529; and E. T. Haefele and E. B. Steinberg, *Government Controls on Transport: An African Case (Zambia)* (Washington, D.C.: Brookings Institution, 1965).

Table 5.2   Daily Newspaper Circulation per 10,000 Population, 1978 (A), 1972 (B), 1966 (C), 1960 (D) and Total Daily Circulation (in hundreds) 1976 (E).

Definition: Total average circulation of daily newspapers divided by the country's population.

Comments: In 1978, Congo, Gabon and Ghana lead Africa in newspaper readership by a wide margin. In general, the English-speaking countries have newspaper circulation rates that are higher than in the French-speaking countries. There are exceptions to this general tendency, however, mainly as a function of levels of economic development and the number of foreigners resident in the country.

```
Range =          349.00
Mean =            78.78
Standard Deviation =         90.82
```

Population Percent Cum.	Country	Rank	Country Name	A	Range Decile	B	C	D	E
.45	.45	1.0	Congo	349	1	8	16	12	500
3.96	3.51	2.0	Ghana	310	2	300	291	300	3450
4.12	.16	3.0	Gabon	283		39	11	0	150
4.35	.23	4.0	Botswana	230	4	222	0	0	170
4.64	.29	5.0	Namibia	191	5			120	180
6.59	1.95	6.0	Angola	180		150	87	91	1200
8.24	1.65	7.0	Zambia	178		130	68	48	930
9.23	.99	8.0	Sierra Leone	170	6	176	63	68	500
11.49	2.26	9.0	Zimbabwe	160		150	150	320	1090
11.68	.19	10.0	Guinea-Bissau	110	7	10	41	23	60
16.28	4.60	11.0	Kenya	100	8	138	72	115	1560
16.44	.16	12.0	Swaziland	98					50
37.44	21.00	13.5	Nigeria	97		41	66	69	5270
42.60	5.16	13.5	Tanzania	97		39	29	25	1580
45.08	2.48	15.0	Madagascar	90		80	87	81	590
45.61	.53	16.0	Liberia	80		45	51	9	80
47.83	2.22	17.0	Ivory Coast	72		97	81	24	530
49.49	1.66	18.0	Malawi	60	9	30			310
49.66	.17	19.0	Gambia	55		41	45	63	30
51.30	1.64	20.0	Senegal	50		61	57	67	250
52.87	1.57	21.5	Guinea	40		12	7	2	200
55.86	2.99	21.5	Mozambique	40		59	74	35	420
58.27	2.41	23.0	Cameroon	39		23	34	14	280
59.02	.75	24.0	Togo	32	10	62	59	13	70
68.73	9.71	25.0	Ethiopia	21		18	15	20	520
72.68	3.95	26.0	Uganda	20		75	73	73	23
80.97	8.29	27.0	Zaire	17		92	31	15	450
81.35	.38	28.0	Lesotho	12		16	0	0	13
82.38	1.03	29.5	Somalia	10		14	22	9	40
88.62	6.24	29.5	Sudan	10		9	5	5	190
89.95	1.33	31.0	Niger	6		5	4	3	30
91.23	1.28	32.5	Burundi	5		1	0	0	2
93.10	1.87	32.5	Mali	5		6	7	2	30
94.44	1.34	34.0	Chad	4		2	5	2	15
95.44	1.00	35.5	Benin	3		7	8	15	10
97.41	1.97	35.5	Upper Volta	3		4	3	0	15
97.87	.46	37.0	Mauritania	2		4	0	0	30
99.23	1.36	38.0	Rwanda	1		0	0	0	2
99.81	.58	40.0	Central African R	0		3	3	4	0
99.91	.10	40.0	Djibouti	0		0	0	0	0
100.00	.10	40.0	Equatorial Guinea	0		33	40	32	0

SOURCE: *Black Africa* second edition.

Table 5.3   Telephone Receivers per 10,000 Population, 1977 (A), 1972 (B), 1967 (C), 1963 (D) and Total Number of Telephones in Thousands 1977 (E).

Definition: The total number of telephone receivers divided by the total population.

Comments: Telephones are obviously an important means of personal communications since they allow for direct communication and interaction at considerable distances. Most telephones in these countries, however, tend to be concentrated in the cities and often in the largest city. The countries with high telephone ownership tend to be high per capita income countries and, conversely, the low per capita income countries tend to have low telephone distribution.

```
Range     =      610.00
Mean      =       84.73
Standard Deviation =        130.33
```

Population Percent			Country		A	Range Decile	B	C	D	E
Cum.	Country	Rank	Name							
.29	.29	1.0	Namibia		620	1	432	390	374	46
.45	.16	2.0	Gabon		600		216	86	62	15
2.71	2.26	3.0	Zimbabwe		290	6	254	224	215	198
2.87	.16	4.0	Swaziland		170	8	138	103	88	9
5.09	2.22	5.0	Ivory Coast		130	9	91	59	35	67
5.32	.23	6.5	Botswana		120		73	50	27	8
5.42	.10	6.5	Equatorial Guinea		120					3
5.52	.10	8.5	Djibouti		110		171			3
7.17	1.65	8.5	Zambia		110		131	114	89	53
11.77	4.60	10.0	Kenya		100		78	61	58	144
12.22	.45	11.5	Congo		90			103	92	12
13.86	1.64	11.5	Senegal		90		102	67	26	39
17.37	3.51	13.0	Ghana		70	10	56	42	45	67
17.54	.17	14.5	Gambia		60		53	38	20	3
20.53	2.99	14.5	Mozambique		60		58	29	26	52
20.72	.19	16.0	Guinea-Bissau		53		63	28	18	4
22.67	1.95	17.5	Angola		50		55	40	25	32
23.66	.99	17.5	Sierra Leone		50		42	28	25	15
26.14	2.48	21.0	Madagascar		40		37	135	30	32
27.80	1.66	21.0	Malawi		40		32	23	18	22
32.96	5.16	21.0	Tanzania		40		31	23	19	64
33.71	.75	21.0	Togo		40		29	16	18	10
37.66	3.95	21.0	Uganda		40		33	31	24	46
40.07	2.41	24.0	Cameroon		37		34	9	8	30
41.07	1.00	27.0	Benin		30		28	19	14	10
50.78	9.71	27.0	Ethiopia		30		21	15	9	79
51.16	.38	27.0	Lesotho		30		31	20	8	4
51.69	.53	27.0	Liberia		30		41	30	28	7
57.93	6.24	27.0	Sudan		30		32	30	27	62
58.51	.58	30.0	Central African R		26		28	19	17	5
60.08	1.57	33.0	Guinea		20		19	17	13	10
60.54	.46	33.0	Mauritania		20		12	25	8	1
61.87	1.33	33.0	Niger		20		9	8	6	8
82.87	21.00	33.0	Nigeria		20		17	14	12	121
91.16	8.29	33.0	Zaire		20		18	14	21	48
92.19	1.03	36.0	Somalia		18		20	17	12	6
93.47	1.28	39.0	Burundi		10		12	9	8	4
94.81	1.34	39.0	Chad		10		13	11	8	7
96.68	1.87	39.0	Mali		10		10	16	10	6
98.04	1.36	39.0	Rwanda		10		7	4	3	4
100.00	1.97	39.0	Upper Volta		10		9	6	4	6

SOURCE: *Black Africa* second edition.

Table 5.4 Commercial Vehicles per 10,000 Population, 1976 (A), 1972 (B), 1966 (C), 1958 (D) and Total Number of Commercial Vehicles in Hundreds, 1976 (E).

Definition: The total number of commercial vehicles divided by country's population.

Comments: Commercial vehicles are the lifeline of economic development. The rapidly growing and wealthier countries tend to be the ones with high rates of commercial vehicle ownership.

```
Range =        2827.00
Mean =          536.76
Standard Deviation =        574.38
```

Population Percent		Country		A	Range Decile	B	C	D	E
Cum.	Country	Rank	Name						
.10	.10	1.0	Djibouti	2870	1	2222	1147	493	31
.39	.29	2.0	Namibia	1648	5				
2.04	1.65	3.0	Zambia	1548		1030	390	366	784
2.20	.16	4.0	Swaziland	1429	6	778	838		71
2.36	.16	5.0	Gabon	1420		1184	448	682	73
2.59	.23	6.0	Botswana	1299		778	346	132	92
4.85	2.26	7.0	Zimbabwe	1099	7	1027	579	890	700
5.30	.45	8.0	Congo	937		700	556	493	130
7.71	2.41	9.0	Cameroon	665	8	616	400	398	512
8.24	.53	10.0	Liberia	657		840	625	250	100
10.72	2.48	11.0	Madagascar	645		560	461	335	501
12.94	2.22	12.0	Ivory Coast	632		1268	800	307	435
13.11	.17	13.0	Gambia	620		510	536	241	31
15.06	1.95	14.0	Angola	589	9	583	317	216	357
19.66	4.60	15.0	Kenya	538		172	196	141	743
21.30	1.64	16.0	Senegal	515		578	526	494	250
24.81	3.51	17.0	Ghana	431		341	235	238	459
25.56	.75	18.0	Togo	319	10	306	226	147	70
33.85	8.29	19.0	Zaire	316		260	180	171	764
33.95	.10	20.0	Equatorial Guinea	310					
34.95	1.00	21.0	Benin	305		275	206	103	95
40.11	5.16	22.0	Tanzania	280		269	200	97	418
40.49	.38	23.0	Lesotho	268		279	58	59	32
41.82	1.33	24.0	Niger	250		200	128	90	118
42.01	.19	25.0	Guinea-Bissau	220		229			11
42.59	.58	26.0	Central African R	213		168	183	171	39
44.25	1.66	27.0	Malawi	205		174	170	126	106
45.24	.99	28.0	Sierra Leone	202		426	324	112	63
46.81	1.57	29.0	Guinea	190		263	230	269	95
47.84	1.03	30.0	Somalia	176		272	240	152	60
49.81	1.97	31.0	Upper Volta	166		144	103	76	101
51.15	1.34	32.0	Chad	159		162	160	114	63
72.15	21.00	33.0	Nigeria	136		119	65	44	952
74.02	1.87	34.0	Mali	133		169	119	84	76
80.26	6.24	35.0	Sudan	132		139	128	131	270
81.62	1.36	36.0	Rwanda	118		80	31	24	48
84.61	2.99	37.0	Mozambique	106		238	186	110	
85.07	.46	38.0	Mauritania	83		456	251	149	43
89.02	3.95	39.0	Uganda	80		78	77	88	89
90.30	1.28	40.0	Burundi	55		67	4	18	22
100.00	9.71	41.0	Ethiopia	43		49	31	39	131

SOURCE: *Black Africa* second edition.

Chapter 6
Religion

The three major religious traditions in contemporary Africa are African traditional religion, Islam, and Christianity. Traditional religion, which consists of a wide variety of localized religious practices and beliefs, is presently declining in institutional vigor and importance, giving way to Islam and Christianity. The underlying philosophy or world view common to African traditional religions has by no means shared in this decline, however. It persists in important ways such as the African adaptations of Islam and Christianity, the continued demand for the divinatory powers, witchcraft protection, and healing skills of traditional practioners, and in other aspects of developing African cultures.

Islam has been an important religious influence in Africa south of the Sahara, especially since the days of Ibn Yasin, an eleventh century Muslim missionary who established himself among the Berbers in contemporary Mauritania. Christianity has an even longer history of contact back to the fourth century introduction of Coptic Christianty to the Kingdom of Axum (present-day Ethiopia). The Ethiopian Orthodox Church remains today the most important Christian Church in Ethiopia. How-

ever, the centuries-long contact between Roman Catholic Portugal and Central and West Africa, which began in the fifteenth century, was ultimately unsuccessful in establishing a lasting mission.

A sustained Christian missionary effort on the part of Protestants and Roman Catholics finally occurred in the nineteenth century. Today, as shown in Figure 6.1, the northern part of Black Africa is heavily Muslim, while certain countries to the south, such as Gabon, are almost entirely Christian. Present indications suggest an accelerated movement towards these two major world religions so that by the 1990's avowed adherents of traditional African religion will be a very small minority in Black Africa. Table 6.1 presents some estimates for the distribution of African believers from 1900—2000 made by Dr. David B. Barrett in 1970. According to Barrett, in the years to come Islamic growth will only equal Black Africa's population growth, whereas Christian growth will continue to surpass it so that before the end of the century African Christians will come to outnumber African Muslims for the first time.

TABLE 6.1   David Barrett's Estimate of Percentage Affiliation to Religions in Africa, 1900—2000.

| | | | | | | Projection* | |
	1900	1920	1940	1960	1970	1980	2000
Traditional	68	60	49	35	25	19	0
Muslim	28	31	37	42	42	42	42
Christian	4	9	14	23	32	39	54

Table calculated from Figure II, David B. Barrett, "Analytical Methods of Studying Religious Expansion in Africa," *Journal of Religion in Africa* 3 (1970):34. Christian and Traditional estimates are based on government, not church, estimates.

*Barrett used a lower Christian expansion rate in his future projection in order to keep his estimates on the conservative side.

Figure 6.1

Religion in Africa

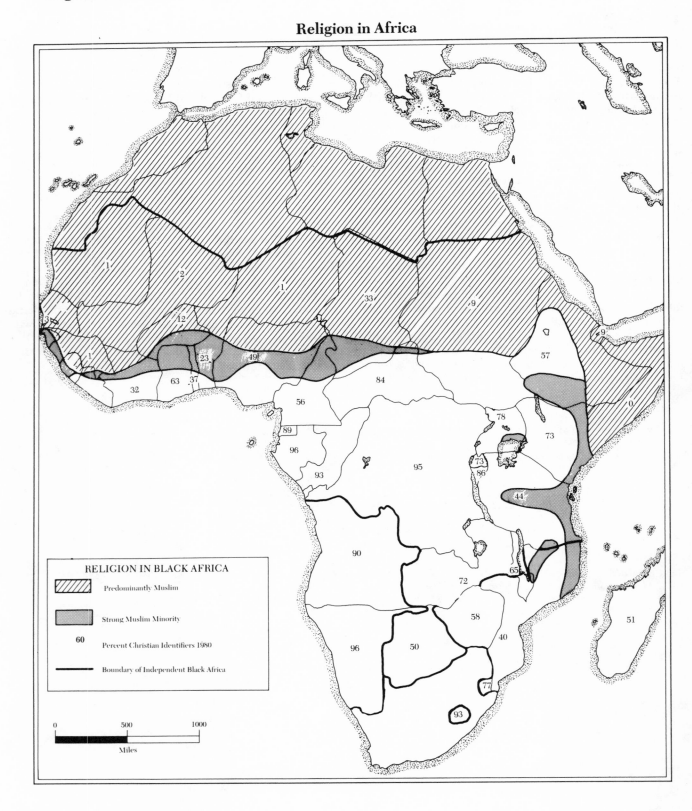

RELIGION IN BLACK AFRICA

- Predominantly Muslim
- Strong Muslim Minority
- **60** Percent Christian Identifiers 1980
- Boundary of Independent Black Africa

0   500   1000

Miles

Table 5.1   Radios per Thousand Population, 1978 (A), 1970 (B), 1965 (C), 1960 (D) and Total Number of Radios in Thousands, 1976 (E).

Definition: The number of radio receivers in the country divided by the total population. These figures are intended to be estimates of actual receivers rather than licenses.

Comments: The rate of growth of radio ownership in Africa, as in much of the developing world, has been phenomenal over the last decade. This has meant that mass communications over large areas no longer requires literate consumers of the printed page. In most of Black Africa the radio stations are owned by governments and have broadcasts in both the national and various important local languages.

```
Range =        224.00
Mean =          67.17
Standard Deviation =         55.32
```

Population Percent Cum.	Population Percent Country	Rank	Country Name	A	Range Decile	B	C	D	E
.10	.10	1.0	Equatorial Guinea	231	1	244	222		80
.63	.53	2.0	Liberia	221		115	100	78	265
.79	.16	3.0	Gabon	178	3	124	78	48	96
.95	.16	4.0	Swaziland	147	4	71	21	6	80
1.05	.10	5.5	Djibouti	133	5	74	94	62	15
2.71	1.66	5.5	Malawi	133		80	24	9	1100
4.93	2.22	7.0	Ivory Coast	118	6	14	15	17	900
5.10	.17	8.0	Gambia	111		108	115	9	63
13.39	8.29	9.0	Zaire	101		60	3	3	2582
16.90	3.51	10.5	Ghana	100		82	71	22	100
17.19	.29	10.5	Namibia	100		80		35	100
18.18	.99	12.0	Sierra Leone	99		76	44	4	325
18.41	.23	13.0	Botswana	85	7	35	8	4	62
39.41	21.00	14.0	Nigeria	76		23	7	4	5500
45.65	6.24	15.0	Sudan	74	8	35	23	1	1325
46.11	.46	16.0	Mauritania	65		44	29	12	100
48.52	2.41	17.5	Cameroon	62		31	19	3	500
48.97	.45	17.5	Congo	62		54	44	14	92
49.55	.58	19.5	Central African R	56		29	21	10	105
51.19	1.64	19.5	Senegal	56		63	64	48	268
52.19	1.00	21.0	Benin	53		31	15	3	180
54.67	2.48	22.0	Madagascar	47	9	43	31	15	130
56.93	2.26	23.0	Zimbabwe	42		27	26	16	90
61.53	4.60	24.5	Kenya	36		37	39	9	530
62.86	1.33	24.5	Niger	36		36	13	1	180
63.05	.19	26.0	Guinea-Bissau	29	10	8	7	4	16
64.33	1.28	27.0	Burundi	26		18	10	6	110
65.90	1.57	28.5	Guinea	25		23	21	13	121
68.89	2.99	28.5	Mozambique	25		11	9	6	250
69.27	.38	31.0	Lesotho	23		5	5	5	30
70.30	1.03	31.0	Somalia	23		18	14	12	80
71.05	.75	31.0	Togo	23		20	18	4	50
72.70	1.65	33.0	Zambia	22		18	12	5	120
74.04	1.34	35.0	Chad	20		16	8	3	85
79.20	5.16	35.0	Tanzania	20		11	10	4	325
83.15	3.95	35.0	Uganda	20		22	24	15	250
85.10	1.95	37.5	Angola	19		17	15	11	125
86.46	1.36	37.5	Rwanda	19		8	5	3	85
88.43	1.97	39.0	Upper Volta	17		16	10	1	110
90.30	1.87	40.0	Mali	14		12	6	2	90
100.00	9.71	41.0	Ethiopia	7		6	6	5	215

SOURCE: *Black Africa* second edition.

Islam and Christianity have been important forces for change in Africa. Each embodies a distinctive universalistic culture which it transmits to its converts through the teachings of its religious leaders, its religious ceremonies, and special experiences such as the Muslim pilgrimage to Mecca. In the modern era Christianity, as the religion of the colonial powers, came to enjoy high prestige with those Africans who aspired to elite positions in the modern social structure. One of the special attractions of Christianity was the widespread network of mission schools. Developed from the beginning of missionary work in each area, so as to instruct the new believers in the Bible, these schools quickly broadened to serve a wider clientele, providing a fuller curriculum and attracting financial support from the colonial governments. As a consequence, the colonial governments, especially the British, opened relatively few secular government schools. Until recently it was not uncommon to find that 60—75 percent of the schools in a country were still owned by the churches although this pattern has undergone dramatic change. Islam offers Koranic religious instruction through local Koranic schools, and various Islamic modernist movements have sought to adapt to the modern, technological world within an Islamic framework.

It is important to realize that both Christianity and Islam are internally differentiated in significant ways in Africa. The major types of Christianity are well known to most Western readers. In Africa they are: 1) the Ethiopian Orthodox Church; 2) Roman Catholicism, which is strongest in the non-Muslim, former French and Belgium colonies, but which is also strong in Eastern Nigeria and Tanzania; 3) Protestantism, which is strongest in the former British colonies and which includes a large number of different types of churches ranging from the Anglicans to the Jehovah's Witnesses; and 4) the African Independent Churches.

The independent churches are Christian groups which separated from the original, missionary-founded Christian churches. Led by Africans, a very large number of the individual churches can be grouped into two major types. The Ethiopian or African independent churches tend to keep to the form of Christianity held by their parent church, but substitute African leadership. The prayer-healing (or Zionist or Aladura—a Yoruba word meaning someone who prays) churches, on the other hand, adapt Christianity to the traditional African forms of worship and world view in certain important respects. For example, their leaders are often called prophets and are believed to have the power to heal through prayer and holy water and to divine through visions. Their worship services use drums and dancing. They are more concerned with the this-worldly help that religion can pro-

vide to believers, an emphasis of traditional religion, than with other-worldly salvation, an emphasis of the missionaries. The prayer-healing churches look to the Bible as the source of religious authority and forbid their members to have anything to do with traditional religion. Independent Christianity, especially the prayer-healing variety, is expanding rapidly in Africa today in those countries which have large numbers of Protestant Christians.

Although to the non-Muslim Islam tends to be seen as far more homogeneous, Islamic differentiation is considerable and important in Black Africa. Of primary importance are the Sufi (mystical) movements which are the predominant form of Islam in Africa. These are denominations organized around a primary Muslim saint which supplement the authority of the Koran with direct revelation. The major Sufi brotherhoods are the Qadiriyya, which is strong in both West and East Africa, and the Tijaniyya which is limited to West Africa. Within each of these brotherhoods there are numerous factions. Some of these factions have become identified with modern reforms such as the Mouridiyya in Senegal, a branch of the Qadiriyya with a "socialist" orientation, which organized some of the most powerful of the peanut cooperatives in Senegal and has been actively involved in modern politics. A branch of the Tijaniyya, under the leadership of Ibrahim Niass of Senegal, has organized its followers in modern-sector activities and has been largely responsible for the intensive revival of Arabic literacy which has occurred in Islamic West Africa in the past twenty years.

Two further expressions of Islam are the Wahabi and Mahdi movements. The former are puritanical, fundamentalist reactions against the excesses of sufism while the latter are based on the claims of particular individuals to the role of the Mahdi or Islamic messiah who is believed to come to earth when the end of the world is at hand. The Ahmadiyya are the followers of a Pakistani Mahdi. This group is very missionary minded and has become strong in West Africa.

A final differentiation in African Islam is the different character of Islam in East and West Africa. Islam spread to these areas in quite different ways with important consequences for the present expression of the religion. In East Africa Islam spread down the coast through the migrations of various Arab groups over the centuries. These groups did not engage in active proselytization, but over time Black Africans became Muslim and a coastal Muslim culture developed. Swahili, the language of this culture, is basically a Bantu language with a large number of Arab loan-words. In West Africa Islam was spread in the interior through the efforts of African not Arab Muslims. An important factor in this spread was large scale military offensives against non-Muslim kingdoms. The resulting Islam, dominated by the Sufi orders, developed its own centers of Islamic learning and was thus more independent of mainstream Islamic culture than East African Islam.

Unlike Christianity, Islam has not spawned the equivalent of the independent churches. This is because Islam is relatively tolerant of various traditional African customs such as polygyny and the concern for this-worldy religious help, especially in the early stages of Islamization. Moreover, the Sufi orders provide an experiential religion and there are Muslim clerics who perform healing and divinatory activities within the Muslim framework.

The data presented in the following tables are taken from data compiled by David Barrett for the recently published *World Christian Encyclopedia*. Barrett has been indefatigible in locating published and unpublished census and sample survey data for Africa. In one instance he worked in a rat-infested basement of a government building in Nairobi to find the unpublished results of the religion question in the 1948 Kenya census. These materials were destroyed soon after he worked with them. His data are, therefore, the best available and supersede the estimates reported in the first edition of *Black Africa*. Because they were compiled on the basis of a different principle they should not be compared with the earlier data in *Black Africa* in order to calculate growth rates.

There are important limitations to even Barrett's data, however. In the first place a number of countries never included a religion question in their census. Secondly, a number of countries that did, did so only at an earlier time, therefore requiring the extrapolation from that time to the present using estimates (which are, of course, a matter of judgment) developed by Barrett. Finally some of these censuses, such as those for Congo, Central African Republic, Chad and Upper Volta, were not full modern enumerations, but sample censuses.

Bibliography

Books on religion in Africa usually specialize in one of the three major religious traditions—an exception is Geoffrey Parrinder's paperback, *Religion in Africa* (Baltimore, Md.: Penguin Books, 1969), which devotes a third of the book each to traditional religion, Christianity, and Islam. This is a satisfactory, though rather dull book, which is weakest in its treatment of traditional religions. Important bibliographies include: Harold W. Turner, *Bibliography of New Religious Movements in Primal Societies*, Vol. I, Black Africa (Boston: G. K. Hall, 1977); Irving I. Zaretsky and Cynthia Shambaugh, *Spirit Possession and Spirit Mediumship in Africa and Afro-America: An Annotated Bibliography* (New York: Garland, 1979) and Samir M. Zoghby, *Islam in Sub-Saharan Africa: A Partially Annotated Guide* (Washington, D.C.: Library of Congress, 1978). The *Journal of Religion in Africa* (Leiden: E. J. Brill, Publisher) publishes articles on all aspects of African religion.

There are six general books on African traditional religion, all by Christian ministers who are sympathetic to the African world view. Perhaps the best introduction to the subject is the sensitive interpretation of African religion by John V. Taylor, *The Primal Vision: Christian Presence Amid African Religion* (London: SCM Press, 1963), which is now available in paperback. Placide Temples, a Belgian Catholic Priest, has written a famous book based on his work in Zaire, *Bantu Philosophy* (Paris: Presence African, 1945, 1959). See also John S. Mbiti's detailed study, *African Religions and Philosophy* (New York: Praeger, 1969), Noel Q. King's *Religions of Africa* (New York: Harper and Row, 1970); E. Bolaji Idowu's *African Traditional Religion: A Definition* (Maryknoll, N.Y.: Orbis, 1973), and Benjamin C. Ray, *African Religions: Symbol, Ritual, and Community* (Englewood Cliffs, NJ: Prentice Hall, 1975). T. O. Ranger has influenced a whole generation of African historians on traditional religion as an important topic for historical analysis. This approach is exemplified in Ranger and I. N. Kimambo (eds., *The Historical Study of African Religions* (Berkeley, Calif.: University of California, 1972).

Most descriptive anthropological studies of particular tribes (ethnographies) include a chapter on religion. A number of anthropologists have written monographs on religion alone, such as E. E. Evans-Pritchard, *Nuer Religion* (London: Oxford University Press, 1956); Godfrey Lienhardt, *Divinity and Experience: The Religion of the Dinka* (London: Oxford University Press, 1961); S. F. Nadel, *Nupe Religion* (London: Oxford University Press, 1954); M. C. Marwick, *Sorcery in its Social Setting: A Study of Northern Rhodesian Chewa* (Manchester, England: Manchester University Press, 1965); and Victor Turner, *The Forest of Symbols: Aspects of Ndembu Ritual* (Ithaca, N.Y.: Cornell University Press, 1967). E. Bolaji Idowu's *Olodumare: God in Yoruba Belief* (London: Longmans, 1961) is a major work by an African theologian.

Daryll Forde has edited *African Worlds: Studies in the Cosmological Ideas and Social Values of African Peoples* (London: Oxford University Press, 1954) and Meyer Fortes and Germaine Dieterlen have edited *African Systems of Thought: Studies Presented and Discussed at the Third International African Seminar* (London: Oxford University Press, 1965). Both these books probe the African world view, as does a series of excellent articles by Robin Horton in the British Journal, *Africa:* "Destiny and the Unconscious in West Africa," 31 (1961):110—116; "Ritual Man in Africa," 34 (1964):85—104; and "African Traditional Thought and Western Science" in two parts, 37 (1967):50—71 and 155—187. John Middleton and E. H. Winter have edited a book on *Witchcraft and Sorcery in East Africa* (New York: Praeger, 1963), and Lucy Mair has published a good popular introduction to the subject, *Witchcraft* (New York: World University Library, 1969). A work on a related topic is Kwasi Wiredu, *Philosophy and African Culture* (New York: Cambridge University Press, 1980).

For the best brief introduction to Christianity in Africa, see Parrinder's book noted above. Recent books on Christianity in Africa include: Adrian Hastings, *A History of African Christianity, 1950-1975*, (New York: Cambridge University Press, 1979); Edward Fashole-Luke et al., *Christianity in Independent Africa*, (Bloomington, Ind: Indiana University Press, 1978); and George Bond et al., eds., *African Christianity: Patterns of Religious Continuity*, (New York: Academic Press, 1979). C.P.Grove's monumental four-volume history of Christian missions in Africa, *The Planting of Christianity in Africa* (London:Butterworth, 1948-1958), has an excellent index and good footnotes, which make it possible for the student to learn about the history of Christianity in any particular country. See the *Journal of Religion in Africa*, and especially the *Bulletin, Society for African Church History* for periodic bibliographies on Christian missions and African Christianity.

Notable histories of Christianity in individual countries include Roland Oliver, *The Missionary Factor in East Africa* (London: Longmans, 1952), and two important studies by Nigerian historians: J. F. A. Ajayi, *Christian Missions in Nigeria 1841-1891: The Making of a New Elite* (London:Longmans, 1965) and E. A. Ayandele, *The Missionary Impact on Modern Nigeria 1842-1941: A Political and Social Analysis* (London:Longmans, 1966).

Studies of contemporary Christianity include a scholarly collection edited by C. G. Baeta, *Christianity in Tropical Africa: Studies Presented and Discussed at the Seventh International African Seminar* (London: Oxford University Press, 1968) and the following monographs: H. Debrunner, *A Church Between Colonial Powers: The Church in Togo* (London: SCM Press,

1960); John V. Taylor, *The Growth of the Church in Buganda* (London: SCM Press, 1960); John V. Taylor and Dorothea Lehmann, *Christians of the Copperbelt* (London: SCM Press, 1961); E. Anderson, *Churches at the Grass-Roots* (London: Longmans, 1968) (on Congo); Marshall W. Murphree, *Christianity and the Shona* (New York: Humanities Press, 1969). and B. A. Pauw, *Christianity and the Shona Tradition* (New York: Oxford University Press, 1975).

The primary source of data for Protestant Christian membership in Africa is the *World Christian Handbook*, published by the World Dominion Press in London. Editions of the work appeared in 1949, 1952, 1957, 1962, and 1968. Roman Catholic data are contained in the Eglise Vivant, *Bilan du Monde*, published in Paris by Casterman in 1958-1959 and 1964. A combined book of World Christian statistics is now available by David Barrett, *The World Christian Encyclopedia* (Nairobi: Oxford University Press, 1982). Recent works include A. Hastings *A History of African Christianity, 1950-1975.* (New York: Cambridge University Press, 1979) and G. Bond and others eds. *African Christianity: Patterns of Religious Continuity.* (New York: Academic Press, 1979).

Two general works on African independent churches are David B. Barrett's quantitative survey in *Schism and Renewal in Africa: An Analysis of Six Thousand Contemporary Religious Movements* (Nairobi: Oxford University Press, 1968) and G. C. Oosthuizens's essentially theological analysis, *Post-Christianity in Africa: A Theological and Anthropological Study* (Grand Rapids, Mich.: Erdmans, 1968). On independent religious movements see Benetta Jules-Rosette, ed., *The New Religions of Africa* (Norwood, NJ: Ablex, 1979).

Among the major monographs on the independent churches are Bengt Sundkler's pioneering study, *Bantu Prophets in South Africa* (London: Oxford University Press, 1948, rev. ed., 1961); C. G. Baeta's *Prophetism in Ghana: A Study of Some "Spiritual" Churches* (London: SCM Press, 1962); F. B. Welbourn, *East African Rebels* (Oxford: Oxford University Press, 1961); M. L. Daneel, *Old and New in Southern Shona Independent Churches*, Vol. 1 (The Hague: Mouton, 1971); H. W. Turner's two-volume study of the church of the Lord (Aladura) in West Africa, *Africa Independent Church* (Oxford: Clarendon Press, 1967); J. D. Y. Peel's sociological study, *Aladura: A Religious Movement Among the Yoruba* (London: Oxford University Press, 1968) and Sheila S. Walker, *The Religious Revolution in the Ivory Coast: Prophet Harris and the Harrist Church* (Chapel Hill, NC: University of North Carolina Press, 1983).

One of the best introductions to Islam in Africa for general readers is the short book by J. S. Trimingham, *The Influence of Islam upon Africa* 2nd ed. (New York:

Longman, 1980) a Christian missionary and Islamic expert, who wrote this book as a summary of the results of his extensive comparative researches into contemporary Africa Islam which were published earlier in a series of scholarly volumes: *Islam in the Sudan* (1949), *Islam in Ethiopia* (1952), *Islam in West Africa* (1959), *A History of Islam in West Africa* (1962) and *Islam in East Africa* (1964) which should be consulted for more detailed descriptions of Islam in particular countries or tribes. Another excellent though dated introduction is the ninety-six page essay by I. M. Lewis, in his edited book, *Islam in Tropical Africa* (London: Oxford University Press, 1966). For a simplified introduction to the form of Islam in Africa, See John N. Paden and Edward W. Soja, *The African Experience*, Vol. II Syllabus (Evanston, Ill.: Northwestern University Press, 1970). A second edited work on African Islam besides the one mentioned above edited by Lewis, is James Kritzeck and William H. Lewis, *Islam in Africa* (New York: Van Nostrand Reinhold, 1969). A helpful essay by Ibrahim Abu-Lughod, "Africa and the Islamic World" in John H. Paden and Edward W. Soja (eds.), *The African Experience*, Vol. I (Evanston, Ill.: Northwestern University Press, 1970) emphasizes the links between Black and North Africa.

The role of Islam in contemporary African politics is considered in: Vernon McKay, "Islam and Relations Among the New African States," in J. H. Proctor (ed.), *Islam and International Relations* (New York: Praeger, 1964); Ali H. Mazrui, "Islam, Political Leadership and Economic Radicalism in Africa," in Mazrui, *On Heroes and Uhuru Worship* (London: Longman, 1967), pp. 157-79; and J. N. Paden *Religion and Political Culture in Kano* (Berkeley, Calif.: University of California Press, 1973).

Monographs on special subjects include J. N. D. Anderson, *Islamic Law in Africa* (London: HMSO, 1954); Humphrey J. Fisher's study of the Pakistani Islâmic sect, *Ahmadiyyah: A Study in Contemporary Islam in the West African Coast* (London: Oxford University Press, 1963); and Horace Miner, *The Primitive City of Timbuctoo* (Princeton, N. J.: Princeton University Press, 1953). Sources of data on Islam besides Trimingham and Froelich, cited above, are Louis Massingnon, *Annuaire du monde musulman* (Paris: LeRouc, 1962) and *Islam en Afrique* (Brussels: Pro Mundi Vita, 1972).

Table 6.1   Estimated Percent Identifiers with Traditional African Religions, 1980 (A), 1970 (B), 1966 (C)

Definition: Estimated percent of the population who identify with traditional African religions.

Comments: Those who *identify* with a particular religion when asked about their religion by someone such as a census-taker are often a much larger group than those who actually exercise membership in the religious group. In the case of African traditional religions, however, this is not the case. Because Islam and Christianity are the prestige religions in most African countries today, many people who actually practice traditional religion prefer to identify with Islam or Christianity.

The range in the percent who identify with traditional religion is large. There is no single explanation of why the populations of Benin, Upper Volta, Mozambique, Zambia, and other countries at the upper end of the distribution have resisted Islam and Christianity, but the answer probably lies in a combination of historical factors and the characteristics of the important ethnic groups. The cumulative population percent column shows that only a small percent of the total 41 country population live in countries with a large number of traditional religionists.

Range = 61.00
Mean = 21.90
Standard Deviation = 17.62

Population Percent Cum.	Country	Rank	Country Name	A	Range Decile	B	C
1.00	1.00	1.0	Benin	61	1	67	67
1.99	.99	2.0	Sierra Leone	52	2	54	63
2.18	.19	3.0	Guinea-Bissau	51		52	58
2.41	.23	4.0	Botswana	49		56	71
5.40	2.99	5.0	Mozambique	48	3	58	67
7.88	2.48	6.0	Madagascar	47		49	61
8.63	.75	7.0	Togo	46		56	64
10.60	1.97	8.0	Upper Volta	45		55	72
12.82	2.22	9.5	Ivory Coast	44		49	59
13.35	.53	9.5	Liberia	44		50	60
15.61	2.26	11.0	Zimbabwe	40	4	46	48
17.18	1.57	12.0	Guinea	30	6	31	34
18.83	1.65	13.0	Zambia	27		34	70
20.17	1.34	14.5	Chad	23	7	27	40
25.33	5.16	14.5	Tanzania	23		32	37
27.74	2.41	16.0	Cameroon	22		32	36
31.25	3.51	17.5	Ghana	21		33	35
31.41	.16	17.5	Swaziland	21		28	40
36.01	4.60	19.5	Kenya	19		28	36
37.67	1.66	19.5	Malawi	19		25	46
39.54	1.87	21.5	Mali	18	8	20	34
40.90	1.36	21.5	Rwanda	18		29	57
47.14	6.24	23.0	Sudan	17		21	36
48.42	1.28	24.0	Burundi	14		25	35
52.37	3.95	25.0	Uganda	13		22	34
52.95	.58	26.5	Central African R	12	9	20	48
54.28	1.33	26.5	Niger	12		14	15
63.99	9.71	28.5	Ethiopia	11		14	23
64.16	.17	28.5	Gambia	11		12	16
66.11	1.95	30.0	Angola	10		17	45
66.49	.38	31.5	Lesotho	6	10	13	19
87.49	21.00	31.5	Nigeria	6		11	15
87.59	.10	33.0	Equatorial Guinea	5		7	11
87.88	.29	34.0	Namibia	4		5	11
88.04	.16	36.0	Gabon	3		3	24
89.68	1.64	36.0	Senegal	3		4	14
97.97	8.29	36.0	Zaire	3		8	34
98.42	.45	39.5	Congo	0		1	36
98.52	.10	39.5	Djibouti	0		0	0
98.98	.46	39.5	Mauritania	0		0	1
100.00	1.03	39.5	Somalia	0		0	0

SOURCES: *Black Africa*, second edition.

Table 6.2   Estimated Percent Identifiers with Islam, 1980 (A), 1970 (B), and 1966 (C).

Definition: Estimated percent of the population who identify with Islam.

Comments: In Islam there is no official church hierarchy, and hence, there are no membership rolls. The individual's self definition is the sole criterion for "membership". It is very clear, however, when an individual regards himself as a Muslim, since participation in the five pillars (repetition of the creed, daily prayers, alms giving, observance of the Ramadan Fast, and the pilgrimage to Mecca), are public activities. Black African Muslims vary considerably in the degree of their orthodoxy. Nevertheless, over time, through the process of Islamization, individuals and ethnic communities undergo the radical change described in Trimingham, *The Influence of Islam upon Africa, op. cit.*

Range = 100.00
Mean = 29.90
Standard Deviation = 33.08

Population Percent Cum.	Country	Rank	Country Name	A	Range Decile	B	C
1.03	1.03	1.0	Somalia	100	1	100	99
1.49	.46	2.0	Mauritania	99		99	96
1.59	.10	3.5	Djibouti	91		87	90
3.23	1.64	3.5	Senegal	91		90	82
4.56	1.33	5.0	Niger	88	2	86	85
4.73	.17	6.0	Gambia	85		84	80
6.60	1.87	7.0	Mali	80	3	78	65
12.84	6.24	8.0	Sudan	73		71	60
14.41	1.57	9.0	Guinea	69	4	68	65
35.41	21.00	10.0	Nigeria	45	6	44	50
36.75	1.34	11.0	Chad	44		42	50
38.72	1.97	12.0	Upper Volta	43		35	22
39.71	.99	13.0	Sierra Leone	39	7	38	30
39.90	.19	14.0	Guinea-Bissau	38		35	33
45.06	5.16	15.0	Tanzania	33		31	23
54.77	9.71	16.0	Ethiopia	31		31	40
56.99	2.22	17.0	Ivory Coast	24	8	23	23
59.40	2.41	18.0	Cameroon	22		20	15
59.93	.53	19.0	Liberia	21		19	15
60.68	.75	20.0	Togo	17	9	13	8
64.19	3.51	21.5	Ghana	16		14	19
65.85	1.66	21.5	Malawi	16		16	12
66.85	1.00	23.0	Benin	15		14	15
69.84	2.99	24.0	Mozambique	13		12	12
71.20	1.36	25.0	Rwanda	9	10	8	1
75.15	3.95	26.0	Uganda	7		6	6
79.75	4.60	27.0	Kenya	6		6	4
80.33	.58	28.0	Central African R	3		3	5
82.81	2.48	29.0	Madagascar	2		2	1
84.09	1.28	32.5	Burundi	1		1	1
84.54	.45	32.5	Congo	1		0	0
84.64	.10	32.5	Equatorial Guinea	1		1	0
84.80	.16	32.5	Gabon	1		1	1
93.09	8.29	32.5	Zaire	1		2	1
95.35	2.26	32.5	Zimbabwe	1		1	0
97.30	1.95	38.5	Angola	0		0	0
97.53	.23	38.5	Botswana	0		0	0
97.91	.38	38.5	Lesotho	0		0	0
98.20	.29	38.5	Namibia	0		0	0
98.36	.16	38.5	Swaziland	0		0	0
100.00	1.65	38.5	Zambia	0		0	0

SOURCE: *Black Africa* second edition.

Table 6.3   Estimated Percent Identifiers with Christianity, 1980 (A), 1970 (B), and 1966 (C).

Definition: Estimated percent of the population who identify with Christianity. This is different from the churches' official membership figures which are lower.

Comments: The major Christian types are the Ethiopian Orthodox church (an ancient form of Christianity found only in Ethiopia), the Roman Catholic Church, the various Protestant denominations, and the African independent Churches (see Table 6.4). This variable includes all these Christians.

Christianity is growing rapidly in many African countries, especially in Central and East Africa, and some argue that its growth rate for Black Africa exceeds Islam's. Roman Catholicism is strongest in the former French colonies and the former Belgian Congo, although two-thirds of Zambia's Christians are Roman Catholic and Lesotho, Nigeria, and Tanzania have large Catholic minorities. Protestant churches have evolved from the status of foreign-controlled mission churches to the status of national churches under the control of indigenous pastors and laity.

```
Range =            96.00
Mean =             47.59
Standard Deviation =          33.13
```

Population Percent Cum.	Country	Rank	Country Name	A	Range Decile	B	C
.16	.16	1.5	Gabon	96	1	96	75
.45	.29	1.5	Namibia	96		95	89
8.74	8.29	3.0	Zaire	95		90	65
9.19	.45	4.5	Congo	93		92	64
9.57	.38	4.5	Lesotho	93		86	81
11.52	1.95	6.0	Angola	90		83	55
11.62	.10	7.0	Equatorial Guinea	89		88	89
12.90	1.28	8.0	Burundi	86	2	74	64
13.48	.58	9.0	Central African R	84		77	47
17.43	3.95	10.0	Uganda	78		69	60
17.59	.16	11.0	Swaziland	77		70	60
22.19	4.60	12.5	Kenya	73	3	64	58
23.55	1.36	12.5	Rwanda	73		62	42
25.20	1.65	14.0	Zambia	72		65	30
26.86	1.66	15.0	Malawi	65	4	59	42
30.37	3.51	16.0	Ghana	63		53	46
32.63	2.26	17.0	Zimbabwe	58		52	45
42.34	9.71	18.0	Ethiopia	57	5	55	37
44.75	2.41	19.0	Cameroon	56		47	49
47.23	2.48	20.0	Madagascar	51		49	38
47.46	.23	21.0	Botswana	50		43	29
68.46	21.00	22.0	Nigeria	49		45	35
73.62	5.16	23.0	Tanzania	44	6	36	40
76.61	2.99	24.0	Mozambique	40		30	21
77.36	.75	25.0	Togo	37	7	30	28
77.89	.53	26.0	Liberia	35		31	25
79.23	1.34	27.0	Chad	33		31	10
81.45	2.22	28.0	Ivory Coast	32		28	18
82.45	1.00	29.0	Benin	23	8	19	18
84.42	1.97	30.0	Upper Volta	12	9	10	6
84.61	.19	31.0	Guinea-Bissau	10		13	9
84.71	.10	33.0	Djibouti	9		13	10
85.70	.99	33.0	Sierra Leone	9	10	13	10
91.94	6.24	33.0	Sudan	9		8	7
93.58	1.64	35.0	Senegal	6		7	4
93.75	.17	36.0	Gambia	3		6	4
95.62	1.87	37.0	Mali	2		3	4
97.19	1.57	39.0	Guinea	1		2	1
97.65	.46	39.0	Mauritania	1		1	1
98.98	1.33	39.0	Niger	1		1	0
100.00	1.03	41.0	Somalia	0		0	0

SOURCES: *Black Africa* second edition.

Table 6.4   Thousands of Estimated Affiliators of African Independent Churches per Million Population, 1980 (A), and 1970 (B).

Definition: Data are for thousands of estimated affiliators of African Independent Churches per million population. An affiliator of a Church - a narrower category than identifier - is either a member or an adherent. The data are those reported by the churches themselves, corrected when possible for over-counts. The source defines independency as "the formation and existence within a tribe of any organized religious movement...which claims the title Christian...and which has either separated by secession from a mission church or an existing African independent church, or has been founded outside the mission churches as a new kind of religious entity under African initiative and leadership."

```
Range =            230.00
Mean =             43.78
Standard Deviation =          61.98
```

Population Percent Cum.	Country	Rank	Country Name	A	Range Decile	B
.16	.16	1.0	Swaziland	230	1	220
8.45	8.29	2.0	Zaire	201	2	198
13.05	4.60	3.0	Kenya	171	3	158
16.56	3.51	4.0	Ghana	158	4	129
18.82	2.26	5.0	Zimbabwe	136	5	123
19.35	.53	6.0	Liberia	133		127
19.51	.16	7.0	Gabon	121		121
19.80	.29	8.0	Namibia	88	7	86
22.02	2.22	9.0	Ivory Coast	82		76
23.67	1.65	10.0	Zambia	78		68
23.90	.23	11.0	Botswana	72		62
24.28	.38	12.0	Lesotho	69	8	64
45.28	21.00	13.0	Nigeria	60		55
45.73	.45	14.0	Congo	30	9	30
47.39	1.66	15.0	Malawi	27		25
49.80	2.41	16.5	Cameroon	22	10	20
52.28	2.48	16.5	Madagascar	22		20
53.28	1.00	18.0	Benin	18		16
55.23	1.95	19.0	Angola	13		12
55.33	.10	20.5	Equatorial Guinea	12		12
56.08	.75	20.5	Togo	12		9
60.03	3.95	22.0	Uganda	9		8
61.02	.99	23.0	Sierra Leone	8		7
61.60	.58	24.0	Central African R	7		6
64.59	2.99	25.0	Mozambique	6		5
69.75	5.16	26.0	Tanzania	5		4
71.09	1.34	27.0	Chad	4		3
73.06	1.97	28.0	Upper Volta	1		1
74.34	1.28	35.0	Burundi	0		0
74.44	.10	35.0	Djibouti	0		0
84.15	9.71	35.0	Ethiopia	0		0
84.32	.17	35.0	Gambia	0		0
85.89	1.57	35.0	Guinea	0		0
86.08	.19	35.0	Guinea-Bissau	0		0
87.95	1.87	35.0	Mali	0		0
88.41	.46	35.0	Mauritania	0		0
89.74	1.33	35.0	Niger	0		0
91.10	1.36	35.0	Rwanda	0		0
92.74	1.64	35.0	Senegal	0		0
93.77	1.03	35.0	Somalia	0		0
100.00	6.24	35.0	Sudan	0		0

SOURCE: *Black Africa* second edition

Chapter 7.

POLITICAL DEVELOPMENT

The transfer of formal sovereignty from European colonial powers to independent Black African governments in the 41 countries described in this book began in Sudan in 1956 and is not yet complete since Namibia is still occupied by South Africa. Liberia, independent since the middle nineteenth century, and the ancient Ethiopian empire are, of course, exceptions to this general observation and other non-independent countries in Africa still await liberation. In what is now two decades since independence, for most of these countries, they have faced three central and formidable tasks of political development: (1) the adaptation of political institutions inherited or transferred from colonial experience to the needs and cultures of African peoples; (2) the unification of ethnically diverse populations into national political communities with a shared identity and political culture, and (3) the mobilization of citizens and natural resources for the attainment of the political goals of national autonomy, social justice, and individual freedom. All this was to be done while confronting neocolonialism, cold war imperialism, economic poverty by world standards, and the "great expectations" generated by the struggle for independence.

The dynamism of African nationalism after the Second World War brought legal sovereignty to the inhabitants of most of the continent's colonies by 1960. Since then, the citizens of these new countries have had to adjust to their colonial heritage of balkanized political boundaries which took no account of the heterogeneous traditional African political loyalties and cultures, or of the geopolitical requirements for viability in the contemporary world economy. Despite the ideological promise of Pan-Africanism, and attempts at political and economic integration (e.g. the Federation incorporating Senegal and Sudan in 1960, and the East African Common Market), contemporary African politics remains closely linked to the colonial definition of political boundaries, and to the problems attendant on the exceptionally rapid devolution from colonial autocracy to internal sovereignty within these boundaries.

Particularly important in this latter connection has been the adoption of European arrangements for democratic government through the regularized electoral competition of more than one political party. In some Black African countries the struggle for independence was successfully organized by single mass parties with clearly formulated programs and organization, and these parties became the clearly predominant focus of political identification and institutional means to power, despite attempts by colonial governments to organize parties in opposition to them. This pattern of single-party dominance was particularly true for former French colonies like Senegal, Ivory Coast, Guinea, Niger, and C.A.R., but it was also characteristic of the political development of Malawi and Tanzania among former British colonies. In most African nations, however, the transfer of electoral politics was accompanied by a proliferation of factions and political parties organized around personalities, regional or ethnic constituencies, and the potentially integrating effects of party organizations were not achieved. The complexity, cost and conflict associated with the development of multiple party systems was further exaggerated in some countries like Nigeria and Zaire by federal or quasi-federal arrangements, with consequent party competition and organization at regional as well as national levels. The most striking feature of political development in most of these countries, therefore, has been the movement towards simplification in the numbers of political parties, and in many places the development of the one-party state. But there remains, nevertheless, great variation in the ways in which African parties and governments provide for mass participation through electoral competition and representation, local organization and public information, and a great deal of research remains to be done on the kinds of variation in political party organization and support, and their effects on the stability and legitimacy of African governments.

The development of national bureaucracies, legal systems, and military and police forces has been another major source of problems in African political development. The inheritance of colonial administrative organizations, legal codes, military structures and equipment, and the status and salaries of the colonial bureaucratic system has posed grave difficulties. The very late devolution of administrative responsibility in the bureaucracies, courts and armies of African states has meant a severe limitation on the experience and training of upper echelon officers in these institutions. The duplication or multiplication of these institutions in sub-national African political communities has created confusion and role-strain in the adjudication of competing claims from national authorities and local constituencies. Because of the serious restrictions in neo-colonial economies on the access to capital and wealth, political institutions have been seen as major avenues to personal profit, and patronage, corruption and inefficiency have tended to be more widespread than the Weberian model of rule-bound, legal, rational and impartial administration would have led us to expect. Colonial practices of recruiting disproportionate numbers of members of single ethnic groups to military or bureaucratic employment because of their superior access to education, or, in the case of army rank and file, because of their lack of such access, have often meant that bureaucratic and military institutions have become sources of political conflict rather than conflict regulation. And the very recency of the colonial experience meant that legislative and bureaucratic officials had more experience initially in opposition than government, and that military personnel have had as much experience in opposition as they have in submission to African politicians. Despite, therefore, the continuation of the colonial model of centralism and hierarchy in government, the institutionalization of African political organizations is beset by problems of central-local tensions, functionalism and intensive competition, inexperience in political office and a pervasive tradition of opposition to central government on the part of those who do not hold political office.

In addition to the importance of the institutionalization of the political organization responsible for the regulation of and succession to political power, critical roles in African political development have to be played by other organizations whose functions, while less overtly political, are concerned with the socialization of the citizen, whose commitment, loyalty and obedience to national authority is the mainstay of political development. While levels of electoral participation by African citizens have been high by international standards, aggregate electoral participation figures give no indication of degree of satisfaction and regime support of participating citizens, and of the degree to which this is a function of participation in institutions like churches, schools and universities, trade unions, and various urban voluntary associations and economic groups. Information on these questions is hard to find, and there is as yet no body of survey research describing African voting behavior. What information we do have suggests that urbanization, participation in an industrial economic organization, and advanced schooling increases the likelihood of voting, political awareness and national identification, although it is apparent that none of these institutions have eradicated ethnic loyalties, cultural differentiation and ethnocentrism. It is this persistence of ethnic identification and difference, which constitutes the greatest threat to the political development of African states, for it increases the number of different interests to be satisfied by government, the possible sources of opposition and conflict, and reduces the ability of governments in these states to mobilize national constituencies and support based on the growth of class or other supra-ethnic solidarities. Whether these 'weaknesses' of the culturally plural state also ensure that authoritarian rule cannot be long maintained we will determine as history unfolds.

In the last analysis, political development is evaluated not by the nature of institutional organization or by the homogeneity and unity of national populations, but by the degree to which members of particular political systems are rewarded by benefits from the policies of governments. In general, it is appropriate to say that while Africans expected improved futures after independence, their 'rising expectations' have not outrun their capabilities, and their governements have greatly surpassed the colonial rulers in the provision of opportunities for health, education, information and political participation. But it is in the achievement of economic benefits for African citizens that African governments are faced with their most difficult development task. The problems of African economic development are discussed in the next chapter, but the central political issues can be touched on here. African socialism, while a powerful political.

Figure 7.1 African Party Systems, 1960—82

1960

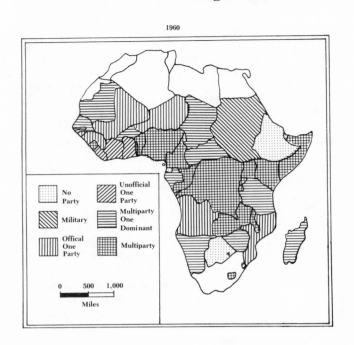

1965

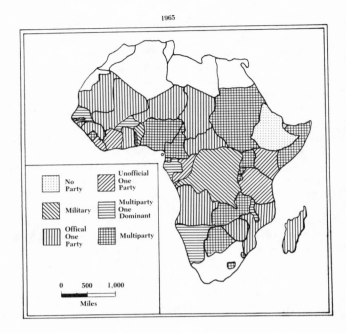

1970

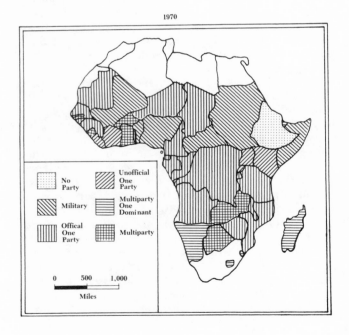

1982

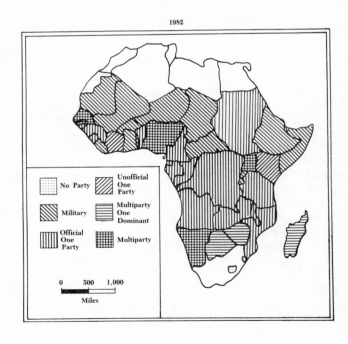

Figure 7.2 Communal Instability in Black African States, 1958—82

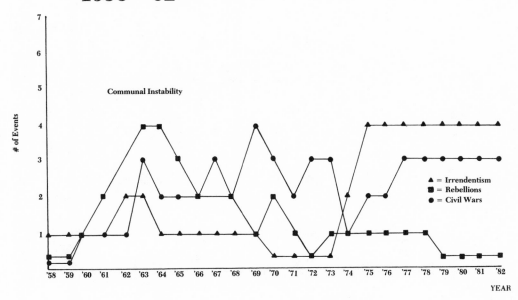

Figure 7.3 Elite Instability in Black African States, 1958—82

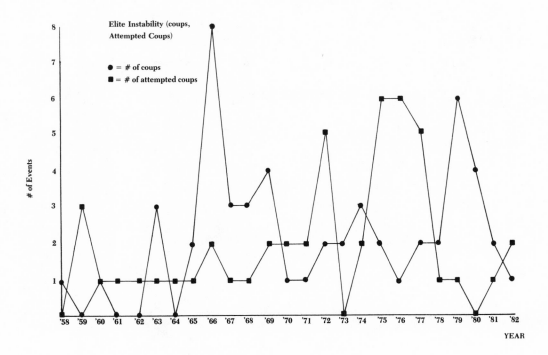

Figure 7.4   Mass Instability in Black African States, 1958—82

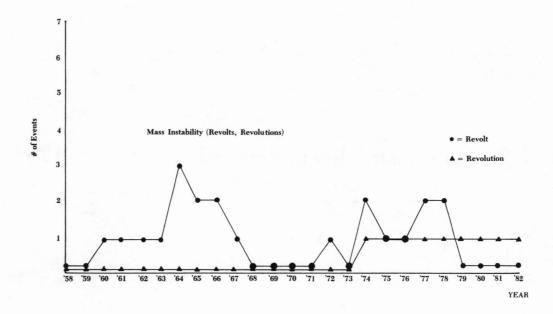

Figure 7.5 Military Regimes in Black Africa
1960—82

1960

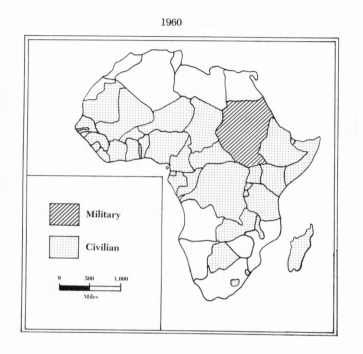

1965

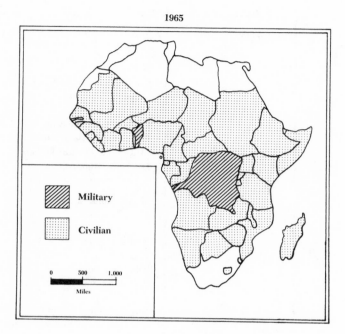

1975

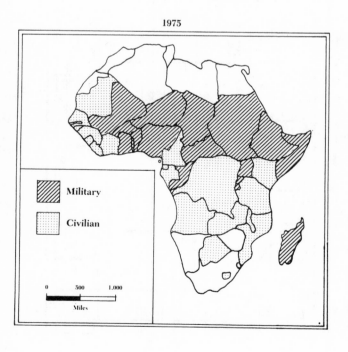

1982

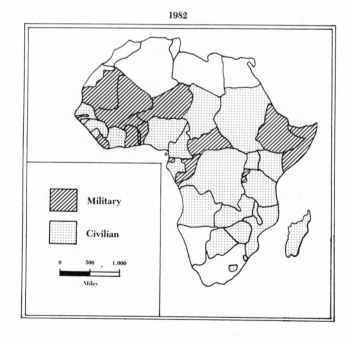

Table 7.6 Leadership Continuity in Black Africa 1956 through
1983

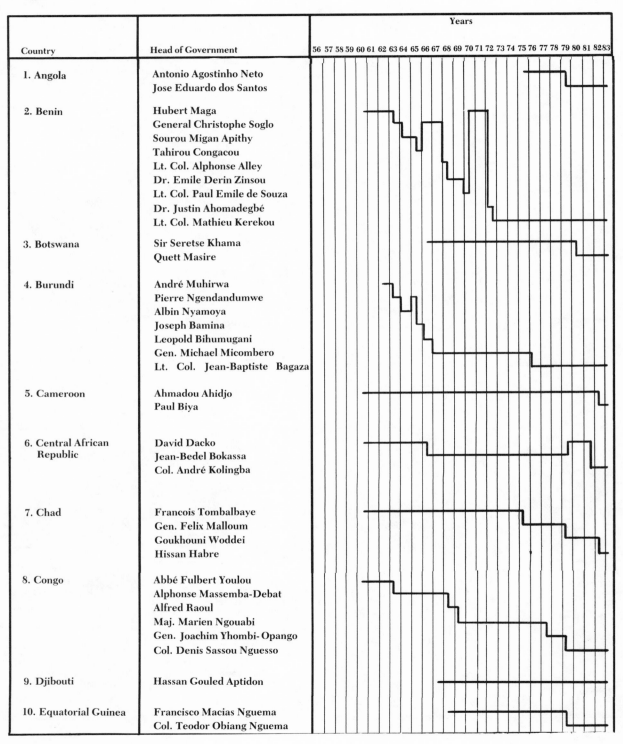

Country	Head of Government	Years
		56 57 58 59 60 61 62 63 64 65 66 67 68 69 70 71 72 73 74 75 76 77 78 79 80 81 82 83
1. Angola	Antonio Agostinho Neto	
	Jose Eduardo dos Santos	
2. Benin	Hubert Maga	
	General Christophe Soglo	
	Sourou Migan Apithy	
	Tahirou Congacou	
	Lt. Col. Alphonse Alley	
	Dr. Emile Derin Zinsou	
	Lt. Col. Paul Emile de Souza	
	Dr. Justin Ahomadegbé	
	Lt. Col. Mathieu Kerekou	
3. Botswana	Sir Seretse Khama	
	Quett Masire	
4. Burundi	André Muhirwa	
	Pierre Ngendandumwe	
	Albin Nyamoya	
	Joseph Bamina	
	Leopold Bihumugani	
	Gen. Michael Micombero	
	Lt. Col. Jean-Baptiste Bagaza	
5. Cameroon	Ahmadou Ahidjo	
	Paul Biya	
6. Central African Republic	David Dacko	
	Jean-Bedel Bokassa	
	Col. André Kolingba	
7. Chad	Francois Tombalbaye	
	Gen. Felix Malloum	
	Goukhouni Woddei	
	Hissan Habre	
8. Congo	Abbé Fulbert Youlou	
	Alphonse Massemba-Debat	
	Alfred Raoul	
	Maj. Marien Ngouabi	
	Gen. Joachim Yhombi-Opango	
	Col. Denis Sassou Nguesso	
9. Djibouti	Hassan Gouled Aptidon	
10. Equatorial Guinea	Francisco Macias Nguema	
	Col. Teodor Obiang Nguema	

	Country	Head of Government	Years
			56 57 58 59 60 61 62 63 64 65 66 67 68 69 70 71 72 73 74 75 76 77 78 79 80 81 82 83
11.	Ethiopia	Haile Selassie I Gen. Aman M. Andom Brig. Gen. Teferi Bante Lt. Col. Mengistu Haile-Mariam	
12.	Gabon	Leon M'Ba Omar Bongo	
13.	Gambia	Sir Dawda Jawara	
14.	Ghana	Dr. Kwame Nkrumah Lt. Gen. Joeseph Ankarah Brig. Gen. A. A. Afrifa Dr. Kofi Busia Gen. Ignatius Kuti Acheampong Gen. Frederick W. K. Akuffo Fl. Lt. Jerry Rawlings Dr. Hila Limann	
15.	Guinea	Ahmed Sekou Touré	
16.	Guinea (Bissau)	Luis de Almeida Cabral Maj. Nino Vieira	
17.	Ivory Coast	Felix Houphouet-Boigny	
18.	Kenya	Jomo Kenyatta Daniel Arap Moi	
19.	Lesotho	Chief Leabua Jonathan	
20.	Liberia	William V. S. Tubman William R. Tolbert Jr. Samuel K. Doe	
21.	Madagascar	Philibert Tsiranana Gen. Gabriel Ramanantsoa Col. Richard Ratsimandrava Gen. Gilles Andriamahazo Com. Didier Ratsiraka	
22.	Malawi	Dr. Hastings Kamazu Banda	
23.	Mali	Modibo Keita Moussa Traoré	
24.	Mauritania	Moktar Ould Daddah Moustapha Ould Salek Mahmoud Ould Louly Mohamed Khouna Ould	
25.	Mozambique	Samora Moises Machel	

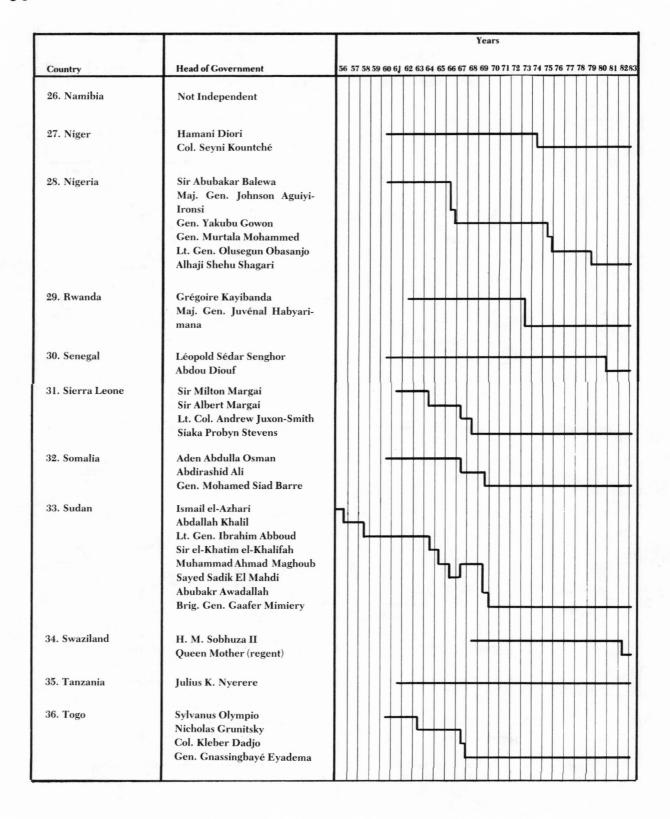

Country	Head of Government	Years
		56 57 58 59 60 6J 62 63 64 65 66 67 68 69 70 71 72 73 74 75 76 77 78 79 80 81 8283
26. Namibia	Not Independent	
27. Niger	Hamani Diori Col. Seyni Kountché	
28. Nigeria	Sir Abubakar Balewa Maj. Gen. Johnson Aguiyi-Ironsi Gen. Yakubu Gowon Gen. Murtala Mohammed Lt. Gen. Olusegun Obasanjo Alhaji Shehu Shagari	
29. Rwanda	Grégoire Kayibanda Maj. Gen. Juvénal Habyari-mana	
30. Senegal	Léopold Sédar Senghor Abdou Diouf	
31. Sierra Leone	Sir Milton Margai Sir Albert Margai Lt. Col. Andrew Juxon-Smith Siaka Probyn Stevens	
32. Somalia	Aden Abdulla Osman Abdirashid Ali Gen. Mohamed Siad Barre	
33. Sudan	Ismail el-Azhari Abdallah Khalil Lt. Gen. Ibrahim Abboud Sir el-Khatim el-Khalifah Muhammad Ahmad Maghoub Sayed Sadik El Mahdi Abubakr Awadallah Brig. Gen. Gaafer Mimiery	
34. Swaziland	H. M. Sobhuza II Queen Mother (regent)	
35. Tanzania	Julius K. Nyerere	
36. Togo	Sylvanus Olympio Nicholas Grunitsky Col. Kleber Dadjo Gen. Gnassingbayé Eyadema	

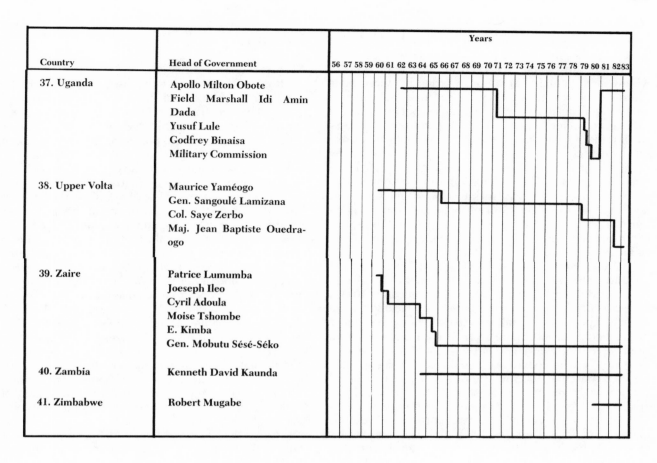

Country	Head of Government	Years
		56 57 58 59 60 61 62 63 64 65 66 67 68 69 70 71 72 73 74 75 76 77 78 79 80 81 82 83
37. Uganda	Apollo Milton Obote Field Marshall Idi Amin Dada Yusuf Lule Godfrey Binaisa Military Commission	
38. Upper Volta	Maurice Yaméogo Gen. Sangoulé Lamizana Col. Saye Zerbo Maj. Jean Baptiste Ouedra-ogo	
39. Zaire	Patrice Lumumba Joeseph Ileo Cyril Adoula Moise Tshombe E. Kimba Gen. Mobutu Sésé-Séko	
40. Zambia	Kenneth David Kaunda	
41. Zimbabwe	Robert Mugabe	

symbol in most African countries, has not deterred most African governments from a conscious encouragement of foreign private capital, and even in those few countries where such a policy has been rewarded by appreciable rates of economic growth (as in Ivory Coast, most noticeably), the ideals of African socialism are belied by a continuing economic control by foreign interests, by very small rates of expansion in the modern employment sector, by consequent very high unemployment, and by the increasingly disproportionate enrichment of the small African bourgeoisie. There is not yet a revolutionary African working class - since work is a privilege. But there may be, and the chances of peaceful political development in Africa are contingent in large part on the success of governments in revising the economic structure of the countries they rule.

The enormity of the problems posed by the tasks of institutionalization, integration and economic growth in Africa, and the relative difficulty experienced by African governments in surmounting them, is reflected in the history of political instability in the 41 states considered in this book. All told there were at least fifty successful coups d'état in twenty-five of these countries in the period between independence and January 1983 and the number continues to grow; there have been protracted and intensely violent civil wars in Zaire, Nigeria, Ethiopia, Sudan, Chad and Angola and numerous instances of violent action by rebellious or irredentist ethnic groups in these and other countries. But popular images of chaos and inevitable instability, of militarism and dictatorship in Africa are far from adequate. There is considerable variance in the intensity of political instability in this set of states; military juntas have handed back political power to civilians in Sierra Leone, Ghana, Nigeria and Upper Volta, and have allowed for very considerable civilian participation in the governments of Zaire and Nigeria. Intense ethnic conflict has not resulted in civil war in countries like Kenya and Zambia, and in Tanzania, at least, there is an example of a unique experiment in democratic government and socialist economic policy which holds great promise for the future of African political development. The student of African political development, at any rate, is challenged to describe the variation and change in institutional organization, public opinion, political behavior and public policy, and to develop empirical explanations of these factors which are likely to decrease the probability of violence in African political life, and increase the probability of security, material welfare, and individual choice in the lives of the citizens of African states.

The Military

It is useful to separate the discussion of the military in Africa from the general discussion of political development. The peculiar importance of the military is related to the relative ease with which members of the armed forces can seize political power, as the history of military coups d'état in Africa already attests. Expertise in the technology of violence, and the commitment to hierarchical authority and secrecy in decision-making, are the hallmarks of military life. They allow the military an overwhelming strategic advantage in disrupting civilian politics, and instill in the military an incompetence in the business of politics should they choose to dabble in it. For politics and political development demand publicity rather than secrecy, participation rather than hierarchy, and persuasion rather than violence. Questions about the military's obedience to civilian authority in the preservation of public order in African states are related to the historical development of armed forces in colonial Africa as well as to patterns of post-colonial political development.

Colonial governments created African armies to put down internal resistance to their conquests of African territory and later considerably expanded the size of their armed forces from Africa in order to obtain assistance in the World Wars as well as wars of liberation in their colonial territories. The number of Africans in the allied armies in the world wars was in the hundreds of thousands. Many Africans saw military service in the French Indo-China war, in the Algerian war, and in the subjugation of resistance movements in Kenya and Cameroon. The colonial authorities preferred to choose the rank and file recruits from what they perceived to be the more "bellicose" and illiterate ethnic groups, and to recruit officers, when they finally chose to do so, from the more educated and "civilized" ethnic groups. In many cases, therefore, those recruitment policies created conflicts within the armed forces between members of different ethnic groups, making the tasks of national integration in the society at large more difficult for civilian authorities. Generally, the very late Africanization of the officer corps also meant that the new national armies had very inexperienced officers, and that competition for elite officer status was particularly pronounced. Furthermore, the political experience of the colonial armed forces was often confined to opposing the African politicians whom, after independence, they were required to obey. This affected both armed forces personnel and politicians, who, in cases like Congo, Ghana and Mali, chose to develop special presidential guards, independent of regular army control, thereby accentuating the civil-military conflicts deriving from the colonial experience.

In the post-colonial era, the military has become an obvious alternative elite to the members of civilian government, and a number of characteristics of the civilian political process have tended to increase the likelihood of military intervention. The development of the centralized party-state in Africa has not dealt as easily with the autonomy of the army as it has with that of the bureaucracy, courts, and trade unions. Civilian involvement in the "business" of the military, as in the direction of the Ghanaian force in the Congo, the "retiring" of senior officers in the Ghanaian army, and the concerted effort to promote an ethnically representative officer corps in Nigeria, may be seen as factors influencing military intervention in those countries. The manifestations of civilian corruption and ethnic conflict in African civilian life has particularly affected members of the military who are trained in a puritanical code of military conduct and punishment, and in an orientation towards the nation as the focus of loyalty and the locus of power. Also, African officers trained at metropolitan military schools in the fear of Communist countries and in the use and appreciation of West European arms and equipment, have often balked at movements by their civilian governments to balance the preponderant influence of Western neo-colonial relationships. However, in the case of armies which have had closer contacts with socialist countries, armies may, at least nominally, be more to the left than their civilian predecessors, e.g. Congo, Somalia, Sudan, Central African Republic and Benin. Finally, the great difficulty of achieving economic growth in contemporary African nations has made the economic burden of supporting larger and technically up-to-date armies more difficult than the military would like, and civilian governments' inabilities to satisfy demands of the army for increased salaries, veterans' employment, new uniforms and equipment, and growth in manpower are sources of civil-military conflict in these countries.

Bibliography

Anyone contemplating an analysis of contemporary African political development should be familiar with at least some of the complexity of pre-colonial African political systems, and some of the history of African politics during the colonial era. A good introduction to the basis of political order in pre-colonial African societies, and the historical development of increasingly complex institutional arrangements in African political systems before the advent of colonialism, is given in Basil Davidson, *The African Genius* (Boston: Little Brown, 1970).

More technical discussions of the variety of traditional African political structures are given in the work of anthropologists contained in: M. Fortes and E. E. Evans-Pritchard, eds., *African Political Systems* (New York: Oxford University Press, 1940); Isaac Schapera, *Government and Politics in Tribal Societies* (London: Watts, 1965); John Middleton and David Trait, eds., *Tribes Without Rulers* (London: Routledge and Kegan Paul, 1958). A useful summary of this literature is given in Lucy Mair, *Primitive Government* (Baltimore: Penguin, 1962), and a fascinating analysis of the process rather than structure of African political life is Max Gluckman, *Politics, Law and Ritual in Tribal Society* (Chicago: Aldine, 1965).

African politics during this colonial era are discussed with varying emphasis by members of different academic disciplines. Historians have been interested in African resistance to colonial rule, which was much more considerable than the colonial histories had suggested. A useful selection of writings on African resistance is contained in Part I of R. I. Rotberg and Ali A. Mazrui eds., *Power and Protest in Black Africa* (New York: Oxford University Press, 1970). Sociologists and anthropologists have been interested in the cultural and institutional adaptation to colonial rule, and the social basis of protest against colonialism as exemplified in syncretistic religious movements. For example, Lloyd Fallers has discussed the problems of African officials in a colonial system of indirect-rule in *Bantu Bureaucracy: A Century of Political Evolution Among the Basoga of Uganda* (Chicago: University of Chicago Press, 1962), and a comprehensive discussion of the African response to colonialism is contained in Georges Balandier, *The Sociology of Black Africa: Social Dynamics in Central Africa* (New York: Praeger, 1970 originally published in French in 1955). Useful compilations of articles discussing a wide variety of issues are Immanuel Wallerstein ed., *Social Change: The Colonial Situation* (New York: Wiley, 1966) and Victor Turner ed., *Colonialism in Africa ca. 1870-1960* Vol III *Profiles of Change: African Society and Colonial Rule* (New York: Cambridge University Press, 1971). A subject of particular interest to political scientists has been the growth of nationalism in colonial Africa. Excellent treatments of this subject are: Thomas C. Hodgkin, *Nationalism in Colonial Africa* (London: Muller, 1956); James S. Coleman, *Nigeria: Background to Nationalism* (Berkeley: University of California Press, 1958); R. I. Rotberg, *The Rise of Nationalism in Central Africa: The Making of Malawi and Zambia, 1873-1964* (Cambridge: Harvard University Press, 1965); Carl G. Rosberg, Jr. and John Nottingham, *The Myth of the "Mau Mau": Nationalism in Kenya* (New York: Praeger, 1966); and W. B. Cohen *Rulers of Empire: The French Colonial Service in Africa* (Stanford: Hoover Institution Press, 1971).

Associated with the rise of nationalism, but also with the organization of African politics after independence, is the articulation of political thought and ideology in Africa. Much early intellectual and organizational work was devoted to Pan-Africanism which is described in I. Geiss' *The Pan-African Movement: A History of Pan Africanism in America, Europe and Africa* (New York: Africana, 1974). Important original writings of contemporary thought are associated with the names of many of the heads of African governments, but the following are particularly notable as statements of the meaning of African Socialism, Pan-Africanism and of the African position vis-a-vis foreign powers: Kwame Nkrumah, *Africa Must Unite* (New York: Praeger, 1964); Nkrumah, *Neo-Colonialism: The Last Stage of Imperialism* (London: T. Nelson, 1965); Leopold Senghor, *On African Socialism* (New York: Praeger, 1964); Mamadou Dia, *The African Nations and World Solidarity* (New York: Praeger, 1961); Julius Nyerere, *Democracy and the Party System* (Dar es Salaam: Tanganyika Standard Ltd., 1965); and Nyerere *Ujamaa: Essays on Socialism* (Dar Es Salaam: Oxford University Press, 1968). Articles on the political thought of Patrice Lumumba by Rene Lemarchand, Kwame Nkrumah by Kenneth Grundy and Sekou Touré by Charles F. Andrian are contained in W. A. E. Skurnik ed. *African Political Thought: Lumumba, Nkrumah and Touré* (Denver: University of Denver, Monograph Series in World Affairs, vol. 5, 1968). A study of Lumumba by one of his contemporaries is T. Kanza *Conflict in the Congo: The Rise and Fall of Lumumba* (Baltimore: Penguin, 1972).

A series of commentaries on the nature of African socialism is given in Carl G. Rosberg, Jr. and Thomas Callaghy, eds., *Socialism in Sub-Saharan Africa: A New Assessment*, (Berkeley: University of California Press, 1979). An introduction to the historical and intellectual background of Pan-Africanism is Colin Legum, *Pan-Africanism: A Short Political Guide* (London: Pall Mall, 1962), which should be read in conjunction with the evaluation of the political histories of Pan-Africanism in Immanuel Wallerstein, *Africa: The Politics of Unity* (New York: Random House, 1967) and Imanuel Geis, *The Pan-*

African Movement: A History of Pan-Africanism in America, Europe and Africa (New York: Africana, 1974). See also Ras Makonnen, *Pan-Africanism from Within* (New York: Oxford University Press, 1973) and E. Mbuyinga, *Pan-Africanism or Neo-Colonialism: The Bankrupcy of the O. A. U.* (London: Zed Press, 1982. Excellent case studies of attempts at unification, and the political inhibition of economic integration are: Claude E. Welch Jr., *Dream of Unity: Pan-Africanism and Political Unification in West Africa* (Ithaca: Cornell University Press, 1966); Joeseph Nye Jr., *Pan-Africanism and East African Integration* (Cambridge: Harvard University Press, 1965); and Arthur Hazelwood ed., *African Integration and Disintegration: Case Studies in Economic and Political Union* (New York: Oxford University Press, 1967). A useful review of the political thought of a number of African political leaders is O. Otite ed. *Themes in African Political Thought* (Enugu: Fourth Dimension, 1978).

The literature on contemporary African politics may be approached first by looking at very general, comparative, theoretical or critical treatments of the subject. A work of major significance as an ideological interpretation of third world politics and as a prophetic forecast of the problems of post-colonial politics in Africa is Frantz Fanon, *The Wretched of the Earth* (New York: Grove Press, 1965). An intensely critical but more empirically detailed work that is specifically concerned with African politics is René Dumont, *False Start in Africa* (New York: Praeger, 1966), which may be contrasted with the equally critical but quite different diagnosis in Stanislav Andreski, *The African Predicament: A Study in the Pathology of Modernization* (London: Joeseph, 1968). A work of major importance by a political scientist that attempts to summarize the problems and the nature of African politics, and which is far-removed from the ideological and polemical stance of Fanon, Dumont or Andreski, is Aristide R. Zolberg, *Creating Political Order* (Chicago: Rand McNally, 1966). Recent studies include books by Crawford Young *Ideology and Development in Africa* (New Haven: Yale University Press, 1982) and Donald S. Rothchild and R. L. Curry *Scarcity, Choice and Public Policy in Middle Africa* (Berkeley: University of California Press, 1978). For a study of Tanzania's political philosophy see J. R. Nellis, *A Theory of Ideology: The Tanzanian Example* (New York: Oxford University Press, 1973) and the review by E. J. Kahn Jr., *The First Decade: A Report on Independent Africa* (New York: Norton, 1972).

These introductory arguments should be supplemented by the very extensive case study literature on African countries. The bibliographies in Part V give the major case studies written for each Black African country, but we can mention here the Cornell University Press,

Westview Press, Scarecrow Press and Praeger series as excellent sources. Praeger has published case studies on countries for which there is very little alternative information in summary form such as for Malawi, Mauritania and Zambia, and that Press has also issued a useful discussion of politics in French-speaking Africa by G. de Lusignan, *French Speaking Africa since Independence* (New York: Praeger, 1964) and an excellent example of political journalism in Walter Schwartz, *Nigeria* (New York: Praeger, 1968). Other works of interest are: P. M. Gukiina, *Uganda: A Case Study in African Political Development* (South Bend: University of Notre Dame Press, 1970); M. Owusu, *Uses and Abuses of Political Power: A Case Study of Continuity and Change in the Politics of Ghana* (Chicago: University of Chicago Press, 1970); and P. Foster and A. R. Zolberg eds., *Ghana and the Ivory Coast: Perspectives on Modernization* (Chicago: University of Chicago Press, 1971).

The literature relating to the theoretical and analytic discussion of political development in Africa is for the most part based on empirical reference to single countries, and the comparative analysis of African politics is somewhat underdeveloped. One should, however, look at James Coleman's chapter on sub-Saharan Africa in Gabriel Almond and James S. Coleman eds. *The Politics of Developing Areas* (Princeton: Princeton University Press, 1960) which should be read in conjunction with Almond's famous theoretical introduction to that volume. An attempt to do theoretically informed comparative analysis, using the very different cases of South Africa, Somalia, Tanzania and the Ivory Coast is by C. Potholm, *Four African Political Systems* (Englewood Cliffs: Prentice Hall, 1970).

The literature on institutional development in African political systems is very extensive. One can begin with the very difficult, but very interesting work of David Apter, whose *Ghana in Transition* (New York: Atheneum, 1963) is an attempt to discuss the problems of institutional transfer in the context of social science theory, and particularly to deal with the role of charismatic leadership as a means to political development. Apter has also discussed the politics of Uganda immediately prior to independence in *The Political Kingdom in Uganda* (Princeton: Princeton University Press, 1961, revised 1967) where he develops a typology of political systems in the transition from traditional to modern political organization. The general theoretical issues arising from this research are elaborated in Apter's *The Politics of Modernization* (Chicago: University of Chicago Press, 1965), which may be a useful guide to the issues of political development as they are conceived of by contemporary political scientists. A recent review of the transfer of power from the colonial country to the indigenes is P. Gifford and W. R. Louis *The Transfer of Power in Africa: Deco-*

lonization 1940-1960 (New Haven: Yale University Press, 1982).

The very abstract issues discussed by Apter can be related to the rich and detailed literature on the development of different political institutions in African states after independence. The changing role of traditional authorities in these countries is discussed in a series of case studies collected in the anthology: Michael Crowder and O. Ikime eds. *West African Chiefs: Their Changing Status Under Colonial Rule and Independence* (New York: Africana, 1972).

The most intensive research on African political institutions is that relating to the development of political parties, and here one may still read with profit the excellent analysis of parties in French-West Africa contained in Ruth Shachter-Morgenthau, *Political Parties in French-Speaking West Africa* (Oxford: Clarendon Press, 1964) and the general discussion in Thomas Hodgkin, *African Political Parties* (Oxford: Oxford University Press, 1964). The best of the case studies of parties in single countries are R. Sklar, *Nigerian Political Parties* (Princeton: Princeton University Press, 1963); A. Zolberg, *One-Party Government in the Ivory Coast* (Princeton: Princeton University Press, 1965) and H. Bienen's *Tanzania: Party Transformation and Economic Development* (Princeton: Princeton University Press, 1967 revised 1970) all of which relate the role of parties to the integration of national political communities and to the development of legitimate central authority in these countries. These books are complimented by an excellent anthology which deals explicitly with the issue of national integration and with the variety of different organizational and ideological styles of political party development; James S. Coleman and Carl C. Rosberg, Jr., *Political Parties and National Integration* (Berkeley: University of California Press, 1964). For the role of parties and the military see Henry Bienen *Armies and Parties in Africa* (New York: Africana, 1978).

There is far less published on the development of other political institutions in Africa such as the bureaucracy, the legal system, local government, trade unions, and the role of institutions such as churches, universities, schools and voluntary organizations in political life. For some insights into the nature of bureaucracy in Africa, there is the general summary of organizational procedures in A. L. Adu, *The Civil Service in New African States* (New York: Prager, 1965) and the case study of the transfer of colonial and metropolitan systems of local government, and the perpetuation of centralization, autocracy and the "generalist" administrator in Martin Stanisland, "Colonial Government and Populist Reform: The Case of the Ivory Coast - I and II." *Journal of Administration Overseas* X (January-April, 1971): 33-42 and 113-126. Political scientists have become particularly interested in the description of local-level politics in Africa, in

an attempt to get beneath the fragile structure of national institutions to the everyday political behavior of the average African citizens. The kinds of issues attracting attention are dealt with in an issue of the *Canadian Journal of African Studies* 3 (1969) no 1 edited by Norman N. Miller; and for an example of an excellent and brief case study of local politics one may look at Colin Leys, *Politicians and Policies: An Essay on Acholi, Uganda 1962-1965* (Nairobi: East African Publishing House, 1967).

For introductions to the role of trade unions in African states, there is the general discussion of Ioan Davies, *African Trade Unions* (Baltimore: Penguin, 1966); the useful chapter on trade unions by Butler and Berg in Coleman and Rosberg, *Political Parties and National Integration* op. cit.; Richard Sandbrook, "Patrons, Clients and Unions: The Labour Movement and Political Conflict in Kenya," *Journal of Commonwealth Political Studies* 10 (March 1972): 3-27; W. Ananaba, *The Trade Union Movement in Nigeria* (New York: Africana, 1970), and U. Damachi et al., eds., *Industrial Relations in Africa*, (New York: St. Martin's Press, 1979).. For a class analysis see Richard Sandbrook and Robin Cohen, eds., *The Development of an African Working Class*, (Toronto: University of Toronto Press, 1976).

Studies of national integration as an aspect of political development are increasing in number. Two very clearly analyzed cases on well articulated theoretical arguments are Brian Weinstein, *Nation-Building on the Ogooue* (Cambridge: M. I. T. Press) and W. R. Johnson, *The Cameroon Federation: Political Integration in a Fragmentary Society* (Princeton: Princeton University Press, 1970). While not specifically concerned with the theory of integration, Martin Kilson, *Political Change in a West African State: A Study of the Modernization Process in Sierra Leone* (Cambridge: Harvard University Press, 1966) has a very interesting discussion of the growth of new systems of class stratification and the problems of integration between the new elites and the mass public in Africa, and there is some useful material on the role of African elites in P. C. Lloyd ed. *The New Elites in Tropical Africa* (New York: Oxford University Press, 1966) as well as his *Africa in Social Change*, rev ed. (Harmondsworth: Penguin, 1972). Also see Rene Lemarchand's "Political Clientism and Ethnicity in Tropical Africa: Competing Solidarities in Nation Building," *American Political Science Review* 66 (March 1972): 68-90, and Crawford Young, *The Politics of Cultural Pluralism*, (Madison: University of Wisconsin Press, 1976). The role of religious elites in the development of national political integration is very usefully discussed in Lucy Behrman, *Muslim Brotherhoods and Politics in Senegal* (Cambridge: Harvard University Press, 1970); John N. Paden, *Religion and Political Culture in Kano* (Berkeley: University of California Press, 1973) and D. B. Cruise O'Brien, *The Mourides of Senegal: The Political and Economic Orga-*

nization of an Islamic Brotherhood (Oxford: Clarendon Press, 1971). The effects of education on the development of a national political culture in the mass public can be assessed in a preliminary fashion from the ambitious comparative survey reported in Otto Klineberg and Marisa Zavalloni, Nationalism and Tribalism Among African Students (New York: Humanities Press, 1969). See the education chapter for further entries on the political role of education. The political role of African students is assessed in W. J. Hanna, et al., eds., University Students and African Politics, (New York: Africana, 1974) and Joel D. Barkan, An African Dilemma (New York: Oxford University Press, 1975).

A useful introduction to the literature on political instability in African states is Aristide R. Zolberg, "The Structure of Political Conflict in the New States of Tropical Africa," American Political Science Review 62 (March 1968): 70-87. Case studies of military intervention in Africa are collected by Henry Bienen ed., in The Military Intervenes (New York: Russell Sage, 1968); Claude E. Welch, Jr., The Soldier and the State in Africa (Evanston: Northwestern University Press, 1970) and Robert I. Rotberg and Ali Mazrui eds. Power and Protest in Black Africa (New York: Oxford University Press, 1970). A comparative summary and explanation of military intervention in Africa is Ruth First, Guns and Power in Africa (New York: Pantheon, 1971). For treatments of civil war and communal violence in African countries, there is the excellent discussion of Zanzibar by Michael Lofchie, Zanzibar, Background to Revolution (Princeton: Princeton University Press, 1965); discussions of rebellion in Uganda, Cameroon, and Zaire (Congo-Kinshasa) in the Rotberg and Mazrui anthology referred to above; analyses of communal violence in Northern Nigeria by J. Paden and R. Cohen, both contained in Melson and H. Wolpe eds. Nigeria: Modernization and the Politics of Communalism (East Lansing: Michigan State University Press, 1970). More recent analyses are T. O. Odetola Military Regimes and Development: A Comparative Analysis of African States (Boston: Allen and Unwin, 1982); R. H. Jackson and C. G. Rosberg, Personal Rule in Africa (Berkeley: University of California Press, 1982); and Samuel Decalo, Coups and Army Rule in Africa (New Haven: Yale University Press, 1976).

The study of the African military remains seriously short of detailed case studies of military organization and personnel. There is a conspicuous exception in Robin Luckham, The Nigerian Military (New York: Cambridge University Press, 1971), but the practical difficulties of obtaining information on the backgrounds and attitudes of armed forces personnel in most countries makes it very difficult to evaluate the degree to which military intervention is a function of the internal organization of armies. Another study on the Nigerian army is N. J. Miners' The Nigerian Army: 1956-1966 (London: Methuen, 1971). Overviews of the military role in Africa are A. R. Zolberg's "The Military Decade in Africa," World Politics 25 (Jan. 1973): 309-331; U. O. Eleazu, "The Role of the Army in Politics: A Reconsideration of Existing Theories and Practices," Journal of the Developing Areas 7 (1973): 265-286; and Peter C. Lloyd, Clashes, Crises, and Coups: Themes in the Sociology of Developing Countries (London: MacGibbon and Kee, 1971). See the comparative case studies in E. Lefever, Spear and Scepter: Army, Police and Politics in Tropical Africa (Washington: Brookings Institution, 1970); Anton Bebler ed., Military Rule in Africa: Dahomey, Ghana, Sierra Leone and Mali (New York: Praeger, 1973); and the novel class analysis in A. A. Mazrui, "The Lumpen Proletariat and the Lumpen Militariat: African Soldiers as a New Political Class," Political Studies XXI (March 1973): 1-12.

An excellent discussion of the general problems of public order and military intervention in Africa, which contains a good deal of information on the early organization of armies in Ghana, Kenya and Nigeria, in particular, is J. M. Lee, African Armies and Civil Order (New York: Praeger, 1969). Another useful and very brief discussion of the general problem is M. J. V. Bell, Army and Nation in Sub-Saharan Africa (London: Institute for Strategic Studies, Adelphi Paper no. 21, 1965), and those issues are also addressed in W. F. Gutteridge's several books: Armed Forces in New States (London: Oxford University Press, 1962), Military Institutions and Power in the New States (London: Pall Mall, 1965), and Military Regimes in Africa (New York: Barnes and Noble, 1975). Gutteridge has some useful comparative information on the historical development of African military forces. Recent studies of the military include Samuel Decalo, Coups and Army Rule in Africa: Studies in Military Style, (New Haven: Yale University Press, 1976) and A. A. Mazrui, ed., The Warrior Tradition in Modern Africa (Atlantic Highlands, NJ: Humanities Press, 1979).

An interesting short discussion of political instability in Africa in terms of the images of the military as the guardian of civil order on the one hand and as the source of militarism on the other is Kenneth W. Grundy, Conflicting Images of the Military in Africa (Nairobi: East African Publishing House, 1968). One should look also at the earlier items dealing with political instability for some useful evaluations of military intervention in Africa. Comparative information on the size and cost of African armed forces in 1966 was compiled from David Wood's The Armed Forces of African States (London: Institute for Strategic Studies, Adelphi Paper no. 27, 1966) and a later version with new data by the same author is The Armed Forces of African States, 1970 (London, Institute for Strategic Studies, Adelphi Paper No. 67). Aside from the Institute for Strategic Studies, and the American Arms Control and Disarmament Agency useful sources of information on the size, equipment and budget of African armies are R. Sellers ed., *Armed Forces of the World: A Reference Handbook* 3rd. ed. (New York: Praeger, 1971); the annual *African Contemporary Record* (London: Af-

rica Research Ltd.); and the various periodicals such as *West Africa, Africa, Africa Report, Africa Confidential, Europa Yearbook, Africa Research Bulletin* and *Africa Digest*. For a comprehensive bibliography see R. B. Shaw and R. L. Sklar, *A Bibliography for the Study of African Politics* (Waltham, MA: Crossroads Press, 1977), 2 Vols.

Table 7.1 **Number of Political Parties in the Period from Independence to 1980 (A), and Independence to 1972 (B).**

Definition: All political parties that were legal (i.e. not banned for the entire period) at some time during the period Independence to January 1, 1980 were counted, even if they resulted from mergers or splits.

Comments: Most of these countries that have had a large number of parties (e.g. seven or more) have suffered from some severe form of political instability such as a coup d'état. Conversely, the countries that had only one party from independence tended to have a more settled political existence in terms of serious political instability. See Part II for a discussion of these issues.

```
Range =        27.00
Mean =          6.72
Standard Deviation =      5.54
```

Population Percent Cum.	Country	Rank	Country Name	A	Range Decile	B
3.51	3.51	1.0	Ghana	27	1	11
24.51	21.00	2.0	Nigeria	19	3	
32.80	8.29	3.0	Zaire	17	4	1
35.21	2.41	5.0	Cameroon	13	6	1
41.45	6.24	5.0	Sudan	13		12
43.42	1.97	5.0	Upper Volta	13		9
44.42	1.00	7.5	Benin	11		1
46.90	2.48	7.5	Madagascar	11		6
47.93	1.03	9.0	Somalia	10	7	7
48.31	.38	11.0	Lesotho	8	8	5
49.30	.99	11.0	Sierra Leone	8		4
50.95	1.65	11.0	Zambia	8		5
51.12	.17	13.5	Gambia	7		4
56.28	5.16	13.5	Tanzania	7		1
56.51	.23	18.0	Botswana	6		6
57.79	1.28	18.0	Burundi	6		1
58.37	.58	18.0	Central African R	6		1
58.82	.45	18.0	Congo	6		1
58.98	.16	18.0	Gabon	6		1
59.14	.16	18.0	Swaziland	6		5
59.89	.75	18.0	Togo	6		1
59.99	.10	24.0	Djibouti	5	9	0
60.09	.10	24.0	Equatorial Guinea	5		0
60.55	.46	24.0	Mauritania	5		1
61.91	1.36	24.0	Rwanda	5		2
65.86	3.95	24.0	Uganda	5		2
67.20	1.34	27.5	Chad	4		2
71.80	4.60	27.5	Kenya	4		2
72.33	.53	29.5	Liberia	3		1
73.99	1.66	29.5	Malawi	3		1
75.86	1.87	31.0	Mali	2	10	0
77.81	1.95	35.0	Angola	1		3
79.38	1.57	35.0	Guinea	1		1
79.57	.19	35.0	Guinea-Bissau	1		2
81.79	2.22	35.0	Ivory Coast	1		1
84.78	2.99	35.0	Mozambique	1		4
86.11	1.33	35.0	Niger	1		1
87.75	1.64	35.0	Senegal	1		3
97.46	9.71	39.0	Ethiopia	0		0

```
DATA NOT AVAILABLE OR NOT APPLICABLE
FOR THE FOLLOWING COUNTRIES

Namibia       Zimbabwe
```

SOURCE: *Black Africa*: second edition.

Table 7.2 **Voting Turnout at Independence.**

Definition: The number of persons actually casting a vote in the national legislative election closest to, but before, the date of independence, as a percent of the total population in that year.

Comments: Since the rules for determining who is eligible to vote vary considerably, it was not generally possible to determine the percent of potential voters who voted. We have used the total population as a base, instead. While in some countries nearly every adult voted, in others only a small proportion voted. It should be noted that countries with low percentages tended to be countries that suffered political breakdowns thereafter.

```
Range =        61.00
Mean =         24.94
Standard Deviation =     13.71
```

Population Percent Cum.	Country	Rank	Country Name	A	Range Decile
.16	.16	1.0	Swaziland	62	1
.54	.38	2.0	Lesotho	52	2
1.90	1.36	3.0	Rwanda	46	3
4.12	2.22	4.0	Ivory Coast	45	
4.58	.46	5.5	Mauritania	38	4
6.84	2.26	5.5	Zimbabwe	38	
7.01	.17	7.5	Gambia	37	5
8.66	1.65	7.5	Zambia	37	
9.11	.45	9.5	Congo	34	
9.27	.16	9.5	Gabon	34	
9.37	.10	11.0	Equatorial Guinea	33	
11.78	2.41	12.0	Cameroon	30	6
13.42	1.64	13.0	Senegal	28	
13.95	.53	14.0	Liberia	27	
15.23	1.28	15.0	Burundi	26	
15.46	.23	16.5	Botswana	23	7
16.21	.75	16.5	Togo	23	
17.78	1.57	19.0	Guinea	22	
22.38	4.60	19.0	Kenya	22	
24.35	1.97	19.0	Upper Volta	22	
25.35	1.00	22.0	Benin	20	
26.38	1.03	22.0	Somalia	20	
34.67	8.29	22.0	Zaire	20	
36.01	1.34	24.0	Chad	19	8
37.88	1.87	25.0	Mali	18	
58.88	21.00	26.0	Nigeria	16	
62.83	3.95	27.0	Uganda	15	
72.54	9.71	28.0	Ethiopia	13	9
73.87	1.33	29.0	Niger	12	
77.38	3.51	30.0	Ghana	11	
83.62	6.24	31.0	Sudan	10	
84.20	.58	32.5	Central African R	8	
85.19	.99	32.5	Sierra Leone	8	
86.85	1.66	34.0	Malawi	3	10
92.01	5.16	35.0	Tanzania	1	

```
DATA NOT AVAILABLE OR NOT APPLICABLE
FOR THE FOLLOWING COUNTRIES

Angola        Djibouti      Guinea-Bissau  Madagascar
Mozambique    Namibia
```

SOURCE: *Black Africa* second edition.

Table 7.3   Percentage of the Vote Cast for the Winning Party in the Election Closest to, but Before, the Date of Independence.

Definition: The winning party is the party from which the government executive (cabinet), or head of government, if a coalition, is chosen.

Comments: In all but seven countries, the new states began independence with a ruling party that had a clear-cut majority of the total vote. In two instances, there were countries with just 50% of the vote and five countries, usually those with a multiplicity of parties, had less than a majority of the votes.

```
Range =        92.00
Mean =         64.77
Standard Deviation =        23.27
```

Population Percent		Rank	Country Name	A	Range Decile
Cum.	Country				
2.22	2.22	1.5	Ivory Coast	100	1
2.68	.46	1.5	Mauritania	100	
3.21	.53	3.5	Liberia	99	
4.87	1.66	3.5	Malawi	99	
5.45	.58	5.0	Central African R	89	2
5.68	.23	6.0	Botswana	87	
7.32	1.64	7.5	Senegal	83	
12.48	5.16	7.5	Tanzania	83	
13.76	1.28	9.0	Burundi	81	3
13.92	.16	10.0	Swaziland	80	
15.28	1.36	11.0	Rwanda	78	
15.38	.10	13.0	Djibouti	77	
16.95	1.57	13.0	Guinea	77	
18.28	1.33	13.0	Niger	77	
20.15	1.87	15.5	Mali	76	
21.18	1.03	15.5	Somalia	76	
22.83	1.65	17.0	Zambia	70	4
24.17	1.34	18.0	Chad	68	
26.43	2.26	19.0	Zimbabwe	62	5
26.60	.17	21.0	Gambia	60	
27.35	.75	21.0	Togo	60	
29.32	1.97	21.0	Upper Volta	60	
29.77	.45	23.0	Congo	58	
33.28	3.51	24.0	Ghana	57	
37.88	4.60	25.0	Kenya	54	6
41.83	3.95	26.0	Uganda	52	
44.24	2.41	27.5	Cameroon	50	
44.40	.16	27.5	Gabon	50	
45.39	.99	29.0	Sierra Leone	46	
45.77	.38	30.0	Lesotho	42	7
45.87	.10	31.0	Equatorial Guinea	39	
66.87	21.00	32.0	Nigeria	28	8
75.16	8.29	33.0	Zaire	25	9
76.16	1.00	34.0	Benin	16	10
82.40	6.24	35.0	Sudan	8	

```
DATA NOT AVAILABLE OR NOT APPLICABLE
FOR THE FOLLOWING COUNTRIES
```

Angola	Ethiopia	Guinea-Bissau Madagascar
Mozambique	Namibia	

SOURCE: *Black Africa* second edition.

Table 7.4   Elite Instability, Independence to 1979 (A), Independence to 1975 (B), Independence to 1969 (C), and 1970-1975 (D).

Definition: A numerical weight was given to coups d'état (5), attempted coups (3), and plots (1). The index is the sum of the scores for all such events coded for a given country during the period from Independence through December 31, 1979, etc. See *Black Africa* for full definitions. Each country's index is divided by the number of years in the period Independence through December 1979.

Comments: The number of countries which have suffered at least one successful coup d'état is about half of the 41 countries reviewed in this book. Even for those that did not have a coup, some form of elite instability was experienced by all but a few African states.

```
Range =        2.82
Mean =         .79
Standard Deviation =        .69
```

Population Percent		Rank	Country Name	A	Range Decile	B	C	D
Cum.	Country							
3.95	3.95	1.0	Uganda	2.82	1	2.05	1.11	3.17
4.95	1.00	2.0	Benin	2.26	2	2.55	2.80	2.17
5.40	.45	3.0	Congo	2.16	3	2.09	2.47	1.50
11.64	6.24	4.0	Sudan	2.04		1.70	1.57	2.00
15.15	3.51	5.0	Ghana	1.68	5	1.28	1.02	1.83
16.43	1.28	6.0	Burundi	1.47		1.48	2.13	.67
16.53	.10	7.0	Equatorial Guinea	1.36	6	1.25	6.67	.17
16.91	.38	8.0	Lesotho	1.30		1.20	.31	1.67
17.66	.75	9.0	Togo	1.21		1.72	2.16	.17
25.95	8.29	10.0	Zaire	1.16		1.42	2.11	3.67
26.53	.58	11.0	Central African R	1.11	7	.72	.86	.50
28.10	1.57	12.5	Guinea	.95		1.10	.63	2.00
49.10	21.00	12.5	Nigeria	.95		1.18	1.29	1.00
50.09	.99	14.0	Sierra Leone	.94		1.16	1.26	1.00
51.43	1.34	15.5	Chad	.79	8	.78	.54	1.17
53.40	1.97	15.5	Upper Volta	.79		.78	.75	.83
55.35	1.95	17.0	Angola	.75				
56.38	1.03	18.0	Somalia	.68		.65	.84	.33
56.84	.46	19.0	Mauritania	.58		.07		.17
66.55	9.71	20.0	Ethiopia	.54	9	.43	.27	.83
69.03	2.48	21.5	Madagascar	.53		.39	.63	
70.90	1.87	21.5	Mali	.53		.53	.76	.17
72.23	1.33	23.0	Niger	.52		.46	.11	1.00
72.39	.16	24.0	Swaziland	.45		.69		.83
72.58	.19	25.0	Guinea-Bissau	.40				
74.22	1.64	26.0	Senegal	.32		.39	.65	
75.58	1.36	27.0	Rwanda	.29		.37	0	.83
80.18	4.60	28.5	Kenya	.25	10	.25	.17	.33
83.17	2.99	28.5	Mozambique	.25				
88.33	5.16	30.0	Tanzania	.22				
88.49	.16	31.5	Gabon	.16		.20	.32	
90.71	2.22	31.5	Ivory Coast	.16		.20	.22	.17
91.24	.53	33.0	Liberia	.14		.38	.40	.33
93.65	2.41	34.0	Cameroon	.11		.06	.10	
95.30	1.65	35.0	Zambia	.07		.09	0	.17
95.53	.23	37.0	Botswana	0		0	0	0
95.70	.17	37.0	Gambia	0		0	0	0
97.36	1.66	37.0	Malawi	0		0	0	0

```
DATA NOT AVAILABLE OR NOT APPLICABLE
FOR THE FOLLOWING COUNTRIES
```

Djibouti	Namibia	Zimbabwe

SOURCES: *Black Africa* second edition..

Table 7.5   Communal Instability, Independence to 1979 (A), Independence to 1975 (B), Independence to 1969 (C), and 1970-1975 (D).

Definition: A numerical weight was given to civil wars (5), rebellions (4), irredentism (3), and ethnic violence (1). The index was computed by multiplying the score for each event by the number of years in which it was reported in any country, and by summing the resultant products. The computations are based on the period from Independence to January 1, 1980. Each country's index was divided by the number of years in this period for that country.

Comment: Conflict between communally-defined groups is not as widespread as that between elites as a comparison of this table and the preceding one will make clear. Nevertheless, in some countries, mostly large culturally plural ones, there has been very severe communally-based violence. The scope and frequency of occurence of this type of violence varies considerably over the years.

```
Range =          6.25
Mean =            .72
Standard Deviation =        1.36
```

Population Percent Cum.	Country	Rank	Country Name	A	Range Decile	B	C	D
1.95	1.95	1.0	Angola	6.25	1	5.00		5.00
11.66	9.71	2.0	Ethiopia	4.37	4	3.48	2.87	5.00
13.00	1.34	3.0	Chad	3.63	5	3.20	2.26	4.67
19.24	6.24	4.0	Sudan	2.52	6	2.90	2.79	3.17
27.53	8.29	5.0	Zaire	1.42	8	1.74	2.84	0
32.13	4.60	6.0	Kenya	1.37		1.83	3.67	0
53.13	21.00	7.0	Nigeria	1.26		1.57	2.58	0
54.49	1.36	8.5	Rwanda	1.18	9	1.48	2.00	.83
58.44	3.95	8.5	Uganda	1.18		1.52	2.64	.17
59.72	1.28	10.0	Burundi	.88		1.11	.67	1.67
61.94	2.22	11.0	Ivory Coast	.47	10	.59	.54	.67
63.81	1.87	12.0	Mali	.42		.53	.87	0
65.46	1.65	13.0	Zambia	.27		.36	.77	0
65.91	.45	14.5	Congo	.26		.33	.54	0
68.39	2.48	14.5	Madagascar	.26		.26	0	.67
69.42	1.03	16.0	Somalia	.21		.26	.42	0
72.93	3.51	17.0	Ghana	.18		.21	.31	0
73.93	1.00	19.0	Benin	.10		.13	.11	.17
76.34	2.41	19.0	Cameroon	.10		.06	.10	0
76.80	.46	19.0	Mauritania	.10		.13	.22	0
77.79	.99	21.0	Sierra Leone	.05		.07	.11	0
78.02	.23	29.5	Botswana	0		0	0	0
78.60	.58	29.5	Central African R	0		0	0	0
78.70	.10	29.5	Equatorial Guinea	0		0	0	0
78.86	.16	29.5	Gabon	0		0	0	0
79.03	.17	29.5	Gambia	0		0	0	0
80.60	1.57	29.5	Guinea	0		0	0	0
80.79	.19	29.5	Guinea-Bissau	0		0		0
81.17	.38	29.5	Lesotho	0		0	0	0
81.70	.53	29.5	Liberia	0		0	0	0
83.36	1.66	29.5	Malawi	0		0	0	0
84.69	1.33	29.5	Niger	0		0	0	0
86.33	1.64	29.5	Senegal	0		0	0	0
86.49	.16	29.5	Swaziland	0		0	0	0
91.65	5.16	29.5	Tanzania	0		0	0	0
92.40	.75	29.5	Togo	0		0	0	0
94.37	1.97	29.5	Upper Volta	0		0	0	0

DATA NOT AVAILABLE OR NOT APPLICABLE FOR THE FOLLOWING COUNTRIES

Djibouti   Mozambique   Namibia   Zimbabwe

SOURCE: *Black Africa* second edition.

Table 7.6   Armed Forces per 100,000 Population, 1978 (A), 1972 (B),
1967 (C) and 1963 (D).

Definition: Excludes police and gendarmerie, but includes Army, Navy
and Air Force. Value is divided by national population.

Comments: There is a great deal of variation in the relative size of African military forces relative to the country's population. This ranges
from some especially high values such as Somalia, Guinea-Bissau and
Mauritania to one country which has no army at all. Most of the large
armies are in countries with active wars.

```
Range =        1590.00
Mean =          352.98
Standard Deviation =          322.16
```

Population Percent Cum.	Population Percent Country	Rank	Country Name	A	Range Decile	B	C	D
1.03	1.03	1.0	Somalia	1590	1	510	357	221
1.22	.19	2.0	Guinea-Bissau	1000	4			
1.68	.46	3.0	Mauritania	860	5	90	91	52
11.39	9.71	4.0	Ethiopia	750	6	174	149	142
11.84	.45	5.0	Congo	730		176	209	92
11.94	.10	6.0	Djibouti	727				
13.89	1.95	7.0	Angola	720				
14.05	.16	8.0	Gabon	670		237	169	132
14.15	.10	9.0	Equatorial Guinea	606	7	333	0	0
15.72	1.57	10.0	Guinea	507		148	135	155
15.88	.16	11.0	Swaziland	433	8	0	0	0
16.11	.23	12.0	Botswana	430		0	0	0
16.64	.53	13.0	Liberia	410		261	369	364
22.88	6.24	14.0	Sudan	400		240	129	102
28.04	5.16	15.0	Tanzania	380		83	16	41
29.69	1.65	16.0	Zambia	360		129	76	92
31.95	2.26	17.0	Zimbabwe	340				
52.95	21.00	18.0	Nigeria	280	9	472	81	15
55.43	2.48	19.0	Madagascar	250		58	64	48
57.07	1.64	20.0	Senegal	240		143	150	81
58.41	1.34	21.0	Chad	210		98	26	25
59.69	1.28	22.5	Burundi	200		85	30	28
60.44	.75	22.5	Togo	200		60	87	16
68.73	8.29	24.0	Zaire	190		218	216	213
69.31	.58	25.0	Central African R	180		177	41	42
72.82	3.51	26.0	Ghana	170		204	196	119
73.20	.38	27.0	Lesotho	146	10	0	0	0
75.61	2.41	28.0	Cameroon	140		73	64	58
77.48	1.87	29.5	Mali	130		69	74	75
80.47	2.99	29.5	Mozambique	130				
81.47	1.00	31.0	Benin	120		78	72	49
83.69	2.22	32.0	Ivory Coast	110		99	112	117
88.29	4.60	34.0	Kenya	90		59	48	32
89.95	1.66	34.0	Malawi	90		25	22	43
91.92	1.97	34.0	Upper Volta	90		31	30	22
93.25	1.33	36.5	Niger	80		50	37	41
94.61	1.36	36.5	Rwanda	80		71	76	34
98.56	3.95	38.0	Uganda	50		121	76	31
99.55	.99	39.0	Sierra Leone	30		53	78	82
99.72	.17	40.0	Gambia	0		0	0	0

DATA NOT AVAILABLE OR NOT APPLICABLE
FOR THE FOLLOWING COUNTRIES

Namibia

SOURCE: *Black Africa* second edition.

Table 7.7   Defense Budget as a Percent of the Gross National Product (GNP) 1977 (A), 1972 (B), 1967 (C) and 1963 (D).

Definition: Total amount spent on military goods and services as a percent of all expenditures on goods and services in the economy. See *Black Africa* for this measure as a percent of total government expenditures.

```
Range =           13.80
Mean =             3.09
Standard Deviation =        2.53
```

Population Percent Cum.	Country	Rank	Country Name	A	Range Decile	B	C	D
1.03	1.03	1.0	Somalia	13.8	1	6.2	4.6	3.5
1.22	.19	2.5	Guinea-Bissau	7.1	5			
1.68	.46	2.5	Mauritania	7.1		2.0	1.4	4.3
3.94	2.26	4.0	Zimbabwe	6.8	6			
4.39	.45	5.0	Congo	5.2	7	4.7	3.3	2.0
4.55	.16	6.0	Swaziland	4.3		0	0	0
6.12	1.57	8.0	Guinea	4.2		4.0	4.3	2.6
27.12	21.00	8.0	Nigeria	4.2		4.4	2.8	1.1
32.28	5.16	8.0	Tanzania	4.2		2.4	.9	.2
38.52	6.24	10.0	Sudan	4.0	8	5.2	3.3	1.9
38.75	.23	11.0	Botswana	3.8		0	0	0
40.62	1.87	12.0	Mali	3.5		2.4	2.4	2.7
41.96	1.34	13.5	Chad	3.4		5.2	3.9	.5
43.93	1.97	13.5	Upper Volta	3.4		1.3	1.2	1.1
47.88	3.95	15.5	Uganda	3.1		5.4	1.5	.2
49.53	1.65	15.5	Zambia	3.1		5.2	1.4	2.0
59.24	9.71	18.0	Ethiopia	2.8		2.6	2.3	1.9
61.72	2.48	18.0	Madagascar	2.8		1.4	1.6	1.5
62.47	.75	18.0	Togo	2.8		1.4	1.8	.7
65.46	2.99	20.0	Mozambique	2.4	9			
66.74	1.28	22.5	Burundi	2.2		2.1	1.5	.9
67.32	.58	22.5	Central African R	2.2		2.1	2.0	.7
69.54	2.22	22.5	Ivory Coast	2.2		1.3	1.4	.1
71.18	1.64	22.5	Senegal	2.2		1.9	2.1	1.1
72.84	1.66	25.0	Malawi	2.1		.4	.5	.5
73.84	1.00	26.0	Benin	2.0		1.7	1.9	.6
76.25	2.41	28.0	Cameroon	1.6		1.9	2.2	2.6
80.85	4.60	28.0	Kenya	1.6		1.3	1.2	.7
82.21	1.36	28.0	Rwanda	1.6		1.7	1.8	2.2
82.74	.53	30.0	Liberia	1.1	10	1.1	1.3	1.9
83.73	.99	31.0	Sierra Leone	1.0		.8	.6	.7
85.06	1.33	32.0	Niger	.8		.7	.8	1.0
93.35	8.29	33.0	Zaire	.7		3.8	4.1	1.8
93.51	.16	34.0	Gabon	.5		1.6	1.1	1.3
97.02	3.51	35.0	Ghana	.4		1.5	3.0	2.0
97.40	.38	36.0	Lesotho	.1		0	0	0
97.57	.17	37.0	Gambia	0		0	0	0

DATA NOT AVAILABLE OR NOT APPLICABLE FOR THE FOLLOWING COUNTRIES

Angola   Djibouti   Equatorial Guinea   Namibia

SOURCE: *Black Africa* second edition

Chapter 8.

Economic Development

Economic development is a goal that is universally accepted, and it is by reference to the extent to which economic development has been achieved that we most often differentiate nations and people as "modernized" or 'developed." Economic development means a growth in the capacity to produce valued goods and social services. The values of men whose experience of luxury has produced public squalor and ecological disaster may be different from those whose all-encompassing experience is of the need for the necessities of life. Nevertheless, it is clear that all men value some things more than others and strive to attain them. While there are differences in the definition of what is to be valued, and in the policies and theories specifying preferred growth rates, distributions, or organizations for producing what is valued, the universality of the approval of economic development has been assisted by the fact that there has at the same time developed an acceptance of the utility of adopting comparable media of exchange and units of value. This unit of comparison is money, and growing participation in the international money economy has led to a simplification of the means of assessing economic development in terms of increases in national income, which is the monetary value of all final consumption goods and services produced annually in a country.

By this latter criterion, Black African countries constitute the least economically developed geographical region of the world. Of the twenty-one countries in the world with a per capita Gross National Product of less than US$100 in 1968, fourteen were Black African countries. While half of the countries of the world had per capita incomes equal to or greater than US$260, only Gabon, the Ivory Coast, Rhodesia, Namibia, Angola, and Equatorial Guinea had attained this figure and the average GNP per capita for the countries discussed in this book was only about $125. This situation is accented by a consideration of dynamic trends in world economic development. The average annual real growth rate in GNP per capita in African countries (excluding the Republic of

South Africa) during the 1960's averaged only 1.7% which compared with 1.9% for South Asia (Burma, Sri Lanka, India, Bangladesh and Pakistan); 2.3% for Latin American countries, and 3.8% for the industrialized countries of the world (*Annual Report*, World Bank, 1971). This gap worsened in the 1970's for all but the oil exporting countries of Black Africa. The gap, therefore, between the economic development of Black African states and the rest of the world continues to widen, and although African states are achieving a measure of economic development, and though there is considerable variation in the rates of growth in different Black African states, the sombre reality of widespread poverty in Africa needs emphasis, scholarly explanation, and political action.

The explanation of economic development in Africa, as elsewhere, is related to a consideration of the "factors" of production, namely, natural resources, labor and capital, and political arrangements which limit or enhance their productivity. As Chapter 1 of this section pointed out, Africa, though it constitutes 22% of the land mass of the world, contains less than 10% of the world's population, and the African peoples are, generally speaking, the least densely concentrated populations in the world. The development potential of this situation is ambiguous, however. While there is, in one sense, plenty of land for economic utilization, much of the African land surface is desert and poorly enriched soil, and the fertile land areas tend to be densely populated, making increasingly onerous demands for increased productivity.

The key issue of economic growth is the progressive ability to extract a surplus over consumption of valuable commodities from the application of labor to the natural environment. Initially, this means an increasing ability to produce sufficient food for a population's needs with less labor, so that more individuals are released to labor in the production of commodities other than food. (Of course, the process of doing this may require non-agricultural employment to increase before indigenous food supplies do, creating a temporary gap to be filled by imports). What this involves is the transformation of subsistence economies to cash economies, and the transfer of surplus labor in agriculture to productive employment in the manufacturing and service sectors of the economy. Sociologically, this means the progressive differentiation of a society into functionally specialized roles and institutions, and the growing commitment on the part of individuals to work, savings and the accumulation of wealth as high-ranking values.

These changes in the nature of labor in African economies are occuring only very slowly. In 1963, there were only ten Black African countries in which 10% or more of the active population were wage-earners, and the highest percentage was in Gabon where 18% of the active population were employed in the wage economy. In some countries, the public service constitutes most of the wage employment. Correspondingly, the average percentage of the labor force employed in agriculture and cattle-raising in 1968 was 84% and only Ghana had less than 60% of its labor force so employed. What is worse, there is very little increase in the generation of food surpluses by these overwhelmingly agricultural labor forces. Estimates reveal that there has been more than a 50% decline in the agricultural productivity of African labor between 1934 and 1964; (0.4% decline in the per capita output of food in Black Africa between 1955 and 1965), and an increase in the production of non-food crops relative to food crops. Pushed on the one hand by the need for finding food, and pulled, on the other, by the prospects of gainful employment suggested by the greatly increased educational experience which African governments have provided in order to upgrade the productivity of human capital, African labor has been moving rapidly into the urban nexus of the cash economy. Urbanization in Black African countries in recent decades has, in fact, been faster than in any other region of the world, creating a mobilized population for employment in the modern sector of their economies. But the availability of labor is very different from its employment, and the levels of unemployment are extremely high and disguised unemployment even higher.

The ability of an economy to absorb new labor and to increase the production of new and valued goods is a function of the generation of capital, which consists of all those products of labor and natural resources that can be used for further production. Capital can be generated either by saving or borrowing, and the degree to which capital increases the production of new goods is a function of the degree to which capital is invested in technological improvement − i.e. the degree to which capital is used by members of the labor force to produce new means for increasing the energy output of individual human labor.

The generation of capital from internal savings in Black African economies is inhibited by the widespread subsistence orientation of African labor, and by the sociocultural stress on values favoring community reciprocity rather than individual accumulation. This is not to say that changes are lacking. Detailed case study research has indicated great variety in individual initiative and capital accumulation in rural agricultural areas like those studied by Polly Hill in Northern Nigeria and Ghana, but there remains an overwhelming impression of limited savings, limited transference of savings to money, limited transference of cash to capital goods and technological innovation, and limited institutional facilitation of savings and credit for these purposes in most of Black Africa. Because of the limited growth in individual cash income, the tax base from which governments can derive revenue and investment capital is difficult to estimate, and very small by international standards. And the degree to which Black African governments utilize revenue to invest in productive capital is limited by the propensity for these governments to utilize revenue in politically rather than economically advantageous ways − in the development of public works that give the image of modern life a concrete manifestation, and in the employment of public officials, who constitute a large percentage of the wage and salaried labor force in many Black African countries.

The results are that gross investment in Black African countries lags considerably behind equivalent rates for most other less developed countries (LDC's) and domestic savings rates lag even further behind. African countries depend on the inflow of foreign capital for the financing of 30% of their gross investment compared to the average of 20% in all underdeveloped countries. And foreign capital, as we shall discuss in the next chapter, is often given in support of foreign economic interests, particularly the preservation of a favorable exchange of industrial manufactured goods for primary products and the expansion of foreign private controls over production by the vertical integration of primary production and industrial production in the same corporate firms. From the perspective of Black African states, these developments have meant that the cost of industrial goods and imported energy have substantially increased while those of primary products have remained stable or dropped over a long period excepting a few commodities such as energy (oil and uranium ore), leading to serious deficits in their balances of trade. Recent events seen to indicate more shortages will appear for many primary products in the future and thus this situation may become less severe. Furthermore, the importation of technology as opposed to consumption goods has been severely limited, and the industrial sectors of Black African

Figure 8.1a GNP per capita (US Dollars, market prices) 1970

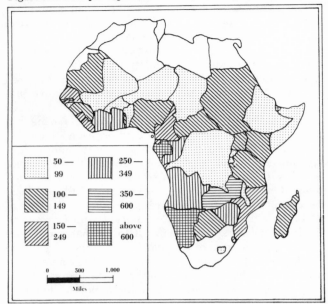

50 — 99		250 — 349	
100 — 149		350 — 600	
150 — 249		above 600	

0   500   1,000
Miles

Figure 8.1b GNP per capita (US dollars, market prices) 1980

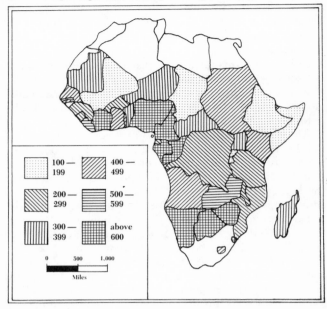

100 — 199		400 — 499	
200 — 299		500 — 599	
300 — 399		above 600	

0   500   1,000
Miles

Figure 8.2a Ave. Annual Real Rate of Growth of GNP Per Capita, 1960-70.

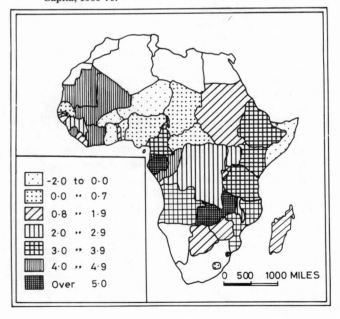

-2·0 to 0·0
0·0 ,, 0·7
0·8 ,, 1·9
2·0 ,, 2·9
3·0 ,, 3·9
4·0 ,, 4·9
Over 5·0

0   500   1000 MILES

Figure 8.2b Ave. Annual Real Rate of Growth of GNP Per Capita, 1970-79.

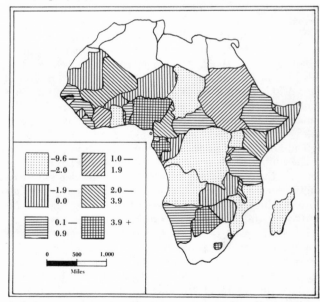

-9.6 — -2.0		1.0 — 1.9	
-1.9 — 0.0		2.0 — 3.9	
0.1 — 0.9		3.9 +	

0   500   1,000
Miles

countries remain small as a result. The average *industrial* Gross Domestic Product per capita in these countries in 1963 was only US$19, which means there is a very limited access to entrepreneurial skills and technological sophistication in the African labor forces. And while foreign capital and private firms continue to be increasingly important in the expansion of national income, there is some evidence to suggest that the overall rate of expansion in the wage-employed population of Black African states is actually decreasing.

Taking the continent as a whole, the prospects for economic development in Black Africa, if this brief introduction is accurate, are not gratifying to those whose interests are the welfare of the peoples of Africa. Nevertheless, there is a great challenge to the student of African affairs to investigate variations in economic development in these countries, and to seek for explanations of those factors which promote or inhibit their economic development.

Bibliography

The ubiquitous commitment to the principle of economic development and the scale of effort required are outlined in such works as R. S. McNamara *One Hundred Countries, Two Billion People: The Dimensions of Development* (New York: Praeger, 1973) and Gunnar Mrydal, *Asian Drama* (New York: Pantheon, 1968). For a background to the conceptual problems of economic development see E. E. Hagen, *The Economics of Development* (Homewood: Irwin, 1966); Hollis B. Chenery, *Structural Change and Development Policy* (New York: Oxford University Press, 1979); M. Chisholm, *Modern World Development* (London: Hutchinson, 1982) and B. W. Hodder, *Economic Development in the Tropics* 3rd ed. (New York: Methuen, 1980). For a review of the problems in the measurement of development see the special issue on development indicators in *The Journal of Development Studies* 8 (April 1972). The previous works are concerned with the general problems of development. For treatments of African economics see P. W. Bell and M. P. Todaro *Economic Theory: An Integrated Text with Special Reference to Tropical Africa and Other Developing Areas* (New York: Oxford University Press, 1970); M. P. Todarao *Economic Development in the Third World* (New York: Longman, 1981); and E. H. Whetham and J. I. Currie, *The Economics of African Countries* (New York: Cambridge University Press, 1971).

For a review of the economic trends in developing countries including Africa see UNCTAD, *Identification of the Least Developed Among Developing Countries*, TB/B/269 (New York: United Nations, August 1969) and R. Robinson, *Developing the Third World: Experiences of the Nineteen Sixties* (New York: Cambridge University Press, 1971). as well as the seven volume series by the International Monetary Fund, *Surveys of African Economies* (Washington, D.C.) that have come out in recent years and cover many of the African countries. The case study literature is reported on in the country sections of Part V. Also the United Nations and the World Bank periodically publish data and reports on African development. A general view of the future is contained in F. S. Arkhurst, *Africa in the Seventies and Eighties: Issues in Development* (New York: Praeger, 1970) and the World Bank's *Accelerated Development in Sub-Saharan Africa.*

Economics, more than any other social science field, is dominated by theoretical and partly competitive models which form the basic orientation for applied economic planning and control. For a review of some of these theories, see G. M. Meier and R. T. Baldwin, *Economic Development: Theory, History, Policy* (New York: Wiley, 1957) and G. M. Meier *Leading Issues in Economic Development* 3rd ed. (New York: Oxford University Press, 1976). For a criticism of such theoretical views in Africa see Gunnar Myrdal, *op. cit.*; Dudley Seers, "Why Visiting Economists Fail," *Journal of Political Economy* 70 (August 1962); Douglas Rimmer, "The Abstraction from Politics: A Critique of Economic Theory and Design with Reference to West Africa," *Journal of Development Studies* 5 (April 1969): 190-204 and a collection of essays by P.T. Bauer, *Dissent on Development* 2nd ed. (London: Weidenfeld and Nicholson, 1977).

More elementary and sometimes oversimplified introductions to African economics are: A. M. Kamarck, *The Economics of African Development* revised edition (New York: Praeger, 1971), G. M. Meier, *International Economics* (New York: Oxford University Press, 1980), and B. W. Hodder, *Economic Development in the Tropics* 3rd ed. (New York: Methuen, 1980). Two edited volumes that usefully discuss some of the realities facing development planners in Africa are S. P. Schatz ed. *Africa South of the Sahara: Developments in African Economics* (London: MacMillan, 1972) and J. S. Uppal and Louis R. Salkever eds. *Africa: Problems in Economic Development* (New York: Free Press, 1972). An older but still useful collection is E. H. Whetham and J. I. Currie, *Readings in the Applied Economics of Africa* Vol I—Microeconomics; Vol 2 Macroeconomics (New York: Cambridge University Press, 1967).

At any point in time, economic and political forces not only interact but are affected by their past histories. For a discussion on these points see John Middleton, *The Effects of Economic Development on Traditional Political Systems South of the Sahara* (The Hague: Mouton, 1966) and S. D. Neumark, *Foreign Trade and Economic Development in Africa: A Historical Perspective* (Stanford: Food Research Institute, 1964). Anthony G. Hopkins in *An Economic History of West Africa* (New York: Columbia University Press, 1975) has produced a major work along these lines.

A major aspect of the developing economy is the existence in a country of an economic sector of the same type as in the industrialized countries centering around factories, financial agencies such as banks and stock exchanges, and other aspects of the so-called "modern" economies. In contrast to this sector there will be a large part of the population who exist as subsistence farmers often on a similar basis to their predecessors of two or three centuries ago. This situation or structural characteristic of an economy is called "dualism." Early works identifying this phenomenon were J. S. Furnival, *Colonial Policy and Practice* (New York: Cambridge University Press, 1948) and J. H. Boeke, *Economics and Economic Policy of Dual Societies* (New York: Institute of Pacific Relations, 1953) which was a review of previous work on the subject by Boeke. A model of the working of such an economy is Lloyd Reynolds, "Economic Development with Surplus Labor: Some Complications," *Oxford Economic Papers* 21 (March 1969): 89-103. For the economic implications in African economies see P. Ndegwa and J. P. Powelson, *Employment in Africa: Some Critical Issues* (Geneva: International Labour Office, 1973); M. Blaugh, *Education and the Employment Problem in Developing Countries* (Geneva: International Labour Office, 1973); G. Hunter, "Employment Policy in Tropical Africa: The Need for Radical Revision," *International Labour Review* 105 (Jan. 1972): 35-58; Guy Hunter, *Modernizing Peasant Societies: A Comparative Study in Africa and Asia* (London: Oxford University Press, 1969); and C. R. Wharton ed. *Subsistence Agriculture and Economic Development* (Chicago: Aldine, 1969). The concept of disguised unemployment while difficult to operationalize is useful. An extensive bibliography on this phenomenon is available in *Development Digest* (July 1966) and a thorough review of the difficulties in applying Western concepts of unemployment to labor in Asia is presented in Gunnar Myrdal, *Asian Drama*, op. cit.

A series of more recent works on the political economy of Africa are: Richard Harris, ed., *The Political Economy of Africa*, (New York: Halsted, 1975); P. C. W. Gutkind and I. Wallerstein, *The Political Economy of Contempo-*

rary Africa, (Beverly Hills, CA: Sage, 1976) and D. Cohen and J. Daniel, eds., *The Political Economy of Africa*, (New York: Longman, 1981).

The mobilization of domestic resources is the *sine qua non* of economic development. In this process, the generation of capital, or that part of production which is used to increase productive capabilities such as new factories, roads, machines, etc., plays a prominent role. For a statement of the role of capital see S. H. Frankel, "Capital and Capital Supply in Relation to the Development of Africa," in E. A. G. Robinson ed., *Economic Development for Africa South of the Sahara* (New York: St. Martin's Press, 1964); and for reviews of sources of capital including rural capital formation see Polly Hill, *Rural Capitalism in West Africa* (London: Cambridge University Press, 1970); G. K. Helleiner, "The Fiscal Role of the Marketing Boards in Nigerian Economic Development, 1947-61," *Economic Journal* LXXIV (September 1964): 582-610; M. F. Lofchie, *The State of the Nations: Constraints on Development in Independent Africa* (Berkeley: University of California Press, 1971); and S. P. Schatz, *Economics, Politics, and Administration in Government Lending: The Regional Loans Boards of Nigeria* (Ibadan: Oxford University Press, 1970). For criticism of the capitalist model of accumulation see the article and book by Giovanni Arrighi and John S. Saul, "Socialism and Economic Development in Tropical Africa," *Journal of Modern African Studies* 6 (1968): 141-169; and *Essays on the Political Economy of Africa* (New York: Monthly Review Press, 1973); and the *Arusha Declaration* (Dar Es Salaam: TANU, 1967).

The mobilization of resources including human resources must be followed by decisions about allocating investment. See the following for discussions of various aspects of this issue: G. Helleiner, "Development Policies for Africa in the 1970's," *Canadian Journal of African Studies* 4 (Fall 1970): 285- 304; Lauchlin Currie, *Accelerating Development* (New York: Wiley, 1969); S. Charkravarty, *The Logic of Investment Planning* (Amsterdam: North Holland, 1960) and E. E. Jucker-Fleetwood, *Money and Finance in Africa* (New York: Praeger, 1964).

One of the major investment allocation decisions relates to the choice of emphasis between industrialization and agriculture. While these issues can become very involved and technical, a view of African industry and its future is provided by A. F. Ewing in *Industry in Africa* (London: Oxford University Press, 1968). For the role of agriculture in African development see William O. Jones, "Increasing Agricultural Productivity in Tropical Africa," in E. F. Joulson, *Economic Development in Africa* (Oxford: Blackwell, 1965); William H. Allan, *The African Husbandman* (Edinburgh: Oliver and Boyd, 1965);

Clifton R. Wharton, Jr., ed. *Subsistence Agriculture and Economic Development* (Chicago: Aldine, 1969); U. J. Lele, *The Design of Rural Development: Lessons From Africa* (Baltimore: Johns Hopkins University Press, 1975); R. Palmer and N. Parson, eds., *The Roots of Poverty in Central and Southern Africa* (Berkeley: University of California Press, 1977); A. K. Smith and C. E. Welch, Jr., eds., *Peasants in Africa* (Waltham, MA: Crossroads Press, 1978); K. R. M. Anthony et al., *Agricultural Change in Tropical Africa* (Ithaca: Cornell University Press, 1979) and Robert Bates and Michael Lofchie, eds., *Agricultural Development in Africa* (New York: Praeger, 1980). See also Alan Berg, *The Nutrition Factor: Its Role in National Development* (Washington, D.C.: Brookings Institution, 1973) and D. F. Owen, *Man in Tropical Africa: The Environmental Predicament* (New York: Oxford University Press, 1973).

Individual country studies are available for most countries and are detailed in the country bibliographies in Part V of this book. Some sources can also be found in the foreign relations and education chapters. Various collections of studies have been compiled. Some such sources are: J. C. de Wilde, "The Manpower and Employment Aspects of Selective Experiences of Agricultural Development in Tropical Africa," *International Labour Review* 104 (Nov. 1971); 367-386; Rene Dumont, *False Start in Africa* 2nd ed. (New York: Praeger, 1969); Peter Robson and D. A. Lury eds. *The Economics of Africa* (Evanston: Northwestern University Press, 1969); John C. de Wilde, et al., *Experiences with Agricultural Development in Tropical Africa* Vol I and Vol II (Baltimore: Johns Hopkins University Press, 1967); and I. G. Stewart and H. Ord eds., *African Primary Products and International Trade* (Edinburgh: Edinburgh University Press, 1965). Typical country studies relevant to some of the critical development issues are: P. C. Garlick, *African Traders and Economic Development in Ghana* (New York: Oxford University Press, 1971); G. K. Helleiner, *Peasant Agriculture, Government and Economic Growth in Nigeria* (Homewood: Irwin, 1966) and W. O. Jones, *Marketing Staple Food Crops in Tropical Africa* (Ithaca: Cornell University Press, 1972).

As rural-urban migration increases so does the problem of absorbing the new arrivals into the labor force. Most African urban areas have large unemployed groups and even larger groups of the underemployed. See Robert Loken, *Manpower Development in Africa* (New York: Praeger, 1969); Ellot Berg, "Major Issues of Wage Policy in Africa," in A. M. Rose ed. *Industrial Relations and Economic Development* (New York: St. Martin's, 1966): and International Labour Organization, *Employment Policies in Africa: 3rd African Regional Conference* (Geneva: ILO, 1969). A particular study of an industrial environment is Margaret Peil's *The Ghanaian Factory Worker: Industrial Man in Africa* (London: Cambridge University Press, 1972).

The attempt to drastically speed up economic development in the mid and late twentieth century has been a trying one for economists as well as farmers, workers and bureaucrats. The continual re-appraisal of plans and the attempt to improve or replace them goes on. One issue is the relation between development and the market pricing system. For discussions of this see P. Marris and A. Somerset, *African Businessmen: A Study of Entrepreneurship and Development in Kenya* (London: Routledge and Kegan Paul, 1971) and E. J. Berg, "Socialism and Economic Development in Tropical Africa," *Quarterly Journal of Economics* (November 1968).

The choice of alternative development plans is explored in A. Seidman, *Comparative Development Strategies in East Africa* (Nairobi: East African Publishing House, 1973); M. Todaro, *Development Planning: Models and Methods* (Nairobi: Oxford University Press, 1971); A. Waterson, *Development Planning: Lessons of Experience* (Baltimore: Johns Hopkins University Press, 1965) and W. A. Lewis, *Development Planning* (New York: Harper and Row, 1966).

For evaluations of planning and expectations about future needs see, M. Faber and D. Seers, eds., *The Crisis in Planning* Vol I *The Issue*, and Vol II *The Experience* (London: Chatto and Windus, 1972) and G. K. Helleiner, "Beyond Growth Rates and Plan Volumes: Planning for Africa in the 1970's," *Journal of Modern African Studies* 10 (1972).

Additional bibliographic sources include C. W. Bergquist *Alternative Approaches to the Problem of Development: A Selected and Annotated Bibliography* (Durham, NC: Carolina Academic Press, 1979) and J. P. Powelson, *A Select Bibliography on Economic Development, with Annotations* (Boulder: Westview, 1979).

Table 8.1   Percent Labor Force in Agriculture and Animal Husbandry, 1977 (A), 1970 (B) and 1960 (C).

Definition: The percent of the active adult labor force over 15 years of age who are engaged in agriculture or cattle-raising as their occupation.

Comments: In all but three of the countries a majority of the labor force is engaged in agriculture or cattle-raising as their primary occupation. Nevertheless, there are some significant variations. About half of the countries have eighty percent or more of their population so engaged, while a few, notably Congo, Djibouti, and Benin have less than half of their populations in agriculture. As the process of urbanization goes on, these percentages will decrease, although Africa still has many urban dwellers who go out to the surrounding countryside to farm during the appropriate season while maintaining their residence in the city.

```
Range =          56.00
Mean =           75.54
Standard Deviation =           13.70
```

Population Percent Cum.	Country	Rank	Country Name	A	Range Decile	B	C
1.33	1.33	1.5	Niger	92.0	1	92.3	95.2
2.69	1.36	1.5	Rwanda	92.0		93.2	95.4
2.79	.10	3.0	Equatorial Guinea	90.0		79.9	83.7
3.37	.58	4.0	Central Afri. R	89.0		91.3	94.1
5.24	1.87	5.0	Mali	88.7		91.0	94.0
5.62	.38	6.0	Lesotho	88.0		89.7	93.4
6.96	1.34	7.5	Chad	87.0		90.1	94.4
8.62	1.66	7.5	Malawi	87.0		89.1	92.5
9.90	1.28	9.0	Burundi	85.0	2	87.2	90.0
10.36	.46	10.0	Mauritania	84.3		87.5	91.2
12.84	2.48	12.5	Madagascar	84.0		89.4	92.8
18.00	5.16	12.5	Tanzania	84.0		86.0	89.3
21.95	3.95	12.5	Uganda	84.0		85.9	89.4
23.92	1.97	12.5	Upper Volta	84.0		86.8	91.5
24.11	.19	15.0	Guinea-Bissau	83.8		87.0	90.9
24.34	.23	17.0	Botswana	83.0		86.7	92.0
25.91	1.57	17.0	Guinea	83.0		84.7	88.2
26.94	1.03	17.0	Somalia	83.0		84.7	87.9
29.16	2.22	19.0	Ivory Coast	82.0		84.5	88.8
38.87	9.71	20.0	Ethiopia	81.0		84.1	88.1
39.04	.17	21.0	Gambia	79.2	3	81.9	85.3
43.64	4.60	22.5	Kenya	79.0		82.1	85.8
49.88	6.24	22.5	Sudan	79.0		82.0	85.7
50.04	.16	24.0	Gabon	77.9		81.4	84.8
51.68	1.64	25.0	Senegal	77.0		79.7	83.6
59.97	8.29	26.0	Zaire	76.0		79.3	83.4
60.13	.16	27.0	Swaziland	75.4		81.1	89.1
62.54	2.41	28.0	Cameroon	73.8	4	75.9	78.5
63.07	.53	29.0	Liberia	73.0		75.6	80.7
63.36	.29	30.0	Namibia	70.0			
64.11	.75	31.5	Togo	69.0	5	73.3	79.5
65.76	1.65	31.5	Zambia	69.0		72.8	78.7
66.75	.99	33.0	Sierra Leone	68.0		71.5	77.7
69.74	2.99	34.0	Mozambique	67.0		73.0	81.1
71.69	1.95	35.0	Angola	60.0	6	63.7	69.4
92.69	21.00	36.5	Nigeria	56.0	7	62.1	70.8
94.95	2.26	36.5	Zimbabwe	56.0		62.1	70.8
98.46	3.51	38.0	Ghana	54.0		58.4	63.8
99.46	1.00	39.0	Benin	47.0	9	49.7	54.5
99.56	.10	40.0	Djibouti	40.0	10		
100.00	.45	41.0	Congo	36.0		41.8	51.7

SOURCE: *Black Africa* second edition.

112 Comparative Profiles

Table 8.2 Per Capita Energy Consumption in Kilograms of Coal Equivalent, 1977 (A), 1970 (B), 1965 (C) and 1960 (D).

Definition: Total consumption of energy within the country divided by the total population.

Comments: Some observers argue that energy consumption is a more meaningful measure of economic development than the more usual index of per capita income. In any case, energy consumption is an essential part of any industrialization process. The range of variation on this variable is considerable, and it is not surprising that most of the high per capita income countries appear high in this table as well. The exceptions to this observation are high income countries whose source of wealth is primary production of a type that does not use large amounts of energy.

```
Range =        1695.00
Mean =          190.81
Standard Deviation =        300.47
```

Population Percent Cum.	Country	Rank	Country Name	A	Range Decile	B	C	D
.16	.16	1.0	Gabon	1707	1	897	248	187
.26	.10	2.0	Djibouti	748	6	441	716	292
2.52	2.26	3.0	Zimbabwe	598	7	692	581	
4.17	1.65	4.0	Zambia	483	8	495	493	
4.70	.53	5.0	Liberia	402		454	202	86
6.92	2.22	6.0	Ivory Coast	356		228	153	76
7.38	.46	7.0	Mauritania	198	9	144	75	18
9.33	1.95	8.0	Angola	185		155	104	86
10.97	1.64	9.0	Senegal	175	10	139	134	121
14.48	3.51	10.0	Ghana	167		173	105	106
20.72	6.24	11.0	Sudan	165		130	81	52
25.32	4.60	12.0	Kenya	141		135	126	143
25.77	.45	13.0	Congo	140		194	118	119
28.76	2.99	14.0	Mozambique	138		138	101	114
31.17	2.41	15.0	Cameroon	122		91	59	55
52.17	21.00	16.0	Nigeria	107		52	53	34
53.16	.99	17.0	Sierra Leone	103		134	64	31
53.33	.17	18.0	Gambia	102		51	33	24
54.36	1.03	19.0	Somalia	96		39	26	19
55.11	.75	20.0	Togo	95		67	39	23
55.21	.10	21.5	Equatorial Guinea	92		65	149	123
56.78	1.57	21.5	Guinea	92		98	100	65
59.26	2.48	23.0	Madagascar	76		71	46	38
59.45	.19	24.5	Guinea-Bissau	71		63	54	19
67.74	8.29	24.5	Zaire	71		81	75	87
72.90	5.16	26.0	Tanzania	65		62	52	41
76.85	3.95	27.0	Uganda	56		74	39	30
77.85	1.00	28.0	Benin	55		42	32	39
79.51	1.66	29.0	Malawi	51		46	38	
80.09	.58	30.0	Central African R	41		63	34	37
81.42	1.33	31.0	Niger	37		25	13	5
83.29	1.87	32.0	Mali	30		21	23	15
84.63	1.34	33.5	Chad	23		25	18	10
86.60	1.97	33.5	Upper Volta	23		13	11	5
96.31	9.71	35.0	Ethiopia	19		33	14	8
97.67	1.36	36.0	Rwanda	18		11	9	11
98.95	1.28	37.0	Burundi	12		15	15	11

DATA NOT AVAILABLE OR NOT APPLICABLE FOR THE FOLLOWING COUNTRIES

Botswana   Lesotho   Namibia   Swaziland

SOURCE: *Black Africa* second edition.

Table 8.3   Gross Domestic Investment (GDI) as a Percent of Gross Domestic Product 1977 (A), 1970 (B), 1965 (C) and 1960 (D), and Total GDI 1977 (E) in millions of US Dollars at 1975 prices.

Definition: The total value of new buildings, equipment, and inventories accumulated during the relevant years as a percent of GDP. Right hand column has the total figure for GDI in 1977 in millions of US dollars.

Comments: Rostow has characterized the rate of capital accumulation as the critical parameter in reaching a point where economic development is "self-sustaining." He suggests that a level of around 15 percent is the minimum for a process of development to start and continue.

```
Range =        62.50
Mean =         21.88
Standard Deviation =        11.78
```

Population Percent Cum.	Population Percent Country	Rank	Country Name	A	Range Decile	B	C	D	E
.16	.16	1.0	Gabon	67.8	1	34.6	30.8	50.1	1877.0
.62	.46	2.0	Mauritania	51.8	3	20.5	16.3	37.4	230.0
.85	.23	3.0	Botswana	37.6	5	42.2	6.1	8.4	113.9
1.88	1.03	4.0	Somalia	35.4	6	18.1	17.3	15.0	78.2
2.63	.75	5.0	Togo	32.1		14.4	22.4	10.8	127.0
2.82	.19	6.0	Guinea-Bissau	32.0					
23.82	21.00	7.0	Nigeria	31.1		14.9	18.3	13.2	9003.1
24.20	.38	8.0	Lesotho	29.9	7	10.2	11.5	2.0	32.9
26.42	2.22	9.0	Ivory Coast	27.3		22.1	19.0	14.6	1758.9
28.07	1.65	10.0	Zambia	25.9		27.1	24.7	23.9	208.4
30.04	1.97	11.0	Upper Volta	25.1		11.4	9.7	9.5	57.0
30.57	.53	12.0	Liberia	24.9		14.5	12.7	20.9	115.1
31.90	1.33	13.0	Niger	23.3	8	18.0	15.2	12.5	126.2
32.48	.58	14.0	Central Afri. R	22.5		18.9	21.4	19.6	48.8
34.89	2.41	15.0	Cameroon	21.7		14.9	15.1	10.6	460.9
39.49	4.60	16.0	Kenya	21.2		24.4	14.4	19.7	430.4
41.15	1.66	17.0	Malawi	21.0		26.1	14.2	10.4	101.3
42.72	1.57	18.0	Guinea	20.3		19.8	20.0	4.5	217.9
43.72	1.00	19.0	Benin	20.2		15.2	11.5	15.0	89.9
45.98	2.26	20.0	Zimbabwe	19.0		21.4	15.4	23.3	261.0
54.27	8.29	21.0	Zaire	18.6		25.3	27.8	12.3	246.6
54.44	.17	22.0	Gambia	18.2		8.1	11.7	10.4	20.4
54.89	.45	23.0	Congo	18.1		25.4	18.9	44.9	108.7
55.05	.16	24.0	Swaziland	17.8	9	16.4	33.8	12.9	26.0
60.21	5.16	25.0	Tanzania	17.1		22.5	14.6	14.4	266.7
61.85	1.64	26.0	Senegal	16.9		15.7	11.9	15.5	175.0
63.19	1.34	27.0	Chad	16.6		13.4	9.2	11.3	48.4
65.67	2.48	28.0	Madagascar	15.7		15.6	10.2	11.0	196.6
71.91	6.24	29.0	Sudan	15.3		10.3	9.1	8.6	707.8
73.27	1.36	30.0	Rwanda	14.9		7.0	9.8	6.1	78.0
75.14	1.87	31.0	Mali	14.7		15.2	22.6	13.6	47.4
75.24	.10	32.0	Equatorial Guinea	13.5		19.9	18.6		10.1
78.23	2.99	33.5	Mozambique	13.3		13.2	9.3	9.5	339.2
79.22	.99	33.5	Sierra Leone	13.3		15.8	11.8	15.5	56.1
80.50	1.28	35.0	Burundi	12.3		6.3	5.8	6.3	33.5
90.21	9.71	36.0	Ethiopia	8.9	10	11.5	13.3	11.5	193.0
92.16	1.95	37.0	Angola	7.4		13.1	9.6	11.6	229.8
95.67	3.51	38.0	Ghana	5.5		14.2	17.9	24.4	95.0
99.62	3.95	39.0	Uganda	5.3		13.3	14.0	11.2	57.8

DATA NOT AVAILABLE OR NOT APPLICABLE FOR THE FOLLOWING COUNTRIES

Djibouti   Namibia

SOURCE: *Black Africa* second edition

Table 8.4 Per Capita Gross Domestic Product in US Dollars, 1977 (A), 1972 (B), 1967 (C) and 1960 (D) at Constant 1975 Prices.

Definition: The total value of all final goods and services produced in the country divided by the population.

Comments: Although a few countries are approaching the levels of income of the less-developed European countries, most African countries have income levels which are among the lowest in the world.

```
Range     =    5254.00
Mean      =     377.49
Standard Deviation =         814.58
```

Population Percent Cum.	Country	Rank	Country Name	A	Range Decile	B	C	D
.16	.16	1.0	Gabon	5301	1	1142	818	631
.45	.29	2.0	Namibia	1290	8			
2.67	2.22	3.0	Ivory Coast	863	9	788	698	538
2.77	.10	4.0	Djibouti	809		840	605	294
4.72	1.95	5.0	Angola	432	10	349	209	65
5.17	.45	6.0	Congo	431		426	384	367
5.40	.23	7.0	Botswana	416		159	158	134
5.50	.10	8.0	Equatorial Guinea	349		264	261	
5.69	.19	9.0	Guinea-Bissau	335		252		
26.69	21.00	10.0	Nigeria	329		273	153	178
29.68	2.99	11.0	Mozambique	296		253	164	59
30.14	.46	12.0	Mauritania	295		261	275	178
30.30	.16	13.0	Swaziland	286		287	230	125
30.83	.53	14.0	Liberia	281		295	266	246
33.24	2.41	15.0	Cameroon	277		242	211	189
39.48	6.24	16.0	Sudan	276		180	232	258
41.13	1.65	17.0	Zambia	242		288	284	249
43.39	2.26	18.0	Zimbabwe	241		240	310	259
45.03	1.64	19.0	Senegal	226		226	229	222
46.60	1.57	20.0	Guinea	216		174	161	151
46.77	.17	21.0	Gambia	202		175	196	153
49.25	2.48	22.0	Madagascar	193		214	213	216
50.00	.75	23.0	Togo	169		162	138	94
53.51	3.51	24.0	Ghana	164		163	242	303
54.51	1.00	25.0	Benin	163		149	155	151
59.11	4.60	26.0	Kenya	152		167	138	134
60.10	.99	27.0	Sierra Leone	132		200	202	185
60.68	.58	28.0	Central African R	122		109	109	116
62.01	1.33	29.0	Niger	103		102	118	112
67.17	5.16	30.0	Tanzania	91		94	84	69
71.12	3.95	31.0	Uganda	90		113	54	99
71.50	.38	32.0	Lesotho	88		73	68	54
73.16	1.66	33.0	Malawi	86		83	85	69
74.52	1.36	34.0	Rwanda	75		65	52	119
75.86	1.34	35.0	Chad	74		73	78	86
85.57	9.71	36.0	Ethiopia	72		65	56	47
86.85	1.28	37.0	Burundi	70		65	59	98
88.72	1.87	38.0	Mali	68		58	64	106
90.69	1.97	39.0	Upper Volta	65		68	71	62
91.72	1.03	40.0	Somalia	60		63	58	63
100.00	8.29	41.0	Zaire	47		92	82	80

SOURCE: *Black Africa* second edition

Table   8.5   **Average Annual Percent Growth in Real Per Capita Gross National Product 1970 to 1977 (A), 1965 to 1970 (B), 1960 to 1965 (C), and 1950 to 1960 (D).**

Definition: The percent growth in the total value of all goods and services produced by residents of the country per capita over the period divided by the number of years and normalized by a price index to reflect real rather than inflationary changes.

Comments: This variable is a measure of the level of sustained growth achieved during the period. Some countries such as Botswana, Lesotho, Djibouti and Gabon have done well over this period, but most countries have had a slow or irregular growth pattern and seventeen countries actually had a declining per capita income in the 1970s. This latter group represents one-third of the population of Black Africa. Here, on the average, the per capita incomes of Black Africans were only slightly higher in 1977 than in 1970.

```
Range =          25.00
Mean =             .69
Standard Deviation =        3.82
```

Population Percent Cum.	Country	Rank	Country Name	A	Range Decile	B	C	D
.23	.23	1.0	Botswana	13.5	1	7.8	2.2	1.2
.61	.38	2.0	Lesotho	5.5	4	-.1	6.7	2.8
.71	.10	4.0	Djibouti	4.9				
.87	.16	4.0	Gabon	4.9		1.1	1.9	-.7
1.04	.17	4.0	Gambia	4.9		1.1	1.9	-.7
1.23	.19	6.0	Guinea-Bissau	4.7				
1.39	.16	7.0	Swaziland	3.7		4.1	11.0	6.3
22.39	21.00	8.0	Nigeria	3.3	5	1.9	2.7	1.6
24.05	1.66	9.0	Malawi	3.1		1.5	.6	6.5
30.29	6.24	10.0	Sudan	2.7		-1.0	-.7	3.5
31.86	1.57	11.0	Guinea	2.4		0	1.2	
33.22	1.36	12.0	Rwanda	2.2		5.6	-5.3	-1.2
35.09	1.87	13.5	Mali	2.1		.5	.7	1.0
40.25	5.16	13.5	Tanzania	2.1		3.1	2.6	3.7
40.70	.45	15.5	Congo	1.4		1.2	.6	-.5
41.45	.75	15.5	Togo	1.4		3.9	5.6	-.9
43.86	2.41	17.0	Cameroon	1.2		5.3	1.2	.3
48.46	4.60	18.0	Kenya	1.0	6	4.9	.2	.7
49.04	.58	19.0	Central African R	.9		1.3	-1.7	1.1
51.26	2.22	20.0	Ivory Coast	.5		3.5	6.1	1.5
52.54	1.28	21.0	Burundi	.4		3.3	.5	-3.2
54.18	1.64	22.0	Senegal	.2		-1.2	1.1	
63.89	9.71	23.0	Ethiopia	.1		1.2	2.7	1.7
64.89	1.00	24.5	Benin	-.1		0	.6	
67.15	2.26	24.5	Zimbabwe	-.1		2.4	-.9	
68.80	1.65	26.0	Zambia	-.2		-.1	2.6	3.1
69.26	.46	27.0	Mauritania	-.5		2.0	7.2	
69.79	.53	28.0	Liberia	-.6		3.1	6.1	7.4
71.13	1.34	29.0	Chad	-.9		-.3	-1.3	
72.12	.99	30.5	Sierra Leone	-1.0		1.6	2.1	1.8
74.09	1.97	30.5	Upper Volta	-1.0		1.6	1.0	-.3
75.12	1.03	32.0	Somalia	-1.1		.9	-2.8	10.6
76.45	1.33	33.0	Niger	-1.5	7	-2.9	2.5	
84.74	8.29	34.0	Zaire	-1.7		2.2	1.7	1.1
88.69	3.95	35.0	Uganda	-2.4		2.2	1.8	.5
92.20	3.51	36.0	Ghana	-2.5		.4	.6	-.4
94.68	2.48	37.0	Madagascar	-3.2		2.5	-.7	.5
94.78	.10	38.0	Equatorial Guinea	-5.0	8	.1	11.8	
97.77	2.99	39.0	Mozambique	-6.1		5.9	.2	1.7
99.72	1.95	40.0	Angola	-11.5	10	1.6	4.3	

DATA NOT AVAILABLE OR NOT APPLICABLE
FOR THE FOLLOWING COUNTRIES

Namibia

SOURCE: *Black Africa* second edition

Table 8.6   Thousands of Inhabitants per Physician, 1977 (A), 1970 (B) and 1960 (C).

Definition: The population of the country divided by the number of physicians.

Comments: This is a basic measure of health services available to the population. While it represents only a part of the health personnel, it tends to be reflective of the entire structure. Those countries with high values have few doctors. Hence countries such as Gabon, Zimbabwe, Guinea-Bissau and Congo had a considerable number of doctors for their population size, while Upper Volta, Malawi, Ethiopia and Burundi were especially deficient in the number of physicians. In the latter group of countries much of the population will probably never see a doctor during their lives.

```
Range =       80145.00
Mean =        22488.74
Standard Deviation =        17351.97
```

Population Percent Cum.	Country	Rank	Country Name	A	Range Decile	B	C
9.71	9.71	1.0	Ethiopia	84850	1	74550	91000
11.68	1.97	2.0	Upper Volta	61798	3	92760	100000
13.34	1.66	3.0	Malawi	48500	5	38250	35000
14.62	1.28	4.0	Burundi	45430		59000	63000
17.61	2.99	5.5	Mozambique	42970	6	58260	21000
18.94	1.33	5.5	Niger	42970		58260	71000
20.28	1.34	7.0	Chad	41160		62880	62000
21.64	1.36	8.0	Rwanda	39350		57900	144000
22.64	1.00	9.0	Benin	34280	7	28920	47000
24.51	1.87	10.0	Mali	32459		41490	39000
25.09	.58	11.0	Central Afri. R	29410		38330	37000
29.04	3.95	12.0	Uganda	28330	8	9210	13000
34.20	5.16	13.0	Tanzania	18490	9	20677	21000
34.95	.75	14.0	Togo	18360		27940	35130
35.33	.38	15.0	Lesotho	17800		26290	
36.97	1.64	16.0	Senegal	16450		16640	35000
38.00	1.03	17.0	Somalia	15560		21140	30000
46.29	8.29	18.0	Zaire	15530		30040	63000
47.86	1.57	19.0	Guinea	15500		31090	48000
50.08	2.22	20.0	Ivory Coast	15220		15320	25480
52.03	1.95	21.0	Angola	15000		8460	14000
73.03	21.00	22.0	Nigeria	14810		20530	32000
74.02	.99	23.0	Sierra Leone	14500		17110	26000
74.48	.46	24.0	Mauritania	14140		17210	30000
76.89	2.41	25.0	Cameroon	13980		25960	34000
77.06	.17	26.0	Gambia	13120		18950	
79.54	2.48	27.0	Madagascar	10780	10	11390	8800
81.19	1.65	28.0	Zambia	10370		13520	12860
84.70	3.51	29.0	Ghana	10200		12950	21000
85.23	.53	30.0	Liberia	10050		11590	12000
91.47	6.24	31.0	Sudan	9760		13660	31000
91.70	.23	32.0	Botswana	9600		15460	20870
91.86	.16	33.0	Swaziland	9200		8270	10000
96.46	4.60	34.0	Kenya	8840		7830	10000
96.91	.45	35.0	Congo	7320		9160	13000
99.17	2.26	36.0	Zimbabwe	7030		6370	
99.36	.19	37.0	Guinea-Bissau	6750			
99.52	.16	38.0	Gabon	4705		5210	6120

DATA NOT AVAILABLE OR NOT APPLICABLE
FOR THE FOLLOWING COUNTRIES

Djibouti   Equatorial Guinea Namibia

SOURCE: *Black Africa* second edition

Chapter 9

Foreign Relations

The foreign relations of the governments of African countries are dominated by four principal concerns: (1) neutrality in terms of alignments with the major cold war powers, and the protection of African territorial sovereignty from encroachment by foreign military and economic interests; (2) continental unity with respect to the elimination of colonialism, and the racist oligarchy of the Republic of South Africa; (3) the expansion of export trade to the rest of the world and among the African states; and (4) the procurement of foreign capital to finance indigenous economic development efforts. Success in the pursuit of these aims has been inhibited to some degree by the system of neo-colonialism in which African countries are subject to the overwhelming economic power of their former colonial powers as well as the other major industrial countries of the West, whose economic interests and governments first established colonialism, and now perpetuate its essential economic impact in Africa: by continuing to control most of the continent's manufacturing and mining, and the international markets for tropical agricultural commodities; by supporting the white minority South African regime; and by providing aid as a reward for, or investment in, African participation in the political and economic policy of the West.

African countries form a well-identified bloc in terms of their relatively cohesive and distinctive patterns of voting on the large number of issues debated by the U. N. — a bloc that is fairly well distinguished from those of the major foreign powers and other third-world blocs. The neutrality of African states in the contemporary balance of power has, however, been less sharp than was promised at the time of their independence. African governments have reinforced their alignment with their former colonial rulers by appealing for military assistance in controlling domestic disorder, as in the cases of the Tanzanian army mutiny in 1964, the attempted coup in Gabon in 1964, and the roles more recently of French forces in Chad, Mauritania, and the Central African Republic. Indeed it has been only when the Western powers have

conspicuously refused to continue their "paternal" relationship with former colonies that African governments in those territories have invited closer relations with non-Western powers. The angry and vengeful response of the French to Guinea's vote for immediate independence in 1958 ensured that country's orientation towards the Soviet Union, although the Guinean government has been rigorously careful to balance this alignment with periodic appeals to the USA, and it has now re-established economic and political links with France. Sekou Touré made a state visit to France in 1982 for the first time since independence. Tanzania only accepted Chinese aid for the building of the railroad linking Zambia to Tanzania after failing to secure such assistance from Britain and the United States. And Nigeria accepted military equipment and financial aid from the Soviet Union only after the hesitating response of the British government to the determination of the Nigerian government to maintain the territorial unity of the Federation in the face of the Biafran secession. More recently, African positions on the Law of the Seas, the Arab-Israeli conflict and cold war issues have shown greater independence from Western powers. Also many of the former French colonies are embarking on independent economic and political programs. This is even more urgent than before because of the weakness of the French franc in the 1980s to date and the need for a more independent monetary policy on the part of France as well as the African states. Noteworthy with respect to increasing financial independence are Mauritania, Madagascar, and Chad.

The unity of African states with regard to the eradication of colonial and racist regimes on the continent has, like their non-alignment in balance of power politics, tended during the last decade to become more marked in the breach than the observance. There is no questioning the moral repugnance of colonialism and racism: the African states are united in the United Nations' debates on Southern Africa and colonialism; the OAU supported liberation movements in Guinea-Bissau, Angola, Mozambique, Zimbabwe, Namibia and the Republic of

South Africa, and the governments of Angola, Mozambique, Zaire, Zambia and Tanzania have allowed liberation movements to be headquartered in those countries. But the closeness of African ties to the European powers and the U.S.A., and their need for development assistance capital and expanded foreign trade has introduced a measure of ambivalence in their actions regarding southern Africa, at least until the success of the Cuban forces in Angola and the breaking of the logjam over Rhodesia. For example, only Tanzania temporarily discontinued diplomatic relations with Britain over Britain's failure to enforce full sanctions against the government of the white minority regime in Rhodesia. The Malawi government under Banda has maintained a firm commitment to dialogue and trade with the industrially powerful Republic of South Africa, the government of Madagascar had earlier agreed to cooperate with South Africa in trade and tourism, and the President of the Ivory Coast expressed a willingness to have diplomatic dialogue with the Republic. With the end of white rule in Rhodesia, the pressures appear to be strong enough to initiate significant political change and for the first time it is possible to think of a serious threat to South African white hegemony.

The possibilities of African governments breaking out of the system of neo-colonialism are likely to be determined largely by the future success of indigenous economic development in Africa (see Chapter 8 for a review of economic development), and a critical aspect of foreign relations of these nations is the attempt to gain development capital through policies afffecting foreign trade. Three related problems in this effort can be mentioned: market expansion, product diversification, and the balance of trade.

One aspect of the expansion of Africa's foreign markets is the absolute increase in the volume and value of trade between African countries and the rest of the world. In these terms, the value of trade between African countries and the rest of the world has more than doubled in the 1960's and was 11 billion US dollars in 1969 and 32 billion US dollars in 1979. At the same time, however, the volume of world exports to Africa more than doubled, reaching 10 billion US dollars in 1969 and 29 billion by 1979, leaving a small positive balance of trade for the continent as a whole (*Accelerated Development in Sub-Saharan Africa* World Bank, 1981). Nevertheless, the growth in Africa's export trade and the size of her balance of trade were more impressive than the corresponding features of the development of Latin America and Asia, even though African exports in 1969 were less valuable than those of Latin America and Asia by two and eleven billion US dollars respectively. The experience in the 1970's has been much worse for most of these countries as the huge in-

creases in energy costs have reverberated through the world economy bringing trade recession and restrictions along with substantial inflation which African primary products were least able to defend themselves against. Generally only those with their own energy sources especially the oil exporters were able to advance their economies significantly during the period although some countries such as the Ivory Coast with an agriculturally-based economy were able to continue to grow during the period but at lower rates compared to the 1960's. Recent drops in the real price of energy which appear to be of some duration may stimulate the world economy and thereby the trade picture of African non-oil exporters in this decade.

The restrictive trade relations between colony and metropole established in the colonial era have only gradually changed in the independence era, despite the desirability, from the perspective of African governments, of lessening the dependency on the metropole by expanding the geographical scope of their foreign markets and increasing the competitive interest in Africa's products. A comparison of figures for the percentage of the total trade of Black African countries contributed by trade with their ex-colonial powers between 1962 and 1971 reveals that in 1962 the mean percentage was 40 percent, which dropped to 33 percent in 1968 and to 30 percent in 1971. By 1980 the figure was about the same as the 1971 figure. This overall pattern does hide significant differences between ex-British colonies and ex-French as Table 9.6 makes clear. This pattern of continuing but lessening metropolitan trade dependency is supported by arrangements for trading preferences to former colonies made by the British Commonwealth and the European Economic Community. While these arrangements facilitate the sale of tropical agricultural commodities in Europe, they perpetuate a system in which the controlling decisions affecting crucial portions of Black Africa's foreign trade are made in Europe, not Africa. By 1974, determined efforts were underway to change this and arrangements have now been made with the EEC and its member states to improve the treatment of African products and to encourage more industrial development in Black Africa. How this will work to the benefit of Africans will be apparent only after the shocks to the world economy of sharply higher energy costs have been absorbed and development is allowed to continue at a higher level than in the 1970's.

The markets for African products are largely controlled by demand patterns from the industrial countries and the instability of prices for these goods drastically affects the income accruing to African producers and their governments. The importance of price changes to national economic development increases as the products affected constitute greater proportions of a country's foreign trade. Diversification of the products available for foreign trade is, therefore, an important aspect of attempts to stabilize the inflow of foreign resources to African countries, and to counteract their vulnerability to single-product price changes.

The progress of African governments in the diversification of the product composition of their exports has not been encouraging. The average percent of total exports accounted for by the sale of the countries' principal exports in the 1975-77 period was 57% as shown in Table 9.5. In 1978-79 the three largest exports for each country constituted 79% on the average in African states. United Nations figures show, furthermore, that exports of 20 leading primary commodities in African countries accounted for 65.7% of all exports from Africa (excluding South Africa) in 1960 and that this figure increased to 70.1% in 1965. These trends to maintain high dependence on a small number of products remains into the 1980's. Correspondingly, the percent of all imports to Africa composed of foreign industrial manufactured goods increased from 72% to 75% from 1960 to 1978. The disadvantages of being confined to a limited number of primary products are underlined by the generally decreasing prices offered for many of these products in Africa's major foreign markets. For example, the price of coffee dropped 40% between 1975 and 1982; the price of copper dropped 26%; the price of cotton dropped 34%; and the price of cocoa dropped by 40%. Similar changes can be observed in other commodities such as iron ore, zinc, manganese ore, groundnuts, tea and bananas. While there are cyclical patterns in such price fluctuations it is clearly the case that there is a long-term decline in the price of most African exports relative to the price of their imports.

If the abilities of African governments to finance economic development by the expansion of foreign trade are limited, there remains another direction their foreign policy might take in order to secure foreign capital for development purposes, namely, to secure capital in the form of foreign aid from other governments and multinational lenders such as the World Bank. A short review of the history of aid procurement will reveal, however, that foreign aid is far from being a panacea for the problems of African economic development.

Motivated variously by the need for foreign political allies in cold war international politics, the desirability of expanding foreign markets for their own export trade, and by the ethical commitment to reducing the heavily stratified international class system in which 20 percent of the world's population consumes roughly 85 percent of the world's income, (*One Hundred Countries, Two Billion People* (New York: Praeger, 1973), advanced indus-

trial countries provided the developing countries of the world with 10 to 14 billion dollars a year (net) during the period 1965 to 1970. This figure has risen about fifty percent through the 1970's in real terms (that is, with the figures adjusted for inflation) and the introduction of Arab sources of aid through the banks of the oil-exporting countries or the Arab-African Bank has been significant. However, the Arab sources tend to funnel resources to Islamic countries.   This foreign aid from the official development assistance countries represents a small and declining proportion of the combined Gross National Product of the industrialized countries (from about one half percent in 1969 to about one-third by the 1980's), and the proportion of their GNP put into loans and grants of development assistance from governments has steadily declined from a peak of about 65% in the mid-1960's to about a third now.

Black African countries were receiving about 1/7th of the total net official foreign aid given by the developed countries in the late 1960's and over 50% of all official grants included in aid disbursements. However, the United Kingdom and the United States have been reducing their official aid to Black African states, and while the total official capital flows to this region have increased through the last decade, the proportion of this total made up of grants as opposed to loans has declined, so increasingly foreign aid has meant cumulating public debts in these countries. This situation had grown to alarming proportions by the 1980's. The total external debt of all African countries outstanding at the end of 1965 was 6.3 billion US dollars and it had increased to 9.2 billion in 1969 (*Annual Report* World Bank, 1971). By 1979 the total debt had grown to 32 billion US dollars! Therefore, foreign aid is, in a sense, necessary to pay for foreign aid. What is more, much of the capital assistance given African as well as other developing countries, is "tied" to the purchase of goods and services from the donor countries, thereby limiting the possibilities of stimulating indigenous capital goods industries in the less developed countries. Finally, it can be argued that much of the official public assistance given by industrial countries to Black African countries often has the effect of simply maintaining the existing pattern of neo-colonial dependency by easing the severe balance of payments problems in most of these countries which allows for the continued expansion of private foreign industrial organizations in Africa, the importing of their capital goods, and the repatriation of their profits. This generality hides the intervening differences, however, particularly between former French and British colonies.

The foreign relations of Black African countries will be a critical factor in their future economic and political development, and the mixed record of attempts to obviate the structure of neo-colonialism reported in this chapter should not detract from the importance of careful analysis

of future trends by students of African development and the genuine successes of some countries.

Bibliography

All but two of the countries examined in this book were under colonial control for much of this century. See the following for examination of the effects of this experience as these countries become politically independent states: T. Lloyd "Africa and Hobson's Imperialism," *Past and Present* (May 1972): 130-153; W. G. Hynes, *The Economics of Empire: Britain, Africa and the New Imperialism 1870-95* (London: Longman, 1979); Clive Dewey and Anthony G. Hopkins, *The Imperial Impact: Studies in the Economic History of Africa and India* (New York: Humanities, 1978); L. H. Gann and P. Duignan, *Burden of Empire: An Appraisal of Western Colonialism in Africa, South of the Sahara* (Stanford, CA: Hoover Institution Press, 1967); M. Crowder, *West Africa Under Colonial Rule* (Evanston, IL: Northwestern University Press, 1968); D. Crummy and C. C. Stewart ed. *Modes of Production in Africa: The Pre-Colonial Era* (Beverly Hills: Sage, 1981); and W. Rodney, *How Europe Underdeveloped Africa* (London: Bogle-L'Ouverture, 1972). Two useful commentaries on particular countries are P. Kalck, *Central African Federation: A Failure in De-Colonization* (New York: Praeger, 1971) and R. Cruse O'Brien, "Colonization to Co-Operation? French Technical Assistance in Senegal," *Journal of Development Studies* 8 (Oct. 1971): 45-58.

For a review of the problems of dealing with the continued attempts at economic domination see J. D. Esseks, "Economic Dependence and Political Development in the New States of Africa," *Journal of Politics* (Nov. 1971): 1052-1075; Claude Ake, *A Political Economy of Africa* (New York: Longman, 1981); Timothy W. Shaw and K. A. Heard eds. *The Politics of Africa: Dependence and Development* (New York: Africana, 1979); P. C. W. Gutkind and I. Wallerstein *The Political Economy of Contemporary Africa* (Beverly Hills: Sage, 1976); A. Martin, *Minding Their Own Business: Zambia's Struggle Against Western Control* (London: Hutchinson, 1972); M. Bostock and H. Charles eds. *Economic Independence and Zambian Copper: A Case Study of Foreign Investment* (New York: Praeger, 1972); I. W. Zartman, *The Politics of Trade Negotiations Between Africa and the European Economic Community* (Princeton: Princeton University Press, 1971); and Harry Johnson, "U.S. Economic Policy Towards the Developing Countries," *Economic Development and Cultural Change* 16 (April

Other sources on neo-colonialism in addition to those above are S. Amin's *Neo-Colonialism in West Africa* (Harmondsworth: Penguin, 1973) which has an extensive bibliography and much useful data, Greg Lanning *Africa Undermined* (New York: Penguin, 1981), T. M. Shaw ed. *Alternative Futures for Africa* (Boulder, Colo: Westview Press, 1982), and K. Nkrumah, *Neo-Colonialism: The Last Stage of Imperialism* (New York: International, 1965).

The Organization of African Unity (OAU) as the voice of independent African states is giving political and economic support to the liberation movements fighting the white-dominated regimes in southern Africa. The independent countries bordering this area are also providing sanctuary to guerrillas and refugees. A useful but sometimes controversial summary of this activity is R. Gibson *African Liberation Movements: Contemporary Struggles Against White Minority Rule* (New York: Oxford University Press, 1972). For a review of the economic and political commitment to South Africa from the Western industrial countries see, for example, R. First, J. Steele, and C. Gurney, *The South African Connection* (New York: Barnes and Noble, 1973). A useful series by Penguin on Africa includes C. Desmond, *The Discarded People* (1971); J. Halpern, *South Africa's Hostages* (1965); E. Mondlane, *The Struggle for Mozambique* (1969); B. Davidson, *The Liberation of Guinea* (1969); and M. Benson, *The Stuggle for a Birthright* (1963). Also see Z. Cervenka *The Unfinished Quest for Unity: Africa and the OAU* (London: Friedmann, 1977).

For analyses of the role of aid from government and international public organizations see G. F. Papanek, "The Effect of Aid and Other Resource Transfers on Savings and Growth in Less Developed Countries," *Economic Journal* 82 (Sept. 1972): 934-950; B. Dinwiddy, ed. *Aid Performance and Development Policies of Western Countries: Studies in U.S., U.K., E.E.C., and Dutch Programs* (New York: Praeger, 1973) and Karl Borgin, *The Destruction of a Continent: Africa and International Aid* (San Diego: Harcourt, Brace, Jovanovich, 1982). For data on aid from Western countries see, in addition to the works mentioned earlier, the Organization for Economic Cooperation and Development, *The Flow of Financial Resources to Less Developed Countries 1956-1963* (Paris: OECD, 1964, 1967) and later editions of this continuing series. K. Borgin, *The Destruction of a Continent: Africa and International Aid.* (San Diego: Harcourt, Brace Jovanovich, 1982).

The role of private foreign investment has been widely discussed from quite different viewpoints. For an important analysis by Giovanni Arrighi, a Marxist, see "International Corporations, Labor Aristocracies, and Economic Development in Tropical Africa," in *Imperialism and Underdevelopment* (New York: Monthly Review Press, 1970), pp 220-267. For a major study of American multinational corporations see R. Vernon, *Sovereignty at Bay* (London: Longman, 1971). Two case studies are: D. H. Humphrey, "Private Foreign Investment in Malawi: A Study of the Sugar Corporation of Malawi," *The African Review* 2 (1972): 283-298 and Alice Amsden, *International Firms and Labour in Kenya 1945-1970* (London: Cass, 1971). Another viewpoint is expressed in G. K. Helleiner, "New Forms of Foreign Investment in Africa," *Journal of Modern African Studies* 6 (April 1968): 17-27; and the role of international corporations in the transfer of technology and managerial knowledge is reviewed in J. Baranson, "Transfer of Technical Knowledge by International Corporations to Developing Countries," *American Economic Review, Papers and Proceedings* 56 (May 1966): 259-267.

For a useful bibliography on African international relations see M. DeLancey, *African International Relations: An Annotated Bibliography* (Boulder, Westview Press,

1981) and for a broad based view of the African international situation see A. A. Mazrui, *Africa's International Relations: The Diplomacy of Dependence and Change* (Boulder, Colo: Westview Press, 1977).

Africa has been one of the sites where cold war conflicts have been played out. For works on this subject see R. Pearson ed. *Sino-Soviet Intervention in Africa* (Washington: Council on American Affairs, 1977); A. L. Gavshon, *Crisis in Africa: Battle Ground of East and West* (New York: Penguin, 1981); W. M. LeoGrande, *Cuba's Policy in Africa 1959-1980* (Berkeley: Institute of International Studies, University of California, 1980); and D. E. Albright ed. *Communism in Africa* (Bloomington: Indiana University Press, 1980). Also see H. F. Jackson, *From the Congo to Soweto: U.S. Foreign Policy Toward Africa since 1960.* (New York: Morrow, 1982), and G. Chaliand *The Struggle for Africa: Conflict of the Great Powers* (New York: St. Martin's Press, 1982).

The links with Arab countries especially the oil-exporters have increased considerably over the last decade. See V. T. LeVine and T. W. Luke *The Arab-African Connection: Political and Economic Realities* (Boulder: Westview Press, 1979).

Other sources can be found under the chapters on political development and economic development as well as in the individual case studies cited in the chapters of Part V.

Table 9.1   Total United States Economic Aid 1976-1979 (A), through 1972 (B), through 1968 (C), and 1969 to 1972 (D) in Millions of US Dollars.

Definition: The total amount of economic aid in the form of loans and grants to the country directly from the United States in the period.

Comments: The considerable majority of American aid has gone to a small number of countries, principally states where large American economic and strategic interests are predominant, such as Liberia, Ethiopia, Zaire, Ghana and Nigeria. The ex-French colonies, by contrast, have generally received only token aid.

```
Range       =     180.00
Mean        =      40.39
Standard Deviation =          50.10
```

Population Percent								
Cum.	Country	Rank	Country Name	A	Range Decile	B	C	D
21.00	21.00	1.0	Nigeria	180	1	422	229	192
30.71	9.71	2.0	Ethiopia	179		298	229	69
34.22	3.51	3.0	Ghana	166		300	240	60
39.38	5.16	4.0	Tanzania	152	2	78	62	16
47.67	8.29	5.0	Zaire	122	4	452	405	47
48.20	.53	6.0	Liberia	97	5	296	252	44
52.80	4.60	7.0	Kenya	77	6	97	63	34
54.13	1.33	8.0	Niger	63	7	21	15	6
56.00	1.87	9.0	Mali	55		28	19	11
57.97	1.97	10.0	Upper Volta	52	8	22	11	11
59.61	1.64	11.0	Senegal	48		43	32	14
61.18	1.57	12.0	Guinea	43		109	74	36
63.59	2.41	13.0	Cameroon	36	9	47	27	15
64.62	1.03	14.0	Somalia	35		77	73	7
64.85	.23	15.0	Botswana	34		30	16	16
65.84	.99	16.0	Sierra Leone	30		53	39	15
67.50	1.66	17.0	Malawi	29		29	23	7
68.84	1.34	18.5	Chad	28		10	8	3
69.22	.38	18.5	Lesotho	28		13	4	3
70.87	1.65	20.0	Zambia	24		68	41	28
71.33	.46	21.0	Mauritania	23		6	3	3
72.33	1.00	22.0	Benin	22		14	11	3
78.57	6.24	23.5	Sudan	20		106	107	16
82.52	3.95	23.5	Uganda	20		48	30	16
84.74	2.22	25.5	Ivory Coast	17	10	110	67	49
87.73	2.99	25.5	Mozambique	17		0	0	0
88.48	.75	27.0	Togo	15		18	14	6
89.84	1.36	28.0	Rwanda	13		8	7	2
92.32	2.48	29.0	Madagascar	11		15	13	3
92.48	.16	30.0	Swaziland	9		6	5	5
92.65	.17	31.0	Gambia	7		4	1	3
93.93	1.28	32.0	Burundi	4		10	7	3
95.88	1.95	37.0	Angola	0		0	0	0
96.46	.58	37.0	Central African R	0		8	5	3
96.91	.45	37.0	Congo	0		5	2	3
97.01	.10	37.0	Djibouti	0		0	0	0
97.11	.10	37.0	Equatorial Guinea	0		0	0	0
97.27	.16	37.0	Gabon	0		7	8	0
97.46	.19	37.0	Guinea-Bissau	0		0	0	0
97.75	.29	37.0	Namibia	0		0	0	0
100.00	2.26	37.0	Zimbabwe	0		0	0	0

SOURCE: *Black Africa* second edition

Table 9.2   Total Eastern-bloc Foreign Aid, 1974-1977 (A), 1965-1973 (B) and 1958-1965 (C) in Millions of US Dollars.

Definition: Total aid in the respective periods from the Soviet Union, Poland, Hungary, Czechoslovakia, Rumania, Bulgaria, Albania, East Germany, Yugoslavia, the People's Republic of China, Cuba and Vietnam.

Comments: Only about half of the 41 countries have received any aid at all from the Eastern-bloc countries during the most recent period and only a quarter received amounts exceeding 50 million dollars.

```
Range =        156.00
Mean =          26.61
Standard Deviation =        37.15
```

Population Percent						
Cum.	Country	Rank	Country Name	A	Range Decile	B	C

Cum.	Country	Rank	Country Name	A	Range Decile	B	C
21.00	21.00	1.0	Nigeria	156	1	133	14
27.24	6.24	2.0	Sudan	115	3	303	22
28.81	1.57	3.0	Guinea	84	5	215	119
30.46	1.65	4.0	Zambia	79		263	0
32.87	2.41	5.0	Cameroon	75	6	71	0
35.35	2.48	6.0	Madagascar	69		11	0
38.86	3.51	7.0	Ghana	66		166	164
39.89	1.03	8.0	Somalia	63		212	96
41.86	1.97	9.0	Upper Volta	60	7	51	0
44.85	2.99	10.0	Mozambique	59			
46.18	1.33	11.0	Niger	54		2	0
51.34	5.16	12.0	Tanzania	47		280	51
51.80	.46	13.0	Mauritania	37	8	22	0
61.51	9.71	14.0	Ethiopia	28	9	203	114
61.67	.16	15.0	Gabon	25		0	0
61.86	.19	16.0	Guinea-Bissau	19			
62.03	.17	17.0	Gambia	17		0	0
63.90	1.87	18.0	Mali	14	10	115	2
64.43	.53	19.0	Liberia	11		0	0
65.77	1.34	20.0	Chad	9		57	0
67.72	1.95	21.0	Angola	2			
69.36	1.64	22.5	Senegal	1		9	7
70.11	.75	22.5	Togo	1		45	0
71.11	1.00	32.5	Benin	0		44	0
71.34	.23	32.5	Botswana	0		0	0
72.62	1.28	32.5	Burundi	0		20	0
73.20	.58	32.5	Central African R	0		6	4
73.65	.45	32.5	Congo	0		66	62
73.75	.10	32.5	Djibouti	0		0	0
73.85	.10	32.5	Equatorial Guinea	0		0	0
76.07	2.22	32.5	Ivory Coast	0		0	0
80.67	4.60	32.5	Kenya	0		71	55
81.05	.38	32.5	Lesotho	0		0	0
82.71	1.66	32.5	Malawi	0		0	0
83.00	.29	32.5	Namibia	0			
84.36	1.36	32.5	Rwanda	0		23	0
85.35	.99	32.5	Sierra Leone	0		28	28
85.51	.16	32.5	Swaziland	0		0	
89.46	3.95	32.5	Uganda	0		30	30
97.75	8.29	32.5	Zaire	0		100	0
100.00	2.26	32.5	Zimbabwe	0			

Table 9.3   Average Annual Per Capita net Official Aid from Development Assistance Countries (DAC), in U.S. Dollars, 1976-1978 (A), 1971-1973 (B) and 1967-1969 (C).

Definition: The total aid in U.S. dollars divided by the number of years in the time period. The development assistance countries are the "market economies" which include Western Europe, the United States, Canada, Japan, Australia and New Zealand.

Comments: The distribution is highly unequal. The countries with the highest levels of aid tend to be the countries with the smallest populations.

```
Range =        299.94
Mean =          28.83
Standard Deviation =        47.18
```

Cum.	Country	Rank	Country Name	A	Range Decile	B	C
.10	.10	1.0	Djibouti	300.55	1		
.33	.23	2.0	Botswana	75.35	8	44.49	27.12
.49	.16	3.0	Gabon	65.55		55.45	21.00
.68	.19	4.0	Guinea-Bissau	63.46		14.00	
.84	.16	5.0	Swaziland	60.14	9	5.91	20.81
1.30	.46	6.0	Mauritania	48.78		11.97	7.31
1.75	.45	7.0	Congo	42.59		23.07	31.18
1.92	.17	8.0	Gambia	33.40		9.98	8.91
2.30	.38	9.0	Lesotho	31.26		14.62	15.47
3.05	.75	10.0	Togo	29.49	10	10.77	6.77
4.69	1.64	11.0	Senegal	28.43		14.47	11.41
6.02	1.33	12.0	Niger	24.26		11.93	5.94
7.38	1.36	13.0	Rwanda	22.35		7.94	4.36
9.03	1.65	14.0	Zambia	22.15		6.68	10.56
14.19	5.16	15.0	Tanzania	21.20		5.11	2.84
14.72	.53	16.0	Liberia	21.15		7.40	21.53
15.75	1.03	17.0	Somalia	20.54		10.15	8.78
17.09	1.34	18.0	Chad	20.48		9.02	5.16
19.50	2.41	19.0	Cameroon	20.22		9.53	27.00
21.37	1.87	20.0	Mali	18.34		8.68	3.41
23.34	1.97	21.0	Upper Volta	18.13		7.17	3.48
23.92	.58	22.0	Central African R	18.08		13.28	10.19
24.92	1.00	23.0	Benin	16.19		8.80	5.50
27.14	2.22	24.0	Ivory Coast	15.92		11.92	8.96
28.80	1.66	25.0	Malawi	14.58		6.88	6.41
33.40	4.60	26.0	Kenya	13.20		6.48	5.57
34.68	1.28	27.0	Burundi	13.12		7.19	3.17
40.92	6.24	28.0	Sudan	10.00		1.88	1.35
49.21	8.29	29.0	Zaire	9.64		5.37	4.50
51.69	2.48	30.0	Madagascar	8.83		7.08	4.49
54.68	2.99	31.0	Mozambique	8.46		4.38	1.84
55.67	.99	32.0	Sierra Leone	8.40		4.40	3.42
59.18	3.51	33.0	Ghana	7.86		5.70	8.66
61.13	1.95	34.0	Angola	6.30		5.24	2.76
62.70	1.57	35.0	Guinea	5.68		4.62	2.73
72.41	9.71	36.0	Ethiopia	4.42		2.06	1.72
72.51	.10	37.0	Equatorial Guinea	1.68			
76.46	3.95	38.0	Uganda	1.45		2.37	2.58
78.72	2.26	39.0	Zimbabwe	1.10			
99.72	21.00	40.0	Nigeria	.61		1.51	1.62

DATA NOT AVAILABLE OR NOT APPLICABLE FOR THE FOLLOWING COUNTRIES

Namibia

Table 9.4   Total Trade as a Percent of GNP 1977 (A), 1972 (B) and 1968 (C).

Definition: The sum of imports and exports divided by the Gross National Product and multiplied by 100.

Comments: This is a measure of how dominated the economy is by foreign trade in relation to the size of the economy as measured by the GDP. A few countries are so dependent on trade that the total trade exceeds the total consumption of goods and services produced in the country. Many countries, especially the poor subsistence economies in the interior of the continent, are much less dependent on trade although their elites, nevertheless, tend to consume imported goods.

```
Range =           156.00
Mean =             66.93
Standard Deviation =        39.08
```

Population Percent Cum.	Country Percent	Rank	Country Name	A	Range Decile	B	C
.16	.16	1.0	Swaziland	166	1	128	84
.54	.38	2.0	Lesotho	146	2	81	52
1.07	.53	3.0	Liberia	133	3	110	120
1.24	.17	4.0	Gambia	131		88	95
1.70	.46	5.0	Mauritania	126		83	65
2.15	.45	6.5	Congo	122		43	73
2.31	.16	6.5	Gabon	122		58	96
2.54	.23	8.0	Botswana	119	4	111	69
2.83	.29	9.0	Namibia	101	5		
5.05	2.22	10.0	Ivory Coast	87	6	55	69
6.70	1.65	11.0	Zambia	83		81	109
9.11	2.41	12.5	Cameroon	81		43	49
10.75	1.64	12.5	Senegal	81		47	29
11.78	1.03	14.0	Somalia	80		48	55
13.12	1.34	15.0	Chad	76		31	24
13.87	.75	16.0	Togo	67	7	41	42
34.87	21.00	17.0	Nigeria	65		39	21
35.87	1.00	18.5	Benin	61		48	71
40.47	4.60	18.5	Kenya	61		44	51
41.46	.99	20.0	Sierra Leone	60		46	49
42.04	.58	21.5	Central African R	57		27	39
43.37	1.33	21.5	Niger	57		30	21
51.66	8.29	23.0	Zaire	53	8	65	63
53.32	1.66	24.5	Malawi	52		45	59
55.19	1.87	24.5	Mali	52		29	19
57.67	2.48	26.0	Madagascar	49		36	43
59.93	2.26	27.0	Zimbabwe	48			
61.90	1.97	28.0	Upper Volta	47		20	25
67.06	5.16	29.0	Tanzania	44		46	58
67.25	.19	30.0	Guinea-Bissau	43		25	9
68.61	1.36	31.0	Rwanda	42		22	26
70.18	1.57	32.0	Guinea	31	9	33	27
71.46	1.28	33.5	Burundi	30		25	22
81.17	9.71	33.5	Ethiopia	30		17	18
87.41	6.24	35.0	Sudan	28		33	22
91.36	3.95	36.0	Uganda	25	10	29	51
91.46	.10	37.5	Djibouti	23			
91.56	.10	37.5	Equatorial Guinea	23		67	66
94.55	2.99	39.0	Mozambique	17		21	30
98.06	3.51	40.0	Ghana	15		25	37
100.00	1.95	41.0	Angola	10		41	58

Table 9.5   Principal Export as a Percent of Total Exports 1975-1977 (A), 1970-1972 (B) and 1966-1968 (C).

Definition: The value of the country's principal export divided by the value of all exports for the period.

Comments: More than half of these countries are dependent on a single commodity for at least half of their foreign exchange earnings. Several are almost totally dependent on a single commodity for all their export income. These countries are especially vulnerable to short-term fluctuations in commodity prices.

```
Range =            75.00
Mean =             57.05
Standard Deviation =        21.44
```

Population Percent Cum.	Country Percent	Rank	Country Name	A	Range Decile	B	C
.10	.10	1.0	Djibouti	100	1		
21.10	21.00	2.0	Nigeria	94		73	27
22.38	1.28	3.5	Burundi	91	2	83	84
24.03	1.65	3.5	Zambia	91		93	94
24.20	.17	5.0	Gambia	88		94	95
28.15	3.95	6.0	Uganda	87		53	53
30.10	1.95	7.0	Angola	85	3	28	48
30.56	.46	8.0	Mauritania	83		78	85
30.66	.10	9.5	Equatorial Guinea	80		58	55
30.82	.16	9.5	Gabon	80		42	35
32.18	1.36	11.0	Rwanda	72	4	51	57
32.71	.53	12.5	Liberia	69	5	66	73
34.04	1.33	12.5	Niger	69		51	65
34.49	.45	14.0	Congo	68		58	48
35.52	1.03	15.0	Somalia	63		53	47
37.09	1.57	16.5	Guinea	61	6	66	64
37.28	.19	16.5	Guinea-Bissau	61		83	90
40.79	3.51	18.5	Ghana	58		64	55
41.17	.38	18.5	Lesotho	58		32	60
50.88	9.71	20.0	Ethiopia	56		54	56
51.63	.75	21.0	Togo	54	7	33	37
57.87	6.24	22.0	Sudan	53		61	55
59.21	1.34	24.0	Chad	51		67	80
61.08	1.87	24.0	Mali	51		35	18
62.07	.99	24.0	Sierra Leone	51		61	57
62.65	.58	26.5	Central African R	44	8	40	51
64.31	1.66	26.5	Malawi	44		37	25
72.60	8.29	28.0	Zaire	43		63	61
74.57	1.97	29.0	Upper Volta	41		35	51
74.86	.29	30.5	Namibia	40	9		
76.50	1.64	30.5	Senegal	40		47	75
76.66	.16	32.0	Swaziland	37		24	26
79.07	2.41	33.0	Cameroon	34		25	28
81.29	2.22	34.5	Ivory Coast	33		31	35
83.77	2.48	34.5	Madagascar	33		27	31
84.00	.23	36.5	Botswana	32	10	84	96
89.16	5.16	36.5	Tanzania	32		15	19
90.16	1.00	38.5	Benin	31		32	49
94.76	4.60	38.5	Kenya	31		20	26
97.75	2.99	40.5	Mozambique	25		20	16
100.00	2.26	40.5	Zimbabwe	25			

Table 9.6   Percent of Export Trade with African States 1977 (A), 1972 (B), 1968 (C) and 1960 (D).

Definition: Percent of all trade with Black African states.

Comments: Most African countries have only a fledgling trade with other African countries. The exceptions tend to be interior countries which generally need to import items through the coastal countries.

```
Range =          34.00
Mean =            7.67
Standard Deviation =           7.74
```

Population Percent Cum.	Country	Rank	Country Name	A	Range Decile	B	C	D
1.87	1.87	1.0	Mali	34	1	25	54	53
3.53	1.66	2.0	Malawi	31		12	19	24
5.50	1.97	3.5	Upper Volta	21	4	59	71	84
13.79	8.29	3.5	Zaire	21		2	1	9
17.74	3.95	5.0	Uganda	19	5	9	18	18
20.73	2.99	6.0	Mozambique	17	6	3	7	5
22.37	1.64	7.0	Senegal	12	7	21	12	
26.97	4.60	8.5	Kenya	11		37	39	30
27.43	.46	8.5	Mauritania	11		0	3	55
27.53	.10	10.0	Djibouti	10	8	1		
28.89	1.36	11.0	Rwanda	9		59	67	4
30.84	1.95	12.5	Angola	8		4	5	7
33.25	2.41	12.5	Cameroon	8		10	9	5
33.48	.23	14.0	Botswana	7		5	5	3
34.82	1.34	16.0	Chad	7		23	10	27
37.04	2.22	16.0	Ivory Coast	7		11	8	12
38.37	1.33	16.0	Niger	7		10	30	26
38.95	.58	19.5	Central African R	6	9	6	1	9
39.12	.17	19.5	Gambia	6		1	1	3
40.15	1.03	19.5	Somalia	6		2	1	4
41.80	1.65	19.5	Zambia	6		2	1	5
42.80	1.00	22.5	Benin	5		10,	17	18
44.08	1.28	22.5	Burundi	5		3	1	7
44.53	.45	25.5	Congo	4		14	4	11
54.24	9.71	25.5	Ethiopia	4		8	5	3
54.43	.19	25.5	Guinea-Bissau	4		5	5	5
59.59	5.16	25.5	Tanzania	4		21	18	8
59.75	.16	30.0	Gabon	3	10	15	7	6
63.26	3.51	30.0	Ghana	3		1	1	4
64.83	1.57	30.0	Guinea	3		16	9	10
67.31	2.48	30.0	Madagascar	3		23	21	18
68.06	.75	30.0	Togo	3		1	5	8
68.16	.10	34.5	Equatorial Guinea	2		0	0	0
68.69	.53	34.5	Liberia	2		2	2	0
89.69	21.00	34.5	Nigeria	2		3	2	1
90.68	.99	34.5	Sierra Leone	2		1	0	1
96.92	6.24	37.0	Sudan	1		7	0	1
97.30	.38	39.5	Lesotho	0		0	5	0
97.59	.29	39.5	Namibia	0		0	0	0
97.75	.16	39.5	Swaziland	0		3	2	2
100.00	2.26	39.5	Zimbabwe	0		0	0	0

SOURCE: *Black Africa* second edition

Table 9.7   Trade With Ex-Colonial Power as Percent of Total Trade
1977 (A), 1972 (B), 1968 (C) and 1962 (D).

Definition: The percent of total trade that was transacted with the ex-colonial power in the given year. Since Liberia and Ethiopia have no ex-colonial power, their principal trading partner over the last two decades, the United States, is used to facilitate comparison.

Comments: While most countries continue to maintain strong trading ties with their ex-colonial powers, a comparison with earlier data shows a tendency for most of the ex-British colonies to steadily decrease their trade dependence with Britain, while many ex-French colonies have tended to maintain or even increase their level of trade dependence.

```
Range =        100.00
Mean =          29.76
Standard Deviation =         20.59
```

Population Percent Cum.	Country	Rank	Country Name	A	Range Decile	B	C	D
.29	.29	1.0	Namibia	100	1			
.39	.10	2.0	Djibouti	90	2			
.97	.58	3.0	Central African R	60	4	52	50	59
2.30	1.33	4.0	Niger	49	6	42	56	54
10.59	8.29	5.0	Zaire	48		35	37	32
10.78	.19	6.5	Guinea-Bissau	45		60	90	90
11.24	.46	6.5	Mauritania	45		34	29	55
11.40	.16	8.0	Gabon	44		45	42	61
11.50	.10	9.5	Equatorial Guinea	42		94	81	85
13.14	1.64	9.5	Senegal	42		53	77	74
15.01	1.87	11.0	Mali	41		35	27	15
17.42	2.41	12.0	Cameroon	38	7	43	46	57
18.76	1.34	13.5	Chad	37		31	51	64
20.73	1.97	13.5	Upper Volta	37		40	34	47
23.21	2.48	15.5	Madagascar	33		48	51	65
24.24	1.03	15.5	Somalia	33		29	40	38
26.46	2.22	17.0	Ivory Coast	32		37	41	54
27.45	.99	18.0	Sierra Leone	31		44	48	46
29.11	1.66	19.0	Malawi	30	8	33	33	34
29.86	.75	20.0	Togo	29		33	35	41
30.03	.17	21.0	Gambia	28		34	47	55
30.48	.45	22.0	Congo	26		48	37	51
30.71	.23	23.0	Botswana	25		23	30	35
31.24	.53	24.0	Liberia	24		21	29	43
32.24	1.00	25.0	Benin	23		39	38	69
33.89	1.65	26.0	Zambia	19	9	22	26	30
37.40	3.51	27.5	Ghana	17		17	27	33
38.97	1.57	27.5	Guinea	17		17	13	17
43.57	4.60	29.0	Kenya	16		22	24	30
64.57	21.00	32.5	Nigeria	15		24	30	39
65.93	1.36	32.5	Rwanda	15		20	22	31
72.17	6.24	32.5	Sudan	15		11	15	21
72.33	.16	32.5	Swaziland	15		20	17	20
77.49	5.16	32.5	Tanzania	15		14	23	45
81.44	3.95	32.5	Uganda	15		20	22	20
84.43	2.99	36.0	Mozambique	12		29	46	33
85.71	1.28	37.0	Burundi	9	10	14	21	20
87.66	1.95	38.0	Angola	5		25	45	30
97.37	9.71	39.0	Ethiopia	3		23	34	39
97.75	.38	40.5	Lesotho	0		5	5	10
100.00	2.26	40.5	Zimbabwe	0		0	0	

SOURCE: *Black Africa* second edition

PART IV

CASE STUDIES:

An Introduction to a Methodology

In Part II we presented an elementary introduction to the methodology of cross-national research which was directed primarily at students and others who might wish to use this technique to analyze the comparative data profiles in Part III. This chapter on case studies has the same purpose in relation to the country profiles, which follow in Part V.

The Case Study

The most common form of study of Africa in undergraduate papers and reports is the case study. This approach involves taking one or a small number of examples of the phenomenon of interest and examining them in detail. The reader interested in socialism, for example, might choose to evaluate Tanzania's particular form of socialism, or to compare Tanzania's political economy with that of the more capitalist neighboring country, Kenya, or compare it with the political economics of Guinea and Congo; which are two other countries professing socialism.[4]

In contrast to the comparative method discussed in Part II, the case study method does not restrict one to topics which can be measured on an equivalent basis across units such as a country's GNP per capita, nor is it required to gather comparable data on a large number of cases. It permits probing supposed differences *within* countries, such as the response to modernization of the Yoruba and Ibo peoples of Nigeria. It allows one to study processes in depth, and to choose a case or cases with an eye to the library resources available. Our approach to case studies in this book does take the *country* as the be-

ginning point of reference, however, because in contemporary Africa the national unit is an especially important context for all groups and institutions within its boundaries. Of course, if one is studying pre-colonial Africa, then ethnic groups or kingdoms would probably be the most relevant starting point.

Although the case study method is commonly used, many are unaware that there are several distinct types of case studies and few make the full and most efficient use of the bibliographical sources which are potentially available to them. This essay considers and evaluates four types of case studies most frequently encountered and discusses the research process for each in terms of a step by step procedure with special emphasis on defining the research question and the selection of cases. It is not intended that a study should always proceed in the exact pattern suggested since the research process always involves seizing on sudden insights or opportunities. But these steps provide a convenient logical framework to discuss the various interrelated aspects of undertaking a case study. Frequent reference will be made to the materials in this book, especially those in the next section, which are intended to assist in case studies of Africa.

Four Types of Case Studies

The four types of case studies we will discuss are: 1) Single Country, Descriptive; 2) Single Country, Analytic; 3) Single Country, Comparative; and 4) Multiple Country, Comparative. Each has its advantages and disadvantages.

Single Country Descriptive: Case Study Type I

The purpose in a descriptive study is to gain a general understanding of a single country. In most cases, such a study is undertaken because of a special interest in a particular African country—perhaps a visit to the country is planned or one has a friend from that country and wishes to become familiar with it. Because this type of approach is so diffuse, it does not lend itself to successful research papers which normally require a focal point. Very often, however, those who wish to undertake one of the other types of case study will *begin* their research by carrying out a preliminary descriptive study of a country in order to decide on a more narrowly defined research question. The method of the single country descriptive study, therefore, is relevant to the interests of many, especially those who are in the topic-selection stage. The steps for this type are as follows:

Step 1 - Case Selection.

This depends on the individual's interest and the library resources available.

Step 2 - Overview.

First, locate an authoritative and recent general book on the country and read it to gain an overview and interpretation of the country's history and social structure. The country bibliographies in the next section will be of considerable help in locating such books, although satisfactory general works of this kind are not available in English for some of the French-speaking Black African countries.

Step 3 - Review.

Next, the reader's understanding of the basic characteristics of the country, its population, and its history should be reviewed. The following questions cover many of the major topics which should be included for an overall understanding of a particular country.

a. *Geography*.

What is the physical situation of the country? Is it landlocked? How good are its port facilities (if it has ports). What type of vegetation does it have and how is it distributed? What is the rainfall distribution?

b. *Population*.

How big is the population and what is the population per square mile? How fast is the population growing and how serious are the population pressures? How is the population differentiated in terms of ethnic groups and in terms of linguistic types? (*Black Africa: A Comparative Handbook* presents the linguistic situation in each country, and also gives the basic data on the ethnic differentiation of the Black African countries.) What are the characteristics of the ethnic groups in terms of type of subsistence (agricultural or nomadic or both), political system (hierarchical to egalitarian), descent rule (patrilineal, matrilineal, etc.), etc. How is the population distributed throughout the country? In many African countries this distribution is very uneven.

c. *History*.

What was the precolonial history of the various ethnic groups in the country? Who was the colonial ruler and how and when was the conquest accomplished? Were there European settlers or special European interests in the country (in terms of mines, plantations, etc.)? How repressive was the colonial period? How was independence accomplished?

d. *Politics*.

What is the present political system (monarchy, federation, etc.)? What is the political party situation? Who is the head of government, how long has he been in office and with which ethnic group is he identified? What is the professed ideology of the government and to what extent is the ideology expressed in concrete programs? What is the basis of support for the government and the sources (potential or actual) of opposition? To what degree is the government oriented to, or dependent upon, Western or Eastern bloc nations, and why? What role does the military play in governance? Basic information on the head of government and political parties is given in Part V.

e. *Economic Development*.

What are the country's major resources? Which of them are presently being exploited and what are the expectations for the future? What are the arrangements for their exploitation and how favorable are the terms to the country? What are the basic agricultural crops and which ones enter the cash economy, such as cocoa, which is exported by Ghana and Nigeria? How much industrialization has taken place and what are the prospects for future industrialization? What percent of the labor force are wage earners, what percent work in factories? What are the objectives of the development plan and how is development to be financed? What is the health of the economy in terms of balance of payments, inflation, and growth? Which groups control the economy; which benefit and which do not?

f. *Social*.

What is the form of the educational system and how extensive has been primary, secondary, and university education? Which are the major cities, how rapidly have they been growing, and how severe are the urban problems? What is the impact of Christianity and/or Islam?

g. *Uniqueness*.

Even in a single country descriptive study, the reader should try to get a sense of the situation of the country in comparison with other Black African nations. (See the comparative data profiles in Part III for some quantitative comparisons and the essay in Part I for a qualitative picture of the overall patterns for Africa. Also consult the maps throughout the book.) What are the unique features of the country? Part Five gives some suggestions on this for each of the countries.

Step 4 - Further Research.

After reviewing his or her knowledge of the country, the student can fill in gaps and add depth by consulting more specialized works. At this point, the country bibliographies in the next section should be helpful because they list the major specialized works for each country. The *Area Handbooks*, where available, provide much detailed information sometimes otherwise unavailable, and contain full but sometimes dated bibliographies. A number of countries' economies are outlined in the multi-volume International Monetary Fund's *Surveys of African Economies*.

II. Single Country Analytic: Case Study Type 2

This type of case study is similar to Type 1 except that here the researcher deliberately narrows his or her focus of attention to a single research question. Instead of learning about Senegal in general, he or she investigates such topics as the role of the Muslim marabouts in Senegalese politics, or the causes of the breakdown of the Mali Federation (into Senegal and Mali), or the contribution that groundnuts (peanuts) make to the Senegalese political economy. The success of an analytic case study

rests on the careful choice of an interesting and meaningful topic which is feasible to undertake with the library and other resources available.

Step 1 - Selection of the Topic.

a. The reader may begin with a research question already in mind. Perhaps he or she has noticed an intriguing anomaly, such as how President Senghor, a Roman Catholic, maintained himself in power for a long period of time when Islam was the predominant religion of Senegal. This could easily lead the student to the marabout topic mentioned above. Or the student may wish to explore a particular body of theory, such as the conditions which promote pan-Africanism (and federations such as Mali) or the Marxian neo-imperialism theory of the continuing economic and political dominance of new nation-states by their former colonial rulers (e.g. the French have heavily subsidized Senegal's groundnut production). If the student begins with a general question, then the problem is to choose the most appropriate example for analysis.

b. Alternatively, many readers begin their study without a particular research question in mind.

(1) In this situation, if the student has a special interest in a particular country, the best approach to topic selection may be to begin with an exploratory descriptive analysis. If the student chooses Somalia, for instance, he or she would first do general reading and then try to narrow his or her interests down to a particular topic for which there exists sufficient literature. This may involve taking some theoretical generalization, such as the proposition that nomadic cattle-herding peoples are much more resistant to modernization than agricultural peoples, and analyzing Somalia as a case study of a nation whose population is primarily nomadic cattle-herders. Again, the reader may seize upon a uniqueness that emerges from an exploratory reading and design the research accordingly. For example, Somalia has experienced one of the highest levels of border disputes in Black Africa, and one might study the reasons for this and its effect on Somalia's political and economic development.

(2) Alternatively the student may prefer to formulate the research question prior to choosing a case of study. In this case the topics covered in the readings should be considered to see if they can be narrowed to a specific conceptual category such as urbanization, education, political development, or economic development. Once a category has been identified, work can begin at formulating a specific research question, such as those suggested above. The topic bibliographies in Part III should assist in topic selection.

In general, the quicker one is able to narrow the focus, the better, because the specific research question will require careful work in locating sources. The question should be as unambiguous and specific as possible.

Step 2 - Case Selection

The reader may have selected a case before selecting a topic, but if not, the next step is to choose a case. The most important criteria for case selection are: 1) personal interest; 2) appropriateness to the research problem; and 3) availability of sources. *Appropriateness* is the most difficult of these criteria to ascertain. Obviously one does not study Gabon if one is interested in the urbanization patterns of former nomadic cattle-herders since there are none in Gabon. One would instead select one of the Sahelian countries of the West African savanna or other cattle herding areas. In principle, one would like to find the *crucial case*. The *crucial case* in scientific method is one that is considered representative of the universe of relevant cases and hence, one from which generalizations to all other cases could be made. But as Prezworski and Teune have pointed out, it is at the national level where many of the most serious threats to validity and confounding factors in a comparison are commonly found. Someone interested in national integration may want to study and compare the countries that have had the most difficulties in national integration, such as Benin or Zaire, or countries which have had little apparent trouble over integration, such as Malawi or Ivory Coast. But, it must be kept in mind that specific characteristics of each country selected may not be characteristic of the general pattern. The use of tables in Part III to identify some of these anomalies can be useful.

Step 3 - Search for Sources.

This step is similar to step 3 for descriptive case studies, and those suggestions are relevant here. At this stage the researcher should consult Appendices 1 and 4 where we discuss bibliographical sources for African studies and the journals in the field. The more specific the research topic, the quicker one can winnow relevant from irrelevant sources. For example, someone who is studying the Kwilu rebellion in Zaire, and has a general understanding of Zaire's politics and social structure, can use a major study like Crawford Young's *Politics in the Congo* by consulting the index and going directly to the nine page references listed under "Kwilu." Likewise, he or she can quickly consult the indexes to journals such as *Africa Report* and the *Journal of Modern African Studies* for articles relevant to the topic. There are also references to the Kwilu Rebellion in the Zaire section of Part V of this book.

Step 4 - Developing the Argument.

As the student reviews the literature, he or she will often find differences of opinion about the topic. Was the Kenyan Mau-Mau movement a nationalist rebellion or a tribal aberration? Should Ghana lay its development emphasis on agricultural or industrial development? Who killed Lumumba and why? These topics and many others have been debated in the literature. The use of such differences of opinion can focus a paper's argument. Their resolution, or the demonstration that they can't be resolved with the information at hand, is a worthwhile and feasible intellectual exercise for undergraduate research.[2] These procedures are the same as those in types 3 and 4 and will not be repeated there.

III. Single Country Comparative: Case Study Type 3

Types 3 and 4 share the analytical focus of Type 2, but add the element of *comparison of more than one case*. In the Type 3 study, the comparison is within the boundaries of a single social or political unit (e.g. an ethnic unit or a country) while in the Type 4 study the comparison is either between such units or between comparable elements of two or more countries. To continue the Senegalese example used earlier, if a Type 2 study examined the political role of Muslim marabouts, a Type 3 study would perhaps compare the marabout role with that of the Senegalese Roman Catholic clergy and a Type 4 study, to anticipate, might compare the political role of the marabouts of Senegal with that of Mauritania's marabouts.

Comparison permits the researcher to begin to generalize about the conditions under which certain activities occur, while the single case, properly interpreted, only allows the researcher to say that *"in this instance this is what happened"* or, if he or she is working with a theory, that it is or is not supported. If Senengalese marabouts do have considerable political influence one might risk inference from this single case that African Muslim leaders generally exert unique political influence. If a comparison with Senegalese Roman Catholic clergy showed that they too exerted considerable political influence, this generalization would have to be dropped or qualified. If an inter-country comparison of Senegal with Mauritania showed that the Maurtanian marabouts did not have much political influence, then the generalization that Muslim leaders always exert political influence is called into question. The student undertaking such a comparison would then probe to see what special conditions in Senegal resulted in the prominent political role taken by its marabouts. He or she might conclude that the Senegalese marabouts' economic role as owners of large groundnut plantations accounts for the difference.[3] To confirm this one could try to find another case where Muslim leaders have a significant economic base and see whether they have a similar political role.[4] Of course, comparisons may confirm as well as disprove hypotheses.

Step 1 - Selection of the Topic

Many of the considerations discussed under this step for Type 2 studies are relevant here with the further addition that the student is looking for a topic which is amenable to comparison within a particular country. Some of the types of units which the student may want to compare are ethnic groups, regions, cities, and elites. In the African context some of the most interesting and feasible intra-country comparisons are between ethnic groups. The differential response to modernization of the Aboure and the Bete peoples in the Ivory Coast; the different political position of the Kikuyu and Luo in Kenya; and a comparison of the response to Christianity on the part of the Yoruba, Bini, Ibo and Hausa peoples of Nigeria are examples of possible ethnic intra-country comparisons.

Step 2 - Case Selection

Personal interest, appropriateness to the research problem and availability of sources are all as important in Type 3 case selection as they are in Type 2 except that instead of looking for the relevant case, the student should look for a *key comparison*.

A key comparison is one in which two cases differ with respect to the variable of most interest to the researcher *while having as much else in common as possible*. In such a situation there is a better chance of discovering what is responsible for the difference. Let us say, for example, that one is interested in the factors which promote the spread of Christianity and decided to compare ethnic groups in one country. If one chooses Nigeria and decides to compare the Yoruba, who are a third or more Christian, with the Hausa, who are less than 1% Christian, it will be found that, although the two groups are somewhat similar in size, they have several important differences which will make it difficult to learn much about the factors encouraging the spread of Christianity. In the *first* place, Islam has been the religion of some Hausa for centuries, whereas Islam is a relative newcomer to the Yoruba. *Second,* because the Hausa live in the savannah while the Yoruba habitat is primarily rain forest there are important differences in their economies and social structure. *Third,* the Hausa live away from the sea and consequently European influence was delayed in reaching them while the Yoruba territory runs to the sea and European influence was early. For these and other reasons the cases are not comparable because the Hausa were far less exposed to Christian missionary efforts and already possessed a universal religion (Islam). A much more appropriate comparison for this research question would be the Yoruba and Bini peoples. The Bini, who have relatively few Christians, share a number of similarities with the neighboring Yoruba including a shared culture, similar habitat, a similar lack of exposure to Islam, and early European influence.

Step 3 - Search for Sources

The comments made for Types 1 and 2 under this step are relevant here too. Country bibliographies and handbooks will give references to the literature on the various ethnic groups and cities.[5] The student should recognize that there is considerable variation in the information available for such intra-country units. A small and relatively unimportant ethnic group may be the subject of several excellent anthropological monographs because it happened to be studied by a prolific scholar whereas another larger group, which happens to be of special interest to the student, may only be described in a few obscure journal articles because it has not yet come under the scrutiny of a publishing scholar. Special care is needed in finding sources for Type 3 studies, therefore, and their availability should be ascertained as early as possible.

IV. Multiple Country Comparative: Case Study Type 4

Step 1 - Selection of the Topic.

Students in the topic formulation stage can either explore the differences between two or more countries which attract their interest until a specific research question emerges or they can select a general topic such as political stability and then narrow it to a specific research question before deciding which countries to use as cases.

In the *first strategy,* two or more countries which vary on a variable of interest are chosen (see Step 2 below for the method of choosing cases). The research question simply may be to explain why country A is different from country B on that variable or, after preliminary research, the student may narrow the comparison further. For example, a general question would be: Why is Kenya more industrialized than Tanzania?, while a more specific question would be: What is the role of ideology in the differential industrialization of Kenya and Tanzania?

In the *second strategy,* the student takes a topic of interest and formulates a research question which is amenable to a multi-country comparative study. As noted earlier, the topic bibliographies in Part III are a helpful source for theoretical generalizations. There are a number of ways to approach the problem of topic selection using these resources, four of which are presented in the following:

1.) Begin with a general theoretical statement which is not made with special reference to Africa and explore its applicability to several African countries. Samuel Huntington (1965) suggests, for example, that social mobilization produces political instability while Seymour Lipset (1960) has argued that economic development sustains democratic and stable political systems—which is the case for Africa?

2.) Take a cross-national generalization about Africa which may or may not have been tested using cross-national research and probe it in more depth using two or three countries. Raymond Hopkins (1966) argues that Christian missionary activity has promoted economic development in Africa. He studied the question using cross-national methodology and a 10-country sample of African countries. This question could be explored using two or three carefully selected countries (or alternatively 41 countries in a comparative study using the data in Part III).

3.) Take a scholarly monograph on a particular country and compare its conclusions with the situation in one or two other countries. As indicated in their title, Robert Clower et. al. conclude, in *Growth Without Development: An Economic Survey of Liberia* (Evanston, Ill.: Northwestern University Press, 1966), that the undeniable growth of Liberia's economy has not resulted in the development of the country. To what extent is this true of other countries?

4.) Take a monograph or journal article which compares two or three African countries on a topic and make the same comparison between two or three more countries. Victor T. LeVine published a study of the coups in Upper Volta, Benin (Dahomey) and the Central African Republic (Rotberg and Mazrui: 1970). He finds in each of these three cases the "national economy and the political system were either on the point of collapse or in serious difficulty" prior to the coups. Several other nations which have had coups could be examined to explore the conditions under which collapses promote coups.[6]

Step 2 - Case Selection

As in Type 3 studies, the *key comparison* is the reader's goal. The tables in Part III should be of great help in choosing which countries to study if the student's topic is measured by one of the variables in those tables. Among the factors which the student may want to "hold constant" are: population size, wealth, colonial history (e.g.

French or British colonial ruler) and natural resources. The student will most likely want to choose countries which have large differences on the variable studied (e.g. countries which have experienced a great deal more or less than average economic growth) or on a variable which is related to that variable (e.g. comparing two countries which have had much economic growth but which differ in permitting or not permitting opposition political parties).

Step 3 - Search for Sources

The country bibliographies in Part V will be of particular relevance in Type 4 studies.

Conclusion: Stages of Research Development

In this chapter we have described in some detail the characteristics and procedures appropriate to the case study method of analysis. We have done this because of the ubiquitousness of the case study among students and other readers who are encountering the study of Africa. Much of this book will, hopefully, be of use to this activity. In concluding we would like to portray the spectrum of research approaches and briefly comment on their complimentarities.

As the reader of this essay may have noticed, as we work from Type 1 to Type 4 case studies we move to increasing generality and representativeness. Less obvious, perhaps, is that the breadth of focus increased and the number of variables being examined declined. Thus we move in one direction to increase our breadth and generality and in the other to increase our depth and detail. Which point on this spectrum is appropriate for a student's work will be determinend by a host of factors; some structural such as library and research facilities; some individual such as personal interest; some situational such as a course chosen or particular current events. But ultimately research must have *both* breadth and depth to prosper.

Footnotes

¹ Many examples of research questions given here are drawn from Economics, Political Science and Sociology. In survey courses on Africa the student usually is able to choose a research problem from one of several disciplines. The case study method described here is applicable to other disciplines including history, psychology and literature.

² At all times the student should avoid setting up a straw man and spending time demolishing arguments that are not taken seriously for good reason by contemporary thinkers. He should, however, consider *every* argument carefully before dismissing it. Sometimes arguments are rejected out of hand by contemporary thinkers because they are not "fashionable," or they may be rejected for ideological reasons. Someone who thinks matters through and examines what really happened without regard to conventional wisdom may discover a new aspect of reality, although it is not likely to be as dramatic as Copernicus' "discovery" that the earth goes around the sun.

³ This is only one of a number of differences between the cases. For example, Mauritania proclaims itself to be a Muslim country while Senegal does not. Any interpretation should take into account all the possible relevant differences and show why some are more relevant than others in explaining the difference.

⁴ The process of generalization from cases is codified in social science methodological theory. The chapter in this book on cross-national comparative research presents a portion of this theory which is applicable to that form of comparison. Essentially this theory specifies the conditions under which the student can form generalizations. Students wishing to go deeper into this topic than is possible in this treatment should consult standard methods texts. (See Appendix 3.)

⁵ A special source for many African ethnic groups is the multi-volume *Ethnographic Survey of Africa* published by the International African Institute. The series consists of short summary monographs, each on a different ethnic group, and includes extensive bibliographies.

⁶ LeVine himself in his article gives examples of other countries which suffered both political and economic collapses prior to a coup and countries which had only a political collapse before a coup.

Part V

INTRODUCTION

The nature of the aggregate indicators on dimensions such as ethnic pluralism, language, urbanization, political patterns, and political instability in Part III was, in many cases, dependent on the judgments of the authors. Part V provides specific information about the basis of some of our judgments. It consists of 41 chapters, one for each country discussed. Each chapter contains five parts: (1) country map and a summary of basic information, (2) elite political instability patterns, (3) country features of especial interest, and (4) a basic bibliography.

It should be emphasized that the data presented in Part V does *not* provide a comprehensive profile of the countries included. There are sources which do this, such as the annual *Africa South of the Sahara*; Jeune Afrique's *Annuaire de l'afrique et du moyen orient* 1981-82 etc; and the earlier Jeune Afrique Yearbooks, *Africa 69/70*, etc. Our purpose is to give comparable, detailed data on a relatively few dimensions. The brief descriptions that follow discuss the nature of the data, our definitions and intentions, and the basic sources used. The reliability of these data are similar to those presented in the other parts of this book. In general, less information was available to us for the former French and Portuguese colonies. These sections can be used by those doing country studies as a reference and guide to works on the country.

Country Map

Each map has been drawn to show the location of the country's ethnic units, and cities with a population of 20,000 or over. These cities are called "major cities" on the map's legend and are indicated by a circle. We also give the locations of a number of the smaller population centers, which are shown by black dots, but only rarely have we named these centers. The map also shows the country's major communication linkages in the form of roads, railroads, and major rivers. Special attention has been given to the places where these linkages cross the country's boundaries. The principal sources for urban locations, spelling, and major transport networks, were *The Times Index Gazetteer of the World* (Boston: Houghton Mifflin Co., 1966), *The Atlas of Africa* (New York: Free Press, 1973), P. Ady, *Oxford Regional Economic Atlas: Africa* (Oxford: Clarendon Press, 1965), *Africa 69/*

70, the *United States Board on Geographic Names/Gazetteer* and the various U.S. Department of State *Background Notes*. The sources for the ethnic unit locations are the works cited in the ethnic patterns sections in the second edition of *Black Africa* and George Peter Murdock, *Africa: Its Peoples and Their Culture History* (New York: McGraw-Hill, 1959). The locations of the ethnic "units" should be considered as rough approximations. The reader should note that these "units" are not usually coterminous with ethnic identity groups or "tribes" (see II below).

I. Basic Information

The population data is from several sources including *World Population 1977* (Washington, D.C., 1977) and the *World Population Data Sheet* which is published by the Population Reference Bureau, Inc. (1755 Massachusetts Avenue, N.W., Washington, D.C. 20036). The Population Reference Bureau uses unpublished materials from the Population Division of the United Nations which are from the 'medium variant' set of projections. These estimates are in general accord with other independently derived estimates.

The *United Nations Demographic Yearbook* and *Africa South of the Sahara* were the sources for the country size data. The major exports are given for 1979 or later when available, otherwise they are for the latest year. The sources for the export data are *International Financial Statistics*. Language data are from the estimates as detailed in *Black Africa* second edition.

II. Elite Political Instability Patterns

This section contains a brief tabular summary, Table 1, of the elite instability events in the country's post-independence history, if there were any. The second edition of *Black Africa* provides much more detail on these and other political instability events.

III. Country Features Worthy of Special Study

In this section we include a list of aspects of that country which would be of particular interest to those doing case studies.

IV. Selected References

An effort was made to include recent, English language (if possible), references which would give the reader access to the best available information on each country. The references are selective and preference was given to books which provide overall coverage on bibliographical, general, political, economic, and social topics.

The various country handbooks published by the United States government are often very useful summaries of the literature on African countries. Cornell University Press brought out a series of country books, primarily by political scientists. The Scarecrow Press series of "historical dictionaries" for each country in Africa is nearly complete and some are of considerable value. Westview Press also is actively building a series of country studies for the states of Black Africa. The former French African countries posed special bibliographic problems because of the relative unavailability of literature in English on them. We tried to compensate for this by referencing the appropriate sections of the comprehensive books by Virginia Thompson and Richard Adloff, and the somewhat less satisfactory book by Guy de Lusignan, *French-Speaking Africa since Independence* (New York: Pall Mall, 1969). However, this is useful only for the earlier periods.

1. Angola

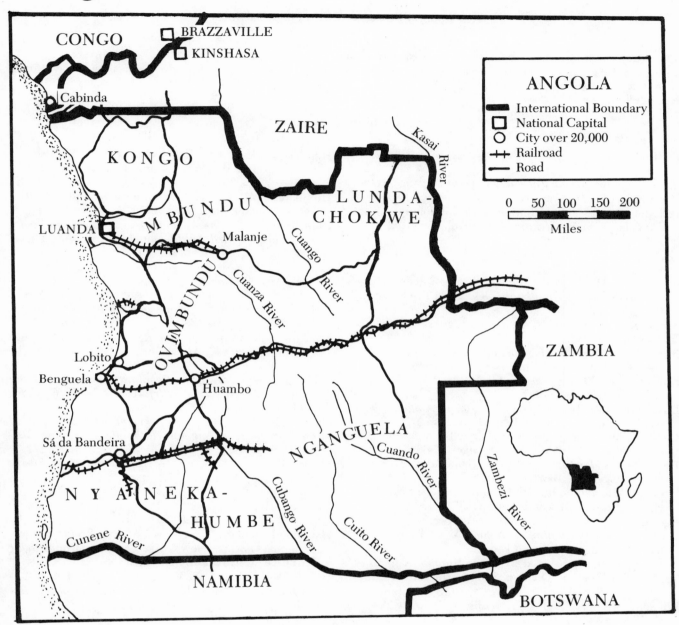

I. Basic Information

Date of Independence: November 11, 1975
Former Colonial Ruler: Portugal
Estimated Population (1980): 6,759,000
Area Size (equivalent in U.S.): 481,354 sq. mi. (Texas, Oklahoma, New Mexico, Louisiana)

Most Widely Spoken Languages: Umbundu—40%; Kimbundu—25%

Date of Last Census: 1970
Major Exports 1973 as Percent of Total Exports: coffee—27 percent; crude petroleum—30 percent; diamonds—10 percent; iron ore—6 percent; fish and fish products—7 percent.

Official Language: Portuguese

II.   Elite Political Instability

TABLE 1.1   Elite Instability (Post-Independence)

Date	Event
1. May 2, 1977	Attempted Coup (MPLA leaders who were recently ousted try to take power.)

III.   Country Features Worthy of Special Study

1. Formerly had the largest white population in Africa outside of the Republic of South Africa and Namibia.
2. Long period of guerrilla activity preceding independence and a succeeding civil war with considerable involvement by the major non-African foreign powers as well as by Zaire and South Africa.
3. Potentially a very wealthy country.

IV. Selected References

BIBLIOGRAPHY

Martin, Phyllis. *Historical Dictionary of Angola*. Metuchen, N.J.: Scarecrow Press, 1980.

Pélissier, René. "Contribution á la bibliographie de l'Angola." *Genève-Afrique* 15, 2 (1976): 136—152.

GENERAL

Abshire, David M and Michael Samuels (eds.) *Portuguese Africa: A Handbook*. New York: Frederick A. Praeger, 1969.

Africa Report, Special Issue on Portuguese Africa. 12 (November 1967).

Birmingham, David. *The Portuguese Conquest of Angola*. London: Oxford University Press, 1965.

Chilcote, Ronald. *Portuguese Africa*. Englewood Cliffs, N.J.: Prentice-Hall, 1967.

Davidson, Basil. *In the Eye of the Storm, Angola's People*. Middlesex, England: Penguin Books, 1974.

Davis, John A. and James K. Baker (eds.) *Southern Africa in Transition*. New York: Praeger, 1966.

Duffy, James. *Portugal in Africa*. Cambridge: Harvard University Press, 1962.

Egero, B. *Mozambique and Angola*. Uppsala: Scandinavian Institute of African Studies, 1977.

Egerton, F. Clement C. *Angola in Perspective: Endeavour and Achievement in Portuguese West Africa*. London: Routledge and Kegan Paul, 1957.

U.S. Department of the Army. *Area Handbook for Angola*. Washington, D.C.: U.S. Government Printing Office, 1979.

Wheeler, Douglas and René Pélissier. *Angola*. New York: Praeger, 1971.

POLITICAL

Barnett, Don and Roy Garvey. *The Revolution in Angola*. Indianapolis, In.: The Bobbs Merill Co., 1972.

Bender, Gerald J. *Angola under the Portuguese: The Myth and the Reality*. Berkeley: University of California Press, 1978.

Chilcote, Ronald. *Emerging Nationalism in Portuguese Africa*. Stanford: Hoover Institution Press, 1972.

Chilcote, R. H. (ed.) *Protest and Resistance in Angola and Brazil*. Berkeley: University of California Press, 1972.

Harsch, Ernest and Tony Thomas. *Angola, The Hidden History of Washington's War*. N.Y.: Pathfinder Press, Inc., 1976.

Henderson, Laurence W. *Angola: Five Centuries of Conflict*. Ithaca, N.Y.: Cornell University Press, 1979.

Humbaraci, A. and N. Muchnik. *Portugal's African Wars*. London: MacMillan, 1974.

Klinghoffer, A. J. *The Angolan War: A Study in Soviet Policy in the Third World*. Boulder, Colo.: Westview, 1980.

Legum, Colin and Tony Hodges. *After Angola*. New York: Africana Publishing Corp., 1976.

Serrans, Carlos Mireina Henriques. "Angola (1961—1976), Bibliogrofia" *Journal of Southern African Affairs* 2 (1977): 295—32.

Marcum, John. *The Angolan Revolution, 1950—1962*. Cambridge, Mass.: Massachusetts Institute of Technology Press, 1969.

Marcum, J. A. *The Angolan Revolution: Volume II, Exile Politics and Guerrilla Warfare, 1962—1976*. Cambridge: MIT Press, 1978.

Okuma, Thomas. *Angola in Ferment: The Background and Prospects of Angolan Nationalism*. Boston: Beacon Press, 1962.

Stockwell, John. *In Search of Enemies: A CIA Story*. N.Y.: W. W. Norton and Company, Inc., 1978.

ECONOMIC

Hammond, Richard J. *Portugal's African Problem: Some Economic Facets*. New York: Carnegie Endowment for Peace, 1962. Occasional Paper, No. 21.

Hance, William and I. S. Van Dongen. "The Port of Lobito and the Benguela Railway." *Geographical Review*, 46 (October 1956): 460–487

SOCIAL

Davidson, Basil. *In the Eye of the Storm: Angola's People*. New York: Doubleday, 1972.

Edwards, A. C. *The Ovimbundu Under Two Sovereignties*. London: Oxford, 1962.

Estermann, Carlos. *The Ethnography of Southwestern Angola, Volume 1: The Non-Bantu Peoples: The Ambo Ethnic Group*. New York: Africana Publishing Company, 1976.

Heimer, F. W. (ed.). *Social Change in Angola*. Munich: Weltforum Verlag, 1974.

International Labour Organisation. *Official Bulletin*, 45 (April 1962), Supplement II: 1-253.

Samuels, Michael. *Education in Angola, 1873—1914*. New York: Columbia University Teachers College Press, 1970.

2. Benin

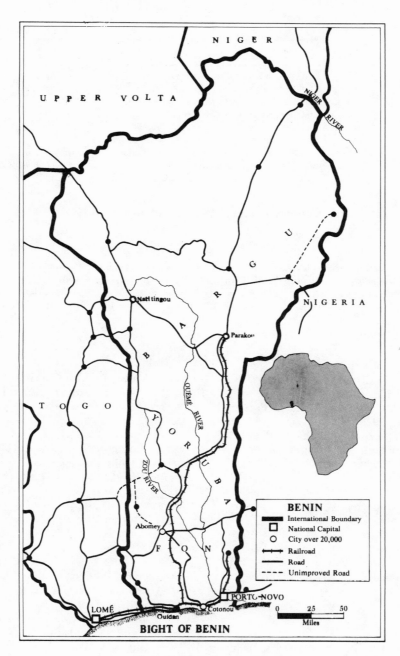

I. Basic Information

Date of Independence: August 1, 1960

Former Colonial Ruler: France

Change in Boundaries: Formerly part of the French West Africa Federation

Former Name: Dahomey (name change to Benin on December 1, 1975)

Most Widely Spoken Languages: Fon-Ewé—60%; Yoruba—14%

Estimated Population (1980): 3,464,000

Area Size (equivalent in U.S.): 43,484 sq. mi. (Tennessee)

Date of Last Census: 1961

Major Exports 1977 as Percent of Total Exports: palm products—23 percent; cotton lint—21 percent; cocoa beans—11 percent.

Official Language: French

II. Elite Political Instability

TABLE 2.1   **Elite Instability (Post-Independence)**

Date	Event
1. October 28, 1963	Coup d'État (Gen. Soglo overthrows Pres. Maga.)
2. December 22, 1965	Coup d'État (Gen. Soglo replaces Pres. Apithy.)
3. December 17, 1967	Coup d'État (Lt. Col. Alley overthrows General Soglo.)
4. December 10, 1969	Coup d'État (Army overthrows President Zinsou.)
5. February 23, 1972	Coup Attempt (Attempted coup by Kouandeté foiled.)
6. October 26, 1972	Coup d'État (Lt. Col. Kerekou overthrows Pres. Maga.)
7. January 21, 1975	Coup Attempt (Attempted coup by armored car unit led by Capt. Assogba.)
8. January 16, 1977	Coup Attempt (Foreign mercenaries land at Cotonou airport but fail to take over country.)

III.   Country Features Worthy of Special Study

1. Benin was a major slave center in West Africa.
2. Political conflict between peoples of three main cities (excluding Cotonou) is at the center of politics.
3. Has had one of the highest levels of elite instability in all the Black African countries especially in the 1960s.
4. Benin has a surplus educated wage-earning class, many of whom worked in other French-speaking West African countries, but were forced to return to Benin after these countries became independent. As a result 75% of Benin's national budget is expended on civil servants.

IV. Selected References

GENERAL

Cornevin, Robert. *Le Dahomey*. (2nd. ed.) Paris: Presses Universitaires de France, 1976

Decalo, S. *Historical Dictionary of Dahomey*. (People's Republic of Benin) Metuchen, N.J.: Scarecrow Press, 1976.

Morgan, W. B. and J. C. Pugh. *West Africa*. London: Methuen, 1969.

Pliya, Jean. *L'Histoire de mon pays*. Cotonou: Imprimerie Nationale du Dahomey, 1967.

Ronen, Dov. *Dahomey: Between Tradition and Modernity*. Ithaca, N.Y.: Cornell University Press, 1975.

Thompson, Virginia and Richard Adloff. *French West Africa*, pp. 139—145. Stanford, Ca.: Stanford University Press, 1957.

POLITICAL

Amir, Samin. *Neo-Colonialism in West Africa*. Harmondsworth, U.K.: Penguin, 1973.

Carter, Gwendolen M. (ed.) *Five African States*, N.Y.: Cornell University Press, 1963.

Decalo, S. *Coups and Army Rule in Africa*. New Haven: Yale University Press, 1976.

de Lusignan, Guy. *French-Speaking Africa since Independence*, pp. 159—169. London: Pall Mall Press, 1969.

Glélé, Maurice-A. *Naissance d'un État Noir*. Paris: Librairie Generale de Droit et de Jurisprudence, 1969.

La Republique de Dahomey. Paris: Berger Levrault, 1969.

Lemarchand, René. "Dahomey: Coup within a Coup." *Africa Report*, 13 (June 1968), pp. 46—54.

LeVine, Victor T. "The Coups in Upper Volta, Dahomey and the Central African Republic." In *Power and Protest in Black Africa*, eds. Robert I. Rotberg and Ali A. Mazrui, pp. 1035—1071. New York: Oxford University Press, 1970.

Terray, Emmanuel. "Les Revolutions Congolaise et *Dahomeenne* de 1963: Essai d'Interpretation." *Revue Française de Science Politique*, (October 1964), pp. 917—942.

Thompson, V. *West Africa's Council of Entente*. Ithaca, N.Y.: Cornell University Press, 1972.

ECONOMIC

International Monetary Fund. "Dahomey." In *Surveys of African Economics*, Vol. 3, Washington, D.C.: I.M.F., 1970.

Serreau, Jean. *Le Developpement à la base au Dahomey et au Senegal*. Paris: Librairie Generale de Droit et de Jurisprudence, 1966.

SOCIAL

Herskovitz, M. *Dahomey: An Ancient West African Kingdom*. Evanston, Ill.: Northwestern University Press, (1938), 1967.

Tardits, Claude. *Porto Novo: Les nouvelles generations africaines entre leur traditions et l'Occident*. The Hague: Mouton, 1958.

3. Botswana

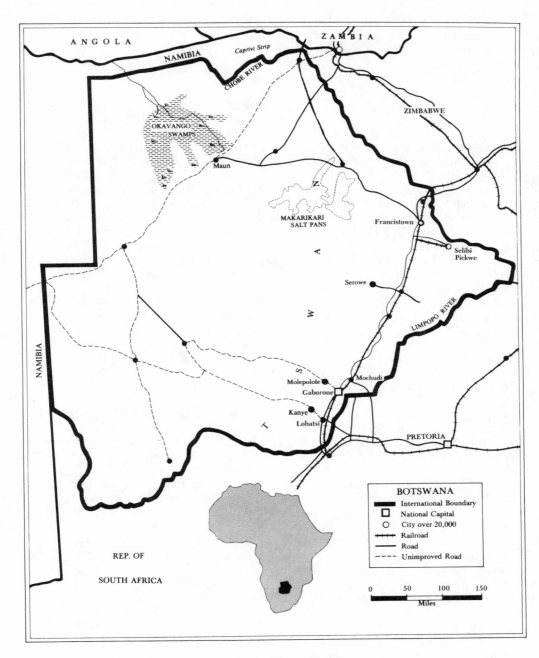

I. Basic Information

Date of Independence: September 30, 1966
Former Colonial Ruler: United Kingdom
Former Name: Bechuanaland
Estimated Population (1980): 787,000
Area Size (equivalent in U.S.): 231,805 sq. mi. (twice Arizona)

Most Widely Spoken Languages: Setswana—98%; Shona—1%

Major Exports 1977 as Percent of Total Exports: diamonds—31 percent; meat and meat products—27 percent; copper-nickel matte—26 percent

Official Languages: English, Tswana

III.   Country Features Worthy of Special Study

1. Buffer state between black and white controlled Africa.
2. Newly discovered mineral wealth coupled with small population gives promise of rapid development.
3. Ethnically homogeneous.

IV. Selected References

BIBLIOGRAPHY

Mohome, Paulus, and John B. Webster. *A Bibliography of Bechuanaland*. Occasional Bibliography No. 5. Syracuse, N.Y.: Syracuse University Program of Eastern African Studies, 1966.

Mutter, Theo and Bernhard Weimer. *Botswana Research Directory 1976: A Compilation of Projects and Reports*. Gaborone: National Institute for Research in Development and African Studies, Documentation Unit, 1977.

Stevens, R. P. *Historical Dictionary of the Republic of Botswana*. Metuchen, N.J.: Scarecrow, 1975.

Webster, John B., et al. *A Supplement to a Bibliography on Bechuanaland*. Occasional Bibliography No. 12. Syracuse, N.Y.: Syracuse University Program of Eastern African Studies, 1968.

GENERAL

Alverson, Hoyt. *Mind in the Heart of Darkness: Value and Self-Identity among the Tswana of Southern Africa*. New Haven, Conn.: Yale University Press, 1978.

Cervenka, Z. *Republic of Botswana: A Brief Outline of its Geographical Setting, History, Economy, and Politics*. Uppsala: Scandanavian Institute of African Studies, 1970.

Cervenka, Z., C. Donat, H. Lab and W. Lonski. *Botswana, Lesotho, and Swaziland*. Bern: Neue Reihe, 1974.

Chirenje, J. Mutero. *A History of Northern Botswana, 1850—1910*. Cranbury, N.J.: Fairleigh Dickinson University Press, 1977.

Dale, Richard. *Botswana and Its Southern Neighbor*. Athens, Ohio: Ohio University, 1970.

Griffiths, W.R. (Comp.) *Botswana: Some Basic Geographical Facts*. Gaborone: Government Printer, 1970.

Munger, Edwin S. *Bechuanaland, Pan-African Outpost or Bantu Homeland?* London: Oxford University Press, 1965.

Sillery, Anthony. *Botswana: A Short Political History*. London: Methuen, 1974.

Stevens, Richard. *Lesotho, Botswana and Swaziland*. London: Pall Mall Press, 1967.

Young, Bertram A. *Bechuanaland*. London: Her Majesty's Stationery Office, 1966

POLITICAL

Colclough, C. and S. McCarthy. *The Political Economy of Botswana*. New York: Oxford University Press, 1979.

Halpern, J. *South Africa's Hostages*. Baltimore: Penguin Books. 1965.

Khama, Seretse. *Botswana: A Developing Democracy in Southern Africa*. Uppsala, Scandanavian Institute of African Studies, 1970.

Kuper, Adam. *Kalahari Village Politics: An African Democracy*. Cambridge: Cambridge University Press, 1970.

MacArtney W. A. J. "Botswana Goes to the Polls." *Africa Report* 14 (December 1969): 28—30.

Parson, Jack. "Political Culture in Rural Botswana: A Survey Result." In *Journal of Modern African Studies*, London, December 1977, pp. 639—650.

Picard, Louis A. "Bureaucrats, Cattle, and Public Policy: Land Tenure Changes in Botswana." *Comparative Political Studies* 13:313—56.

Schapera, Isaac. *Government and Politics in Tribal Societies*. New York: Schocken, 1970.

Vengroff, R. *Botswana: Rural Development in the Shadow of Apartheid*. Cranbury, N.J.: Fairleigh Dickinson University Press, 1977.

ECONOMIC

Colclough, Christopher and S. McCarthy. The *Political Economy of Botswana*. New York: Oxford University Press, 1980.

Hartland-Thunberg, Penelope. *Botswana: An African Growth Economy*. Boulder, Col.: Westview Press, 1978.

Hogblom, Goran. *Botswana*. Uppsala: Agricultural College of Sweden, 1973.

International Monetary Fund. "Botswana" in *Surveys of African Economies*. Vol. 5. Washington, D.C.: I.M.F., 1973.

Reynolds, Norman. *Rural Development in Botswana*. Capetown: University of Capetown, School of Economics, 1977.

Selwyn, Percy. *Industries in the Southern African Periphery*. London: Croom Helm, Ltd., 1975.

Smith P. *Botswana: Resources and Development*. Pretoria: African Institute, 1970.

SOCIAL

Rose, Brian. "Education in Botswana, Lesotho and Swaziland." In *Education in Southern Africa*, ed. B. Rose. London: Collier-Macmillan, 1970.

Russell, Margo and Martin. *Afrikaners of the Kalahari: White Minority in a Black State*. London: Cambridge University Press, 1979.

Schapera, Isaac. *The Tswana*. Ethnographic Survey of Africa. Southern Africa, Pt. 3. London: International African Institute, 1953.

Vivelo, Frank R. *The Herero of Western Botswana: Aspects of Change in a Group of Bantu-Speaking Cattle Herders*. St. Paul, Minn.: West Publishing Co., 1976.

4. Burundi

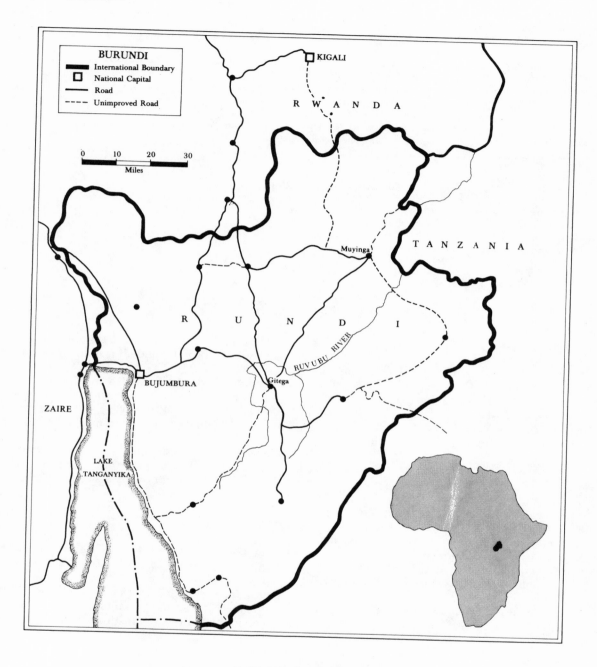

I. Basic Information

Date of Independence: July 1, 1962
Former Colonial Ruler: Belgium
Change in Boundaries: Split from pre-independence UN
 Trust territory of Ruanda-Urundi in 1962
Former Name: Urundi (in Ruanda-Urundi)
Estimated Population (1980): 4,429,000

Area Size (equivalent in U.S.): 10,747 sq. mi. (New
 Hampshire and Delaware)
Date of Last Census: 1970/71
Major Export 1978 as Percent of Total Exports: coffee—
 85 percent.

Most Widely Spoken Languages: Kirundi—90%;
 Swahili—5%

Official Language: French

II. Elite Political Instability

TABLE 4.1   Elite Instability (Post- Independence)

Date	Event
1. January 15, 1965	Assassination of Prime Minister Albin Nyamoya.
2. October 18, 1965	Coup Attempt (Hutu attempt to take power.)
3. July 8, 1966	Coup d'État (Mwami [king] deposed by his son.)
4. November 28, 1966	Coup d'État (Capt. Micombero takes power from Ntare.)
5. March 1972	Coup Attempt (King Ntare V returns to take power and is killed shortly thereafter.)
6. November 2, 1976	Coup d'État (Micombero ousted by army.)

III.   Country Features Worthy of Special Study

1. One of the most densely populated states in Africa.
2. Long history of ethnic conflict (Hutu-Tutsi) and political instability.
3. One of the few countries where a tribal minority has clung to power.
4. One of the poorest countries in the world.

IV. Selected References

BIBLIOGRAPHY

Nahayo, S. "Contribution à la bibliographie des ouvrage relatifs au Burundi (Afrique Central)" in 3 parts. *Geneve-Afrique*, 10, 1; 10, 2; 11, 1 (1971—72) pp. 92—99; 100—11; 94—104.

Nyambariza, Daniel. *Le Burundi: essai à une bibliographie 1959—1973*, Bujumbura: Université du Burundi,

GENERAL

Lemarchand, René. *Rwanda and Burundi*. New York: Praeger, 1970.

Nsanze, T. *L'Edification de la Republique du Burundi*. Brussels: Remarques Africaines, 1970.

U.S. Department of the Army. *Area Handbook for Burundi*. Washington, D.C.: Government Printing Office, 1969.

Weinstein, W. *Historical Dictionary of Burundi*. Metuchen, N.J.: Scarecrow, 1976.

POLITICAL

Bowen, Michael, *Passing By: The United States and Genocide in Burundi, 1972*. Washington: Carnegie Endowment for International Peace, 1973.

Chronique de Politique Etrangère. *Decolonisation et Independence de Rwanda et du Burundi*. Brussels: Institut Royal des Relations Internationales, 1963.

Lemarchand, René. "Political Instability in Africa: The Case of Rwanda and Burundi." *Civilisations*, 16 (1966): 307—337.

Lemarchand, René. "Social Change and Political Modernisation in Burundi." *Journal of Modern African Studies*, 4 (1966): 401—433.

Melady, Thomas P. *Burundi: The Tragic Years*. Maryknoll, N.Y.: Orbis, 1974.

Weinstein, Warren. *Political Conflict and Ethnic Strategies: A Case Study of Burundi*. Syracuse, N.Y.: Syracuse University, Maxwell School of Citizenship and Public Affairs, 1976.

ECONOMIC

International Monetary Fund. "Burundi" in *Surveys of African Economies*, Vol. 5. Washington, D.C.: I.M.F., 1973.

Leurquin, Philippe P. *Agricultural Change in Ruanda-Burundi 1945—1960*. Stanford, Calif.: Stanford University Food Research Institute, 1963.

SOCIAL

Baeck, L. *Étude socio-economique du centre extra-coutumier d'Usumbura*. Brussels: Academie Royale des Sciences Coloniales, 1957.

Liege Université. Foundation pour les recherches scientifiques au Congo Belge et au Ruanda-Urundi. *Le problème de l'enseignement dans le Ruanda-Urundi*. Elizabethville: C.E.P.S.I., 1958.

5. Cameroon

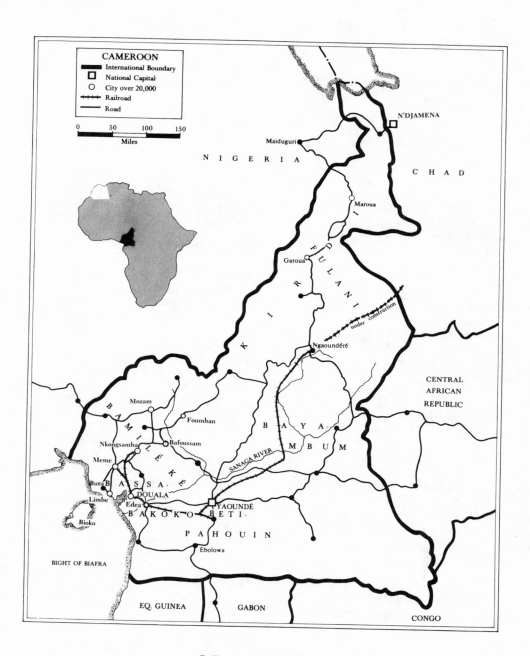

I. Basic Information

Date of Independence: January 1, 1960 (West Cameroon became independent in October, 1961)

Former Colonial Rulers: France and United Kingdom

Changes in Boundaries: The Southern Cameroons (British) voted to become part of the Cameroon Republic (French) on February 11, 1961

Former Names: Cameroun (Fr.), Kamerun (Ger.), Cameroon Federal Republic

Most Widely Spoken Languages: Beti-Pahouin—24%; Bamiléké—18%

Estimated Population (1980): 8,332,000

Area Size (equivalent in U.S.): 183,569 sq. mi. (Oregon and Washington)

Date of Last Census: 1976

Major Exports 1978 as Percent of Total Exports: coffee—29 percent, cocoa and derivatives—34 percent, wood—12 percent, aluminum—4 percent, cotton products—4 percent

Official Language: French

III. Country Features Worthy of Special Study

1. Cameroon is the only Black African country resulting from the union of a former British and a former French colony. As such it had to face unique problems of integration.
2. Especially diverse ethnically.
3. Despite such considerable diversity it is one of the most stable countries in Africa.

IV. Selected References

BIBLIOGRAPHY

Delancey, Mark and Virginia Delancey. *A Bibliography of Cameroon*. New York: Africana, 1975.

LeVine, V. T. and R. P. Nye. *Historical Dictionary of Cameroon*. Metuchen, N.J.: Scarecrow, 1974.

GENERAL

De Lancey, M. *Cameroon*. Boulder, Colo.: Westview, 1981.

Eyongetoh, Tambi and Robert Brain. *A History of the Cameroon*. London: Longman, 1974.

Lembezat, Bertrand. *Le Cameroun*. Paris: Nouvelles Editions Latines, 1965.

LeVine, Victor T. *Cameroon Federal Republic*. Ithaca, N.Y.: Cornell University Press, 1971.

LeVine, Victor T. *The Cameroon: From Mandate to Independence*. Berkeley, Ca.: University of California Press, 1964.

Mveng, Englebert. *Histoire du Cameroun*. Paris: Presence Africaine, 1963.

Rubin, Neville. *Cameroun: An African Federation*. New York: Praeger, 1971

U.S. Department of the Army. *Area Handbook for the United Republic of Cameroon*. Washington, D.C.: Government Printing Office, 1974.

POLITICAL

Ardener, Edwin. "The Nature of Reunification of Cameroon." In *African Integration and Disintegration*, ed. A. Hazelwood. London: Oxford University Press, 1967.

Azarya, Victor. *Aristocrats Facing Change: The Fulbe in Guinea, Nigeria, and Cameroon*. Chicago: University of Chicago Press, 1978.

Boyast, J. F. "One-Party Government and Political Development in Cameroun." *African Affairs*, 72 (April 1973): 125—144.

Gardinier, David E. *Cameroon: United Nations Challenge to French Policy*. London: Oxford University Press, 1963.

Joseph, R. A. *Radical Nationalism in Cameroun: Social Origins of the U.P.C. Rebellion*. Oxford: Clarendon Press, 1977.

Johnson, Willard R. *The Cameroon Federation: Political Integration in a Fragmentary Society*. Princeton, N.J.: Princeton University Press, 1969.

de Lusignan, Guy. *French-Speaking Africa Since Independence*: 121-132. New York: Praeger, 1969.

Welch, Claude, Jr. *Dream of Unity*. Ithaca, N.Y.: Cornell University Press, 1966.

ECONOMIC

Clignet, R. *The Africanization of the Labor Market: Educational and Occupational Segmentation in the Cameroons*. Berkeley: University of California Press, 1976.

Clignet, R. "Economic Development and Employment in Eastern Cameroon." *International Labour Review*, 85 (June 1962): 601—611.

Green, R. H. "The Economy of Cameroon Federal Republic." In *The Economies of Africa*, eds. P. Robson and D. A. Lury, pp. 236—286. Evanston, Ill.: Northwestern University Press, 1969.

Hugon, Philippe. *Analyse du sous-developpment en Afrique Noire: l'exemple de l'economie du Cameroun*. Paris: Presses Universitaires de France, 1968.

International Monetary Fund. "Federal Republic of Cameroon." In *Surveys of African Economies*, Vol. 1. Washington, D.C.: I.M.F., 1968.

Kendrick, Robin. *A Survey of Labor Relations in Cameroon*. Ann Arbor, Mich.: University of Michigan, 1976.

Ndongoko, Wilfred A. *Planning for Economic Development in a Federal State: The Case of Cameroon, 1960—1971*. München, Weltforum Verlag, 1975.

Wells, Frederick A. *Studies in Industrialization: Nigeria and the Cameroons*. London: Oxford University Press, 1962.

SOCIAL

Ardener, Edwin, et al. *Plantation and Village in the Cameroons: Some Economic and Social Studies*. London: Oxford University, 1960.

Guillard, Joanny. *Golonpoui: analyse des conditions de modernisation d'un village du Nord-Cameroun*. Paris: Mouton, 1965.

Meek, C. K. *Land Tenure and Land Administration in Nigeria and the Cameroons*. London: Her Majesty's Stationery Office, 1957.

Vernon-Jackson, H. O. H. *Language, Schools and Government in Cameroon*. New York: Teachers College Press, 1967.

Weekes-Vagliani, W. *Family Life and Structure in Southern Cameroon*. Paris, OECD, 1976.

6. Central African Republic (CAR)

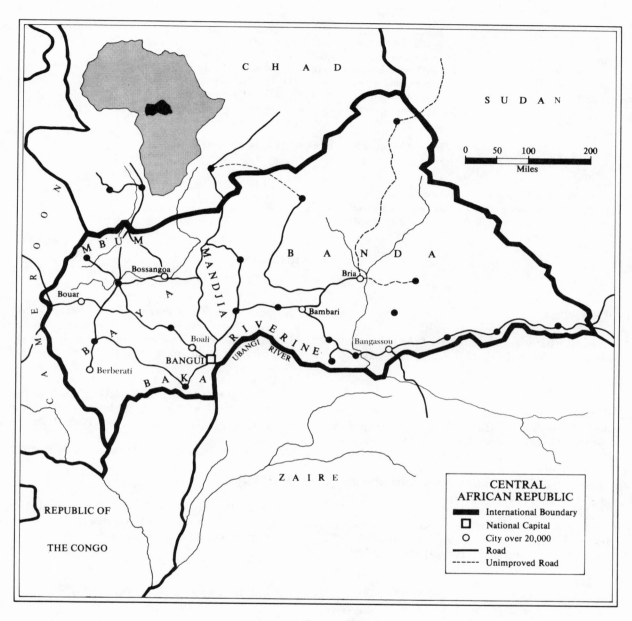

I. Basic Information

Date of Independence: August 13, 1960
Former Colonial Ruler: France
Change in Boundaries: Formerly part of French Equatorial Africa
Former Names: Ubangi-Shair, Oubangui-Chari, Central African Empire
Estimate Population (1980): 1,996,000*
Area Size (equivalent in U.S.): 240,535 sq. mi. (Texas and Minnesota)

Most Widely Spoken Languages: Banda—31%; Baya—29%; Sango—25%

Date of Last Census: 1975 (sample survey)
Major Exports 1978 as Percent of Total Exports: diamonds—38 percent; coffee—30 percent; wood—16 percent.

Official Language: French

*The 1968 census figure of 2,255,536 is not accepted by international agencies.

II.   Elite Political Instability

TABLE 6.1   Elite Instability (Post- Independence)

Date	Event
1. January 1, 1966	Coup d'État (Col. Bokassa overthrows Pres. Dacko.)
2. February 5, 1976	Coup Attempt (Army men unsuccessfully attempt to assassinate Bokassa.)
3. September 23, 1979	Coup d'État (While out of the country, Bokassa is deposed by Dacko backed by French troops.)
4. September 1, 1981	(Colonel Kolingba takes power from Dacko apparently with Dacko's cooperation.)
5. March 3, 1982	(Army units attempt to overthrow Kolingba but are repulsed.)

III.   Country Features Worthy of Special Study

1. Very sparsely populated with severe transportation problems.
2. Continued presence of large numbers of French government officials.
3. Landlocked and dependent on Cameroon and Congo for access to the sea.

IV. Selected References

BIBLIOGRAPHY

Kalck, Pierre. *Historical Dictionary of the Central African Republic*. Metuchem, N.J. Scarecrow, 1980.

GENERAL

Ballard, John A. "Four Equatorial States: Congo, Gabon, Ubangi-Shari, Chad." In *National Unity and Regionalism in Eight African States*, ed. Gwendolen M. Carter, pp. 231—329. Ithaca, N.Y.: Cornell University Press, 1966.

Kalck, P. *Historie de la republique centrafricaine des origins prehistoriques a nos jours*. Paris: Berger-Levrault, 1974.

Thompson, Virginia and Richard Adloff. *The Emerging States of French Equatorial Africa*, pp, 385—425. Stanford, Calif.: Stanford University Press, 1960.

POLITICAL

de Lusignan, Guy. *French-Speaking Africa since Independence*, pp. 108—114. London: Pall Mall Press, 1969.

Kalck, Pierre. *The Central African Republic*: *A Failure in de-Colonization*. New York, Praeger, 1971.

LeVine, Victor T. "The Central African Republic: Insular Problems of an Inland State." *Africa Report*, 10 (November 1965): 17—23.

LeVine, Victor T. "The Coups in Upper Volta, Dahomey and the Central African Republic." In *Power and Protest in Black Africa*, eds. Robert I Rotbert and Ali A. Mazrui, pp. 1035—1071. New York: Oxford University Press, 1970.

Péan, Pierre. *Bokassa ler*. Paris, ed. A. Moreau, 1977.

ECONOMIC

International Monetary Fund. "The Central African Republic." In *Surveys of African Economies*, Vol. 1. Washington, D.C.: I.M.F., 1968.

SOCIAL

Lebeuf, Jean-Paul. *Bangui*. Paris, 1954.

7. Chad

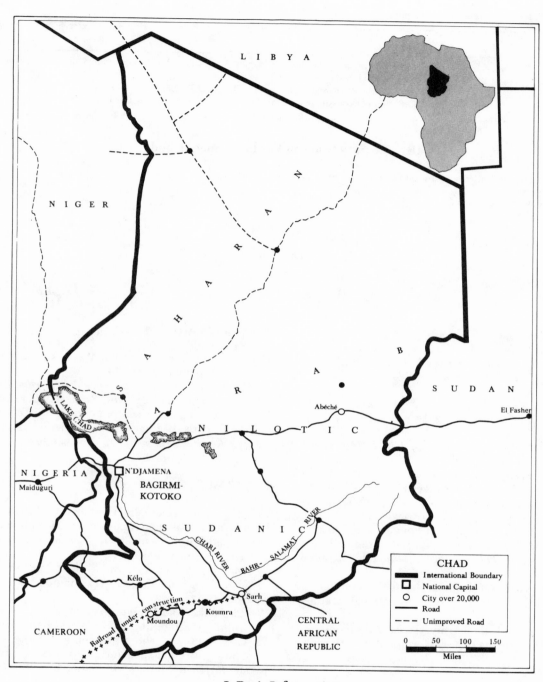

I. Basic Information

Date of Independence: August 11, 1960
Former Colonial Ruler: France
Change in Boundaries: Formerly part of French Equatorial Africa
Estimated Population (1980): 4,627,000

Most Widely Spoken Languages: Mande—44%; Kru-Bassa—37%

Area Size (equivalent in U.S.): 496,000 sq. mi. (Texas, new Mexico, and Oklahoma)
Date of Last Census: 1968
Major Exports 1978 as Percent of Total Exports: cotton—69 percent; cattle—10 percent.

Official Language: English

II. Elite Political Instability

TABLE 7.1 Elite Instability (Post- Independence)

Date	Event
1. April 13, 1975	Coup d'État (Army units under the Acting Army Chief of Staff, Gen. Noel Odingar, overthrow Tombalbaye who was killed in the fighting.)
2. April, 1976	Coup Attempt (Assassination attempt by FROLINAT against Malloum.)
3. March 31, 1977	Coup Attempt (Assassination against Malloum by members of the Garde Nomade fails.)

III. Country Features Worthy of Special Study

1. Prolonged violent conflict between Arabs and Black Africans.
2. Landlocked country.
3. Severely affected by 1970's drought.

IV. Selected References

BIBLIOGRAPHY

Bibliographie du Tchad (sciences humaines) 2nd ed revue et corrigee 1970. Ndjamena, 1974.

GENERAL

Decalo, S. *Historical Dictionary of Chad.* Metuchen, N.J.: Scarecrow Press, 1977.

De Proni, I. "Population, production and culture in the plains-society of northern Cameroon and Chad: the anthropologist in development projects." *Current Anthropology*, 1978 v. 9, pp. 42—57, 208—09.

Digulmbaye, Georges, and Robert Langue. *L'Essence du Tchad.* Paris: Presses Universitaires de France, 1969.

Hugot, Pierre. *Le Tchad.* Paris: Nouvelle Editions Latines, 1965.

Thompson, Virginia, and Richard Adloff. *Conflict in Chad.* Berkeley: Institute of International Studies, 1981.

U.S. Department of the Army. *Area Handbook for Chad.* Washington, D.C. Government Printing Office, 1972.

POLITICAL

Ballard, John A. "Four Equatorial States: Congo, Gabon, Ubangi-Shari, Chad." In *National Unity and Regionalism in Eight African States*, ed. Gwendolen M. Carter, pp. 231—329. Ithaca, N.Y.: Cornell University Press, 1966.

Bouquet, Christian. *Tchad: genèse d'un conflit.* Paris: L'Harmattan, 1982.

Decraene, Philippe. "Chad at World's End." *Africa Report*, 13 (January 1968): 54.

de Lusignan, Guy. *French-Speaking Africa since Independence*, pp. 114-21. New York: Praeger, 1969.

Le Cornec, Jacques. *Histoire Politique du Tchad de 1900 à 1962.* Paris: R. Pichon et R. Durand-Auzias, 1963.

Lycett, Andrew. "Chad's Disastrous Civil War." *Africa Report*, 23, 5, pp. 4—7.

ECONOMIC

Cabot, Jean. *Le Tchad* 2nd ed. Paris: PUF, 1978.

International Labour Organization. "Employment Position and Problems in Chad." *International Labour Review*, 85 (1962): 500—07.

International Monetary Fund. "Chad." In *Surveys of African Economies*, Vol. 1. Washington, D.C.: I.M.F., 1968.

World Bank. *Chad: Development Potential and Constraints.* Washington, D.C.: World Bank, 1974.

Yansane, Aguibou: Some problems of monetary dependency in French-speaking West African States. *Journal of African Studies*, vol. 5, no. 4, 1978: 444-76.

SOCIAL

Lebeuf, Annie. *Les Populations du Tchad.* Paris: Presses universitaires de France, 1959.

8. Congo

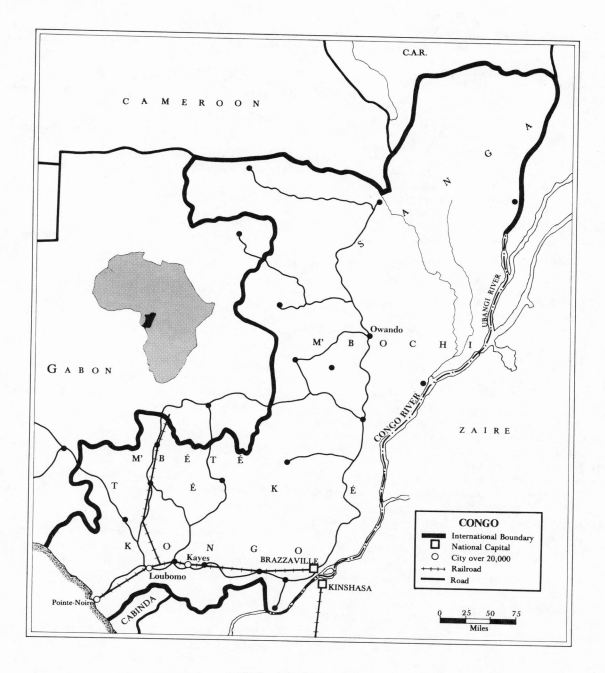

I. Basic Information

Date of Independence: August 15, 1960
Former Colonial Ruler: France
Change in Boundaries: Formerly part of French Equatorial Africa
Former Names: Moyen Congo; Congo (Brazzaville)
Estimated Population (1980): 1,544,000
Most Widely Spoken Languages: Kikongo—52%; Teke—20%

Area Size (equivalent in U.S.): 132,047 sq. mi. (Montana)
Date of Last Census: 1974
Major Exports 1977 as Percent of Total Exports: Crude petroleum—53 percent; timber—17 percent.
Official Language: French

II.   Elite Political Instability

TABLE 8.1   **Elite Instability (Post-Independence)**

Date	Event
1. August 15, 1963	Coup d'État (Army forces Youlou's resignation; Massemba-Debat replaces him.)
2. May 13, 1968	Coup attempt (Unnamed mercenaries led by Jacques Debreton, a European, captured some prisoners in an attempted coup.)
3. August 3, 1968	Coup d'État (Capt. Ngouabi overthrows Massemba-Debat.)
4. November 7, 1969	Coup Attempt (Fourteen people were sentenced to death for participating in a coup attempt about which little is known.)
5. March 22—23, 1970	Coup Attempt (Lt. Kikanga leads an invasion from Zaire in an attempted coup d'état.)
6. February 22, 1972	Coup Attempt (Lt. Ange Diawar, a leftist revolutionary, tries to overthrow Ngouabi, and is hunted and killed in April 1973.)
7. March 18, 1977	Coup Attempt (Ngouabi assassinated by members of the Palace Guard who fail to take control of the government.)
8. February 8, 1979	Coup d'État (Gen. Yhombi-Opango overthrown by the army.)

III.   Country Features Worthy of Special Study

1. Avowedly a revolutionary socialist state.
2. Highest level of urbanization of all the Black African countries.
3. A small population that is relatively well off but beset by internecine conflict.

IV. Selected References

GENERAL

Sautter, Gilles. *De l'Atlantique au fleuve Congo, une geographie du sous-peuplement: Republique du Congo; Republique Gabonaise.* 2 vols. Paris: Mouton, 1966.

Soret, Marcel. *History du Congo: Capitale Brazzaville.* Paris: Berger-Levrault, 1978.

Thompson, V. and R. Adloff. *Historical Dictionary of the Congo (Brazzaville).* Metuchen, N.J.: Scarecrow Press, 1974.

U.S. Department of the Army. *Area Handbook for People's Republic of the Congo (Congo Brazzaville).* Washington, D.C.: Government Printing Office, 1971.

Vennetier, Pierre, *Geographie du Congo-Brazzaville.* Paris: Gautheir-Villars, 1966.

Wagret, Jean Michel. *Histoire et sociologie politiques de la Republique du Congo (Brazzaville).* Paris: Librarie Generale de Droit et de Jurisprudence, 1963.

POLITICAL

Ballard, John A. "Four Equatorial States: Congo, Gabon, Ubangi-Shari, Chad." In *National Unity and Regionalism in Eight African States,* ed. Gwendolen M. Carter, pp. 231—329. Ithaca, N.Y.: Cornell University Press, 1966.

Calvocoress, P. *The Congo in World Politics since 1945,* pp. 340—53. London: Longman, 1977.

de Lusignan, Guy. *French-Speaking Africa since Independence,* pp. 91—100. London: Pall Mall Press, 1969.

Gause, René with Viriginia Thompson and Richard Adloff. *The Politics of Congo-Brazzaville.* Stanford, Calif.: Hoover Institution Press, 1973.

Terrary, Emmanuel. "Les Revolutions Congolaise et Dahomeenne de 1963: Essai d'Interpretation." *Revue Française de Science Politique* (October 1964): 917—42.

ECONOMIC

Amin, Samir and Catherin Coquery-Vidrovitch. *Histoire Économique du Congo, 1888—1968.* Paris: Editions Anthropos. 1969.

Bertrand, Hugues. *Le Congo: formation sociale et mode à developpement economique.* Paris: Maspero, 1975.

International Monetary Fund. "Congo-Brazzaville." In *Surveys of African Economies,* Vol. 1. Washington, D.C.: I.M.F., 1968.

SOCIAL

Andersson, Efrain. *Churches at the Grass Roots: A Study of Congo-Brazzaville.* London: Lutterworth, 1968.

Andersson, Efrain. *Messianic Popular Movements in the Lower Congo.* Uppsala: Almqvist and Wiksells, 1958.

Balandier, Georges. *Sociologie actuelle de L'Afrique Noire,* 2nd. Ed. Paris: Presses universitaires de France, 1963.

Ctoce-Spinelli, Michel. *Les enfants de Poto-Poto.* Paris: Editions Bernard Grasset, 1967.

Elbou, Marie. *La formation de la conscience nationale en Republique populaire du Congo.* Paris, Anthropos, 1977.

Lissouba, Pascal. *Conscience du développement et democratic ,* Dakar: Nouvelles Editions Africaines, 1975.

9. Djibouti

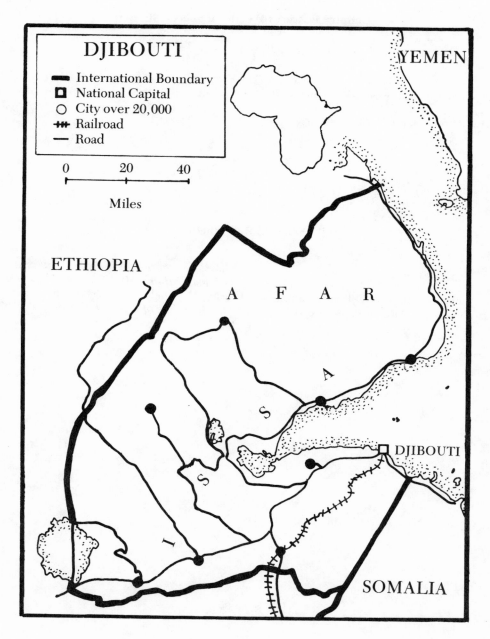

I. Basic Information

Date of Independence: June 27, 1977
Former Colonial Ruler: France
Change in Boundaries: Before independence it was known as the French territory of the Afars and the Issas.
Former Name: French Somaliland
Most Widely Spoken Language: Arabic

Estimated Population (1980): 361,000
Area Size (equivalent in U.S.): 8,800 sq. mi. (New Hampshire)
Date of Last Census: 1976
Major Exports 1976 as Percent of Total Exports: skins and leather—4 percent
Official Language: Arabic

III.   Country Features Worthy of Special Study

1. Country a focus of conflict between Somalia which seeks to integrate the Somali population and Ethiopia which depends on the port of Djibouti for much of its supplies.
2. A largely desert country, Ethiopia's principal outlet to the sea.

IV. Selected References

BIBLIOGRAPHY

Clarke, W. Sheldon. "The Republic of Djibouti—an introduction to Africa's newest state and a review of related literature and sources." *Current Bibliography of African Affairs*, 10 (1977—1978), 3—31.

Clarke, W. Sheldon. *A Developmental Bibliography for the Republic of Djibouti*. (Djibouti), (1979), (246) p.

10. Equatorial Guinea

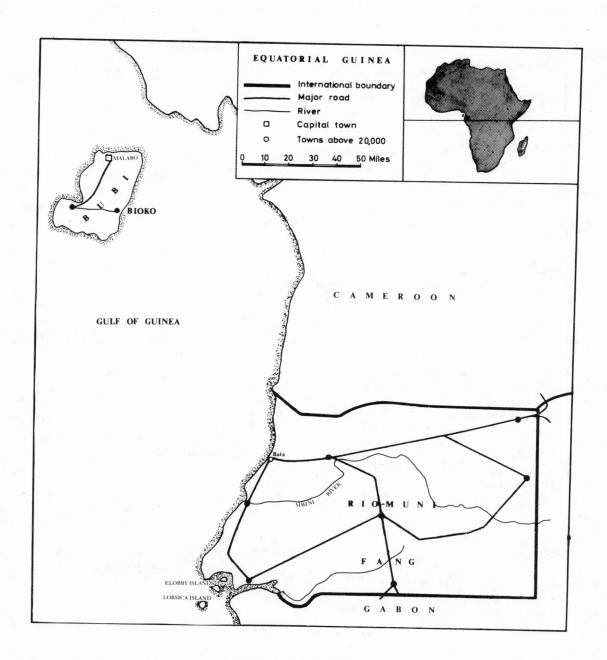

I. Basic Information

Date of Independence: October 12, 1968
Former Colonial Ruler: Spain
Change in Boundaries: The former Rio Muni and Fernando Po were merged
Former Names: Rio Muni and Fernando Po
Estimated Population (1980): 340,000*
Area Size (equivalent in U.S.): 10,830 sq. mi. (Vermont)
Date of Last Census: 1960

Most Widely Spoken Language: Fang—85%

Major Exports as Percent of Total Exports: no information available—principal exports are cocoa, coffee and timber

Official Language: Spanish

*Reports indicate that a large part of the country's population fled to neighboring countries (Gabon and Cameroon)

II.   Elite Political Instability

TABLE 10.1   Elite Instability (Post- Independence)

Date	Event
1. March 5, 1969	Attempted Coup (Foreign Minister, Antanasio Ndongo attempted to overthrow Nguema.)
2. March 15—20, 1969	Coup d'État (President suspends the constitution.)
3. August 3, 1979	Coup d'État (Macias Nguema overthrown by Army.)

III.   Country Features Worthy of Special Study

1. Only former Spanish colony in equatorial Africa.
2. Country composed of three non-contiguous parts.
3. Smallest population of all Black African countries.

IV. Selected References

BIBLIOGRAPHY

Berman, S. *Spanish Guinea: An Annotated Bibliography*. Washington, D.C.: Catholic University Libraries, 1961.

Liniger-Goumaz, M. *Historical Dictionary of Equatorial Guinea*. Metuchen, N.J.: The Scarecrow Press, Inc., 1979.

Liniger-Goumaz, M. *Guinea Ecuatorial: Bibliografia General*. Bern: Commu. Natu. Suisse UNESCO, 2nd. edition (no date); 1st edition (1974).

GENERAL

Great Britain Foreign Office Historical Section. *Spanish and Italian Possessions: Independent States*. Greenwich, Conn.: Greenwood Press, 1969.

Pelissier, René. *Etudes Hispano-guineennes*. Paris: 1967.

Pelissier, René. *Los Territorios Espanoles de Africa*. Madrid: C.S.I.C., 1964.

Pelissier, René. "Spanish Guinea—An Introduction." *Race*, 6 (October 1964): 117—128.

POLITICAL

"African Political Parties in Equatorial Africa, 1968." *Africa Report*, (March 1968).

Pelissier, René. "Uncertainties in Spanish Guinea." *Africa Report* (March 1968): 16—18.

ECONOMIC

International Monetary Fund. "Equatorial Guinea" in *Surveys of African Economies*, vol. 5. Washington, D.C.: I.M.F., 1973.

Kobel, Armen Eric. *La Republique de Guinée équatoriale*. Berne, Copy Quick, 1976.

Pelissier, R. "Autopsy of a Miracle." *Africa Report*, 1970, no. 75, pp. 10—14.

11. Ethiopia

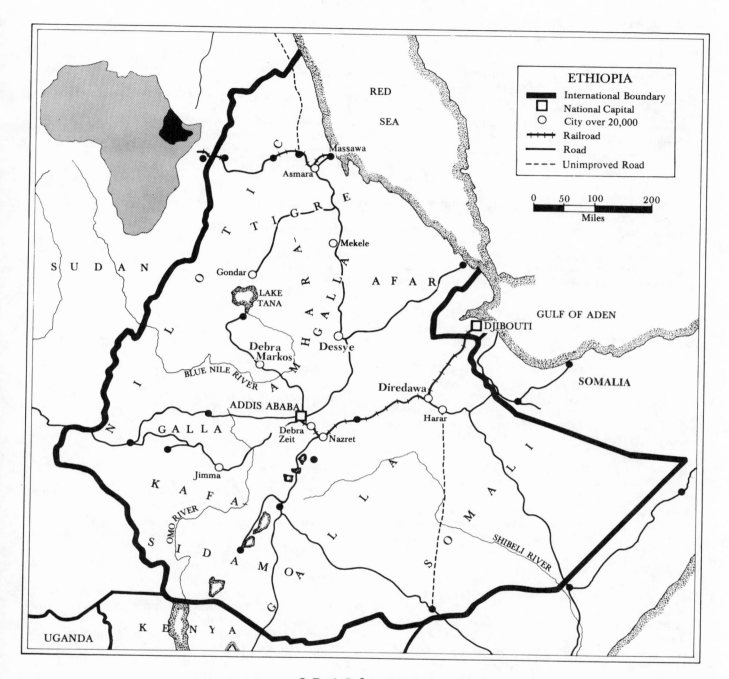

I. Basic Information

Date of Independence: Ancient kingdom
Former Colonial Ruler: None
Change in Boundaries: Eritrea added in 1952
Former Name: Both Ethiopia and Abyssinia are ancient names for the nation
Estimated Population (1980): 33,598,000

Most Widely Spoken Languages: Gallinya—50%; Amharic—40%

Area Size (equivalent in U.S.): 471,778 sq. mi. (Texas and Montana)
Date of Last Census: None ever held
Major Exports 1976 as Percent of Total Exports: coffee—56 percent; hides and skins—9 percent; pulses (seeds)—10 percent; oil seeds—5 percent.

Official Language: Amharic

II. Elite Political Instability

TABLE 11.1   Elite Instability (Post- Independence)

Date	Event
1. December 14—17, 1960	Coup Attempt (Staged while Selassie was out of the country. He returned and defeated the attempt led by members of the Imperial Guard.)
2. November 22, 1974	Coup d'État (Gen. Andon is killed after an internal dispute with other leaders of the provisional Military Government.)
3. February 3, 1977	Coup d'État (Gen. Benti murdered by Army units under Col. Mengistu and others.)
4. November 12, 1977	Coup d'État (Col. Atnafu executed under orders of Col. Mengistu.)

III. Country Features Worthy of Special Study

1. Traditional Amhara-Tigre culture is at the peasant rather than the tribal level of social organization, unlike most of Black Africa. It is especially resistant to social change.
2. Formerly the only absolute monarchy in independent Black Africa and the world's oldest continuing Christian-based kingdom.
3. Amalgamation of Ethiopia with Eritrea had led to a civil war and poses a long-term problem.
4. In February, 1975 Black Africa's most ambitious land reform was announced by the military regime.

IV. Selected References

BIBLIOGRAPHY

Brown, Clifton F. *Ethiopian Perspectives: A Bibliographical Guide to the History of Ethiopia*. Westport, Conn. Greenwood Press, 1978.

Darch, Colin. *A Soviet View of Africa: An Annotated Bibliography on Ethiopia, Somalia and Djibouti*. Boston: G. K. Hall, 1980.

Hidaru, Alaul and Dessalegn Rahmato (eds.). *A Short Guide to the Study of Ethiopia: A General Bibliography*. Washington, D.C.: African Bibliographic Center, 1976.

Marcus, Harold G. *The Modern History of Ethiopia and the Horn of Africa: A Select and Annotated Bibliography*. Stanford, Calif.: Hoover Institution Press, 1972.

GENERAL

Buxton, D. R. *The Abyssinians*. New York: Praeger, 1970.

Caputo, Robert. "Ethiopia: Revolution in an Ancient Empire." *National Geographic* 163, 5, 614—645.

Hess, Robert. *Ethiopia: The Modernization of Autocracy*. Ithaca, N.Y.: Cornell University Press, 1970.

Levine, Donald N. *Greater Ethiopia: The Evolution of a Multiethnic Society*. Chicago: University of Chicago Press, 1974.

Lipsky, George. *Ethiopia*. New Haven, Conn.: HRAF Press, 1962.

Rosenfeld, Chris Prouty. *Historical Dictionary of Ethiopia*. Metuchen, N.J.: Scarecrow Press, 1981.

Ullendorff, Edward. *The Ethiopians: An Introduction to Country and People*. 3rd ed.

U.S. Department of the Army. *Area Handbook for Ethiopia*, 3d ed. Washington, D.C.: U.S. Government Printing Office, 1971.

POLITICAL

Clapham, C. *Haile Selassie's Government*. New York: Praeger, 1969.

Farer, Tom J. *War Clouds on the Horn of Africa: The Widening Storm*. N.Y. Carnegie Endowment for International Peace 1979.

Gilkes, P. *The Dying Lion: Feudalism and Modernization in Ethiopia*. New York: St. Martin's Press, 1975.

Greenfield, Richard. *Ethiopia: A New Political History*. New York: Praeger, 1965.

Legum, C. *Ethiopia: The Fall of Haile Selassie's Empire*. New York: Africana, 1975.

Markakis, John and Asmelash Beyene. "Representative Institutions in Ethiopia." *Journal of Modern African Studies*, 5 (1967): 193—219.

Markakis, John and Nega Ayele. *Class and Revolution in Ethiopia*. Nottingham: Spokesman, 1978.

Ottaway, M. "Social Classes and Corporate Interest in the Ethiopian Revolution." *Journal of Modern African Studies* 14, 3 (1976): 469—86.

Ottaway, Marina and David. *Ethiopia: Empire in Revolution*. New York: Africana Publishing Co., 1978.

Perham, M. *The Government of Ethiopia*. London: Oxford University Press, 1964.

Potholm, Christian P. *Liberation and Exploitation: The Struggle for Ethiopia*. Washington, D.C.: University Press of America, 1976.

Schwab, P. *Haile Selassie I, Ethiopia's Lion of Judah*. Chicago: Nelson.

Schwab, Peter. *Decision-Making in Ethiopia*. Rutherford, N.J.: Fairleigh-Dickinson University Press, 1972.

Sherman, Richard. *Eritrea: The Unfinished Revolution*. New York: Praeger, 1980.

Trevaskis, G. *Eritrea: A Colony in Transition, 1941—52*. London: Oxford University Press, 1960.

Valdes, Vivo Raul. *Ethiopia's Revolution.* New York: International Publishers, 1977.

ECONOMIC

Bequele, A. and E. Chole. *A Profile of the Ethiopian Economy.* Addis Ababa: Oxford University Press, 1969.

Ginzberg, Eli and Herbert A. Smith. *Manpower Strategy for Developing Countries: Lessons from Ethiopia.* New York: Columbia University Press, 1967.

U.S. Department of Agriculture, Economic Research Service, Foreign Regional Analysis Division. *A Survey of Agriculture in Ethiopia.* ERS-Foreign 254. Washington, D.C.: Government Printing Office, 1969.

SOCIAL

Bender, M.L. et al. (eds) *Language in Ethiopia.* London: Oxford University Press, 1976.

Comhaire, Jean. "Urban Growth in Relation to Ethiopian Development." *Cultures et Developpment,* 1 (1968): 25—40.

Derus, Jacques. "Addis Ababa—Genese d'un Capitale Imperiale." *Revue Belge de Geographie,* 88 (1965): 283—314.

Korten, D. C. *Planned Change in a Traditional Society: Psychological Problems of Modernization in Ethiopia.* New York: Praeger, 1972.

Legesse, A. *Gada: Three Approaches to the Study of African Society.* New York: Free Press, 1973.

Levine, Donald. *Wax and Gold: Tradition and Innovation in Ethiopian Culture.* Chicago: University of Chicago Press, 1966.

Pankhurst, Richard. "The Foundation and Growth of Addis Ababa." *The Ethiopian Observer,* 6 (1962): 33—61.

Shack, W. A. *The Central Ethiopian: Amhara, Tigrina, and Related Peoples.* London: International African Institute, 1976.

Tamrat, Taddesse. *Church and State in Ethiopia.* New York: Oxford University Press, 1972.

Trimingham, John S. *Islam in Ethiopia.* London: Oxford University Press, 1952.

Ullendorif, Edward. *The Semitic Languages of Ethiopia: A Comparative Phonology.* London: Taylor's (Foreign) Press, 1955.

12. Gabon

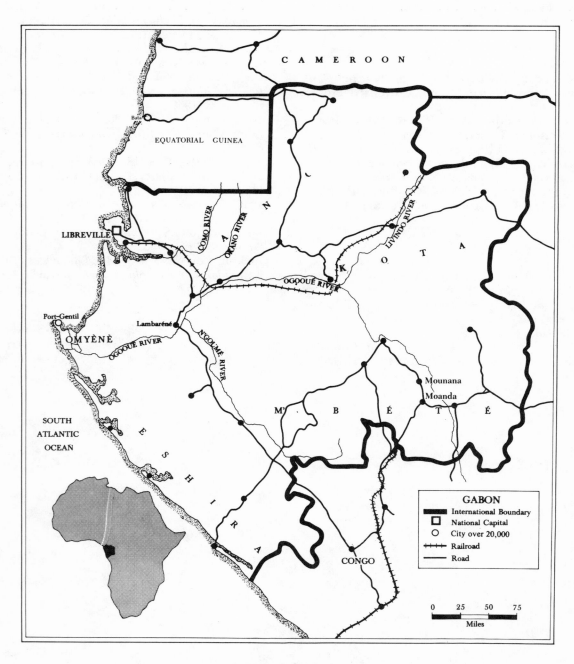

I. Basic Information

Date of Independence: August 17, 1960
Former Colonial Ruler: France
Change in Boundaries: Formerly part of French equatorial Africa
Estimated Population (1980): 549,000 (1970 census figure of 950,000 has not been accepted by international agencies)

Most Widely Spoken Languages: Fang—50%; Eshira—20%

Area Size (equivalent in U.S.): 102,000 sq. mi. (Colorado)
Date of Last Census:
Major Exports (1977) as Percent of Total Exports: crude petroleum—78 percent.
Official Language: French

II. Elite Political Instability

TABLE 12.1   Elite Instability (Post- Independence)

Date	Event
1. February 18—20, 1964	Attempted Coup (Army elements put down by French paratroopers.)

III.   Country Features Worthy of Special Study

1. Very high level of per capita income but little development of the country except for the cities and the mineral exporting areas.
2. Strong continued French presence.
3. High level of enrollment in primary and secondary education.
4. Lowest population growth rate in Black Africa.
5. Major railroad project underway to open the interior to development.

IV. Selected References

BIBLIOGRAPHY

Centre Culture Saint-Exupéry. *Ouvrages sur le Gabon.* Libreville, Centre de documentation. Saint-Exupéry, 1978.

Weinstein, Brian. "Gabon: A Bibliograhic Essay." *Africana Newsletter*, 1, no. 4, 1963.

GENERAL

Bouquerel, J. *Le Gabon.* Paris: Presses Universitaires de France, 1970.

Gardinier, David. *Historical Dictionary of Gabon.* Metuchen, N.J.: Scarecrow, 1981.

Lasserre, Guy. *La France d'Outre-mer.* Paris: Larousse, 1979.

Sautter, Gilles. *De l'Atlantique au fleuve Congo, une geographie du sous-peuplement.* Republique du Congo: Republique Gabonaise, 2 vols. Paris: Mouton, 1966.

Thompson, Virginia and Richard Adloff. *The Emerging States of French Equatorial Africa*, pp. 343—384. Stanford, Calif.: Stanford University Press, 1960.

Weinstein, Brian. *Gabon: Nation Building on the Ogooue.* Cambridge: Massachusetts Institute of Technology Press, 1966.

POLITICAL

Ballard, John A. "Four Equatorial States: *Congo, Gabon, Ubangi-Shari, Chad.*" In *National Unity and Regionalism in Eight African States*, ed. Gwendolen M. Carter, pp. 231—329. Ithaca, N.Y.: Cornell University Press, 1966.

Darlington, C. and A. *African Betrayal.* New York: McKay, 1968.

de Lusignan, Guy. *French-Speaking Africa since Independence*, pp. 100—108. London: Pall Mall Press, 1969.

ECONOMIC

France Ministere de la cooperation. *Gabon: donées statistiques sur les activities, economiques, culturelles et socialles.* Paris: 1976.

"Gabon: une expansion rapide." *Europe-Franco-Outremer* (October 1969): 12—62.

Hilling, D. "The Changing Economy of Gabon: Developments in a New African Republic." *Geography*, 48 (1963): 155—165.

International Monetary Fund. "Gabon." In *Surveys of African Economies*. Vol. 1. Washington, D.C.: I.M.F., 1968.

SOCIAL

Balandier, Georges, *Sociologie actuelle de l'Afrique noire.* 2nd ed. Paris: Presses universitaires de France, 1963.

Lasserre, Guy. *Libreville, la ville et sa region (Gabon, A.E.F.): etude de geographie humaine.* Paris: Colin, 1958.

13. Gambia

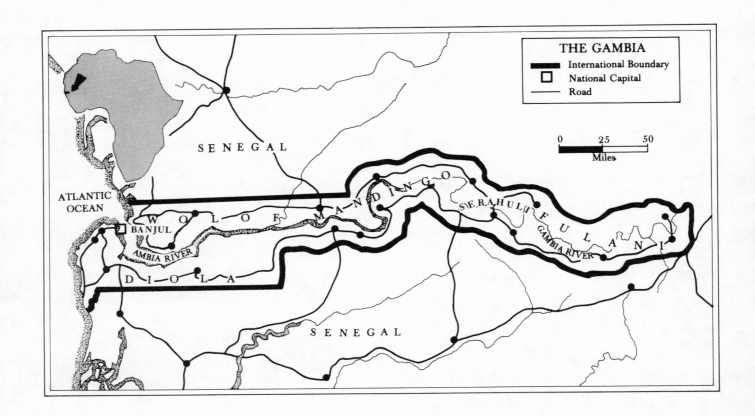

THE GAMBIA
- International Boundary
- National Capital
- Road

0   25   50
Miles

I. Basic Information

Date of Independence: February 18, 1965
Former Colonial Ruler: United Kingdom
Estimated Population (1980): 599,000
Area Size (equivalent in U.S.): 4361 sq. mi. (twice Delaware)

Most Widely Spoken Languages: Mandingo—60%; Fulani—16%

Date of Last Census: 1973
Major Exports 1977—1978 as Percent of Total Exports: groundnuts and derivatives—78 percent.

Official Language: English

II. Elite Political Instability

TABLE 13.1 Elite Instability (Post- Independence)

Date	Event
1. August, 1981	Coup Attempt (Units of the Police Field Force are suppressed by police and Senegalese army units.)

III. Country Features Worthy of Special Study

1. Small, narrow country almost surrounded by Senegal. It has been proposed that the two countries merge.
2. It is among the smallest of all the Black African countries.
3. Gambia is one of the few Black African countries which has more than one political party, although the opposition parties are very weak.

IV. Selected References

BIBLIOGRAPHY

Gamble, D. P. *A General Bibliography of the Gambia*. (up to 31 December 1977), Boston: G.K. Hall, 1979.

Nyang, S. S. "Politics in Post-Independence Gambia." *Current Bibliography of African Affairs*, 8, 2 (1975), 113—126.

GENERAL

Bridges, R. C. and A. Adams, eds. *Senegambia: Colloquium at the University of Aberdeen, April 1974*. Aberdeen: University African Study Group. 1974.

Gailey, Harry A. *A History of the Gambia*. London: Routledge and Kegan Paul, 1964.

Gailey, H. A. *Historical Dictionary of the Gambia*. Metuchen, N.J.: Scarecrow, 1975.

Gray, J. M. *A History of the Gambia*. N.Y.: Barnes and Noble, Inc., 1966.

Tengue, Michael. "The Gambia." *Geographical Magazine* (London), 34 (November 1961): 380—392.

Rice, Berkeley. *Enter Gambia: The Birth of an Improbable Nation*. London: Angus and Robertson, 1968.

Wright, Donald. *Oral Tradition from the Gambia*. Athens, Ohio. Ohio University, Center for International Studies, Africa Program, 1979.

POLITICAL

Daun, Holger. *Change, Conflict Potential and Politics: Two Gambian Case Studies*. Lunds Université, 1977.

Nyang, S. S. *The Historical Development of Political Parties in the Gambia*. Washington, D.C.: Howard University Press, 1975.

Robson, Peter. "Problems of Integration between Senegal and Gambia." In *African Integration and Disintegration*. ed, Arthur Hazelwood, pp. 115—128. London: Oxford University Press, 1967.

Welch, Claude E., Jr. "Unlikely Gambia." *Africa Report*, 10 (Feburary 1965): 5—9.

ECONOMIC

Dunsmore, J. R. et al. *The Agricultural Development of the Gambia: An Agricultural, Environmental and Socioeconomic Analysis*. Surbiton, Surrey: Ministry of Overseas Development, Land Resources Division, 1976.

Haswell, Margaret. *The Nature of Poverty*. London: The Macmillan Press, Ltd., 1975.

International Monetary Fund. "The Gambia." In *Surveys of African Economies*, Vol. 6. Washington, D.C.: I.M.F., 1975.

SOCIAL

Van der Plas, Charles D. *Report of a Socio-Economic Survey of Bathurst and Kombo-St. Mary in the Gambia*. New York: United Nations, 1956.

14. Ghana

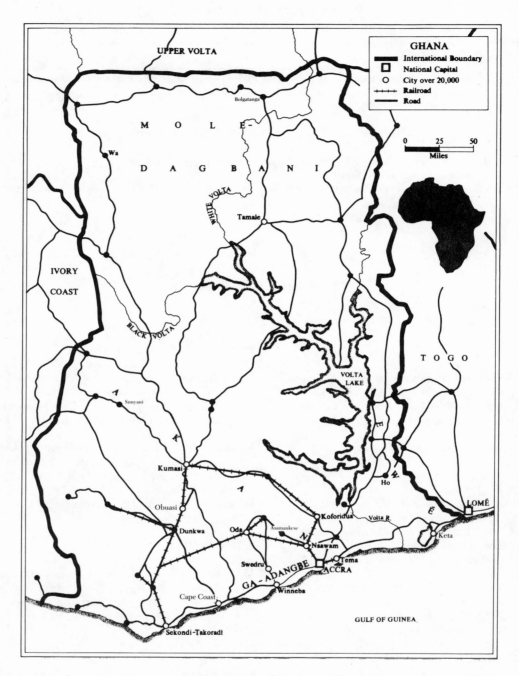

I. Basic Information

Date of Independence: March 6, 1957
Former Colonial Ruler: United Kingdom
Change in Boundaries: Addition of UN Trust Territory "British Togoland" on December 13, 1956
Former Name: Gold Coast

Most Widely Spoken Languages: "Akan"—44%; Mole-Dagbani—16%

Estimted Population (1980) 12,128,000
Area Size (equivalent in U.S.): 92,100 sq. mi. (Wyoming)
Date of Last Census: 1970
Major exports 1975 as percent of total exports: cocoa—59 percent; logs and timber—8 percent; gold—9 percent.

Official Language: English

II. Elite Political Instability

TABLE 14.1 Elite Instability (Post- Independence)

Date	Event
1. February 24, 1966	Coup d'État (Army overthrows Nkrumah while he is out of the country.)
2. April 17, 1967	Attempted Coup (Army elements try to restore Nkrumah.)
3. January 13, 1972	Coup d'État (Army overthrows Busia and restores military rule.)
4. July 5, 1978	Coup d'État (Archeampong forced to resign by fellow officers.)
5. June 4—6, 1979	Coup d'État (Rawlings and other junior officers overthrow military government.)
6. December 31, 1981	Coup Attempt (Rawlings takes power from Limann.)

III.   Country Features Worthy of Special Study

1. Major Pan-Africanist and revolutionary state under Nkrumah (pre-1966).
2. Among most highly educated and modernized of Black African states.
3. One of the lowest percent of labor force in agriculture and cattle raising in Black Africa.

IV. Selected References

BIBLIOGRAPHY

Amedekey, E. Y. (Comp.). *The Culture of Ghana: A Bibliography*. Accra: Ghana University Press, 1971.

Baynham, S. "The Ghanaian Military: A Bibliographic Essay," *West African Journal of Sociology and Political Science* 1, 1 (October 1975): 83—96.

Chand, Attar. "Ghana Since the Coup: A Select Bibliography." *Africa Quarterly* 9 (October—December 1969), 310—315.

Johnson, A. F. *A Bibliography of Ghana, 1930—1961*. London: Longmans for Ghana Library Board, 1964.

GENERAL

Aluko, Olajide. *Ghana and Nigeria, 1957—1970*. N.Y.: Barnes and Noble, 1976.

Apter, David E. *Ghana in Transition*, 2nd rev. ed. Princeton, N.J.: Princeton University Press, 1972.

Dickson, Kwamina B. *An Historical Geography of Ghana*. London: Cambridge University Press, 1969.

Fage, John D. *Ghana: A Historical Interpretation*. Madison: University of Wisconsin, 1959.

Foster, Philip and Aristide R. Zolberg. *Ghana and the Ivory Coast: Perspectives on Modernization*. Chicago: University of Chicago Press, 1971.

Genoud, Roger. *Nationalism and Economic Development in Ghana*. New York: Praeger, 1969.

Jeffries, Richard. *Class, Power and Ideology in Ghana: The Railwaymen of Sekondi*. Cambridge: Cambridge University Press, 1978.

U.S. Department of the Army. *Area Handbook for Ghana*. Washington, D.C.: U.S. Government Printing Office, 1971.

Ward, William E. F. *A History of Ghana*. London: Allen and Unwin, 1966.

POLITICAL

Afrifa, A. A. *The Ghana Coup, 24th February, 1966*. London: Frank Cass, 1966.

Amin, Samir. *Neo-Colonialism in West Africa*. Harmondsworth, Middlesex: Penguin Books, 1973.

Armha, Kwesi. *Nkrumah's Legacy*. London: Rex Collings, 1974.

Austin, Dennis. *Ghana Observed: Essays on the Politics of a West African Republic*. Manchester: University of Manchester Press, 1976.

Austin, Dennis. *Politics in Ghana, 1946—1960*. London: Oxford University Press, 1964.

Austin, D. and F. Luckham, eds. *Politicians and Soldiers in Ghana*. London: Cass, 1975.

Bretton, Henry L. *The Rise and Fall of Kwame Nkrumah*. New York: Praeger, 1966.

Davidson, Basil. *Black Star: A View of the Life and Times of Kwame Nkrumah*. N.Y. Praeger, 1973.

Dowse, Robert E. *Aspects of Ghanaian Development: Studies in Political Sociology*. Totowa, N.J.: Frank Cass, 1979.

Fitch, Bob and Mary Oppenheimer. *Ghana: End of an Illusion*. New York: Monthly Review Press, 1966.

Harvey, William. *Law and Social Change in Ghana*. Princeton: Princeton University Press, 1966.

James, C. L. R. *Nkrumah and the Ghana Revolution*. London: Allison and Busby, 1977.

Jeffries, Richard. "The Ghanaian Election of 1979." *African Affairs*, 79, 316, 397—414.

Jones, Trevor. *Ghana's First Republic, 1960—66: The Pursuit of the Political Kingdom*. London: Methuen, 1976.

Kay, G., ed. *The Political Economy of Colonialism in Ghana: A Collection of Documents and Statistics, 1900—1960*. Cambridge: Cambridge University Press, 1972.

Milburn, J. F. *British Business and Ghanaian Independence*. London: C. Hurst, 1977.

Nkrumah, Kwame. *Ghana, The Autobiography of Kwame Nkrumah*. London: Nelson, 1957.

Nkrumah, Kwame. *Neocolonialism, the Last Stage of Imperialism*. London: Heinemann, 1965.

Nkrumah, Kwame, *Class Struggles in Africa*. N.Y.: International Publishers, 1970.

Ocran, A. K. *A Myth is Broken: An Account of the Ghana Coup d'État of 24 February 1966.* London: Longman, 1968.

Ocran, A. *Politics of the Sword: A Personal Memoir on Military Involvement in Ghana.* London: Rex Collings, 1977.

Omari, T. Peter. *Kwame Nkrumah: The Anatomy of an African Dictatorship.* New York: Africana, 1970.

Owosu, M. *Uses and Abuses of Political Power: A Case Study of Continuity and Change in the Politics of Ghana.* Chicago: University of Chicago Press, 1970.

Pinkney, Robert. *Ghana Under Military Rule.* New York: Barnes and Noble, 1972.

Price, R. M. *Society and Bureaucracy in Contemporary Ghana.* Berkeley: University of California Press, 1975.

Smock, D. R. *The Politics of Pluralism: A Comparative Study of Lebanon and Ghana.* New York: Elsevier, 1975.

Staniland, M. *The Lions of Dagbon: Political Change in Northern Ghana.* New York: Cambridge University Press, 1975.

Thompson, W. S. *Ghana's Foreign Policy, 1957—1966.* Princeton, N.J.: Princeton University Press, 1969.

Woronoff, Jon. *West African Wager: Houphouet Versus Nkrumah.* Metuchen, N.J.: Scarecrow Press, 1972.

ECONOMIC

Amin, Samir. *Trois experiences africaines de developpement: le Mali, le Guinee et le Ghana.* Paris: Presses Universitaires de France, 1965.

Garlick, P. C. *African Traders and Economic Development in Ghana.* New York: Oxford University Press, 1971.

Genoud, Roger. *Nationalism and Economic Development in Ghana.* N.Y.: Praeger, 1969.

Hance, William A. "The Volta River Project: A Study in Industrial Development." In *African Economic Development*, rev. ed., by William A. Hance, pp. 87—114. New York: Praeger, 1967.

Hill, P. *Rural Capitalism in West Africa.* London: Cambridge University Press, 1970.

Howard, Rhoda. *Colonialism and Underdevelopment in Ghana.* New York: Africana Publishing Co., 1978.

International Monetary Fund. "Ghana." In *Surveys of African Economies*, Vol. 6. Washington, D.C.: I.M.F., 1975.

Killick, Tony. *Development Economics in Action: A Study of Economic Policies in Ghana.* New York: St. Martin's Press, 1978.

Killick, A. and R. Szereszewski. "The Economy of Ghana," in *The Economies of Africa*, eds. P. Robson and D. A. Lury, pp. 79—126. Evanston, Ill.: Northwestern University Press, 1969.

Lawson, Rowena. *The Changing Economy of the Lower Volta, 1954—67.* Oxford: Oxford University Press, 1972.

Leith, J. C. *Foreign Trade Regimes and Economic Development: Ghana*, Vol. II. New York: National Bureau of Economic Research, 1974.

Seidman, Ann Willcox. *Ghana's Development Experience: 1951—65.* Nairobi: East African Publishing House, 1978.

Steel, W. F. *Small-Scale Employment and Production in Developing Countries: Evidence from Ghana.* New York: Praeger, 1977.

SOCIAL

Acquah, I. *Accra Survey.* London: University of London Press, 1958.

Agbodeka, F. *Achimota in the National Setting.* Accra: Afram Publishers, 1977.

Arkaifie, R. *Bibliography of the Ewes.* Cape Coast, Ghana, 1976.

Baeta, C. G. *Prophetism in Ghana: A Study of Some "Spiritual" Churches.* London: S.C.M. Press, 1962.

Birmingham, Walter, et al. eds. *A Study of Contemporary Ghana*, Vol. 2, "Some Aspects of Social Structure." London: Allen and Unwin, 1967.

Boateng, E. A. *A Geography of Ghana.* New York: Cambridge University Press, 1966.

Brokensha, David. *Social Change at Larteh, Ghana.* Oxford: Clarendon Press, 1966.

Caldwell, John C. *African Rural-Urban Migration: The Movement to Ghana's Towns.* New York: Columbia University Press, 1969.

Curle, A. *Educational Problems of Developing Societies with Case Studies of Ghana, Pakistan, and Nigeria.* New York: Praeger, 1973.

Field, M. J. *Search for Security: An Ethno-Psychiatric Study of Rural Ghana.* London: Faber and Faber, 1960.

Foster, Philip. *Education and Social Change in Ghana.* Chicago: University of Chicago Press, 1965.

Hilton, T. E. *Ghana Population Atlas.* London: Nelson, 1960.

Kaufert, Joseph M. "Ethnic Unit Definition in Ghana: A Comparison of Culture Cluster Analysis and Social Distance Measures" in John N. Paden, (ed), *Values, Identities and National Integration*, Evanston, Ill.: Northwestern University Press, 1980, pp. 41—52.

Kay, B. *Bringing up Children in Ghana.* London: Allen and Unwin, 1962.

Levine, V. T. *Political Corruption: The Ghana Case.* Stanford: Hoover Institution, 1974.

Parsons, Robert T. *The Churches and Ghana Society.* Leiden: E. J. Brill, 1967.

Peil, Margaret. *The Ghanaian Factory Worker: Industrial Man in Africa.* London: Cambridge University Press, 1972.

Schildkrout, E. *People of the Zongo: The Transformation of Ethnic Identities in Ghana.* New York: Cambridge University Press, 1978.

Wilks, I. *Asante in the Nineteenth Century.* New York: Cambridge University Press, 1975.

15. Guinea

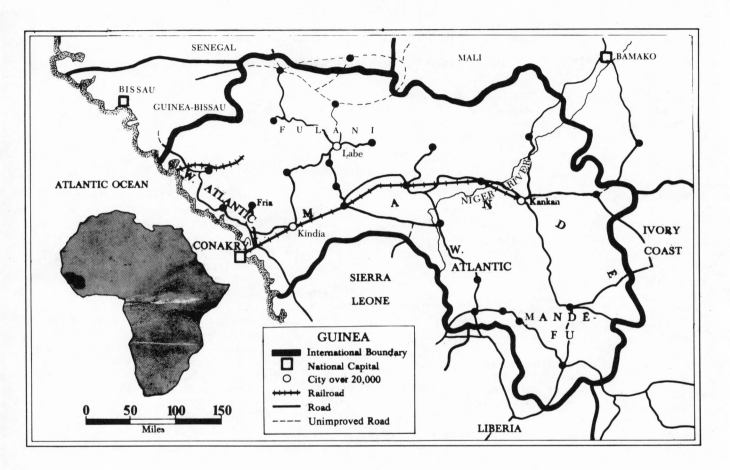

GUINEA
- ▬▬ International Boundary
- ◻ National Capital
- ○ City over 20,000
- ┼┼┼┼ Railroad
- ─── Road
- ----- Unimproved Road

0 50 100 150
Miles

I. Basic Information

Date of Independence: October 2, 1958

Former Colonial Ruler: France

Change in Boundaries: Formerly part of the French West African Federation

Estimated Population (1980): 5,419,000* (the 1972 census result was reported to be 5,143,284 but this may have been for the *de jure* population including those Guineans who have left the country.

Area Size (equivalent in U.S.): 94,926 sq. mi. (Oregon)

Date of Last Census: 1972

Major Exports 1975/1976 as Percent of Total Exports: bauxite—61 percent; alumina—33 percent**

Most Widely Spoken Languages: Malinké—48%; Poular (Fulani)—33%

Official Language: French

*According to a report in *The New York Times* (December 1968), between 500,000 and 1,000,000 Guineans have left the country since independence. *Africa Contemporary Record 1969—70*, p. B 496, says that a population figure "in the region of 3,500,000 has been mentioned for 1967." The Europa Yearbook 1979 (Vol. II, p. 414) reported a 1978 estimate that 1,000,000 Guineans had left the country.

**A large volume of smuggling takes place across the country's borders and no information is available about its composition.

II.   Elite Political Instability

TABLE   15.1   Elite Instability (Post- Independence)

Date	Event
1. February, 1968	Attempted Coup (The government reported that 500 Guinean nationals attempted to enter the country from abroad to overthrow the government.)
2. November 22, 1970	Attempted Coup (Portuguese sponsored "invasion" of Conakry by opponents of the Touré regime.)

III.   Country Features Worthy of Special Study

1. Key sectors of the economy have been nationalized since independence.
2. Rejected continued French colonial domination in a 1958 referendum and tried to pursue a strict non-alignment policy.
3. Large out-migration since independence.
4. Especially high percent of budget spent on education.

IV. Selected References

BIBLIOGRAPHY

Organization for Economic Cooperation and Development. *Bibliographie sur la Guinee*. Paris: O.E.C.D., 1967.

GENERAL

Ameillon, B. *La Guinee: bilan d'une independence*. Paris: Maspero, 1964.

Charles, Bernard. *Guinee*. Lausanne: Editions Rencontre, 1963.

O'Toole, T. E. *Historical Dictionary for Guinea*. Metuchen, N.J.: Scarecrow, 1978.

Riviere, C. (trans. by V. Thompson and R. Adloff) *Guinea: The Mobilization of a People*. Ithaca, N.Y.: Cornell University Press, 1977.

Suret-Canale, J. *La Republique de Guinee*. Paris: Seghers, 1970.

Thompson, Virginia and Richard Adloff. *French West Africa*, pp. 132—138. Stanford, Cal.: Stanford University Press, 1957.

Nelson, H. D. et al. *Area Handbook for Guinea*. 2nd Edition. Washington, D.C.: U.S. Government Printer, 1975.

POLITICAL

Adamolekun, L. *Sekou Touré's Guinea: An Experiment in Nation Building*. London: Methuen, 1976.

Amin, Samir. *Neo-Colonialism in West Africa*. Harmondsworth, Middlesex: Penguin, 1973.

Atwood, William. *The Reds and the Blacks*. New York: Harper and Row, 1967.

Cowan, L. Gray. "Guinea." In *African One-Party States*, ed. Gwendolen M. Carter. Ithaca, N.Y.: Cornell University Press, 1962.

de Lusignan, Guy. *French-Speaking Africa since Independence*. pp. 180—198. New York: Praeger 1969.

DuBois, Victor David. *The Independence Movement in Guinea: A Study in African Nationalism*. Princeton, N.J.: PhD. Thesis available from University Microfilms, 1963.

DuBois, Victor. "Guinea." In *Political Parties and National Integration in Tropical Africa*, pp. 186—215, eds. J. S. Coleman and C. G. Rosberg. Los Angeles: University of California Press, 1964.

Morrow, John H. *First American Ambassador to Guinea*. New Brunswick: Rutgers University Press, 1968.

Touré, Sékou. *Strategie et tactique de la revolution*. 2nd ed. Conakry, Guinea: Bureau de presse de la Presidence de la Republique, 1976.

Zartman, William I. "Guinea: The Quiet War Goes On." *Africa Report*, 12 (November 1967): 67—72.

ECONOMIC

Amin, Samir. *Trois experiences Africaines de developpement*: le Mali, la Guinee et le Ghana. Paris: Presses Universitaires de France, 1965.

Berg, Elliot. "Education and Manpower in Senegal, Guinea, and the Ivory Coast." In *Manpower and Education: Country Studies in Economic Development*, eds. F. B. Harbison and C. Myers. New York: McGraw-Hill, 1965.

O'Connor, M. "Guinea and the Ivory Coast: Contrast in Economic Development," *Journal of Modern African Studies*, X, 3 October 1972, 409—26.

Voss, Joachin. *Guinea*. Bern: K. Schweder, 1967.

SOCIAL

Derman, William. *Serfs, Peasants, and Socialists: A Former Serf Village in the Republic of Guinea*. Berkeley: University of California Press, 1973.

Leunda, X. "La reforme de l'enseignement et son incidence sur l'evolution rurale en Guinee." *Civilisations*, (1972/1973): 232—262.

Stern, T. N. "Political Aspects of Guinean Education." *Comparative Education Review*, 8 (June 1964): 98—103.

16. Guinea-Bissau

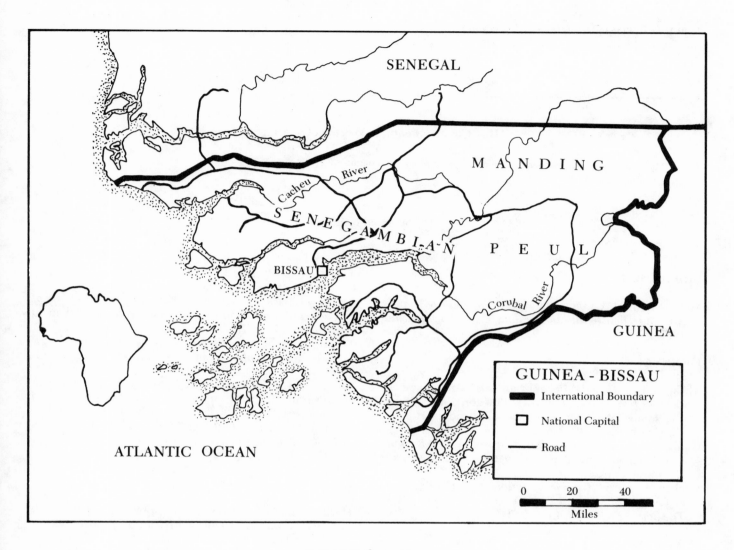

I. Basic Information

Date of Independence: September 10, 1974
Former Colonial Ruler: Portugal
Former Name: Portuguese Guinea
Estimated Population (1980): 646,000*
Area Size (equivalent in U.S.): 13,948 sq. mi. (Mass., R.I. Conn.)
Date of Last Census: 1979

Most Widely Spoken Languages: Creole—60%; Balante—30%; Fulani—20%

Major Exports 1977 as a Percent of Total Exports: groundnuts—60%, fish—19%, palm kernels—13%
Official Language: Portuguese

*After independence, large numbers of refugees were reported to have returned to the country and the population may be somewhat larger than current estimates.

II. Elite Political Instability

TABLE 16.1 Elite Instability (Post- Independence)

Date	Event
1. November 15, 1980	Coup d'État (Cabral ousted by other members of government and army.)

III. Country Features Worthy of Special Study

1. One of the world's poorest countries now trying to recover from a devastating war of liberation.

IV. Selected References

BIBLIOGRAPHY

McCarthy, J. M. *Guinea-Bissau and Cape Verde Islands: A Comprehensive Bibliography*. New York: Garland, 1977.

GENERAL

Abshire, David, and Michael Samuels. *Portuguese Africa—A Handbook*. New York: Praeger, 1969.

Duffy, James. *Portugal in Africa*. Cambridge: Harvard University Press, 1962.

Goult, Denis. *Looking at Guinea-Bissau: A New Nation's Development Strategy*. Washington, D.C., Overseas Development Council, 1978.

Lobban, Richard. *Historical Dictionary of the Republics of Guinea-Bissau and Cape Verde*. Metuchen, N.J.: The Scarecrow Press, Inc., 1979.

POLITICAL

Aaby, Peter. *The State of Guinea-Bissau: African Socialism or Socialism in Africa?* Uppsala, Scandinavian Institute of African Studies, 1978

Cabral, Amilcar. *Revolution in Guinea*. New York: Monthly Review Press, 1970.

Chaliand, Gerard. *Armed Struggle in Africa: With the Guerrillas in Portuguese Guinea*. New York: Monthly Review Press, 1969.

Chilcote, Ronald. *Emerging Nationalism in Portuguese Africa*. Stanford, Calif.: Hoover Institution Press, 1972.

Davidson, Basil. *The Liberation of Guinea*. Harmondsworth, U.K.: Penguin, 1969.

Davidson, Basil. *Growing from Grass Roots: The State of Guinea-Bissau*. London: Committee for Freedom in Mozambique, 1974.

David, Jennifer. *The Republic of Guinea-Bissau: Triumph over Colonialism*. New York: Africa Fund, 1974.

Rudbeck, L. *Guinea-Bissau: A Study in Political Mobilization*. Uppsala: Scandinavian Institute of African Studies, 1974.

Urdang, Stephanie. *Fighting Two Colonialisms, Women in Guinea-Bissau*. N.Y.: Monthly Review Press, 1979.

ECONOMIC

Herbert, E. W. "Portuguese Adaptation to Trade Patterns: Guinea to Angola," *African Studies Review* 17 (September 1974), pp. 411—24.

U.S. Bureau of Labor Statistics. *Labor Conditions in Portuguese Guinea*. Washington, D.C.: U.S. Government Printing Office, 1966.

SOCIAL

Heisel, Don F. "The Demography of the Portuguese Territories: Angola, Mozambique, and Portuguese Guinea," in W. I. Brass et. al. (eds.), *The Demography of Tropical Africa*. Princeton: Princeton University Press, 1968, p. 440—65.

17. Ivory Coast

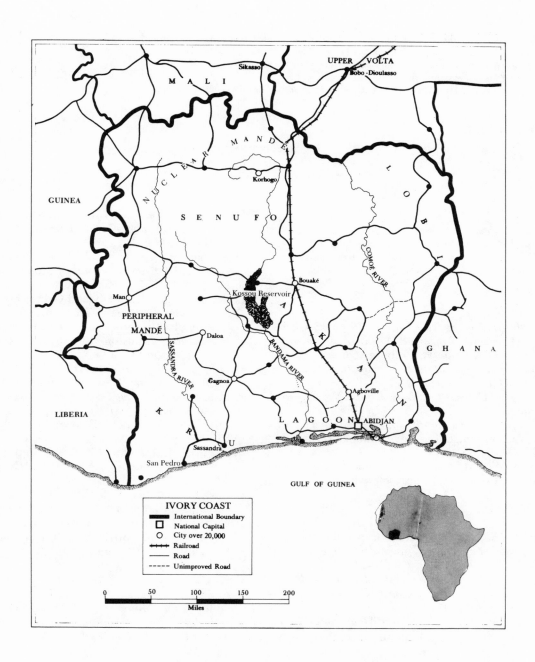

IVORY COAST

▬▬ International Boundary
☐ National Capital
◦ City over 20,000
╂╂╂ Railroad
── Road
---- Unimproved Road

0   50   100   150   200
Miles

I. Basic Information

Date of Independence: August 7, 1960
Former Colonial Ruler: France
Change in Boundaries: Formerly part of the French West African Federation
Estimated Population (1980): 7,662,000

Most Widely Spoken Languages: Akan—27%; Kru-Bété—18%

Area size (equivalent in U.S.): 124,504 sq. mi. (New Mexico)
Date of Last Census: 1975
Major Exports 1976 as Percent of Total Exports: cocoa—33 percent; coffee—25 percent; wood—14 percent.

Official Language: French

III. Country Features Worthy of Special Study

1. Leading exponent of rapid industrial growth via the vehicle of large-scale foreign investment in agriculture and processing industries.
2. Potential problems because of continuing French influence in government administration.
3. Thirty-five to forty percent of its male African labor are immigrants from neighboring countries.
4. Strong pro-Western in orientation with close ties to France.
5. Recent oil strikes mean that Ivory Coast's concentration on agricultural development may change.

IV. Selected References

BIBLIOGRAPHY

Organization for Economic Cooperation and Development. Development Center. *Essai d'une Bibliographie sur la Cote d'Ivoire*. Paris: O.E.C.D., 1964.

GENERAL

Bernheim, M. *African Success Story: The Ivory Coast*. New York: Harcourt, Brace and World, 1970.
Foster, Philip and Aristide R. Zolberg. *Ghana and the Ivory Coast: Perspectives on Modernization*. Chicago: University of Chicago Press, 1972.
Lewis, B. *Ivory Coast*. Boulder, Colo.: Westview—forthcoming.
Roberts, T.D. et al. *Area Handbook for the Ivory Coast*, 2nd ed. Washington, D.C.: Government Printing Office, 1973.
Woronoff, Jon. *West African Wager: Houphouet Versus Nkrumah*. Metuchen, N.J.: Scarecrow Press, 1972

POLITICAL

Cohen, Michael A. "The Myth of the Expanding Center: Politics in the Ivory Coast," *Journal of Modern African Studies*, 11, 2 (June, 1973), 227—246.
Cohen, Michael A. *Urban Policy and Political Conflict in Africa: A Study of the Ivory Coast*. Chicago: University of Chicago Press, 1974.
de Lusignan, Guy. *French Speaking Africa since Independence*, pp. 135—145. London: Pall Mall Press, 1969.
Wallerstein, Immanuel, *The Road to Independence: Ghana and the Ivory Coast*. The Hague: Mouton, 1964.
Zolberg, Aristide. *One-Party Government in the Ivory Coast*. Princeton, N.J.: Princeton University Press, 1964, new ed. 1969.

ECONOMIC

Amin, Samir. *Le Developpement du Capitalisme en Côte d'Ivoire*. Paris: Editions de Minuit, 1967.

Den Tuinder, Bastiaan A. *Ivory Coast: The Challenge of Success*. Baltimore: Johns Hopkins University Press for the World Bank, 1978.
Due, Jean M. "Agricultural Development in the Ivory Coast and Ghana." *Journal of Modern African Studies*, 7 (1969): 637—660.
Lewis, Barbara. "Ethnicity and Occupational Specialization in Ivory Coast: The Transporter's Association," in John N. Paden (ed) *Values, Identities, and National Integration*. Evanston, Ill., Northwestern University Press, 1980, pp.75—90.
Masini, J., et al. *Multinationals in Africa: A Case Study of the Ivory Coast*. New York: Praeger, 1980.
Miracle, Marvin. "The Economy of the Ivory Coast." In *The Economies of Africa*, eds. P. Robson and D. A. Lury, pp. 195—235. Evanston, Ill.: Northwestern University Press, 1969.
Roussel, L. "Employment Problems in the Ivory Coast." *International Labour Review*, 104 (December 1971): 505—526.
Sawadogo, Abdoulaye. *L'agriculture en Côte d'Ivoire*. Paris: Presses universitaires de France, 1977.
Stryker, J. D. *Exports and Growth in Ivory Coast: Timber, Cocoa and Coffee*. New Haven: Yale University, Economic Growth Center, 1972.

SOCIAL

Clignet, Remi. *Many Wives, Many Powers: Authority and Power in Polygynous Families*. Evanston, Ill.: Northwestern University Press, 1970.
Clignet, Remi and Philip Foster. *The Fortunate Few: A Study of Secondary Schools and Students in the Ivory Coast*. Evanston, Ill.: Northwestern University Press, 1966.
Holas, Bohumil. *Le separatisme religieux en Afrique noire: l'example de la Côte d'Ivoire*. Paris: Presses Universitaires de France, 1965.
Joshi, Heather, H. Lubell and J. Monly. *Abidjan, Urban Development and Employment in the Ivory Coast*. Geneva: International Labour Office, 1976.
Salem, Claudel. *Pluralism in the Ivory Coast: The Persistence of Ethnic Identities in the One Party State*. Los Angeles: University of California Press, 1975.

18. Kenya

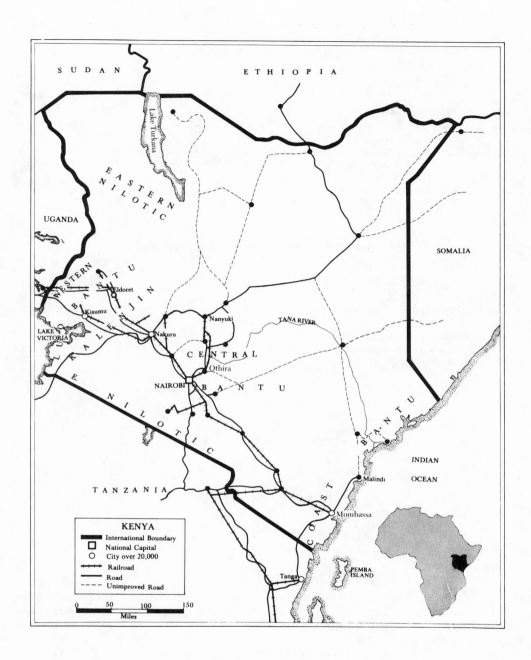

I. Basic Information

Date of Independence: December 12, 1963
Former Colonial Ruler: United Kingdom
Estimated Population (1980): 15,913,000
Area Size (equivalent in U.S.): 224,961 sq. mi. (Nevada and New Mexico)

Most Widely Spoken Languages: Swahili—85%; Kikuyu—25%

Date of Last Census: 1969
Major Exports: 1976 (excluding re-exports to Uganda and Tanzania) as percent of Total Exports: coffee—35 percent; tea—12 percent; petroleum products—12 percent.

Official Language: Swahili

II. Elite Political Instability

TABLE 18.1   Elite Instability (Post-Independence)

Date	Event
1. August 1, 1982	Coup Attempt (Airforce units attempt to take over government but are repulsed in bloody fighting with the army.)

III.   Country Features Worthy of Special Study

1. Pre-independence history of black-white confrontation.
2. Large native-born Asian population.
3. Relatively free-enterprise approach to economic development.
4. Government domination by the Kikuyu ethnic group has led to continued tensions, especially with the Luo.
5. High level of industrialization for Black Africa.

IV. Selected References

BIBLIOGRAPHY

Collison, R. L. comp. *Kenya* (World Bibliographic Series, Santa Barbara, CA: Clio Press, 1982.

Howell, John B. *Kenya: Subject Guide to Official Publications*. Washington, D.C.: Government Printing Office, 1978.

Ndegwa, R. N. *Mau Mau: A Select Bibliography*. Nairobi: Kenyatta University College, 1977.

GENERAL

Harbeson, J. *Nation-Building in Kenya: The Role of Land Reform*. Evanston, Ill.: Northwestern University Press, 1973.

Kaplan, I. et al. *Area Handbook for Kenya*, 2nd edition. Washington, D.C.: Government Printing office, 1976.

Ogut, B. A. *Historical Dictionary of Kenya* Metuchen, N.J.: Scarecrow, 1981.

Ojany, F. F. and Ogendo, R. B. *Kenya: A Study in Physical and Human Geography*. London: Longman, 1973.

POLITICAL

Arnold, G. *Kenyatta and the Politics of Kenya*. London: J.M. Dent, 1974.

Arnold, G. *Modern Kenya*. Harlow, UK: Longman, 1981.

Barkan, J. D. and J. J. Okumu (eds). *Politics and Public Policy in Kenya and Tanzania*. New York: Praeger, 1978.

Barnett, Donald L. and Karari Mjaja. *Mau Mau from Within: Autobiography and Analysis of Kenya's Peasant Revolt*. New York: Monthly Review Press, 1966.

Bennett, George. *Kenya: A Political History—The Colonial Period*. London: Oxford University Press, 1963.

Bienen, Henry. *Kenya: The Politics of Participation and Control*. Princeton, N.J.: Princeton University Press, 1973.

Frost, Richard A. *Race Against Time: Human Relations and Politics in Kenya Beyond Independence*. London: Rex Collings, 1978.

Gertzel, Cherry. *The Politics of Independent Kenya 1963—1968*. London: Heinemann, 1970.

Kenyatta, Jomo. *Suffering Without Bitterness: The Founding of the Kenyan Nation*. Nairobi: East African Publishing House, 1968.

Kitching, G. *Class and Economic Change in Kenya*. New Haven: Yale University Press, 1980.

Murray-Brown, Jeremy. *Kenyatta*. London: George Allen and Unwin, Ltd., 1972.

Odinga, Oginga. *Not Yet Uhuru*. New York: Hill and Wang, 1967.

Ross, Marc Howard. "Political Alienation, Participation, and Ethnicity in the Nairobi Urban Area" in John N. Paden (ed.) *Values, Identities, and National Integration*, Evanston, Ill.: Northwestern University Press, 1980, pp.173—82.

Wipper, Audrey. *Rural Rebels: A Study of Two Protest Movements in Kenya*. New York: Oxford University Press, 1978.

ECONOMIC

Burrows, J. *Kenya: Into the Second Decade: Report of a Mission Sent to Kenya by the World Bank*. Baltimore: Johns Hopkins University Press, 1975.

Hazelwood, A. *The Economics of Kenya*. New York: Oxford University Press, 1980.

Holtham, Gerald and Arthur Hazelwood. *Aid and Inequality in Kenya: British Development Assistance to Kenya*. London: Croom Helm, 1976.

King, J. R. *Stabilization Policy in an African Setting: Kenya 1963—1973*. Studies in the Economics of Africa. Exeter, N.H.: Heinemann, 1979.

Leonard, David K. *Reaching the Peasant Farmer: Organization Theory and Practice in Kenya*. Chicago: University of Chicago Press, 1977.

Leys, Colin. *Underdevelopment in Kenya: The Political Economy of Neo-Colonialism, 1964—1971*. Berkeley: University of California Press, 1975.

Obudho, Robert A. and D.R.F. Taylor. *The Spatial Structure of Development: A Study of Kenya*. Boulder, Colo.: Westview Press, 1979.

Oser, Jacob. *Promoting Economic Development: With Illustrations from Kenya*. Evanston, Ill.: Northwestern University Press, 1967.

Rempel, Henry and William J. House. *The Kenya Employment Problem: An Analysis of the Modern Sector Labour Market*. New York: Oxford University Press, 1978.

Singer, H., and R. Jolly. "Unemployment in an African Setting: Lessons of the Employment Strategy Mission to Kenya." *International Labour Review*, 107 (February 1973): 103—116.

Swainson, N. *The Development of Corporate Capitalism in Kenya, 1918—1977*. Berkeley: University of California Press, 1980.

Van Zwandenberg, R. M. A., and Anne King. *An Economic History of Kenya and Uganda, 1800—1970*. London: Macmillan, 1975.

Wolff, Richard. *The Economics of Colonialism: Britain and Kenya, 1870-1930*. New Haven: Yale University Press, 1974.

SOCIAL

Cour, D. and D. Ghai. *Education and Development: New Perspectives from Kenya*. New York: Oxford University Press, 1975.

Cowan, L. Gray. *The Costs of Learning: The Politics of Primary Education in Kenya*. New York: Columbia Teachers College Press, 1970.

De Bilj, Harm J. *Mombasa: An African City*. Evanston, Ill.: Northwestern University Press, 1968.

Gregory, R. G. *India and East Africa: A History of Race Relations Within the British Empire, 1890—1939*. New York: Oxford University Press, 1972.

Gutto, S. B. O. *The Status of Women in Kenya: A Study of Paternalism, Inequality, and Underprivilege*. Nairobi: Institute of Development Studies, University of Nairobi, 1976.

Hake, A. *African Metropolis: Nairboi's Self-Help City*. London: Chatto & Windus, Ltd. for Sussex University Press, 1977.

Kenyatta, Jomo. *Facing Mount Kenya*. London: Secker and Warburg, 1938.

Lamb, G. *Peasant Politics: Conflict and Development in Murang'a*. New York: St. Martin's Press, 1974.

Marris, P. and A. Somerset. *African Businessmen: A Study of Entrepreneurship and Development in Kenya*. London: Routledge and Kegan Paul, 1971.

Rhoades, John. *Linguistic Diversity and Language Belief in Kenya: The Special Position of Swahili*. Syracuse, N.Y.: Syracuse University, 1977.

Rothchild, Donald. *Racial Bargaining in Independent Kenya: A Study of Minorities and De-colonization*. London: Oxford University Press, 1973.

Sheffield, James R. *Education in Kenya: An Historical Study*. New York: Teachers College Press, 1973.

Whiteley, W. H. *Language in Kenya*. New York: Oxford University Press, 1975.

19. Lesotho

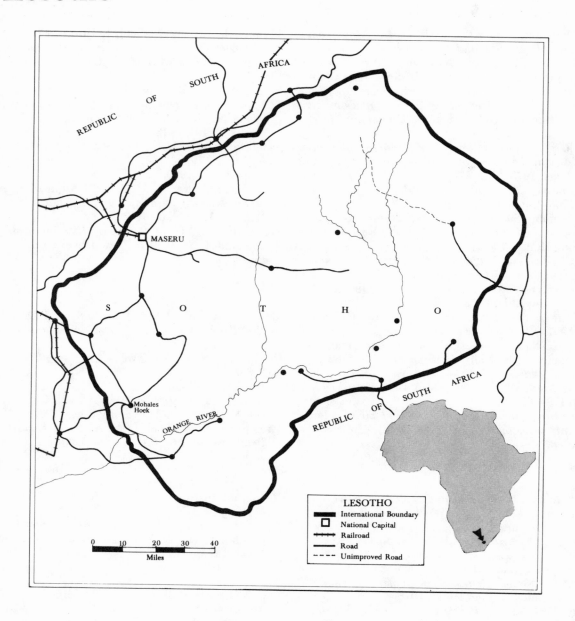

I. Basic Information

Date of Independence: October 4, 1966
Former Colonial Ruler: United Kingdom
Former Name: Basutoland
Estimated Population (1980): 1,332,000
Area Size (equivalent in U.S.): 11,716 sq. mi. (New Hampshire and Delaware)
Most Widely Spoken Languages: Sesotho—99%; Zulu— 1%

Date of Last Census: 1976
Major Exports 1977 as Percent of Total Exports: wool—21 percent; mohair—16 percent; diamonds—10 percent
Official Languages: English, Sesotho

II. Elite Political Instability

TABLE 19.1 Elite Instability (Post-Independence)

Date	Event
1. January 30, 1970	Coup d'État (Chief Jonathan, after apparently losing the election, takes power with the aid of the police and declares the election null.)
2. January 7, 1974	Attempted Coup. (Members of the opposition party, the BCP, attack police stations in an apparent attempt to oust Chief Jonathan.)

III. Country Features Worthy of Special Study

1. Surrounded by the Republic of South Africa.
2. Large part of male population normally away working in the South African mines.
3. Constitutional monarchy.
4. Ethnically very homogeneous.
5. One of the highest Christian percentages in Black Africa.

IV. Selected References

BIBLIOGRAPHY

Haliburton, G. *Historical Dictionary of Lesotho.* Metuchen, N.J.: Scarecrow Press, 1977.

Switzer, Les and Donna Switzer. *The Black Press in South Africa and Lesotho: A Descriptive Bibliographical Guide.* Boston: G. K. Hall, 1979.

Wilken, Gene C. and Carolyn F. Amiet, comps. *Bibliography for Planning and Development in Lesotho.* Fort Collins, Col.: Colorado State University, 1977.

Willet, S. M. and D. Ambrose. *Lesotho: A Comprehensive Bibliography.* Santa Barbara, Ca.: Clio Press, 1980.

GENERAL

Ashton, Hugh, *The Basuto: A Social Study of Traditional and Modern Lesotho* 2nd ed. London: Oxford University Press, 1967.

Central Office of Information Reference Pamphlet. *Lesotho.* London: Her Majesty's Stationery Office, 1966.

Coates, Austin. *Basutoland.* London: Her Majesty's Stationery Office, 1966.

Halpern, Jack. *South Africa's Hostages: Basutoland, Bechuanaland and Swaziland.* Baltimore: Penguin, 1965.

Potholm, C. and Richard Dale, eds. *South Africa in Perspective.* New York: Free Press, 1972.

Sanders, Peter. *Moshoeshoe, Chief of the Sotho.* London: Heinemann, 1975.

Stevens, Richard. *Lesotho, Botswana, and Swaziland.* London: Pall Mall Press, 1967.

POLITICAL

Hammett, I. *Chieftancy and Legitimacy: An Anthropological Study of Executive Law in Lesotho.* Boston: Routledge and Kegan Paul, 1975.

Khaketla, B. M. *Lesotho 1970: An African Coup Under the Microscope.* Berkeley: University of California Press, 1972.

Spence, J. E. *Lesotho: the Politics of Dependence.* London: Oxford University Press, 1968.

Strom, Gabrielle W. *Development and Dependence in Lesotho, the Enclave of South Africa.* Uppsala, Scandinavian Institute of African Studies, 1978.

Weisfelder, Richard. *The Basotho Monarchy: A Spent Force or a Dynamic Political Factor?* Athens, Ohio: Center for International Studies, Ohio University, 1972. Papers in International Studies, Africa Series, No. 16.

ECONOMIC

International Monetary Fund. "Lesotho," in *Surveys of African Economies,* Vol. 5. Washington, D.C.: I.M.F., 1973. .

Leistner, J. M. E. *Lesotho: Economic Structure and Growth.* Pretoria: Africa Institute, 1966.

Manne, W. *Lesotho: A Development Challenge.* Baltimore: Johns Hopkins University Press, 1975.

Strom, Gabrielle W. *Socio-Economic Structure and Authorities in Southern Africa.* Uppsala University. Department of Peace Research, 1975.

Ward, Michael. "Economic Independence for Lesotho," *Journal of Modern African Studies,* 5 (1967): 355—368.

World Bank. *Lesotho: A Development Challenge.* World Bank Country Economic Report Series, Baltimore: John Hopkins University Press, 1975.

SOCIAL

Gerard, Albert S. "Literature of Lesotho." *Africa Report,* 11 (October 1965): 68—70.

Kuper, A. "The Social Structure of the Sotho-Speaking Peoples of Southern Africa," *Africa* 45 1 (1975), Part I, pp. 67—82, Part II.

Rose, Brian. "Education in Botswana, Lesotho and Swaziland." In *Education in Southern Africa,* ed. B. Rose. London: Collier-Macmillan, 1970.

Sheddick, Vernon G. J. *The Southern Sotho.* Ethnographic Survey of Africa. Southern Africa, pt. 2. London: International African Institute, 1953.

Wallman, Sandra. *Take Out Hunger: Two Case Studies of Rural Develoment in Basutoland.* New York: Humanities Press, 1969.

20. Liberia

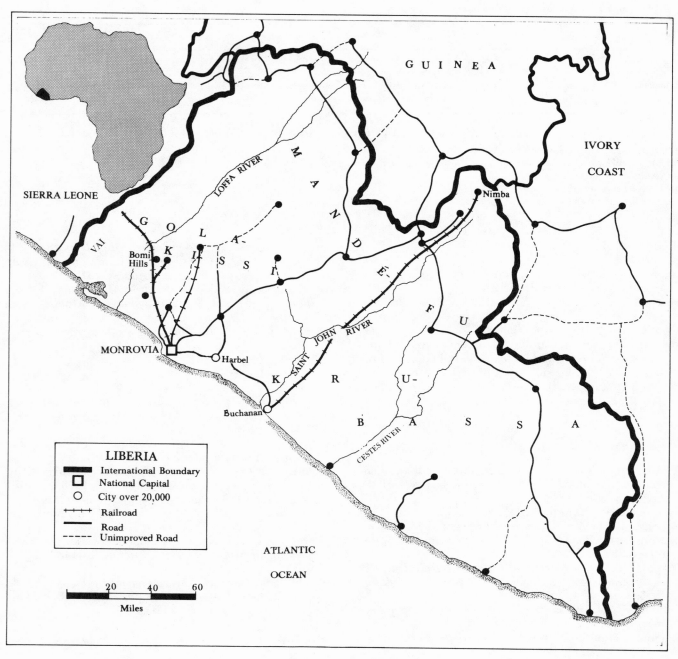

LIBERIA
- ▬▬▬ International Boundary
- ▢ National Capital
- ○ City over 20,000
- ┼┼┼ Railroad
- ─── Road
- - - - Unimproved Road

20 40 60
Miles

I. Basic Information

Date of Independence: 1847
Estimated Population (1980): 1,850,000
Area Size (equivalent in U.S.): 43,000 sq. mi. (Ohio)
Date of Last Census: 1974
Most Widely Spoken Languages: Mande—44%; Kru-
    Bassa—37%

Major Exports as Percent of Total Exports: iron ore—56
percent; rubber—14 percent; coffee—10 per-
cent(1977); diamonds—6 percent; wood—6 per-
cent(1977).

II.   Elite Political Instability

TABLE 20.1   Elite Instability (Post-Independence)

Date	Event
1. June 24, 1955	Attempted Coup (Assassination attempt by associates of former Pres. Barclay.)
2. April 12, 1980	Coup d'État (Coup led by army sergeant Doe, overthrows Tolbert.)

III.   Country Features Worthy of Special Study

1. Country largely dependent on foreign multi-national corporations for development of their resources.
2. "Settlers" have until recently dominated political, economic, and social life in the country.
3. Country never under colonial rule.
4. Long association with the United States.

IV. Selected References

BIBLIOGRAPHY

Holsoe, Sven. *A Bibliography of Liberia*. Part I Book. Part III. Articles. Newark, Del.: Liberian Studies Association, 1971, 1976.

GENERAL

Buell, Raymond L. *Liberia: A Century of Survival, 1847—1947*. Philadelphia: University of Pennsylvania Press, 1947.

Cassell, C. Abayomi. *Liberia: History of the First African Republic*. N.Y.: Fountainhead, 1970.

Clifford, M. L. *The Land and People of Liberia*. Philadelphia: Lippincott, 1971.

Henries, A. Doris Banks. *A Bibliography of President William V. S. Tubman*. London: Macmillan, 1967.

Liberian Studies Journal. Newark, Del.: University of Delaware, Department of Anthropology.

Liebenow, J. Gus. *Liberia, The Evolution of Privilege*. Ithaca, N.Y.: Cornell University Press, 1969.

Smith, Robert A. *William V. S. Tubman, the Life and Work of an African Statesman*. Amsterdam: Van Ditmar, 1967.

U.S. Department of the Army. *Area Handbook for Liberia*, 2nd ed. Washington, D.C.: Government Printing Office, 1972.

Von Grielinski, S., ed. *Liberia in Maps*. New York: Africana, 1972.

Wilson, Charles M. *Liberia: Black Africa in Microcosm*. New York: Harper, 1971.

POLITICAL

Clapham, C. *Liberia and Sierra Leone: An Essay in Comparative Politics*. New York: Cambridge University Press, 1976.

Fraenkel, Merran. "Social Change on the Kru Coast of Liberia." *Africa*, 36 (1966): 154—172.

Holas, Bohumil. *Mission dans l'Est Liberien: Resultats demographiques, ethnologiques et anthropometriques*. Dakar: L'Institut Français d'Afrique Noire, 1952.

Sawyer, Amos, "Social Stratification and National Orientations: Students and Nonstudents in Liberia," in John N. Paden (ed) *Values, Identities, and National Integration: Empirical Research in Africa*, Northwestern University Press, 1980, p. 285—303.

Schulze, W. *A New Geography of Liberia*. London: Longmans, 1973.

Study Committee on Manpower Needs and Educational Capabilities in Africa. *Liberia: Study of Manpower Needs, Educational Capabilites and Overseas Study*, Report 5. New York: Education and World Affairs, 1965.

Lowenkopf, M. *Politics in Liberia*. Stanford: Hoover Institution, 1976.

ECONOMIC

Carlsson, Jerker. *Transnational Companies in Liberia*. Uppsala, Scandinavian Institute of African Studies, 1977.

Dalton, George and A. A. Walters. "The Economy of Liberia." In *The Economies of Africa*, eds. P. Robson and D. A. Lury, pp. 287—315. Evanston, Ill.: Northwestern University Press, 1969.

Hanes, William A. "Iron Ore in Liberia: A Study of the Impact of Mining on a Developing Economy." In *African Economic Development*, rev. ed., pp. 54—86. New York: Praeger, 1967.

International Monetary Fund. "Liberia." In *Surveys of African Economies*, Vol. 6. Washington, D.C.: I.M.F., 1975.

Liberia. Ministry of Planning and Economic Affairs. *Economic Survey of Liberia, 1977*. Monrovia, 1978.

SOCIAL

Fraenkel, Merran. *Tribe and Class in Monrovia*. London: Oxford University Press, 1964.

21. Madagascar

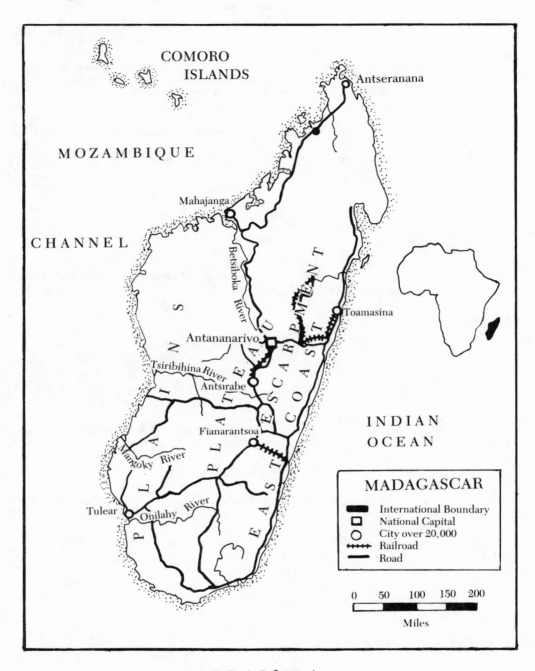

I. Basic Information

Date of Independence: June 26, 1960
Area Size (equivalent in U.S.): 226, 657 sq. miles (Arizona and Nevada)
Former Colonial Ruler: France

Most Widely Spoken Language: Malagasy—96%

Date of Last Census: 1975
Major Exports 1977 as Percent of Total Exports: coffee—48 percent; vanilla—11 percent; cloves—6 percent; petroleum products—6.6 percent (1976).

Official Language: French and Malagasy

TABLE 21.1   Elite Instability (Post-Independence)

Date	Event
1. May 18, 1972	Coup d'État (Gen. Ramanantsoa took over during time of civil strife.)
2. February 11, 1975	Coup Attempt (Members of special mobile police try to overthrow government.)

III.   Country Features Worthy of Special Study

1. Unique mixture of African and Asian racial and cultural backgrounds.
2. Country is entirely situated on one major island (fourth largest in the world) and several small island dependencies.
3. History of close cooperation with France and the recipient of a large amount of French aid which has changed under the current administration.
4. Tends to remain somewhat aloof from African affairs, although it is active in the Organization of African Unity.

IV. Selected References

BIBLIOGRAPHY

Duignan P. *Madagascar (The Malagasy Republic), A List of Materials* etc. Stanford: Hoover Institution, 1962.

Fontvieille, Jean R. *Bibliographie Nationale de Madagascar*, 1956–63. Tananarive, Université de Madagascar, 1971.

GENERAL

Bastian, Georges. *Madagascar: Étude Geographique et Economique.* Tananarive: Fernand Nathan, 1967.

Cadoux, Charles. *La Republique* . Paris: Berger-Levrault, 1969.

Deschamps, Hubert. *Madagascar*, 2nd. ed. Paris, DUF, 1976.

Deschamps, Hubert. *Histoire de Madagascar*. Paris: Berger-Levrault, 1972.

Heseltine, Nigel. *Madagascar.* New York: Praeger, 1971.

Kent, Raymond K. *From Madagascar to the Malagasy Republic.* New York: Praeger, 1963.

Ostheimer, John M., ed. *The Politics of the Western Indian Ocean*, New York: Praeger, 1975.

Pascal, Roger. *La Republique.* Paris: Berger-Levrault, 1965.

Ralaimihoatra, Edouard. *Histoire de Madagascar.* Tananarive: Societe Malagàche d'Edition, 1966.

Thompson, Virginia and Adloff, Richard. *The Malagasy Republic: Madagascar Today.* Stanford: Stanford University Press, 1965.

U.S. Department of the Army. *Area Handbook for the Malagasy Republic.* Washington, D.C.: Government Printing Office, 1973.

POLITICAL

Comte, Jean. *Les Communes Malgaches.* Tananarive: Editions de la Librairie de Madagascar, 1963.

Gaudusson, Jean. *L'Administration Malagache* Paris: Berger Levrault, 1976.

Mannoni, O. *Prospero and Caliban: The Psychology of Colonization.* New York: Praeger, 1964.

Spacensky, Alain. *Madagascar: cinquante ans de vie politique.* Paris: Nouvelles Editions Latines, 1971.

ECONOMIC

Archer, Robert. *Madagascar depuis 1972*, Paris, Editions l'Harmatta, 1976.

Besairie, Henri. *Les resources minerales de Madagascar.* Tenanarive: Imprimerie Nationale, 1961.

Finance Ministère de la Cooperation. *Madagascar Donnes statistique sur les activities economique culturelles et sociales*, Paris, 1976.

Gendarmen, Rene. *L'economie de Madagascar: diagnostic et perspectives de developpement.* Paris: Editions Cujas, 1960.

Minelle, Jean. *L'agriculture á Madagascar.* Paris: Librairie M. Riviers, 1959.

World Bank. *Madagascar: Economic Memorandum on Current Economic Position and Prospects and Selected Development Issues.* Washington, D.C.: 1976.

SOCIAL

Gow, B.A. *Madagascar and the Protestant World.* New York: Holmes and Meier, 1980.

Ruud, Jorgen. *Taboo: A Study of Malagasy Customs and Beliefs.* London: Allen and Unwin, 1960.

Slawecki, L. M. S. *French Policy Towards the Chinese in Madagascar.* Hamden, Conn.: Shoe String Press, 1971.

22. Malawi

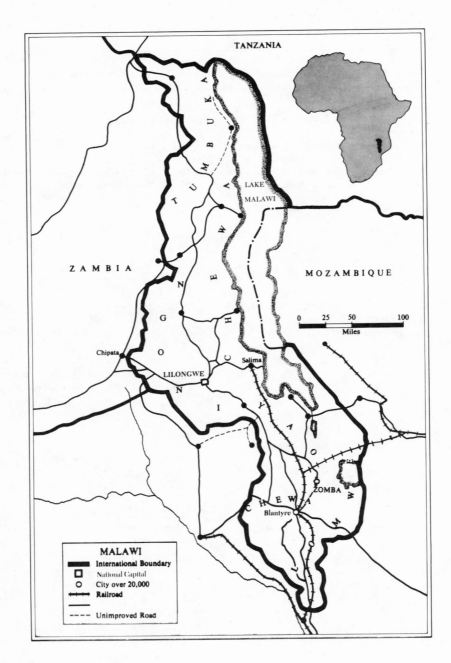

I. Basic Information

Date of Independence: July 6, 1964
Former Colonial Ruler: United Kingdom
Change in Boundaries: Formerly part of Central African
　Federation, 1953-1963
Former Name: Nyasaland
Estimated Population (1980): 5,734,000

Most Widely Spoken Languages: Chichewa—60%;
　Lomwe—19%

Area Size (equivalent in U.S.): 45,747 sq. mi. (including
　9,422 sq. miles of inland water (Louisianna)
Date of Last Census: 1977
Major Exports 1978 as Percent of Total Exports: * to-
　bacco—57 percent; tea—18 percent; sugar—7 per-
　cent; groundnuts—3 percent.

Official Language: Chichewa

*does not include re-exports.

III. Country Features Worthy of Special Study

1. Buffer state between Black Africa and white-controlled Africa. Malawi has tried to cooperate with South Africa and has been unique in maintaining formal diplomatic relations with South Africa.
2. Malawi has adopted a development strategy by emphasizing agricultural development among the small farmers.
3. Identification with ethnic groups less strong than in many other Black African countries.
4. Each year about 100,000 Malawi workers migrate to Zambia or South Africa to work in the mines.

IV. Selected References

BIBLIOGRAPHY

Boeder, R. M. *Malawi*, Santa Barbara, Ca: Clio Press, 1981.

Malawi *National Research Publications 1965—1975*, compiled by National Research Council. Lilongwe: The Council 1976.

GENERAL

Agnew, S. and M. Stubbs, eds. *Malawi in Maps*. New York: Africana, 1972.

Crosby, C. A., *Historical Dictionary of Malawi*, Metuchen, NJ: Scarecrow, 1980.

Debenham, F. *Nyasaland, the Land of the Lake*. London: Her Majesty's Stationery Office, 1955.

Pachai, B. *Malawi: The History of the Nation*. N.Y.: Longmans, 1973.

Pachai, B., ed. *The Early History of Malawi*. Evanston, Ill.: Northwestern University Press, 1972.

Pike, John G. *Malawi: A Political and Economic History*. New York: Praeger, 1968.

Pike, John G. and G. T. Rimmington. *Malawi, A Geographical Study*. London: Oxford University Press, 1965.

Read, Frank E. *Malawi, Land of Promise: A Comprehensive Survey*. Blantyre: R. Parker, 1967.

U.S. Department of the Army. *Area Handbook for Malawi*. Washington, D.C.: Government Printing Office, 1975.

POLITICAL

Jones, Griff. *Britain and Nyasaland*. London: Allen and Unwin, 1964.

Mair, Lucy P. *The Nyasaland Elections of 1961*. London: Athlone Press, 1962.

McCracken, John. *Politics and Christianity in Malawi, 1875—1940: The Impact of the Livingstonian Mission in the Northern Province*. New York: Cambridge University Press, 1977.

McMaster, Carolyn. *Malawi: Foreign Policy and Development*. London: Julian Friedmann, 1974.

Miller, Norman N. *Malawi-Central African Paradox*. Hanover N.H.: American University Field Staff, 1979.

Mufuka, K. N. *Missions and Politics in Malawi*. Kingston, Ontario: Limestone Press, 1977.

Pachai, B. *Land and Politics in Malawi, 1875-1975*. Kingston, Ontario: Limestone Press, 1978.

Short, Phillip. *Banda*. Boston: Routledge and Kegan Paul, 1974.

Williams, J. David. *Malawi: The Politics of Despair*. Ithaca, N.Y.: Cornell University Press, 1978.

ECONOMIC

Hazelwood, Arthur and P. O. Henderson, eds. *Nyasaland: The Economics of Federation*. Oxford: Blackwell, 1960.

Humphrey, David. *Malawi since 1964: Economic Development: Progress and Prospects*, Department of Economics, University of Malawi (1974) Occasional Paper no. 1.

International Monetary Fund. "Malawi." In *Surveys of African Economies*, vol. 4. Washington, D. C.: I.M.F., 1971.

SOCIAL

Malawi National Statistical Office. *Malawi Population Change Survey: Feb. 1970—January 1972*. Zomba: Government Printer, 1973.

Mitchell, J. Clyde. *The Yao Village: A Study in the Social Structure of a Nyasaland Tribe*. Manchester, England: Manchester University Press for Rhodes-Livingstone Institute, 1956.

Mead, Margaret. *Children of Their Fathers: Growing Up Among the Ngoni of Malawi*. New York: Holt, Rinehart and Winston, 1960, 1968.

Rimmington, Gerald T. "Education for Independence: A Study of Changing Educational Administration in Malawi." *Comparative Education*, 2 (1966): 217-223.

Seltzer, George. "High Level Manpower in Nyasaland's Development." In *Manpower and Education: Country Studies in Economic Development*, eds. F. B. Harbison and C. Myers. New York: McGraw-Hill, 1965.

Shepperson, George. *Myth and Reality in Malawi*, Evanston, Ill.: Northwestern University Press, 1976.

Wishlade, R. L. *Sectarianism in Southern Nyasaland*. London: Oxford University Press, 1965.

23. Mali

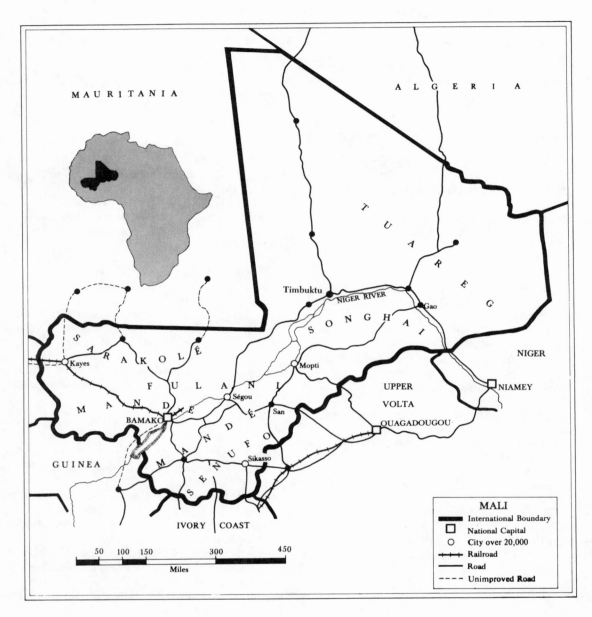

I. Basic Information

Date of Independence: September 22, 1960 (June 20, 1960 as Mali Federation)

Former Colonial Ruler: France

Change in Boundaries: Formerly part of French West African Federation. Part of the Mali Federation (formed with Senegal) from April 4, 1959, to August 20, 1960, when Senegal seceded.

Former Name: Soudan

Most Widely Spoken Languages: Bamana—50%; Fulani—10%

Estimated Population (1980): 6,474,000

Area Size (equivalent in U.S.): 478,767 sq. mi. (Texas, Colorado and Nevada)

Date of Last Census: 1976

Estimated Major Exports 1976 as percent of Total Exports: cotton and cotton products—50 percent; groundnuts—16 percent; live animals—13 percent.

Official Language: French

II. Elite Political Instability

TABLE 23.1 Elite Instability (Post-Independence)

Date	Event
1. November 19, 1968	Coup d'État (Army overthrows the government of Modibo Keita and assumes power.)

III. Country Features Worthy of Special Study

1. Revolutionary socialist state under Modibo Keita until 1968.
2. Landlocked country in the center of the drought belt.
3. One of the poorest countries in the world.

IV. Selected References

BIBLIOGRAPHY

Brasseur, Paule. *Bibliographie Generale du Mali (Anciens Soudan Francais et Haut-Senegal-Niger).* I.F.A.N. catalogues et documents, 16. Dakar: I.F.A.N., 1964.

Brasseur, Paule. *Bibliographie Generale du Mali, 1961–1970.* Dakar, Nouvelles Editions Africaines 1970.

Cutler, C. H. "Mali: A Bibliographic Introduction." *African Studies Bulletin,* 9 (1966): 74–78

Imperato, P. J. *Historical Dictionary of Mali.* Metuchen, N.J.: Scarecrow, 1977.

GENERAL

Imperato, P. J. *Mali, a Handbook of Historical Statistics* Boston: G. K. Hall, 1982.

Thompson, Virginia and Richard Adloff. *French West Africa,* pp. 146-54. Stanford, Ca.: Stanford University Press, 1957.

POLITICAL

Amin, Samir. *Neo-Colonialism in West Africa.* Harmondsworth, Middlesex: Penguin Books, 1973.

Barate, C. *Administration locale et socialisme dans le Mali independant,* 1977. vol. 31, no. 3, pp. 1035–37

de Lusignan, Guy. *French-Speaking Africa since Independence,* pp. 231-49. London: Pall Mall Press, 1969.

Foltz, William J. *From French West Africa to the Mali Federation.* New Haven, Conn.: Yale University Press, 1965.

Hazard, John N. "Marxian Socialism in Africa: The Case of Mali." *Comparative Politics,* 2 (October 1969): 1—15.

Rondos, Alexander G. "What Kind of Handover?" *Africa Report,* vol. 24, 1979.

Hopkins, Nicholas S. *Popular Government in an African Town.* Chicago: University of Chicago Press, 1972.

Synder, Francis G. *One-Party Government in Mali: Transition Toward Control.* New Haven, Conn.: Yale University Press, 1965.

ECONOMIC

Amin, Samir. *Trois Experiences Africaines de Developpement: le Mali, la Guinee et le Ghana.* Paris: Presses Universitaires de France, 1965.

Jouve, Edmond. *La Republique du Mali,* Paris, Berger-Levrault, 1974.

Klaus, E. *Tradition and Progress in the African Village: the Noncapitalist Reforms of Rural Communities in Mali.* N.Y.: St. Martin's Press, 1975.

"Mali" In *Surveys of African Economies,* Vol. 7 Washington, D.C.: International Monetary Fund, 1977.

SOCIAL

Diop, Majhemouf. *Histoire des classes sociales dans l'Afrique de l'Ouest: Le Mali.* Paris: Francois Maspero, 1971.

Meillassoux, Claude. *Urbanisation of an African Community: Voluntary Associations in Bamako.* Seattle: University of Washington Press, 1968.

Milner, Horace. *The Primitive City of Timbuctoo.* rev. ed. Garden City, N.Y.: Anchor Books, 1965.

Ouologuem, Yambo. *Bound to Violence.* New York: Harcourt, Brace and Jovanovich, 1971.

Paques, Viviana. *Les Bambara.* Paris: Presses universitaires de France, 1954

24. Mauritania

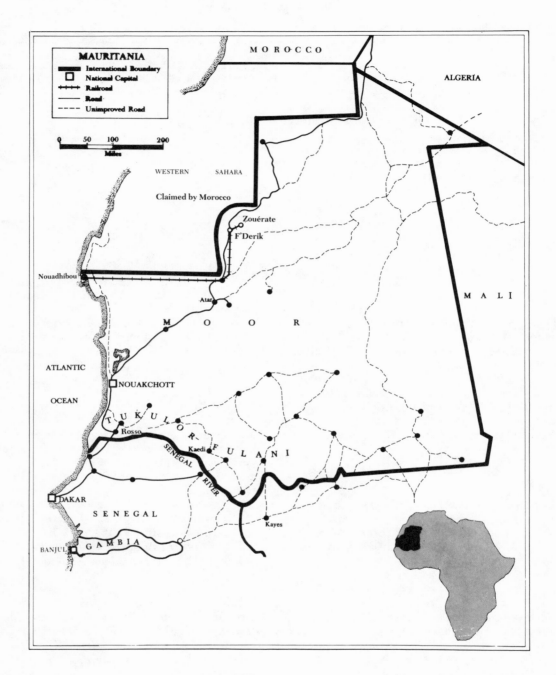

I. Basic Information

Date of Independence: November, 1960
Former Colonial Ruler: France
Change in Boundaries: Formerly part of French West Africa Federation (often grouped with Senegal for census purposes during the colonial period)

Most Widely Spoken Languages: Arabic—90%; Fulani—13%

Estimated Population (1980): 1,588,000
Area Size (equivalent in U.S.): 397,950 sq. mi. (Texas, Colorado and Nevada)
Date of Last Census: 1977
Major Exports 1976 as Percent of Total Exports: iron ore—86 percent.
Official Language: French, Arabic

II. Elite Political Instability

TABLE 24.1   Elite Instability (Post- Independence)

Date		Event
1. July 10, 1978	Coup	(Army under Salek overthrows Pres. Daddah because of dissatisfaction with government policy on the former Spanish Sahara.)
2. April, 1979	Coup	(Lt. Col. Bouceif named Prime Minister and effective head of government over apparent dissatisfaction with Salek's handling of the war.)
3. January, 1980	Coup	(Louly dismissed as a result of power struggle within the military.)
4. March 16, 1981	Attempted Coup	(Exiled army officers lead attack against Presidential Palace and are repulsed.)

III. Country Features Worthy of Special Study

1. Muslim religious-based state.
2. Arab majority in conflict with non-Arabic minority along the Senegalese border.
3. Directly in the drought belt.

IV. Selected References

BIBLIOGRAPHY

Van Maele, Bernard. *Bibliographie Mauritanie.* Nouakchott, Ministere de l'information et de la culture, 1971.

GENERAL

Gerteiny, Alfred G. *Historical Dictionary of Mauritania.* Metuchen, N.J.: Scarecrow, 1981.

Heyman, J. M. "Mauritania: An Annotated Bibliography of Bibliographies." *Current Bibliography of African Affairs.* 1978—79 p. 378-80.

U.S. Department of the Army. *Area Handbook for Mauritania,* Washington, D.C.: Government Printing Office, 1972.

POLITICAL

Chassey. F. de. *Mauritanie, 1900-1975: de l'ordre colonial a l'ordre neo-colonial entre Maghreb et Afrique noire.* Paris, Ed. Antropes, 1978.

de Lusignan, Guy. *French-Speaking Africa since Independence,* pp. 218-230. London: Pall Mall Press, 1969.

Gaudio, Attilio. *Le Dosier de la Mauritanie.* Paris, Nouvelles Edition Latines. 1978.

ECONOMIC

Bradley, P., Raynaut, C., Tarrealba, J. *The Guidimaka Region of Mauritania: A Critical Analysis Leading to a Development Project.* London: International African Institute, 1977.

International Monetary Fund. "Mauritania." In *Surveys of African Economies,* Vol. 3 Washington, D.C.: I.M.F., 1970.

Westebbe, Richard M. *The Economy of Mauritania.* New York: Praeger, 1971.

SOCIAL

Stewart, C. C. and E. K. Stewart, *Mauritania, a Study from the 19th Century.* Oxford: Clarendon Press, 1973.

25. Mozambique

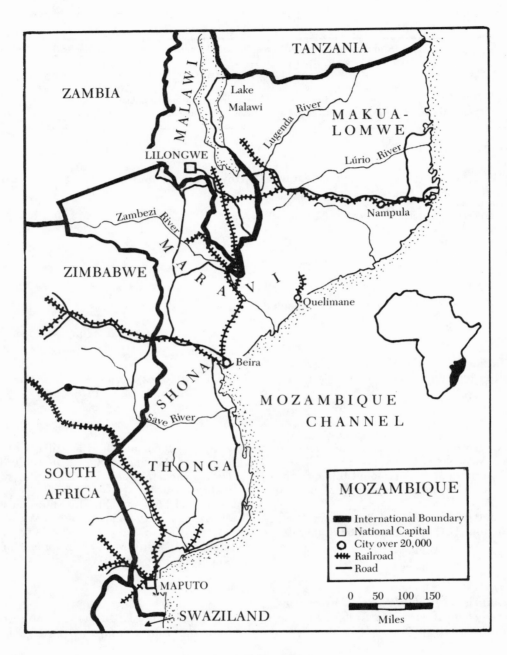

I. Basic Information

Date of Independence: June 25, 1975
Former Colonial Ruler: Portugal
Estimated Population (1980): 10,339,000
Area Size (equivalent in U.S.): 303,769 sq. mi. (Texas and Louisiana)
Date of Last Census: 1970

(Aug, 1980, a census was conducted, but results not available.)
Major Exports 1977 as Percent of Total Exports: cashew nuts—30 percent; textiles—9 percent; cotton—6 percent; sugar—5 percent; vegetable oils—4 percent; tea—8 percent; wood—3 percent.

Most Widely Spoken Languages: Makua—40%; Thonga—23%

Official Language: Portuguese

III.   Country Features Worthy of Special Study

1. Mozambique is located between Zimbabwe and the sea and has a common border with South Africa. This strategic location automatically makes her an important actor in the struggle to erase the last vestiges of non-Black rule in Southern Africa.
2. Along with Guinea-Bissau, it is one of the two countries in Black Africa which came to independence after a prolonged military struggle in which the African opposition was basically unified (unlike Angola).
3. One of the highest percent of population adhering to traditional religion in Black Africa.

IV. Selected References

BIBLIOGRAPHY

Gibson, Mary Jane. *Portuguese Africa: A Guide to Official Publications*. Washington, D. C.: 1967.

GENERAL

Abshire, David, and Michael Samuels (eds.). *Portuguese Africa-A Handbook*. New York: Praeger, 1970.
Bruce, N. *Portugal: The Last Empire*. New York: Halsted Press, 1975.
Chilcote, Ronald. *Portuguese Africa*. Englewood Cliffs, N.J.: Prentice Hall, 1967.
Egego, B. *Mozambique and Angola*. Uppsala: Scandinavian Institute of African Studies, 1977.
Kaplan, I., et al. *Area Handbook for Mozambique*, 2nd ed. Washington, D.C.: U.S. Government Printing Office, 1977.
Swift, Kerry. *Mozambique and the Future*. London: R. Hale, 1975.

POLITICAL

Gann, L. H. "Portugal, Africa, and the Future." *Journal of Modern African Studies*, 13, 1 (1975): 1—18.
Henriksen, T. H. "Portugal in Africa: A Noneconomic Interpretation," *African Studies Review* 16, 3 (December 1973): 405—16.
Humbaraci, A., and N. Muchnik. *Portugal's African Wars*. London: Macmillan, 1974.

Isaacman, Allen. *A Luta Continua: Creating a New Society in Mozambique*. Binghamton, N.Y.: Ferdinand Braudel Center, 1978.
Martins, Elisio. *Colonialism and Imperialism in Mozambique: The Beginning of the End*. Kastrup Denmark African Studies 1974.
Middlemas, K. *Cabora Basssa: Engineering and Politics in Southern Africa*. London: Weidenfeld and Nicholson, 1976.
Mittleman, James H., *Underdevelopment and the Transition to Socialism: Mozambique and Tanzania*, New York: Academic Press, 1981.
Mondlane, Eduardo. *The Struggle for Mozambique*. London: Penguin, 1969.
Paul, J. *Mozambique: Memoirs of a Revolution*. Harmondsworth: Penguin, 1975.
Rees, D. "Soviet Strategic Penetration of Africa," *Conflict Studies* 77 (November 1976): 1—20.

ECONOMIC

Torp, Jens Erik. *Industrial Planning and Development in Mozambique: Some Preliminary Considerations*. Uppsala: The Scandinavian Institute of African Studies, 1979.

SOCIAL

Henriksen, T. H. *Mozambique: A History*. London: Rex Collings, 1978.
Smith, A. K. "The Peoples of Southern Mozambique: An Historical Survey," *Journal of African History*, 14, 4 (1973): 565—80.

26. Namibia

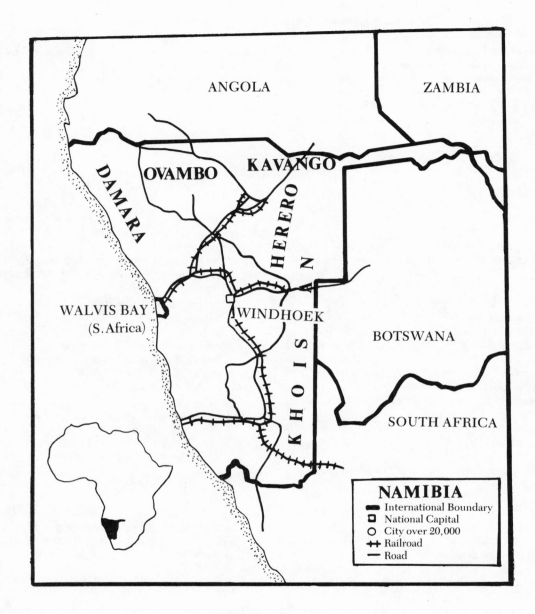

I. Basic Information

Date of Independence: Not Independent as of the end of 1982

Former Colonial Ruler: Germany, South Africa.

Change in Boundaries: Former League of Nations mandated territory administered by South Africa since 1920.

Former Name: South West Africa.

Estimated Population (1980): 1,020,000

Area Size (equivalent in U.S.): 317,827 sq. miles (Louisiana and Texas).

Most Widely Spoken Languages: Ambo, Afrikaans, English.

Date of Last Census: 1970.

Major Exports 1972 as Percent of Total Exports:* diamonds—38 percent; fish products—19 percent; livestock—15 percent; karakul pelts—14 percent.

Official Languages: Afrikaans, English, German

*After 1966 no official export data were released for Namibia. Source for 1972 exports: *Africa South of the Sahara, 1978—79.*

III.   Country Features Worthy of Special Study

1. Small population coupled with most mineral wealth and considerable development infrastructure for such a population.
2. Large European population closely linked to South Africa.
3. Complex ethnic and cultural divisions in population.

IV. Selected References

BIBLIOGRAPHY

Bridgman, J. and D. E. Clarke. *German Africa: A Select Annotated Bibliography.* Stanford: Hoover Institution, 1965.

Schoeman, E., *The Namibian Issue, 1920-1980: A Select and Annotated Bibliography.* Boston: G. K. Hall, 1982.

GENERAL

First, Ruth. *South West Africa.* Harmondsworth: Penguin, 1963.

Serfontein, J. H. P. *Namibia.* London: Rex Collins, 1977.

Winter, Colin. *Namibia.* London: Lutterworth Press, 1977.

POLITICAL

Tatemeyer, G. *Namibia Old and New: Traditional and Modern Leaders in Ovamboland.* London: Hurst, 1974.

SOCIAL

Wellington, J. H. *Southern Africa: A Geographical Study,* London: Oxford University Press, 1978.

Wellington, J. H. *South West Africa and Its Human Issues,* Oxford, Clarendon Press, 1967.

ECONOMIC

Thomas, W. H. *Economic Development in Namibia,* Munich: Grunewald, 1978.

27. Niger

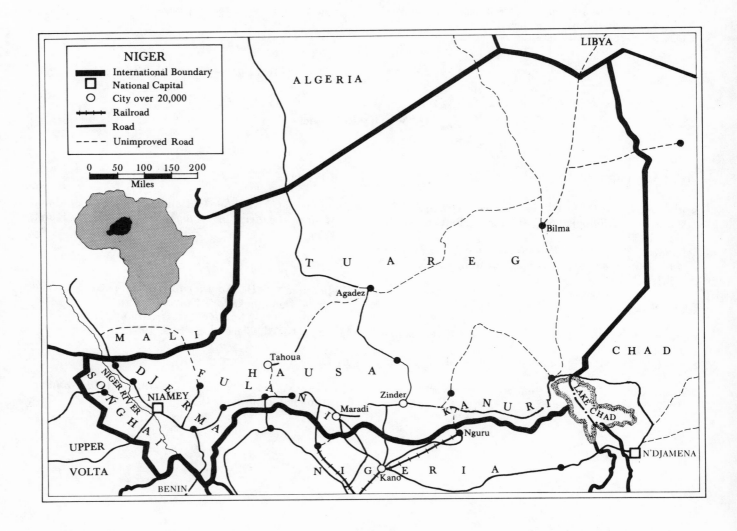

I. Basic Information

Date of Independence: August 3, 1960
Former Colonial Ruler: France
Change in Boundaries: Formerly part of the French West Africa Federation
Estimated Population (1980): 4,832,000
Area Size (equivalent in U.S.): 489,190 sq. mi. (Texas, Nevada, and New Mexico)

Most Widely Spoken Languages: Hausa—81%; Songhai—24%

Date of Last Census: 1977
Major Exports 1978 as Percent of Total Exports*: uranium ore—65 percent.
Official Language: French

*Considerable unrecorded trade takes place across the Niger-Nigeria border particularly in commodities such as groundnuts and livestock. The droughts of the 1970's exacerbated this phenomenon.

II.   Elite Political Instability

TABLE, 27.1   Elite Instability (Post- Independence)

Date	Event
1. April 15, 1974	Coup d'État (Army ousts Pres. Diori.)
2. March 14—15, 1976	Attempted Coup (Army units under Moussa Bayere attempt to take power but are repulsed.)

III.   Country Features Worthy of Special Study

1. Landlocked country with very little water and badly affected by the drought.
2. Major French influence in the development of the country.
3. Very poor in mineral resources except for uranium.

IV. Selected References

BIBLIOGRAPHY

DeCalo, S. *Historical Dictionary of Niger*. Metuchen, N.J.: Scarecrow Press, 1979.

GENERAL

Charlick, R. and J. Thompson. *Niger*. Boulder, Colo.: Westview Press, 1981.

Clair, Andrée. *Le Niger: pays á decouvrir*. Paris: Hachette, 1965.

Donnaint, P. and F. Lancrenon. *Le Niger*. Paris: Presses Universitaires de France, 1976.

Riveieres, Edmond Sere de. *Histoire du Niger*. Paris: Bergere-Levrault, 1965.

POLITICAL

Amin, Samir. *Neo-Colonialism in West Africa*. Harmondsworth, Middlesex: Penguin Books, 1973.

de Lusignan, Guy. *French-Speaking Africa since Independence*, pp. 151-59. London: Pall Mall Press, 1969.

Jouve, E. "Du Niger de Diori Hamani au Gouvernment des Militaires (1974-1977)." *Revue Français Études Politiques Africaines, 149, May 1978, pp. 19-44.*

Thompson, Virginia. "Niger." In *National Unity and Regionalism in Eight African States*, ed. Gwendolen M. Carter. Ithaca, N.Y.: Cornell University Press, 1966.

ECONOMIC

International Monetary Fund. "Niger." In *Surveys of African Economies*, Vol. 3. Washington, D.C.: I.M.F., 1970.

SOCIAL

Van Hoey, Leo F. "The Coercive Process of Urbanization: The Case of Niger." In *The New Urbanization*, eds. Scott Greer, et al. New York: St. Martin's Press, 1968.

28. Nigeria

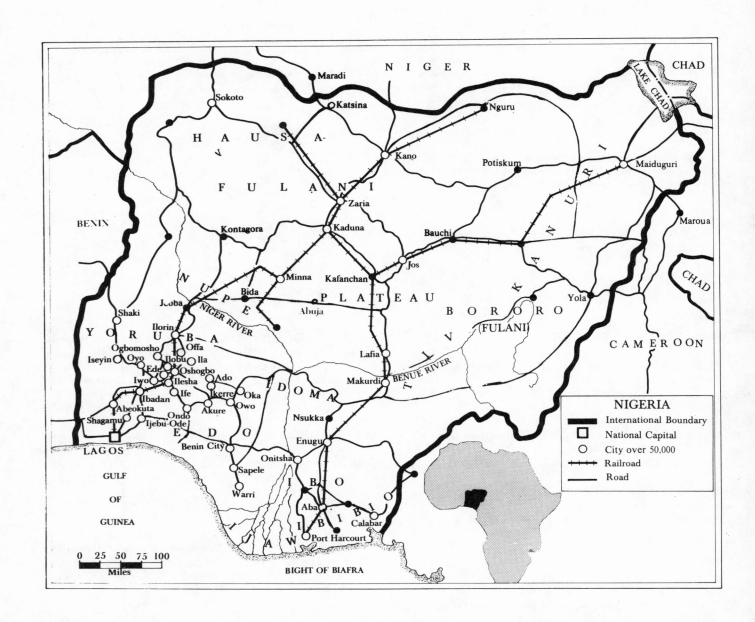

I. Basic Information

Date of Independence: October 1, 1960

Former Colonial Ruler: United Kingdom

Change in Boundaries: Addition of UN Trust Territory of Northern Cameroons on June 1, 1961

Estimated Population (1980): 72,600,000 (Note some estimates are up to 90,000,000)

Most Widely Spoken Languages: Hausa—55%; Yoruba—27%; Ibo—17%

Area Size (equivalent in U.S.): 356,669 sq. mi. (Texas and Colorado)

Date of Last Census: 1973 (Results repudiated by the government in August 1975—currently they use extrapolated 1963 results for government purposes)

Major Exports 1979 as Percent of Total Exports: crude petroleum—94 percent

Official Language: English

II.   Elite Political Instability

TABLE 28.1   Elite Instability (Post-Independence)

Date	Event
1. January 15, 1966	Coup (First Republic toppled with the murder of Balewa, the Prime Minister, and other leaders by a group of army officers.)
2. July 29, 1966	Coup (Military regime of Gen. Ironsi overthrown in a coup in which he is killed. This coup was led by Northern officers fearful of the effects of Ironsi's policies on Northern interests.)
3. July 29, 1975	Coup (Gen. Gowon overthrown by senior military officers while out of the country.)
4. February 13, 1976	Attempted Coup (Gen. Mohammed was murdered but attempt was quickly defeated.)

III.   Country Features Worthy of Special Study

1. Largest population in Africa with the most diverse peoples and cultures.
2. Major oil producer which is generating funds for rapid development, has several major cash crops and resources.
3. Suffered major civil war.
4. One of the two Federations in Black Africa. (Sudan is the other)

IV. Selected References

BIBLIOGRAPHY

Aguolu, C. C. *Nigerian Civil War, 1967—70, An Annotated Bibliography*. Boston: G.K. Hall, 1973.

Aguolu, C. C. *Nigeria: A Comprehensive Bibliography in the Humanities and Social Sciences, 1900—1971*. Boston, G.K. Hall, 1975.

Alati, G. A. and O. G. Tamuno, eds. *Nigerian Publications 1950—1970*. Ibadan: Ibadan University Press, 1977.

Baum, Edward. *A Comprehensive Periodical Bibliography of Nigeria, 1960—1970*. Athens, Ohio: Center for International Studies, Ohio University, 1975. Papers in International Studies, Africa Series, No. 24.

Ita, Nduntuei O. *Bibliography of Nigeria: A Survey of Anthropological and Lingusitic Writings from the Earliest Time to 1966*. New York: Africana, 1971.

GENERAL

Coleman, James S. *Nigeria, Background to Nationalism*. Berkeley: University of California Press, 1958, reprinted 1971.

Crowder, Michael. *The Story of Nigeria*, rev. ed. London: Faber, 1966.

Nelson, H. D. et al. *Area Handbook for Nigeria*, 4th ed. Washington, D.C.: Government Printing Office, 1982.

Onimoloye, S. A. ed. *Biographia Nigeriana: A Biographical Dictionary of Eminent Nigerians*. Boston: G.K. Hall, 1977.

Schwartz, Frederick A. O., Jr. *Nigeria: The Tribes, the Nations, or the Race—The Politics of Independence*. Cambridge: The MIT Press, 1965.

Schwartz, Walter. *Nigeria*. New York: Praeger, 1968.

Udo, Reuben K. *Geographical Regions of Nigeria*. Berkeley: University of California Press, 1970.

Williams, G. *Nigeria: Economy and Society*. Totowa, N.J.: Rowan and Littlefield, 1977.

POLITICAL

Adelayo, Augustus. "Policy-Making in Nigerian Political Administration," London: *Journal of Administration Overseas*, vol. 18, no. 1, January 1979, pp. 4—14.

Akinsanya, A. "The Count Down to Civilian Rule in Nigeria: The Constituent Assembly." London: *Journal of Administration Overseas*, vol. 18, no. 1, January 1979, pp. 34—45.

Arnold, Guy. *Modern Nigeria*. London: Longmans, 1977.

Baker, Pauline H. *Urbanization and Political Change: The Politics of Lagos, 1917—1967*. Berkeley: University of California Press, 1974.

Bienen, H. and V. P. Diejomaoh. *Political Economy of Income Distribution in Nigeria*. New York: Holmes and Meier, 1981.

Biersteker, T. J. *Distortion or Development: Contending Perspectives on the Multinational Corporation*. Cambridge, Mass.: The MIT Press, 1978.

Cohen, Robin. *Labour and Politics in Nigeria: 1945—1971*. New York: Africana, 1974.

De St. Jorre, John. *The Brothers War: Biafra and Nigeria*. Ibadan: Ibadan University Press, 1974.

Dudley, B. J. *Parties and Politics in Northern Nigeria*. London: Cass, 1968.

Dudley, B. J. *Instability and Political Order: Politics and Crisis in Nigeria*. Ibadan: University of Ibadan Press, 1973.

Dudley, B. J. *An Introduction to Nigerian Government*, Bloomington: Indiana University Press, 1982.

Idang, G. J. *Internal Politics and Foreign Policy, 1960—1966*. Ibadan: Ibadan University Press, 1974.

Joseph, Richard. "Political Party and Ideology in Nigeria." *Review of African Political Economy*, no. 18, 1979, pp. 78—90.

Kirk-Greene, A. H. M., ed. *Crisis and Conflict in Nigeria: A Documentary Sourcebook, 1966—1970*, 2 vols. London: Oxford University Press, 1971.

Luckham, R. *The Nigerian Military: A Sociological Analysis of Authority and Revolt 1960—67*. New York: Cambridge University Press, 1971.

Mackintosh, John P., ed. *Nigerian Government and Politics*. Evanston, Ill.: Northwestern University Press, 1966.

Nafziger, E. W. "The Political Economy of Disintegration in Nigeria." *Journal of Modern African Studies*, 1973, pp. 505—36.

Orewa, G. O. "The Role of Traditional Rulers in Administration." In *Quarterly Journal of Administration*, vol. 12, no. 2, January 1978, pp. 151—65.

Oyediran, Oyeleye, ed. *Nigerian Development and Politics under Military Rule, 1966—79*. London: Macmillan, 1979.

Paden, John N. *Religion and Political Culture in Kano*. Berkeley: University of California Press, 1973.

Panter-Brick, S. K., ed. *Nigerian Politics and Military Rule: Prelude to the Civil War*. London: University of London, The Athlone Press, 1970.

Panter-Brick, S. K., ed. *Soldiers and Oil: The Political Transformation of Nigeria*. London: Cass, 1978.

Peil, M. *Nigerian Politics: The People's View*. London: Cassell, 1976.

Post, Kenneth, W. J. and Michael Vickers. *Structure and Conflict in Nigeria, 1960—1965*. Madison: University of Wisconsin Press, 1973.

Segun, M. *Friends, Nigerians, Countrymen*. Ibadan: Oxford University Press, 1978.

Sklar, Richard L. *Nigerian Political Parties: Power in an Emergent African Nation*. Princeton: Princeton University Press, 1963.

Smock, Audrey C. *Ibo Politics: The Role of Ethnic Unions in Eastern Nigeria*. Cambridge, Mass.: Harvard University Press, 1971.

Wayas, John. *Nigeria's Leadership Role in Africa*. London: Macmillan, 1979.

Whitaker, C. S. *The Politics of Tradition: Continuity and Change in Northern Nigeria, 1946—1966*. Princeton: Princeton University Press, 1970.

Wolpe, H. *Urban Politics in Nigeria: A Study of Port Harcourt*. Berkeley: University of California Press, 1974.

Zartman, I. W. *The Political Economy of Nigeria*, New York: Praeger, 1983.

ECONOMIC

Aboyade, Ojetunji. *Foundations of an African Economy*. New York: Praeger, 1966.

Ayida, A. A. and H. M. A. Onitiri, eds. *Reconstruction and Development in Nigeria: Proceedings of a National Conference*. New York: Oxford University Press, 1972.

Dean, Edwin. *Plan Implementation in Nigeria, 1962—1966*. London: Oxford University Press, 1974.

Edundare, R. O. *An Economic History of Nigeria, 1860—1960*. London: Methuen, 1973.

Hay, A. and R. Smith. *Interregional Trade and Monetary Flows in Nigeria, 1964*. London: Oxford University Press, 1970.

Helleiner, G. R. *Peasant Agriculture, Government, and Economic Growth in Nigeria*. Homewood, Ill.: Irwin, 1966.

International Monetary Fund. "Nigeria." In *Surveys of African Economies*, Vol. 6. Washington, D.C.: I.M.F., 1975.

Kilby, Peter, *Industrialisation in an Open Economy: Nigeria, 1945—1966*. London: Cambridge University Press, 1969.

Nafziger, E. W. *African Capitalism: A Case Study in Nigerian Entrepreneurship*. Stanford: Hoover Institution, 1977.

Schatz, S. P. *Nigerian Capitalism*. Berkeley, Calif.: University of California Press, 1977.

Stolper, W. F. *Planning Without Facts: Lessons in Resource Allocation from Nigeria's Development*. Cambridge: Harvard University Press, 1966.

Tims, W. *Nigeria: Options for Long-Term Development*. Baltimore: Johns Hopkins University Press, 1974.

SOCIAL

Abernethy, David B. *The Political Dilemma of Popular Education: An African Case*. Stanford, Calif.: Stanford University Press, 1970.

Adeyeye, Samuel O. *The Co-operative in Nigeria: Yesterday, Today and Tomorrow*. Gottingen: Vandenhoech and Ruprecht, 1978.

Ajayi, J. F. Ade. *Christian Missions in Nigeria: The Making of a New Elite*. Evanston, Ill.: Northwestern University Press, 1965.

Ajayi, J. F. Ade, ed. *City of Lagos*. London: Longman, 1975.

Baldwin, D. E. and C. M. Baldwin. *The Yoruba of South Western Nigeria: An Indexed Bibliography*. Boston: G.K. Hall, 1976.

Bishop, Vaughn F. "Language Acquisition and Value Change in the Kano Urban Area" in John N. Paden ed. , *Values, Identities and National Integration*. Evanston, Ill. Northwestern University Press, 1980, pp. 183-96.

Brann, C. M. B. *Language in Education and Society in Nigeria*. Quebec City, Canada: International Center for Research on Bilingualism, 1974.

Eades, J. S. *The Yoruba Today*. New York: Cambridge University Press, 1981.

Ekanem, I. I. *The 1963 Nigerian Census*. Benin City, Nigeria: Ethiope Publishing, 1972.

Henderson, Richard. *The King in Every Man: Evolutionary Trends in Onitsha Ibo Society and Culture*. New Haven, Conn.: Yale University Press, 1972.

Hill, Polly. *Rural Hausa*: *A Village and a Setting*. New York: Cambridge University Press, 1972.

Hill, Polly. *Population, Prosperity and Poverty*: *Rural Kano, 1900 and 1970*. New York: Cambridge University Press, 1977.

LeVine, Robert A. *Dreams and Deeds*: *Achievement Motivation in Nigeria*. Chicago: University of Chicago Press, 1966.

Lloyd, P.C. *Power and Independence*. Boston: Routledge and Kegan Paul, 1974.

Lloyd, P. C., A. L. Mabogunje, and B. Awe. *The City of Ibadan*. London: Cambridge University Press, 1967.

Lucas, David and McWilliam, John. *Population in Nigeria*: *A Select Bibliography*. Chapel Hill, N.C.: Carolina Population Center, 1974.

Mabogunje, Akin L. *Urbanization in Nigeria*. New York: Africana, 1969.

Marris, P. *Family and Social Change in an African City*. Evanston, Ill.: Northwestern University Press, 1962.

Otite, O. *Autonomy and Dependence*: *The Urhobo Kingdom of Okpe in Modern Nigeria*. Ibadan, Nigeria: University of Ibadan Press, 1973.

Udo, R. K. *Geographical Regions of Nigeria*. London: Heinemann, 1970.

Van den Berghe, P. L. *Power and Privilege at an African University* . London: Routledge and Kegan Paul, 1973.

29. Rwanda

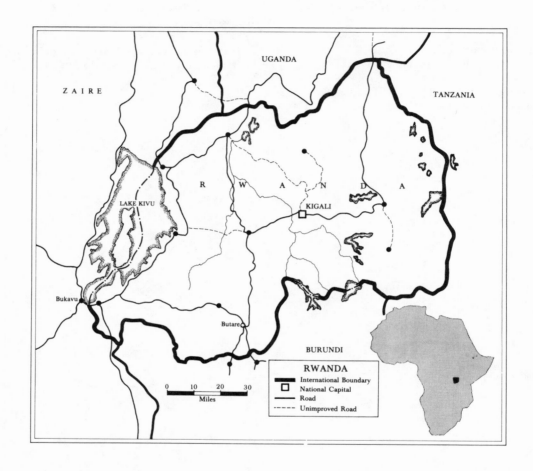

I. Basic Information

Date of Independence: July 1, 1962
Former Colonial Ruler: Belgium
Change in Boundaries: Before Independence it was part of the UN trust territory of Ruanda-Urundi
Former Name: Ruanda
Estimated Population (1980): 4,705,000

Most Widely Spoken Languages: Kinyaranda—98%; Swahili—15%

Area Size (equivalent in U.S.): 10,169 sq. mi. (Vermont)
Date of Last Census: 1978
Major Exports 1976 as Percent of Total Exports: coffee—77 percent; tea—7 percent; cassiterite (tin ore)—6 percent

Official Language: French and Kinyaranda

II. Elite Political Instability

TABLE 29.1 Elite Instability (Post- Independence)

Date	Event
1. July 5, 1973	Coup (Gen. Habyarimana and army overthrow Kayibanda.)

III. Country Features Worthy of Special Study

1. Landlocked country with high population density.
2. Constant friction between the predominant Hutus and the former royalty, the Tutsi.
3. One of the poorest countries in the world.

IV. Selected References

BIBLIOGRAPHY

Clement, Joseph R. A. M. *Essai de Bibliographie de Ruanda-Urundi*. Usumbura: n.p., 1959.
Levesque, Albert. *Contribution to the National Bibliography of Rwanda, 1965—1970*. Boston, G.K. Hall, 1979.

GENERAL

Lemarchand, René. *Rwanda and Burundi*. New York: Praeger, 1970.
Office de l'Information et des Relations Publiques du Congo Belge et du Ruanda-Urundi. *Ruanda-Urundi, Geography and History*. Brussels: 1960.
U.S. Department of the Army. *Area Handbook for Rwanda*. Pamphlet No. 550—84. Washington, D.C.: Government Printing Office, 1969.

POLITICAL

Chronique de Politique Étrangère. *Decolonisation et Independence de Rwanda et du Burundi*. Brussels: Institut Royal des Relations Internationales, 1963.
Codere, Helen. "Political Instability in Africa: The Case of Rwanda and Burundi." *Civilisations*, 16 (1966): 307—337.
Lemarchand, René. "The Coup in Rwanda." In *Power and Protest in Black Africa*, eds. Robert I. Rotberg and Ali Mazui. New York: Oxford University Press, 1970.
Linden, I. *Church and Revolution in Rwanda*. Manchester, Manchester University Press, New York, Africana Publishing Co., 1977.

Weinstein, W. "Military Continuities in the Rwanda State." *Journal of Asian and African Studies*, 12, 1—4, Jan.—Oct. 1977, pp. 48—56.

ECONOMIC

France. *Ministere de la Cooperation Rwanda, donnees statistiques sur les activites culturelles et sociales*. Paris, Le Service, 1975.
International Monetary Fund. "Rwanda." In *Surveys of African Economies*, vol. 5. Washington, D.C.: I.M.F., 1973.
Leurquin, Philipe P. *Agricultural Change in Ruanda-Urundi, 1945—1960*. Stanford, Calif.: Stanford University Food Research Institute, 1963.

SOCIAL

d'Hertefelt, Marcel. "The Rwanda of Rwanda." In *Peoples of Africa*, ed. James L. Gibbs, Jr., pp. 403—440. New York: Holt, Rinehart and Winston, 1965.
Hanf, T., P. V. Dies, W. Mann, J. H. Wolff. *Education et Developpement au Rwanda*. Munich: Weltforum Verlag, 1974.
Harrow, Jean Paul, et. at. *Le Ruanda-Urundi: ses resources naturelles des populations*. Brussels: Les Naturalists Belges, 1956.
Hewbury, M.C. "Ethnicity in Rwanda." *Africa*, 48, 1, 1978, pp. 17—28.
Liege Universite. Foundation pour les recherces scientifiques au Congo Belge et au Rwanda-Urundi. *Le probleme de l'enseignement dans le Ruanda-Urundi*. Elizabethville: C.E.P.S.I., 1958.
Maquet, J. J. *The Premise of Inequality in Ruanda: A Study of Political Relations in a Central African Kingdom*. London: Oxford University Press, 1961.

30. Senegal

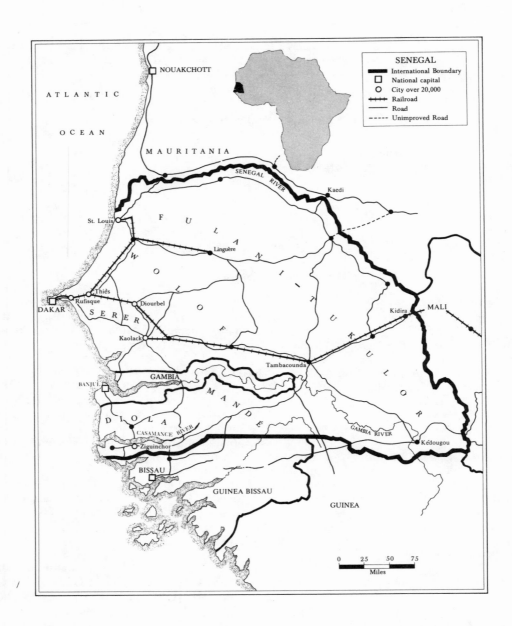

I. Basic Information

Date of Independence: August 29, 1960 (June 20, 1960 as Mali Federation)

Former Colonial Ruler: France

Change in Boundaries: Formerly part of French West African Federation. Part of Federation of Mali (formed with Mali) from April 4, 1959 to August 20, 1960, when Senegal seceded

Most Widely Spoken Languages: Wolof—67%; Pulaar—22%

Estimated Population (1980): 5,665,000

Area Size (equivalent in U.S.): 75,750 sq. mi. (Nebraska)

Date of Last Census: 1976

Major Exports 1977 as Percent of Total Exports: groundnuts and products—48%; phosphates—9%; oilseed cake—8% (1976); petroleum products—7% (1976)

Official Language: French

II. Elite Political Instability

TABLE 30.1 Elite Instability (Post- Independence)

Date	Event
1. December 17, 1962	Attempted Coup (Mamadou Dia, the Prime Minister tries to take over the government from President Senghor and fails.)

III. Country Features Worthy of Special Study

1. Large French population and close links with France pose difficult political problems if country is to develop.
2. Single-produce economy depends on peanuts.
3. High percent Muslim, but President Senghor was a Christian.
4. Dakar long a dominant port and educational center for former French West Africa.

IV. Selected References

GENERAL

Adam, François, and others. *Atlas national du Sénégal.* Paris: Institut Géographique Nationale, 1977.

Colvin, Lucie G. *Historical Dictionary of Senegal,* Metuchen, NJ: Scarecrow, 1981.

Crowder, Michael. *Senegal: A Study in French Assimilation Policy.* rev. ed. London: Methuen, 1967.

Ernst, Harold. *Senegal.* Bonn: R. Schroeder, 1965.

Fougeyrollas, Pierre. *Ou va le Sénégal? Analyse spectrale d'une nation africaine.* Paris: Editions Anthropos, 1970.

Gellar, S. *Senegal.* Boulder, Colo.: Westview Press, 1981.

Klein, Martin A. *Islam and Imperialism in Senegal.* Stanford, Calif.: Stanford University Press, 1967.

Nelson, H. D., et al. *Area Handbook for Senegal,* 2nd ed. Washington, D.C.: Government Printing Office, 1974.

POLITICAL

Behrman, Lucy. *Muslim Brotherhoods and Politics in Senegal.* Cambridge, Mass.: Harvard University Press, 1970.

Costa, E. "Employment Problems and Policies in Senegal." *International Labour Review,* 95 (May 1967): 417—451.

De Lusignan, Guy. *French-Speaking Africa since Independence,* pp. 199—217. London: Pall Mall Press, 1969.

Foltz, William J. *From French West Africa to the Mali Federation.* New Haven, Conn.: Yale University Press, 1965.

Foltz, William J. "Social Structure and Political Behavior of Senegalese Elites." *Behavior Science Notes,* 4 (1969): 145—163.

Hymans, J. L. *Leopold Sedar Senghor: An Intellectual Biography.* Edinburgh: Edinburgh University Press, 1972.

Johnson, G. Wesley, Jr. *The Emergence of Black Politics in Senegal.* Stanford, Calif.: Stanford University Press, 1971.

Markowitz, Irving L. *Leopold Senghor and the Politics of Negritude.* New York: Atheneum, 1969.

Schumacher, Edward. *Politics, Bureaucracy and Rural Development in Senegal.* Berkeley: University of California Press, 1974.

Senghor, Leopold Sedar. *On African Socialism.* New York: Praeger, 1964.

Skurnik, W. A. E. *The Foreign Policy of Senegal.* Evanston, Ill.: Northwestern University Press, 1972.

Zuccarelli, François. *Un Parti Politique Africain: l'Union Progressiste Sénégalaise.* Paris: Librairie Générale de Droit et de Jurisprudence, 1970.

ECONOMIC

Bachmann, Heinz B., et al. *Senegal: Tradition, Diversification and Economic Development.* Washington, D.C.: International Bank for Reconstruction and Development, 1974.

International Monetary Fund. "Senegal." In *Surveys of African Economies,* Vol. 3. Washington, D.C.: I.M.F., 1970.

O'Brien, R. C. ed. *The Political Economy of Underdevelopment: Dependence in Senegal.* Beverly Hills, Ca.: Sage, 1980.

Peterec, Richard J. *Dakar and West African Economic Development.* New York: Columbia University Press, 1967.

Serreau, Jean. *Le développement à la base au Dahomey et au Sénégal.* Paris: Librairie generale de droit et de jurisprudence, 1966.

Cruise O'Brien, Donal B. *The Mourides of Senegal: The Political and Economic Organization of an Islamic Brotherhood.* Oxford: Oxford University Press, 1971.

Cruise O'Brien, Donal B. *Saints and Politicians: Essays in the Organization of a Senegalese Peasant Society.* Cambridge: Cambridge University Press, 1975.

Cruise O'Brien, Rita. *White Society in Black Africa: The French of Senegal.* Evanston, Ill.: Northwestern University Press, 1972.

Pfeffermann, G. *Industrial Labor in the Republic of Senegal.* New York: Praeger Special Study, 1968.

Sankale, M., L. V. Thomas, and P. Fougeyrollas. *Dakar en devenir.* Paris: Présence africaine, 1968.

Sy, Cheikh Tidiana. *La confrérie sénégalaise des Mourides.* Paris: Présence africaine, 1969.

31. Sierra Leone

I. Basic Information

Date of Independence: April 27, 1961
Former Colonial Ruler: United Kingdom
Estimated Population (1980): 3,428,000
Area Size (equivalent in U.S.): 27,699 sq. mi. (South Carolina)

Most Widely Spoken Languages: Temne-Limba—45%; Mendé—36%

Date of Last Census: 1974
Major Exports 1977 as Percent of Total Exports: diamonds—45 percent; cocoa—13 percent; coffee—26 percent; bauxite—6 percent.

Official Language: English

II. Elite Political Instability

TABLE 31.1   Elite Instability (Post-Independence)

Date	Event
1. March 21, 1967	Coup d'État (Army leader refused to accept the election results and declared martial law, two days later younger Army officers overthrow their commander and take power.)
2. April 26, 1968	Coup d'État (Army sergeants take power and install Stevens.)
3. March 23, 1971	Attempted Coup (Attempted coup by Army general was thwarted.)

III. Country Features Worthy of Special Study

1. Mineral wealth the basis of the economy.
2. The country has two large and roughly equal in size ethnic groups around which much of the political strife has centered.
3. In 1967 Sir Albert Margai was defeated in an election—one of the few times an African ruling party was defeated at the polls—but military took over to forestall Stevens taking office.
4. Especially long colonial contact with England. It was a crown colony in 1808.

IV. Selected References

BIBLIOGRAPHY

Luke, Sir Harry C.J. *A Bibliography of Sierra Leone.* Westport, Conn. Negro University Press, 1969.

Switzer John P. *A Bibliography of Sierra Leone 1968—1970.* Freetown, Njala University College, 1973.

Williams, Geoffrey J. *A Bibliography of Sierra Leone, 1925—67.* New York: Africana, 1971.

Zell, Hans M. *A Bibliography of Non-Periodical Literature on Sierra Leone, 1925—66.* Freetown: Fourah Bay College Bookshop, University College of Sierra Leone, 1966.

GENERAL

Abraham, Arthur. *Topics in Sierra Leone History: a Counter Colonial Interpretation.* Freetown: Sierra Leone Publishers, 1976.

Clarke, J.I., ed. *Sierra Leone in Maps.* London: University of London Press, 1966.

Collier, Gershon. *Sierra Leone: Experiment in Democracy in an African Nation.* New York: New York University Press, 1970.

Dalton, K.G. *A Geography of Sierra Leone.* Cambridge: Cambridge University Press, 1965.

Foray, C.P. *Historical Dictionary of Sierra Leone.* Metuchen, N.J.: Scarecrow Press, 1977.

Fourah Bay College Library. *Catalog of the Sierra Leone Collection Fourah Bay College Library,* Boston, G.K. Hall 1979.

Fyfe, Christopher. *A Short History of Sierra Leone.* London: Longmans, 1972.

Kaplan, I., et al. *Area Handbook for Sierra Leone.* Washington, D.C.: U.S. Government Printing Office, 1976.

Kup, A. P. *Sierra Leone: A Concise History.* New York: St. Martin's Press, 1975.

Migeod, Frederick W. *A View of Sierra Leone.* New York: Negro Universities Press, 1970.

Sibthorse, A. B. C. *The History of Sierra Leone.* New York: Humanities Press, 1971.

Walker, James W. *The Black Loyalists.* New York, Africana, 1976.

West, Richard. *Back to Africa: A History of Sierra Leone and Liberia.* London: Cape, 1970.

POLITICAL

Barrows, W. *Grassroots Politics in an African State: Integration and Development in Sierra Leone.* New York: Africana, 1976.

Cartwright, John R. *Politics in Sierra Leone, 1947—1967.* Toronto: University of Toronto Press, 1970.

Cartwright, J. R. *Political Leadership in Sierra Leone.* Toronto: University of Toronto Press, 1978.

Clapham, C. *Liberia and Sierra Leone: An Essay in Comparative Politics.* New York: Cambridge University Press, 1976.

Cohen, Abner, *Politics of Elite Culture: Explorations in the Dramaturgy of Power in a Modern African Society.* Berkeley: University of California Press, 1981.

Cox, Thomas S. *Civil-Military Relations in Sierra Leone: A Case Study of African Soldiers in Politics.* Cambridge: Harvard University Press, 1976.

Kilson, Martin. *Political Change in a West African State: Study of the Modernization Process in Sierra Leone.* Cambridge, Mass.: Harvard University Press, 1966.

ECONOMIC

Bank of Sierra Leone. Research Dept. *Charts on the Economy in Sierra Leone.* Freetown, Bank of Sierra Leone, 1975.

International Monetary Fund. "Sierra Leone." In *Surveys of African Economies,* Vol. 6. Washington, D.C.: I.M.F., 1975.

Jabati. S. A. *Agriculture in Sierra Leone.* N.Y.: Vantage Press, 1978.

Van der Laan, H. L. *The Lebanese Trader in Sierra Leone.* The Hague: Mouton, 1976.

SOCIAL

Banton, M. P. *West African City: A Study of Tribal Life in Freetown*. London: Oxford University Press, 1957.

Makannah, T. J. *The Study of Internal Migration in Sierra Leone: A Review and Bibliography of Recent Literature*, Freetown: Central Statistical Office, 1977.

Spitzer, Leo. *The Creoles of Sierra Leone: Responses to Colonialism, 1870—1945*. Madison, Wis.: University of Wisconsin Press, 1974.

32. Somalia

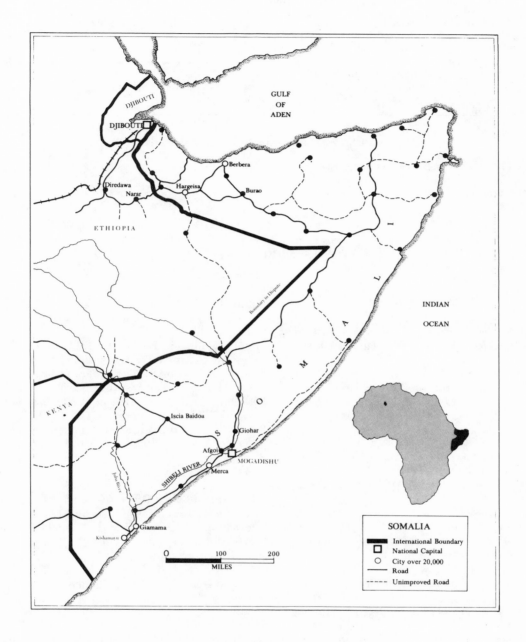

I. Basic Information

Date of Independence: July 1, 1960
Former Colonial Rulers: Italy and United Kingdom
Change in Boundaries At independence, merger of UN
  Trust Territory of Somaliland with British Somaliland
Former Names: Somaliland, British Somaliland
Estimated Population (1980): 3,553,000*
Area Size (equivalent in U.S.): 246,201 sq. mi. (Texas)
Date of Last Census: 1975

Most Widely Spoken Languages: Somali—97%;
  Swahili—3%

Major Exports 1976 as Percent of Total Exports: Livestock, hides and skins—70 percent; bananas—16 percent.
Official Language: Somali (as of 1972)

*There have been reports that the conflict in the Oga-
den has promoted the arrival of one quarter of a million
refugees into Somalia. (*Africa Report*, Sept./Oct. 1980,
p. 31).

II.   Elite Political Instability

TABLE 32.1   Elite Instability (Post-Independence)

Date	Event
1. December 10, 1961	Attempted Coup (By northern army unit.)
2. October 21, 1969	Coup d'État (Army takes over after the assassination of the President.)
3. April, 1978	Coup Attempt (Fails after Barre rallies army units.)

III.   Country Features Worthy of Special Study

1. Population is primarily nomadic pastoral in type but a major effort is being made to shift them to settled agriculture.
2. Center of irredentist movement to unite all the Somali people in the horn of Africa.
3. Ethnic homogeneity but considerable interclan rivalry.
4. Islam is the state religion.

IV.   Selected References

BIBLIOGRAPHY

Krofors, C. and V. H. Narberg. *A Selection List of Literature on Somalia.* Uppsala: Scandanavian Institute of Africa Studies, 1976.

Salad, Mohamed Khalief. *Somalia: A Bibliographical Survey.* Westport, Ct.: Greenwood Press, 1977.

GENERAL

Cahill, K. M.(ed.) *Somalia: A Perspective.* Albany: State University of New York Press, 1980.

Castagno, M. *Historical Dictionary of Somalia.* Metuchen, N.J.: Scarecrow, 1976.

Contini, Paolo. *The Somali Republic: An Experiment in Legal Integration.* London: Cass, 1969.

Hess, Robert L. *Italian Colonialism in Somalia.* Chicago: University of Chicago Press, 1966.

Kaplan, I. et al. *Area Handbook for Somalia.* 2nd ed. Washington, D.C.: Government Printing Office, 1977.

Lewis, I. M. *A Pastoral Democracy.* New York: Holmes and Meier, 1981.

Thompson, Virginia and Richard Adloff, *Djibouti and the Horn of Africa.* Stanford, Ca.: Stanford University Press, 1968.

POLITICAL

Drysdale, John C. S. *The Somali Dispute.* New York: Praeger, 1964.

Laitin, D. D. *Politics, Language and Thought: The Somali Experience.* Chicago: University of Chicago Press, 1977.

Legum, Colin and Lee Bull. The Horn of Africa in Continuing Crisis, N.Y.: Africana, 1979.

Lewis, I. M. *ABBAR: The Somali Drought.* London: International African Institute, 1975.

Potholm, C. P. *Four African Political Systems.* Englewood Cliffs, N.J.: Prentice-Hall, 1970.

Barre, Mohamed Siad. *My Country and My People: Selected Speeches, 1969—74.* Mogadishu: 1974 (June).

ECONOMIC

International Labor Office. *Economic Transformation in a Socialist Framework.* Geneva: ILO. 1977.

International Monetary Fund. "Somalia." In *Surveys of African Economies*, Vol. 2, Washington, D.C.: I.M.F., 1968.

Quarterly Economic Review: Uganda Ethiopia Somalia: London, Economist Intelligence Unit, 1974.

SOCIAL

Box, T. W. "Nomadism and Land Use in Somalia." *Economic Development and Cultural Change*, 19 (1971): 222—228.

Cassanelli, Lee V. "Recent developments in Somali Studies," *Horn of Africa*, vol. 2, no. 1 Jan./Mar. 1979, pp. 36-41.

Lewis, I. M. "Conformity and Contrast in Somali Islam." In *Islam in Tropical Africa*, ed. I. M. Lewis, pp. 252—265. London: Oxford University Press, 1966.

33. Sudan

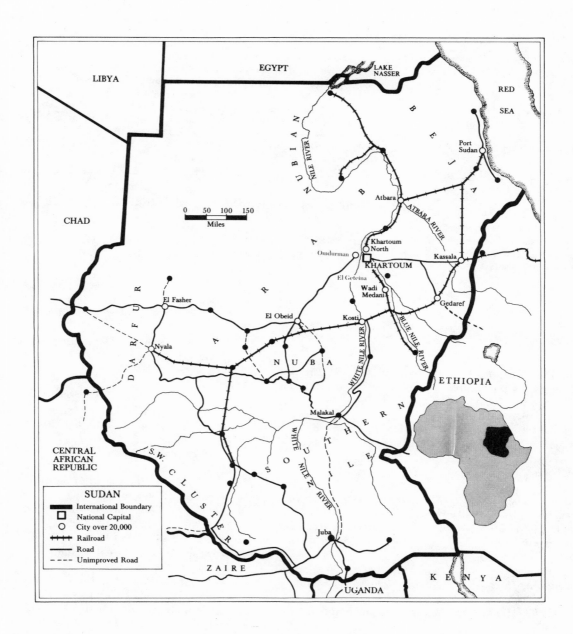

I. Basic Information

Date of Independence: January 1, 1956
Former Colonial Rulers: United Kingdom and Egypt
Former Name: Anglo-Egyptian Sudan
Estimated Population (1980): 21,590,000
Area Size (equivalent in U.S.): 967,500 sq. mi. (Alaska, Texas, and Colorado or nearly one-third the size of continental United States)

Most Widely Spoken Languages: Arabic—65%; Dinka—18%

Date of Last Census: 1973
Major Exports 1976 as Percent of Total Exports: cotton and cotton product—51 percent; groundnuts—20 percent; gum hashab—6 percent; sesame—9 percent.

Official Language: Arabic

II. Elite Political Instability

TABLE 33.1 Elite Instability (Post- Independence)

Date	Event
1. November 17, 1958	Coup d'État (Army takes over from a divided and factious civilian regime.)
2. March 4—9, 1959	Coup Attempt (Army units fail to overthrow government.)
3. May 21—22, 1959	Attempted Coup (Army units attempt to march on the capital and are repulsed.)
4. November 9, 1959	Attempted Coup (Dissident army units fail in coup attempt.)
5. December 18, 1966	Attempted Coup (Army units attempt coup and are repulsed.)
6. May 25, 1969	Coup d'État (Col. Nimeiry overthrows the civilian government.)
7. July 21—23, 1971	Attempted Coup (Army officers fail in attempt to oust Nimeiry.)
8. September 5, 1975	Attempted Coup (Paratroopers fail in attempt.)
9. July 2—3, 1978	Coup Attempt (Army units fail to overthrow Numeiry.)

III. Country Features Worthy of Special Study

1. Former long standing conflict between the Arab north and Black African south.
2. More involved with North Africa and Arab affairs than any other Black African country.
3. Largest country in area in Black Africa.

IV. Selected References

BIBLIOGRAPHY

African Bibliographic Center, Washington. *A Current Bibliography on Sudanese Affairs, 1960—64*. Special Bibliographic Series, Vol. 3, No. 4, 1965. Westport, Conn.: Greenwood, 1965.

Voll, John Obert. *Historical Dictionary of the Sudan*. Metuchen, N.J.: Scarecrow Press, 1978.

GENERAL

Albino, O. *The Sudan: A Southern Viewpoint*. New York: Oxford University Press, 1970.

Barbour, L. M. *The Republic of the Sudan: A Regional Geography*. London: University of London Press, 1961.

Collins, Robert O. *Land Beyond the Rivers: The Southern Sudan, 1898—1918*. New Haven: Yale University Press, 1971.

Conte, C. *The Sudan as a Nation*. Milan, Giuffre Editore, 1976.

El-Mahdi, Mandour. *Short History of the Sudan*. London: Oxford University Press, 1965.

Hassan, Y. Fadi, ed. *Sudan in Africa*. Khartoum: Khartoum University Press, 1971.

Henderson, Kenneth D.   *Sudan Republic*. New York: Praeger, 1965.

Holt, Peter M. *A Modern History of the Sudan*, New York: Grove Press, 1979.

Martin P. F. *The Sudan in Evolution*. Westport, Conn.: Negro Universities Press, 1970.

Oduho, J. and W. Deng. *The Problem of the Southern Sudan*. London: Oxford University Press, 1963.

Nelson, H. D. et al. *Area Handbook for Sudan*, 3rd ed. Washington, D.C.: Government Printing Office, 1973.

Voll, J. O. *Historical Dictionary of the Sudan*. Metuchen, N.J.: Scarecrow, 1978.

POLITICAL

'Abd Al-Rahim, Muddathir. *Imperialism and Nationalism in the Sudan: A Study in Constitutional and Political Development, 1899—1956*. London: Oxford University Press, 1969.

Bechtold, P. K. *Politics and the Sudan: Parliamentary and Military Rule in an Emerging African Nation*. New York: Praeger, 1976.

Beshir, M. O. *The Southern Sudan: Background to Conflict*. New York: Praeger, 1968.

Eprile, Cecil. *War and Peace in the Sudan, 1955—1972*. Newton Abbott, Great Britain: David and Charles, 1974.

Howell, John. "Politics in the Southern Sudan." *African Affairs*, 72 (April 1973): 163—178.

Lees, Francis A. and Hugh C. Brooks. *The Economic and Political Development of the Sudan*. Boulder, Colorado, Westview Press, 1977.

Sylvester, A. *Sudan Under Nimieri*. London: Bodley Head, 1977.

Wai, D. *Secessionist Politics and the International Community: The Case of the Afro-Arab Conflict in the Sudan*. Ph.D. Thesis, Harvard University, 1977.

Wai, Dunstan. "The Sudan: Domestic Politics and Foreign Relations under Nimiery." *African Affairs*, 78, 312, July 1979, pp. 297—317.

Wai, Dunstan, M., ed. *The Southern Sudan: The Problem of National Integration*. London: Cass, 1973.

Woodwar, P. *Condominium and Sudanese Nationalism*. London: Rex Collings, 1979.

Wright, P. *Conflict on the Nile*. London: Heinemann, 1972.

ECONOMIC

Adams, Martin E. and Howell, John. "Developing the Traditional Sector in the Sudan." *Economic Development and Cultural Change*, 27, 3 April 1979, pp. 505—518.

Barnett, Tony. *The Gezira Scheme: An Illusion of Development*. London: Cass, 1977.

Growth Employment and Equity: A Comprehensive Strategy for the Sudan. Geneva: ILO, 1976.

Hance, William A. "The Gezira Scheme: A Study in Agricultural Development." In *African Economic Development*, rev. ed., pp. 31—53. New York: Praeger, 1967.

Osman, Omar and A. A. Suleiman. "The Economy of Sudan." In *The Economies of Africa*, eds. P. Robson and D. A. Lury, pp. 436—470. Evanston, Ill.: Northwestern University Press, 1969.

SOCIAL

Beshir, Mohamed Omer. *Educational Development in the Sudan, 1898—1956*. London: Oxford University Press, 1969.

El Tayeb, S. D. Z. *The Students in the Sudan, 1940—1970*. Khartoum: Khartoum University Press, 1971.

Hassan, Y. F. *The Arabs and the Sudan*. Edinburgh: Edinburgh University Press, 1967.

McLoughlin, J. "The Sudan's Three Towns: A Demographic and Economic Profile of an African Urban Complex." *Economic Development and Cultural Change*, 12: Pt. 1 (October 1963), pp. 70—83; Pt. 2 (January 1965), pp. 158—173; Pt. 3 (April 1964), pp. 186—304.

O'Null, N. "Imperialism and Class Struggle in Sudan". *Race and Class*, 20, 1, Summer 1978, pp. 1—19.

Trimingham, J. S. *Islam in the Sudan*. London: Oxford University Press, 1949.

Warburg, Gabriel *Islam, Nationalism and Trade Unionism in a Traditional Society: The Case of Sudan*. London: Frank Cass, 1978.

34. Swaziland

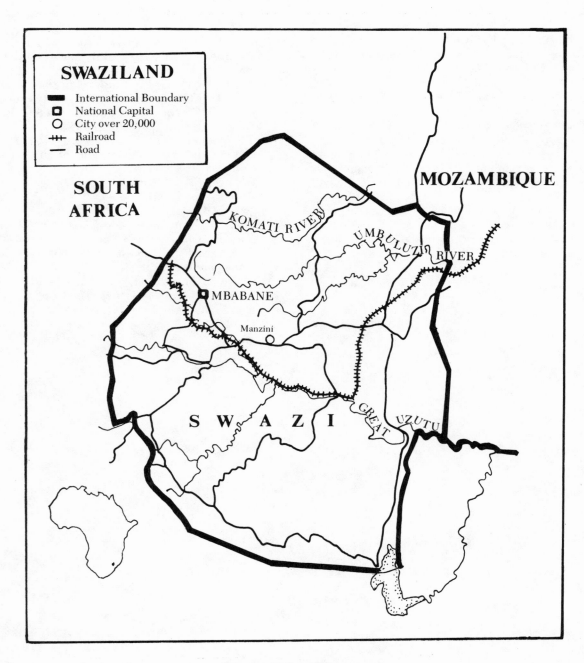

SWAZILAND
- ▬▬ International Boundary
- ☐ National Capital
- ○ City over 20,000
- +++ Railroad
- — Road

SOUTH AFRICA

MOZAMBIQUE

KOMATI RIVER

UMBULUZI RIVER

MBABANE

Manzini

S W A Z I

GREAT UZUTU

I. Basic Information

Date of Independence: September 6, 1968
Former Colonial Ruler: United Kingdom
Estimated Population (1980): 555,000
Area Size (Equivalent in U.S.): 6,704 sq. mi. (New Jersey)

Most Widely Spoken Languages: Siswazi—95%

Date of Last Census: 1976
Major Exports 1975 as Percent of Total Exports: sugar—54% wood and wood products—9% iron—9 % asbestos—7%

Official Language: English and Siswazi

II.   Elite Political Instability

TABLE 34.1   Elite Instability (Post- Independence)

Date	Event
1. April 12, 1973	Coup d'État (King Sobhuza suspends the constitution.)

III.   Country Features Worthy of Special Study

1. Buffer state between black and white ruled Africa; surrounded by South Africa.
2. Monarchy has taken power in a coup, the only successful attempt to do so in Black Africa.

IV. Selected References

BIBLIOGRAPHY

Grotpeter, J. A. *Historical Dictionary of Swaziland*. Metuchen, N.J.: Scarecrow, 1975.
University College of Swaziland. *Swaziland National Bibliography 1973—1976 with current information*. Kwaluseni: University of Botswana and Swaziland, 1977.
Wallace, Charles S. *Swaziland: A Bibliography*. Johannesberg: University of Witwatersrand, 1967.
Webster, John B. and Paulus Mohome. *A Bibliography on Swaziland*. Syracuse: Program of Eastern African Studies, Syracuse University, 1968

GENERAL

Barker, Dudley. *Swaziland*. London: Her Majesty's Stationery Office, 1965.
Matsebula, J. S. M. *A History of Swaziland*. 2nd edition, London: Longmans, 1976.
Stevens, Richard P. *Lesotho, Botswana, and Swaziland: The Former High Commission Territories in Southern Africa*. New York: Praeger, 1971.

POLITICAL

Kuper, H. *Sobhuza II, Ngwenyama and King of Swaziland*. London: Duckworth, 1978.
Potholm, Christian P. *Swaziland: The Dynamics of Political Modernization*. Berkeley: University of California Press, 1972.
Rosenprinz, B. D. *Urbanization and Political Change: A Study of Urban Local Government in Swaziland*. Los Angeles: University of California, 1976.
Szal, R. J. *Inequality and Basic Needs in Swaziland*. Geneva: International Labour Office, 1976.
Van Wyk, Adam Johannes. *Swaziland: A Political Study*. Pretoria: Africa Institute, 1969.

ECONOMIC

Best, Alan C. G. *The Swaziland Railway: A Study in Politico-Economic Geography*. East Lansing: Michigan State University Press, 1966.
Fair, T. J. D., G. Murdock and H. M. Jones. *Development in Swaziland: A Regional Analysis*. Johannesburg: Witwatersrand University Press, 1969.
International Monetary Fund. "Swaziland." In *Surveys of African Economies*, Vol. 5. Washington, D.C.: I.M.F., 1973.
Jones, David. *Aid and Development in Southern Africa: British Aid to Botswana, Lesotho and Swaziland*. London: Croom Helm, 1977.
Selwyn, P. *Industries in the Southern African Periphery: A Study of Industrial Development in Botswana, Lesotho and Swaziland*. London: Croom Helm, in association with the Institute of Development Studies, Sussex, 1975.

SOCIAL

Kuper, Hilda. *The Swazi: A South African Kingdom*. New York: Holt, Rinehart and Winston, 1965.
Marwick, Brian. *The Swazi—An Ethnographic Account of the Natives of the Swaziland Protectorate*. London: Frank Cass, 1966.

35. Tanzania

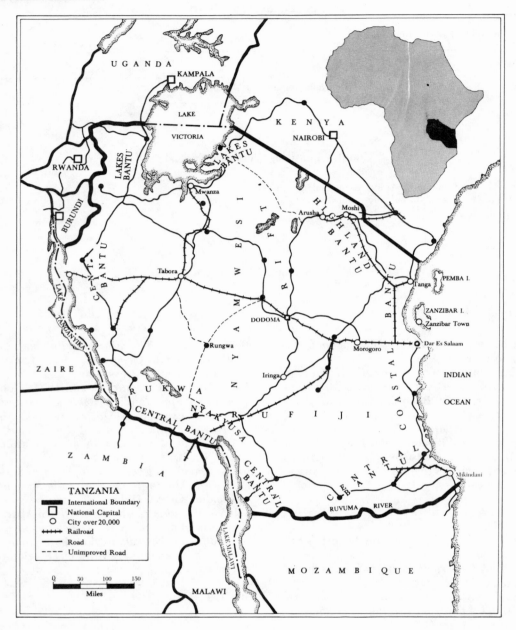

I. Basic Information

Date of Independence: December 9, 1961
Former Colonial Ruler: United Kingdom
Change in Boundaries: April 26, 1964, Tanganyika and
  Zanzibar became the United Republic of Tanganyika
  and Zanzibar; October 29, 1964, name became Tanzania
Former Names: Tanganyika and Zanzibar
Estimated Population (1980): 17,849,000

Most Widely Spoken Languages: Swahili—95%; Sukuma—12%

Area Size (equivalent in U.S.): 364,900 sq. mi. including
  inland waterways (Texas and Colorado)
Date of Last Census: 1974
Major Exports 1975 as Percent of Total Exports (excluding trade with Kenya and Uganda in locally produced goods): coffee beans—19%; cloves—13%; sisal—12%; raw cotton—12%; cashew nuts—9%; diamonds—7%.

Official Language: Swahili

II.   Elite Political Instability

TABLE 35.1   Elite Instability (Post-Independence)

Date	Event
1. April 7, 1972	Coup Attempt (Sheikh Abeid Karume of Zanzibar is assassinated as part of a planned coup d'état.)

III.   Country Features Worthy of Special Study

1. One of the ideological leaders of Africa, Nyerere is attempting to oppose neo-colonialism and to establish a socialist state on a genuinely non-aligned basis.
2. Notable absence of political instability on the mainland.
3. Population is ethnically heterogeneous with no dominant ethnic groups.
4. Unusual "union" with Zanzibar.
5. Very extensive program of rural resettlement into "Ujamaa villages" as part of an ambitious rural development program.

IV.   Selected References

BIBLIOGRAPHY

Bates, Margaret. *A Study Guide for Tanzania*. Boston: Development Program, African Studies Center, Boston University, 1969.

GENERAL

Ayany, S. G. *A History of Zanzibar*. Nairobi: East African Literature Bureau, 1970.

Bienen, Henry. *Tanzania: Party Transformation and Economic Development*, enlarged edition. Princeton, N.J.: Princeton University Press, 1970.

Cliffe, L. *Tanzania*. New York: Praeger, 1970.

Iliffe, John. *A Modern History of Tanganyika*. New York: Cambridge University Press, 1979.

Kaplan, I. ed. *Tanzania: A Country Study*. Washington D.C. Government Printing Office, 1978.

Kimambo, I. N., and A. J. Temu (eds.). *A History of Tanzania*. Nairobi: East Africa Publishing House, 1969.

Kurtz, L. S. *Historical Dictionary for Tanzania*. Metuchen, N.J.: Scarecrow Press, 1978.

Yeager, R. *Tanzania: an African Experiment*. Boulder, Colo.: Westview Press, 1982.

POLITICAL

Bailey, Martin. *The Union of Tanganyika and Zanzibar*. Program of East African Studies. Syracuse, N.Y.: Syracuse University, 1973.

Cliffe, L., and J. Saul (eds.). *Tanzania Socialism-Politics and Policies: An Interdisciplinary Reader*, 2 volumes. Nairobi: East Africa Publishing House, 1972.

Duggan, William R., and John R. Civille. *Tanzania and Nyerere: A Study of Ujamaa and Nationalism*. Maryknoll, N.Y.: Orbis Books, 1976.

Hatch, John. *Two African Statesmen: Kaunda of Zambia and Nyerere of Tanzania*. Chicago: Regenery, 1976.

Hopkins, Raymond. *Political Roles in a New State*. New Haven, Conn.: Yale University Press, 1971.

Hutchison, Alan. "Exorcising the Ghost of Karume." *Africa Report*, 19 (March/April 1974): 46—51.

Hyden, Goren. *Political Development in Rural Tanzania*. Nairobi: East African Publishing House, 1969.

Hyden, Goren. *Beyond Ujamaa in Tanzania*. Berkeley: University of California Press, 1980.

Ingle, Clyde R. *From Village to State in Tanzania: The Politics of Rural Development*. Ithaca, N.Y.: Cornell University Press, 1972.

Kariokia, James N. *Tanzania's Human Relation*. Univ. Park, PA. The Pennsylvania State University Press, 1979.

Liebenow, J. Gus. *Colonial Rule and Political Development in Tanzania*. Nairobi: East African Publishing House, 1972.

Martin, E. B. *Zanzibar: Tradition and Revolution*. London: Hamish, Hamilton, 1978.

Morrison, D. R. *Education and Politics in Africa: The Tanzanian Case*. London: Hurst, 1976.

Mwansasu, Bismarck U., and Cranford Pratt (eds.). *Towards Socialism in Tanzania*. Toronto: University of Toronto Press, 1978.

Nellis, John R. *A Theory of Ideology: The Tanzania Example*. New York: Oxford University Press, 1972.

Nyerere, Julius K. *Freedom and Development: Uhuru n Maendelco*. London: Oxford University Press, 1973.

Nyerere, Julius K. *Freedom and Socialism: Uhuru na Ujamaa*. London: Oxford University Press, 1969.

Nyerere, Julius K. *Ujamaa: Essays on Socialism*. Dar Es Salaam: Oxford Univ. Press, 1968.

Pratt, C. *The Critical Phase in Tanzania, 1945—68: Nyerere and the Emergence of a Socialist Strategy*. London: Cambridge University Press, 1975.

Shivji, I. G. *Class Struggle in Tanzania*. London: Heinemann, 1976.

Samoff, Joel. *Tanzania: Local Politics and the Structure of Power*. Madison, Wis.: University of Wisconsin Press, 1974.

Smith, William Edgett. *We Must Run While They Walk: A Portrait of Africa's Julius Nyerere*. New York: Random House, 1971.

Von Sperber, Klaus W. *Public Administration in Tanzania*. Africa Studies No. 55. New York: Humanities, 1970.

ECONOMIC

Clar, W. Edmund. *Socialist Development and Public Investment in Tanzania, 1964—73*. Toronto: University of Toronto Press, 1978.

Helleiner, G. K. "Socialism and Economic Development in Tanzania." *Journal of Development Studies* (January 1972): 183—204.

International Monetary Fund. "Tanzania." In *Surveys of African Economies*, Vol. 2, Washington, D.C.: I.M.F., 1968.

McHenry, Dean E. *Tanzania's Ujamaa Villages: The Implementation of a Rural Development Strategy*. Berkeley: University of California, Institute of International Studies, 1979.

Nyerere, Julius. *The Economic Challenge: Dialogue or Confrontation*. London: Catholic Inst. of Race Relations, 1975.

Rweyemamu, Justinian. *Underdevelopment and Industrialization in Tanzania*. New York: Oxford University Press, 1973.

SOCIAL

Bennett, N. R. *A History of the Arab State of Zanzibar*. London: Methuen, 1978.

Cameron, J., and W. A. Dodd. *Society, Schools and Progress in Tanzania*. New York: Pergamon, 1970.

Ranger, T. O. *The African Churches of Tanzania*. Nairobi: East African Publishing House, 1969.

Resnick, Idrian (ed.). *Tanzania: Revolution by Education*. New York: Humanities Press, 1969.

Shorter, Aylward. *Chiefship in Western Tanzania*. London: Oxford University Press, 1972.

Stren, Richard E. *Urban Inequality and Housing Policy in Tanzania*. Berkeley, Ca.: Institute of International Studies, 1975.

Sutton, J. E. G. (ed.). "Dar es Salaam: City, Port, and Region." *Tanzania Notes and Records*, 71 (1970).

36. Togo

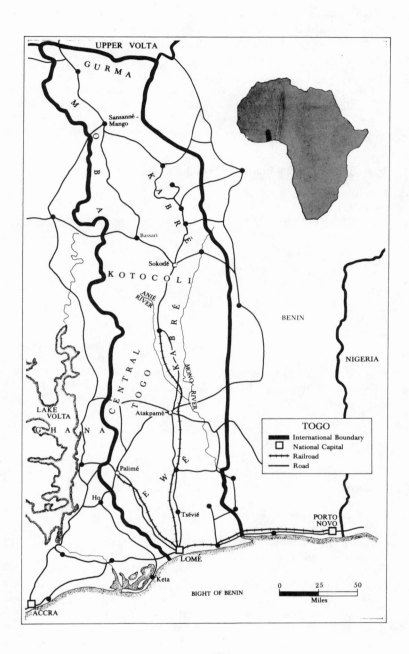

UPPER VOLTA

GURMA

MOBA

Sansanné-
Mango

KABRE

Bassari

Sokodé

KOTOCOLI

ANIE RIVER

KABRÉ

CENTRAL TOGO

MONO RIVER

BENIN

NIGERIA

LAKE
VOLTA

GHANA

Atakpamé

EWE

TOGO
■ International Boundary
□ National Capital
┼ Railroad
— Road

Palimé

Ho

Tsévié

PORTO
NOVO

LOMÉ

Keta

BIGHT OF BENIN

0   25   50

Miles

ACCRA

I. Basic Information

Date of Independence: April 27, 1960
Former Colonial Ruler: France
Former Name: Togoland
Population (1980): 2,596,000
Area Size (equivalent in U.S.): 21,6222 sq. mi. (West Virginia)

Most Widely Spoken Languages: Ewe—50%; Kabre—20%

Date of Last Census: 1970
Major Exports 1977 as Percent of Total Exports: phosphates—49 percent; cocoa—26 percent;* coffee—14 percent.
Official Language: French

*Much of the cocoa is smuggled to Togo by Ghanaian farmers for better prices than they can get in Ghana.

II.   Elite Political Instability

TABLE 36.1   Elite Instability (Post- Independence)

Date	Event
1. January 13, 1963	Coup d'État (Pres. Olympio was killed by non-commissioned army officers.)
2. November 21, 1966	Attempted Coup (Noe Kutuklui called for demonstrations against Grunitsky in a radio broadcast. More than 5,000 people took to the streets in the city of Lomé in response to the call from leading Ewe politician, but the coup attempt was aborted by the army without violence.)
3. January 13, 1967	Coup d'État (Lt. Col. Eyadema, Chief of Staff of the Togolese Army, seized power.)

III.   Country Features Worthy of Special Study

1. Irredentism sentiment with the Ewé of southeastern Ghana.
2. Under German colonial rule until World War I.
3. Carrying out an "authenticity" program to upgrade the relative importance of African rather than French culture.

IV. Selected References

GENERAL

Corevin, Robert. *Le Togo.* 2nd ed. Paris: Presses de Universitaires Francaises, 1973.

Decalo, S. *Historical Dictionary of Togo.* Metuchen, N.J.: Scarecrow Press, 1976.

POLITICAL

Amin, Samir. *Neo-Colonialism in West Africa.* Harmondsworth, Middlesex: Penguin Books, 1973.

Decalo, S. *Coups and Army Rule in Africa: Studies in Military Style.* New Haven: Yale University Press, 1976.

de Lusignan, Guy. *French-Speaking Africa Since Independence*, pp. 170—1979. London: Pall Mall Press, 1969.

Hodges, T. "Eyadema's Unchallenged Rule." *Africa Report* (July/August 1977): 61—64.

Howe, Russell W. "Togo: Four Years of Military Rule." *Africa Report*, 12 (May 1967): 6—12.

Knoll, Arthur J. *Togo under Imperial Germany, 1884— 1914: A Case Study in Colonial Rule.* Stanford: Hoover Institution Press, 1978

Thompson, Virginia. *West Africa's Counil of the Entente.* Ithaca, N.Y.: Cornell University Press, 1972.

ECONOMIC

International Monetary Fund. "Togo." In *Surveys of African Economies*, Vol. 3. Washington, D.C.: I.M.F., 1970.

SOCIAL

Aithnard, K. *Some Aspects of Cultural Policy in Togo.* Paris: UNESCO, 1976.

Debrunner, H. *A Church Between Colonial Powers: The Church in Togo.* London: Lutterworth Press, 1965

Kumekper, T. "Togo" in *Population Growth and Socioeconomic Change in West Africa.* J. Caldwell et al., eds. New York: Columbia University Press, 1975, pp. 720—35.

37. Uganda

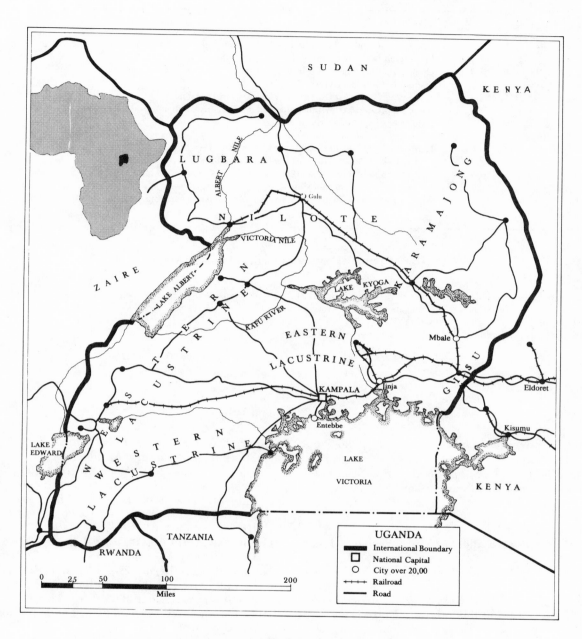

I. Basic Information

Date of Independence: October 9, 1962
Former Colonial Ruler: United Kingdom
Population (1980)*: 13,660,000
Area Size (equivalent in U.S.): 91,133 sq. mi. (Oregon)
Date of Last Census: 1969
Major exports 1977 as Percent of Total Exports: coffee—

93 percent; cotton—2 percent; tea—2 percent (excludes re-exports).
Official Language: English

Most Widely Spoken Languages: Ganda—41%; Swahili—30%

*Since there have been large numbers of refugees in adjoining countries it is difficult to estimate the country's population by extrapolating from previous census figures. Hence, this figure may be an overestimate.

II.   Elite Political Instability

TABLE 37.1 Elite Instability (Post-Independence)

Date	Event
1. February 22, 1966	Coup d'État (Prime Minister Obote suspended the constitution, relieved the President, Sir Edward Mutesa, and declared himself Executive President.)
2. January 26, 1971	Coup d'État (The army led by Maj. Gen. Idi Amin, who had risen from the ranks to become its commander in 1966, seized power.)
3. September 17—28, 1972	Attempted Coup (Pro-Obote forces invade from Tanzania.)
4. March 23—24, 1974	Attempted Coup (Army units attacked Amin at his command post, but he was absent and able to rally loyal troops to put down the attempt.)
5. February 16, 1975	Coup Attempt (Amin's motorcade ambushed—Amin escapes.)
6. August, 1975	Coup Attempt (Tank units try to oust Amin while he is out of the country but are stopped.)
7. June 10, 1976	Coup Attempt(Assassination attempt against Amin fails.)
8. July 1976	Coup Attempt (Army and police leaders attempt to convince Amin to resign but are shot by Amin's men.)
9. June 18, 1977	Coup Attempt (Details not known.)
10. April, 1979	Coup d'État (Amin ousted after invasion of Uganda by anti-Amin forces with major Tanzanian army support.)

III.   Country Features Worthy of Special Study

1. One ethnic group, the Baganda, in whose territory lies the capital, lost their traditional dominant position in the country after independence.
2. Under Amin, country had a policy of expelling most of those of foreign descent.
3. Pattern of especially arbitrary and repressive rule by Amin.
4. Complex problems of rebuilding after the demonstration of the Amin years.

IV. Selected References

BIBLIOGRAPHY

Collison, R. L. *Uganda*. Santa Barbara, CA: Clio Press, 1981.

Gray, Beverly. *Uganda: Subject Guide to Official Publications*. Washington: Library of Congress, 1977.

GENERAL

Col, J. M. *Uganda*. Boulder, Colo.: Westview Press, 1981.

Gertzel, Cherry. *Uganda*. London: Pall Mall Press, 1970.

Gulkina, P. M. *Uganda: A Case Study in African Political Development*. South Bend, Ind.: Notre Dame University Press, 1972.

Ibingira, G. S. K. *The Forging of an African Nation: The Political and Constitutional Evolution of Uganda from Colonial Rule to Independence, 1894—1962*. New York: The Viking Press, 1973.

Jorgensen, J. J. *Uganda: A Modern History*, London: Croom Helm, 1981.

Low, D. A. *Buganda in Modern History*. Berkeley: University of California Press, 1971.

Uganda Government. *Atlas of Uganda*. Entebbe: Department of Lands and Surveys, 1962.

U.S. Department of the Army. *Area Handbook for Uganda*. Washington, D.C.: Government Printing Office, 1969.

POLITICAL

Apter, David F. *The Political Kingdom in Uganda: A Study in Bureaucratic Nationalism*, 2nd ed. Princeton, N.J.: Princeton University Press, 1967.

Gertzel, Cherry. *Party and Locality in Northern Uganda, 1945—1962. London: Althone Press, 1974*.

Gingyera-Pinycwa, A. G. G. *Apollo Milton Obote and His Time*. New York: NOK, 1978.

Gwyn, David. *Idi Amin: Death-Light of Africa*. Boston: Little, Brown, 1977.

Hansen, Holger Bernt. *Ethnicity and Military Rule in Uganda*. Uppsala: The Scandinavian Institute of African Studies, Research Report No. 43, 1977.

Hills, Denis. *The White Pumpkin*. London: George Allen and Unwin, 1975.

Kasfir, N. *The Shrinking Political Arena: Participation and Ethnicity in African Politics with a Case Study of Uganda*. Berkeley: University of California Press, 1975.

Kiwanuka, Semakula. *Amin and the Tragedy of Uganda*. Munich: Weltforum Verlag, 1979.

Kyemba, Henry. *A State of Blood*. N.Y.: Ace Books, 1977.

Leys, Colin. *Politicians and Policies: An Essay on Politics in Acholi, Uganda 1962—65*. Nairobi: East African Publishing House, 1967.

Mamdani, M. *Politics and Class Formation in Uganda*. New York: Monthly Review Press, 1976.

Martin, David. *General Amin*. London: Faber & Faber, 1974.

Mittelman, J. H. *Ideology and Politics in Uganda: From Obote to Amin*. Ithaca: Cornell University Press, 1975.

Strate, J. T. *Post-Military Coup Strategy in Uganda: Amin's Early Attempts to Consolidate Political Support*. Athens, Ohio: Center for International Studies, Ohio University, 1973. Papers in International Studies, Africa Series, No. 18.

ECONOMIC

International Monetary Fund. "Uganda." In *Surveys of African Economies*, Vol. 2, Washington, D.C.: I.M.F., 1968.

Jameson, J. D. (ed.) *Agriculture in Uganda*. New York: Oxford University Press, 1971.

Richards, A. I. et al. (eds.) *Subsistence to Commercial Farming in Present-Day Buganda*. New York: Cambridge University Press, 1973.

SOCIAL

Ainsworth, Mary D. S. *Infancy in Uganda*. Baltimore, Md.: Johns Hopkins Press, 1967.

Brandt. Hartmat, et al. *The Industrial Town as Factor of Economic and Social Development: The Example of Jinja/Uganda*. Munich: Welforum Verlag, 1972.

Curley, Richard T. *Elders Shades and Women: Ceremonial change in Lango, Uganda*. Berkeley: University of California Press, 1973.

Doornbos, Martin, *Not All the King's Men: Inequality as a Political Instrument in Ankole, Uganda*. The Hague: Mouton, 1978

Fallers, Lloyd A., ed. *The King's Men: Leadership and Status in Buganda on the Eve of Independence*. New York: Oxford University Press, 1964.

Fallers, Lloyd A., *Bantu Bureaucracy*. Chicago: University of Chicago Press, 1965.

Scott, Roger. *The Development of Trade Unions in Uganda*. Nairobi: East African Publishing House, 1966.

Southall, A. W. "The Concepts of Elite and Their Formation in Uganda." In *The New Elites in Tropical Africa*, ed. P. C. Lloyd. New York: Oxford University Press, 1966.

Southall, A. W. and P. G. Gutkind. *Townsmen in the Making: Kampala and its Suburbs*. London: Routledge and Kegan Paul, 1957.

Tosh, John. *Clan Leaders and Colonial Chiefs in Lango: The Political History of an East African Stateless Society c. 1800—1939*. New York: Oxford University Press, 1978.

Van Zwanenberg, R. M. A. and Anne King. *An Economic History of Kenya and Uganda, 1900—1970*. London: Macmillan, 1975.

Vincent, Joan. *African Elite: The Big Men of a Small Town*. New York: Columbia University Press, 1971.

38. Burkina Faso (Upper Volta)

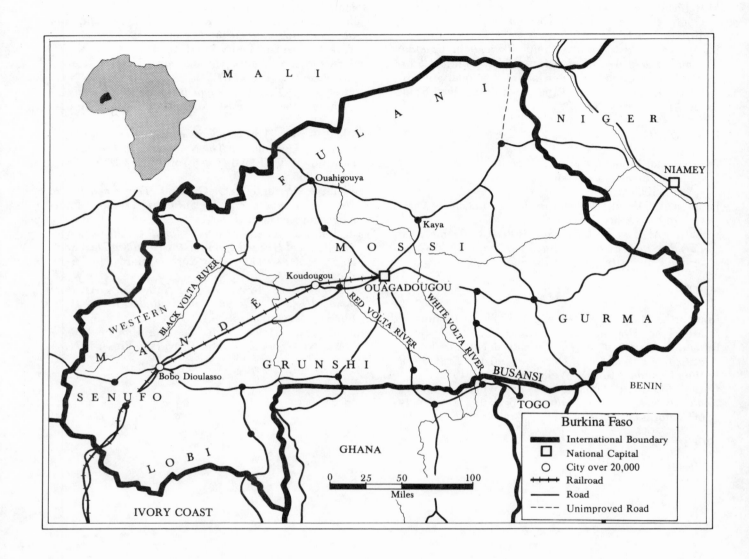

I. Basic Information

Date of Independence: April 5, 1960
Former Colonial Ruler: France
Change in Boundaries: Formerly part of the French West African Federation; administered as part of the Ivory Coast after conquest, administered separately from 1919-1932; administered as part of Mali and the Ivory Coast until 1947

Most Widely Spoken Languages: Mossi—55%; Dyula—21%

Estimated Population (1980): 6,800,000
Area Size (equivalent in U.S.): 103,870 sq. mi. (Colorado)
Date of Last Census: 1975
Major Exports 1977 as Percent of Total Exports: raw cotton — 40 percent; live animals — 29 percent; karite nuts and oil — 14 percent.

Official Language: French

II.   Elite Political Instability

TABLE 38.1   Elite Instability (Post- Independence)

Date	Event
1. January 3, 1966	Coup d'État (Col. Lamizana ousts Pres. Yaméogo over labor dispute.)
2. February 8, 1974	Coup d'État (Pres. Lamizana suspends the constitution and assumes full control. All parties are banned.)
3. November 25, 1980	Coup d'État (Lamizana overthrown by Col. Zerbo—all parties banned.)
4. November 7, 1982	Coup d'État (Col. Zerbo overthrown by Army units.)

III.   Country Features Worthy of Special Study

1. One of the world's least developed economies.
2. At least 750,000 Voltaians emigrate each year for work, especially to the Ivory Coast.
3. Almost half of the population still followed traditional religion in 1980, one of the highest rates of adherence to traditional religion in Black Africa.

IV. Selected References

BIBLIOGRAPHY

African Bibliographic Center, Washington. *French-Speaking West Africa. Upper Volta Today, 1960—1967: A Selected and Introductory Bibliographic Guide.* Westport: Negro Universities Press, 1969.

McFarland, D. M. *Historical Dictionary of Upper Volta.* Metuchen, N.J.: Scarecrow, 1978.

GENERAL

Guilhem, Marcel. *Histoire de las Haute-Volta* . Paris: Ligel, 1964.

Grant, Stephen H. "Getting by with Nothing." *Africa Report*, 18 (May-June 1973): 29-32.

Lippens, P. *La République de Haute Volta.* Paris: Bergère-Levrault, 1972.

Pool, D. I. and S. P. Coulibaly (eds). *Demographic Transition and Cultural Continuity in the Sahel: Aspects of the Social Demography of Upper Volta.* Ithaca, N.Y.: Cornell University, International Population Program, 1977.

Thompson, Virginia and Richard Adloff. *French West Africa*, pp. 171-178. Stanford, Calif.: Stanford University Press, 1957.

POLITICAL

Amin, Samir. *Neo-Colonialism in West Africa.* Harmondsworth, Middlesex: Penquin Books, 1973.

De Lusignan, Guy. *French-Speaking Africa Since Independence.* pp. 145-151. London: Pall Mall Press, 1969.

LeVine, Victor T. "The Coups in Upper Volta, Dahomey and the Central African Republic." In *Power and Protest in Black Africa*, eds. Robert I. Rotberg and Ali A. Mazrui, pp. 1035-1071. New York: Oxford University Press, 1970.

ECONOMIC

International Monetary Fund. "Upper Volta," In *Surveys of African Economies*, Vol. 3. Washington, D.C.: I.M.F., 1970.

SOCIAL

Courel, M. F. et al. "La population de la Haute Volta au recensement de decembre 1975." *Cahiers d'Outre Mer*. 32, 125, pp. 39—65.

Levtzion, Nehemia. *Muslims and Chiefs in West Africa.* Oxford: Clarendon Press, 1968.

Skinner, Elliot P. *African Urban Life: The Transformation of Ouagadougou.* Princeton, N.J.: Princeton University Press, 1974.

Skinner, Elliot P. *The Mossi of the Upper Volta: The Political Development of a Sudanese People.* Stanford, Cal.: Stanford University Press, 1964.

Wettere-Verhasselt, Yole Van. "Bobo-Dioulasso: Le Developpement d'une ville d'Afrique Occidentale." *Les Cahiers d'Outre-Mer*, 35 (Janvier-Mars 1959): 88—94.

39. Zaire

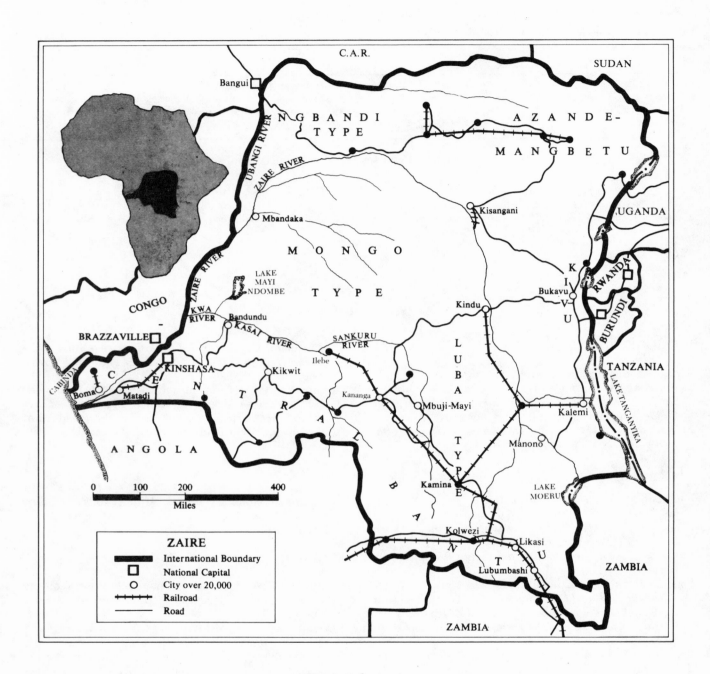

I. Basic Information

Date of Independence: June 30, 1960
Former Colonial Ruler: Belgium
Former names: Belgian Congo, Congo (Leopoldville), Congo (Kinshasa).
Estimated Population (1980): 28,669,000 *Area Size (equivalent in U.S.)*: 906,000 sq. mi. (Alaska, Texas, and Colorado)
Most Widely Spoken Languages: Lingala—40%; Kongo—35%; Swahili—30%

Date of Last Census: 1969-70
Major Exports (1976) as Percent of Total Exports: copper — 42 percent; coffee — 14 percent; cobalt — 13 percent; diamonds — 6 percent.
Official Language: French

II.   Elite Political Instability

TABLE 39.1 Elite Instability (Post-Independence)

Date	Event
1. September 14, 1960	Coup d'État (Col. Mobutu takes power after breakdown of civilian rule.)
2. November 19, 1963	Attempted Coup (Mobutu kidnapped, escapes and puts it down.)
3. November 25, 1965	Coup d'État (Col. Mobutu assumes full powers after parliamentary power struggle.)

III.   Country Features Worthy of Special Study

1. Center of international "cold-war" conflict after independence in 1960.
2. Great mineral wealth coupled with one of the most literate populations in Africa.
3. Second largest country in area in Black Africa and one of the most populous.
4. High percentage of the population are Christian and it has the highest number of adherents of independent churches per capita in Black Africa.
5. Economy heavily dependent on copper and other minerals, and vulnerable to international copper price fluctuations.

IV. Selected References

BIBLIOGRAPHY

Bustin, Edouard. *A Study Guide for Congo-Kinshasa*. Boston: Development Program, African Studies Center, Boston University, 1970.

Liniger-Goumaz. Max. *Bibliographies africaines*. Geneve, Editions du Temps, 1971—74, 2 vols.

GENERAL

Anstey, Roger. *King Leopold's Legacy: The Congo under Belgian Rule, 1908—1960*. London: Oxford University Press, issued under the auspices of the Institute of Race Relations, 1966.

Biebuyck, Daniel and Mary Douglas. *Congo Tribes and Parties*. London: Royal Anthropological Institute, 1961.

Cornevin, Robert. *Le Zaire, ex. Congo Kinshasa*. Paris, P.U.F., 1972.

Merlier, M. *Le Congo de la Colonisation Belge à l'Indépendence*. Paris: Maspero, 1961.

Roth, H. M., et al. *Zaire, A Country Study*, 3rd ed. American University, Washington, D.C., 1979.

Van der linden, Jacques. *La Republique du Zaire*. Paris. Bergère-Levrault, 1975.

POLITICAL

Bustin, E. *Lunda Under Colonial Rule*. Cambridge: Harvard University Press, 1975.

Dayal, R. *Mission of Hammarskjold: The Congo Crisis*. London: Oxford University Press, 1976.

Gerard-Libois, Jules. *Katanga Secession*. Madison: University of Wisconsin Press, 1966.

Heiraz, G. and H. Donnay, *Lumumba: The Last Fifty Days*. N.Y.: Grove Press, 1969.

House, Arthur H. *The U.N. in the Congo: The Political and Civilian Efforts*. Washington, D.C.: University Press of America, 1978.

Kanza, Thomas. *The Rise and Fall of Patrice Lumumba*. London: Rex Collings, 1978.

La Fontaine, J. S. *City Politics: A Study of Leopoldville 1962—1963*. New York: Cambridge University Press, 1970.

Lemarchand, René. Political Awakening in the Congo. Berkeley: University of California Press, 1964.

Lumumba, Patrice. *Congo, My Country*. New York: Praeger, 1962.

Nkrumah, Kwame. *Challenge of the Congo*. London: Thomas Nelson, 1967.

Schatzberg, M. G. *Politics and Class in Zaire: Bureaucracy, Business and Beer in Lisala*. N.Y.: Holmes and Meier, 1979.

Verhaegen, Benoit. *Rebellions au Congo*. 2 vols. Brussels: Centre de recherche et d'information socio-politiques, 1966.

Weiss, Herbert. *Political Protest in the Congo: The Parti Solidaire Africain During the Independence Struggle*. Princeton, N.J.: Princeton University Press, 1967.

Weissman, Stephen R. *American Foreign Policy in the Congo, 1960—1964*. Ithaca, N.Y.: Cornell University Press, 1974.

Williams, Jean-Claude. *Patrimonialism and Political Change in the Congo*. Stanford, Calif.: Stanford University Press, 1972.

Young, Crawford. *Politics in the Congo: Decolonization and Independence*. Princeton, N.J.: Princeton University Press, 1965.

Young, Crawford. "Rebellion and the Congo." In *Power and Protest in Black Africa*, eds. Robert I. Rotberg and Ali A. Mazrui, pp. 969—1011. New York: Oxford University Press, 1970.

ECONOMIC

Gran, Guy, ed. *Zaire, The Political Economy of Underdevelopment*. N.Y.: Praeger, 1979.

International Monetary Fund. "Democratic Republic of the Congo." In *Surveys of African Economies*, Vol. 4, Washington, D.C.: I.M.F., 1971.

Miracle, Marvin P. *Agriculture in the Congo Basin*. Madison: University of Wisconsin Press, 1967.

Pemans, J. P. "The Social and Economic Development of Zaire since Independence: An Historical Outline." *African Affairs*, 74 (April 1975): 143—179.

SOCIAL

Andersson, Efraim. *Messianic Popular Movements in the Lower Congo*. Uppsala: Almqvist & Wiksell, 1958.

Cahier des Relgions Africaines. 9, 17—18 (1975) special issue on Zaire's ethnic groups.

Caulemans, P. "Introduction de l'Influence de l'Islam au Congo." In *Islam in Tropical Africa*, ed. I. M. Lewis, pp. 174—192. London: Oxford University Press, 1966.

MacGaffey, W. *Custom and Government in the Lower Congo*. Berkeley: University of California Press, 1970.

Obenga, Theophile. *Le Zaire*. Paris: Presence Africaine, 1977.

Pons, V. C. *Stanleyville: An African Urban Community Under Belgian Administration*. London: Oxford University Press, 1969.

Reardon, Ruth Slade. "Catholics and Protestants in the Congo." In *Christianity in Tropical Africa*. ed. C. G. Bacta, pp. 83—100. London: Oxford University Press, 1968.

United Nations. Economic Commission for Africa. "Leopoldville and Lagos: Comparative Study of Conditions in 1960." In *The City in Newly Developing Countries*, ed. Gerald Breese, pp. 436—460. Englewood Cliffs, N.J.: Prentice-Hall, 1969.

Vansina, Jan. *Kingdoms of the Savannah*. Madison: University of Wisconsin Press, 1966.

40. Zambia

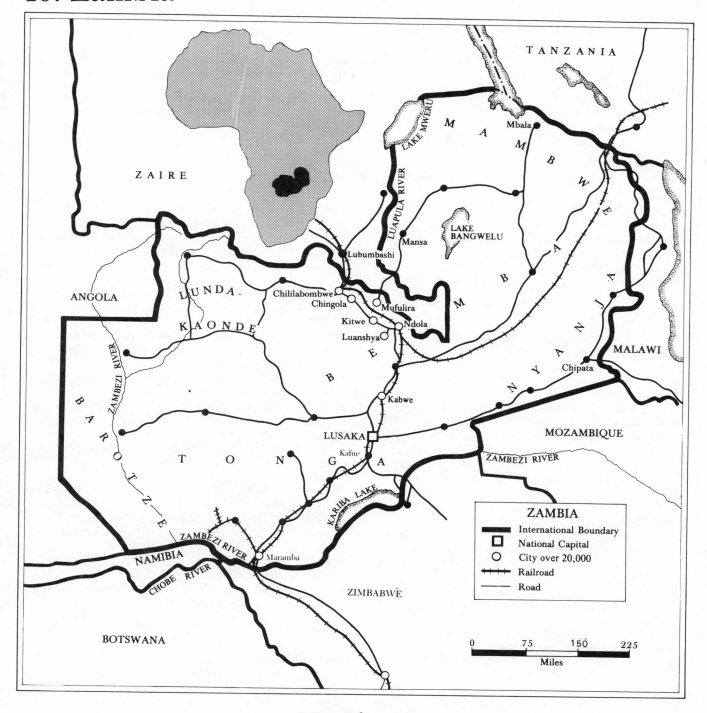

I. Basic Information

Date of Independence: October 24, 1964
Former Colonial Ruler: United Kingdom
Change in Boundaries: Part of the Central African Federation, 1953-1963.
Former Name: Northern Rhodesia

Most Widely Spoken Languages: Bemba—35%; Tonga—18%

Population (1980): 5,725,000
Area Size (equivalent in U.S.): 290,586 sq. mi. (Texas)
Date of Last Census: 1969 (sample census in 1974)
Major Exports 1977 as Percent of Total Exports: copper — percent.

Official Language: English

III.   Country Features Worthy of Special Study

1. Kaunda was a key figure in the Rhodesian conflict which resulted in the establishment of majority rule in Zimbabwe.
2. Had been a fast growing economy, for the first decade after independence but recent events have seen major declines in copper prices, its major source of foreign exchange.
3. Major economic dependence on a single mineral resource, copper, which is vulnerable to international price fluctuations.
4. Kuanda's program, which was begun in June 1975 to establish a "humanist state" of equals in which all private enterprise is to be eradicated.

IV. Selected References

BIBLIOGRAPHY

Grotpeter, John J. *Historical Dictionary of Zambia*. Metuchen, N.J.: Scarecrow Press, 1979.
Rau, W. E. *A Bibliography of Pre-Independence Zambia: The Social Sciences*. Boston: G.K. Hall, 1978.

GENERAL

Davis, D. H. (ed.). *Zambia in Maps*. N.Y.: Holmes and Meier, 1972.
Hall, Richard. *Zambia*. New York: Praeger, 1966.
Hall, Richard. *Zambia, 1890—1964, the Colonial Period*. London: Longman, 1976.
Kaplan, Irving, ed. *Zambia, a Country Study*, 3rd. ed. Washington, U.S. Government Printing Office, 1979.
Martin, A. *Minding Their Own Business: Zambia's Struggle Against Western Control*. London: Hutchinson, 1972.
Robert, Andrews. *A History of Zambia*. N.Y.: Africana, 1976.

POLITICAL

Arglin, Douglas G. and Shaw, Timothy M. *Zambia's Foreign Policy: Studies in Diplomacy and Dependence*. Boulder, Col.: Westview, 1979.
Bates, R. *Unions, Parties, and Political Development: A Study of Mineworkers in Zambia*. New Haven, Conn.: Yale University Press, 1971.
Bates, R. *Rural Responses to Industrialization*. New Haven: Yale University Press, 1976.
Berger, Elena L. *Labor, Race and Colonial Rule: The Copperbelt from 1924 to Independence*. London: Oxford University Press, 1974.
Bond, G. G. *The Politics of Change in a Zambian Community*. Chicago: University of Chicago Press, 1976.
Cervanka, Zdenek and R. Weiss. *Zambia: The First Ten Years 1964—1974*. Stockholm: Swedish-Zambian Association, 1974.
Epstein, A. L. *Politics in an African Urban Community*. Manchester: Manchester University Press, 1958.
Hall, Richard. *The High Price of Principles: Kaunda and the White South*. Rev. ed. Harmondsworth, U.K.: Penguin, 1973.
Kaunda, Kenneth. *Zambia Shall Be Free: An Autobiography*. New York: Praeger, 1963.

Kaunda, Kenneth. *Zambia, Independence and Beyond*. London: Thomas Nelson, 1966.
MacPherson, Fergus. *Kennth Kaunda of Zambia*. Lusaka: Oxford University Press, 1974.
Meebelo, H. S. *Main Currents of Zambian Humanist Thought*. London: Oxford University Press, 1973.
Mulford, David C. *Zambia: The Politics of Independence, 1957—1954*. London: Oxford University Press, 1967.
Ollawa, Patrick E. *Participatory Democracy in Zambia: The Political Economy of National Development*. Elms Court: Arthur H. Stockwell, 1979.
Pettman, Jan. *Zambia: Security and Conflict, 1964—1973*. New York: St. Martin's Press, 1974.
Rotberg, Robert D. *Black Heart: Gore-Browne and the Politics of Multiracial Zambia*. Berkeley: University of California Press, 1977.
Scarritt, James R. "The Decline of Political Legitimacy in Zambia." African Studies Review, 22, 2, Sept. 1979, pp. 13—38.
Scott, I. "Middle Class Politics in Zambia." *African Affairs* (London), 77, 308, July, 1978, pp. 321—34.
Shaw, T. M. "The Foreign Policy of Zambia: An Events Analysis of a New State." *Comparative Political Studies*, 11, 2, July, 1978, pp. 181—209.
Sklar, R. *Corporate Power in an African State*. Berkeley: University of California Press, 1975.
Tordoff, W. (ed.). *Politics in Zambia*. Manchester: Manchester University Press, 1974.

ECONOMIC

Blitzer, Charles R. *Development and Income Distribution in a Dual Economy: A Dynamic Simulation Model for Zambia*. Washington, D.C.: World Bank, 1978.
Bostock, M., and C. Harvey (eds.). *Economic Independence and Zambian Copper: A Case Study of Foreign Investment*. New York: Praeger, 1972.
Dodge, D. J. *Agricultural Policy and Performance in Zambia: History, Prospects, and Proposals for Change*. Berkeley: Institute for International Studies, 1977.
Daniel, Philip. *Africanisation, Nationalisation and Inequality: Miner's Labour and the Copperbelt in Zambian Development*. N.Y.: Cambridge University Press, 1979.

Elliott, Charles (ed.). *Constraints on the Economic Development of Zambia.* New York: Oxford University Press, 1972.

Fry, James. *Employment and Income Distribution in the African Economy.* London: Croom Helm, 1979.

Gordenker, L. *International Aid and National Decisions: Development Programs in Malawi, Tanzania and Zambia.* Princeton: Princeton University Press, 1976.

Hellen, John Anthony. *Rural Economic Development in Zambia, 1890—1964.* Munich: Weltforum Verlag, 1968.

International Monetary Fund. "Zambia." In *Surveys of African Economies,* Vol. 4. Washington, D.C.: I.M.F., 1971.

Kapferrer, B. *Strategy and Transition in an African Factory: African Workers and Indian Management in a Zambian Town.* Manchester: Manchester University Press, 1972.

Simonis, H., and V. E. *Socioeconomic Development in Dual Economies: The Example of Zambia.* Munich: Weltforum Verlag, 1975.

Turok, Ben. *Development in Zambia.* London, Zed Press, 1979.

SOCIAL

Bates, R. H. "Ethnic Competition and Modernization in Contemporary Africa." *Comparative Political Studies,* 6, 4 (January 1974): 457—84.

Brelsford, W. V. *The Tribes of Northern Rhodesia.* Lusaka: Northern Rhodesia Government Printer, 1956.

Brooks, E., and V. Nyirenda (eds.). *Social Development in Zambia: Case Studies.* Lusaka: University of Zambia, 1977.

Heisler, Helmuth. *Urbanization and the Government of Migration: The Inter-relation of Urban and Rural Life in Zambia.* New York: St. Martin's Press, 1974.

Mitchell, J. Clyde and A. L. Epstein. "Occupational Prestige and Social Status Among Africans in Northern Rhodesia," *Africa* 29 (1959): 22—40.

Mwanakatwe, J. M. *The Growth of Education in Zambia Since Independence.* London: Oxford University Press, 1969.

Ohannessian, S., and M. Kashoki (eds.). *Language in Zambia.* London: International African Institute, 1977.

Perrings, Charles. *Black Mine Workers in Central Africa: Industry Strategies and the Evolution of an African Proletariat in the Copperbelt, 1911—1941.* N.Y.: Africana Publishing Co., 1979.

Powdermaker, Hortense. *Copper Town: Changing Africa. The Human Situation on the Rhodesian Copperbelt.* New York: Harper, 1962.

Schuster, Ilsa and M. Glazer. *New Women of Lusaka.* Palo Alto, Calif.: Mayfield, 1979.

Siddle, C. J. "Rural Development in Zambia: A Spatial Analyis," *Journal of Modern African Studies,"* 8 *(July 1970): 271—184.*

41. Zimbabwe

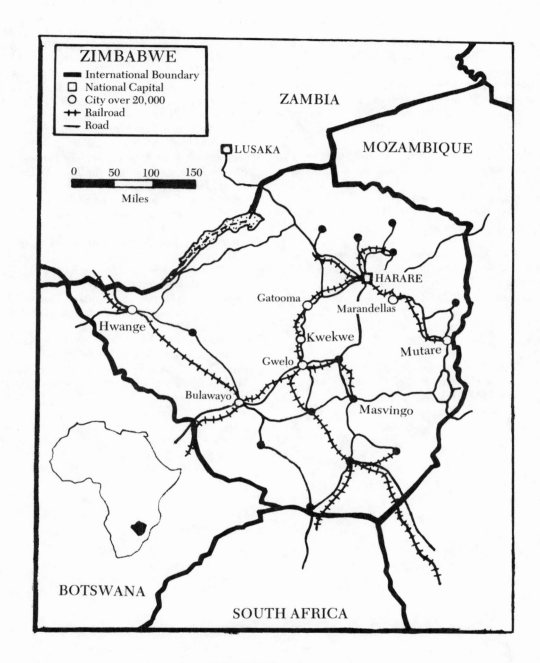

I. Basic Information

Date of Independence: April 19, 1980
Former Colonial Ruler: United Kingdom
Change in Boundaries: Member of the Central African Federationfrom 1953 to 1963.
Former Name: Southern Rhodesia, Rhodesia, Zimbabwe-Rhodesia

Most Widely Spoken Languages: Shona—78%; Ndebele—15%

Estimted Population (1980) 7,820,000
Area Size (equivalent in U.S.): 150,820 sq. mi. (Montana)
Date of Last Census: 1969
Major exports 1978 as percent of total exports: Not known because of the war.

Official Language: English

III.   Country Features Worthy of Special Study

1. Recently emerged from a long conflict over majority rule in the country.
2. Ethnic conflicts threaten the continuance of a political democracy.

IV. Selected References

BIBLIOGRAPHY

Pollak, Oliver B. and Karen Pollak. *Rhodesia/Zimbabwe*. Santa Barbara, Clio Press, 1979.

Rasmussen, R. K. *Historical Dictionary of Rhodesia/Zimbabwe Metuchen*, New Jersey: Scarecrow Press, 1979.

O'Meara, Patrick and Gosebrink, Jean. "Bibliography on Rhodesia." *Africana Journal*, 9,1 1978, pp. 5-42 and 9,2 pp101—112.

GENERAL

Austin, R. *Racism and Apartheid in Southern Africa: Rhodesia*. Paris: UNESCO, 1975.

Blake, R. *A History of Rhodesia*. New York: Knopf, 1978.

Cary, R. and D. Mitchell. *African Nationalist Leaders in Rhodesia: Who's Who*. Bulawayo: Bulawayo Books, 1977.

Lorey, M. *Rhodesia: White Racism and Imperial Response*. Middlesex, England: Penguin Books, 1975.

Nelson, Harold D. *Area Handbook for Southern Rhodesia*. Washington: U.S. Government Printing Office, 1975.

Rhodesia/Zimbabwe 1971—1977. New York: Facts on File Publications, 1978.

Simson, Howard. *Zimbabwe: A Country Study*. Uppsala: Scandanavian Institute of African Studies, 1979.

POLITICAL

Bull, Theodore, ed. *Rhodesia: Crisis of Color*. Chicago: Quadrangle Books, 1967.

Clements, Frank. *Rhodesia, The Course to Collision*. London: Pall Mall Press, 1969.

Good, Robert C. *U.D.I.: The International Politics of the Rhodesian Rebellion*. London: Faber, 1973.

Hills, D. *Rebel People*. New York: Africana Publishing, 1978.

Hirsch, Morris I. *A Decade of Crisis, Ten Years of Rhodesian Front Rule (1963—72)*. Salisbury: Peter Dearlove, 1973.

Hutson, H. P. W. *Rhodesia: Ending an Era*. London: Springwood Books, 1978.

Lake, Anthony. *The "Tar Baby" Option, American Policy Toward Southern Rhodesia*. N.Y.: Columbia University Press, 1976.

Legum, C. *Southern Africa: The Year of the Whirlwind*. New York: Holmes and Meier, 1977.

Meredith, Martin. *The Past is Another Country: Rhodesia 1890—1979*. London: Andre Deutsch, 1979.

Nyangoni, C. and G. Nyandoro, eds. *Zimbabwe Independence Movements*. New York: Barnes and Noble, 1979.

O'Meara, P. *Rhodesia: Racial Conflict or Coexistence?* Ithaca, N.Y.: Cornell University Press, 1975.

Raeburn, M. *Black Fire! Accounts of the Guerrilla War in Rhodesia*. London: Julian Friedmann, 1977.

Sithole, N. *Zimbabwe's Year of Freedom*. Pasadena: Munger Africana Library Notes. 43, 1978.

Sithole, N. *Roots of a Revolution: Scenes from Zimbabwe's Struggle*. New York: Oxford University Press, 1977.

Strack, H. R. *Sanctions: The Case of Rhodesia*. Syracuse: Syracuse University Press, 1978.

Todd, Judith. *The Right to Say No*. London: Sidgwich and Jackson, 1972.

Windrich, E. *The Rhodesian Problem, A Documentary Record 1923—1973*. London: Routledge and Kegan Paul, 1975.

Windrich, E. *Britain and the Politics of Rhodesian Independence*. New York: Africana Publishing, 1978.

ECONOMIC

Clarke, D. G. *The Distribution of Income and Wealth in Rhodesia*. Gwelo: Mambo Press, 1977.

Clarke, D. G. *Foreign Companies and International Investment in Zimbabwe*. London: Catholic Institute for International Relations, 1980

Simson, Howard. *Zimbabwe: A Country Study*. Uppsala: Sandanavian Institute of African Studies, 1979.

Wasserman, Gary. "The Economic Transition to Zimbabwe." *Africa Report*, 23, 6, Nov./Dec. 1978, pp. 39—45.

Zimbabwe-Rhodesia, Government of. *Economic Survey of Zimbabwe-Rhodesia*. Salisbury, 1978.

SOCIAL

Bourdillon, M. F. C. *The Shona Peoples: An Ethnography of the Contemporary Shona, With Special Reference to Their Religion*. Gwelo: Mambo Press, 1976.

Kay, G. and M. Smout, eds. *Salisbury: A Geographical Survey of the Capital of Rhodesia*. New York: Holmes and Meier, 1977.

O'Callaghan, M. *Southern Rhodesia: The Effects of a Conquest Society on Education, Culture and Information*. Paris: UNESCO, 1977.

APPENDIX 1

Selected Data Souces on Africa

The number of sources of data on Africa is very large, including academic journals, private publications, government reports, and institutional reports. The following is a selected list of these sources many of which also cite other published sources. The list of journals and handbooks in Appendix 4 will also be helpful to the reader looking for data on Africa. For general guides to research materials see J. N. Paden and E. Soja *The African Experience*, Vol. IIIb, Guide to Resources (Evanston: Northwestern University Press, 1970); Helen Conover and Peter Duignan *Guide to African Research and Reference Works* (Stanford: Hoover Institution Press, 1972); Gerald Hartwig and William O'Barr, *The Student Africanist's Handbook* (Cambridge, Mass.: Schenkman, 1974); Purnima M. Bhatt, *Scholar's Guide to Washington, D.C. for African Studies* (Washington, D.C.: Smithsonian Institution, 1980) and Hans E. Panovsky *A Bibliography of Africana* (Westport, Conn.: Greenwood Press, 1975).

For sources of data on a wide range of socio-political-economic measures see The United Nations annuals such as the *U.N. Demographic Yearbook*, the *U.N. Statistical Yearbook*, and the Economic Commission for Africa's *Statistical Yearbook*. For economic and trade data see the International Monetary Fund's *International Financial Statistics* (monthly) and *Direction of Trade* (monthly). *The World Bank Atlas* (annual) provides basic income data. A major source is *Europa Yearbook* and its area specific copy, *Africa South of the Sahara*. Also see J. M. Harvey, *Statistics Africa: Sources for Social, Economic and Market research* 2nd edition (Beckenham, England: CBD Research, 1978).

For data on general events, particularly political and government activities, see *West Africa* (weekly); *African Development* (monthly); *Africa* (monthly); *Africa Research Bulletin* (monthly); *Africa Confidential* (forthnightly); and *Africa Diary* (monthly).

For data on individuals see the work by J. Dickie and A. Rake *Who's Who in Africa* (London: African Development, 1973) and the various country 'Who's Who' such as, for example, the *Who's Who for East Africa; Who's Who in Nigeria; Who's Who in Ghana*; and the brief who's who in *Africa: South of the Sahara* (annual).

For general annual reviews of the situation in Africa the best sources are *Africa Contemporary Record; Africa: South of the Sahara* and *Africa* (as published by *Jeune Afrique* in Paris).

Other sources of data can be gleaned from the sources for the tables presented both in this book and in *Black Africa: A Comparative Handbook* (second edition) as well as the country studies in the bibliographies in Parts III and V of this book.

APPENDIX 2

**Correlation Matrix for Variables in Part III
and Listing of Data.**

The following tables present Pearson correlation coefficients for every pair of variables presented in column A in Part III. This table may be used to evaluate how much any two variables covary with each other. If a theoretical rationale is advanced as to *why* two variables in this list should covary (such as turning up the heat on a stove causes the increase in the temperature of water in the pot) then these correlations may be used to evaluate whether the theory is true. The reader should be aware that without such a rationale the imputation of causation is questionable... covariance as such does not demonstrate causation. Further, by chance it is expected that out of a large number of correlations roughly five percent will be large enough to be statistically significant.

The correlation coefficient varies between -1.00 and 1.00; the higher the absolute value of the coefficient the more the two variables are statistically related. A negative sign means that as the value of one variable goes higher the value of the other decreases and, conversely, if the sign is positive then they go up and down together. For example, the correlation coefficient between Per Capita Gross Domestic Product and Number of Secondary Students per 10,000 population is .23, indicating a strong positive relation.

Each variable in the following is identified by a short *number*. These numbers are the table numbers of the variables as presented in the tables of Part III. Readers interested to see how two variables relate to each other should check the table numbers, and then turn to the correlation matrix and find the row with the highest of the two numbers and the column with the value of the lowest of the two numbers.

------- P E A R S O N   C O R R E L A T I O N   C O E F F I C I E N T S -------

	S1.1	S1.2	S1.3	S1.4	S2.1	S2.2	S3.1	S3.2	S3.3	S3.4	S3.5	S4.1	S4.2	S4.3
S1.1	1.0000													
S1.2	.4517*	1.0000												
S1.3	.0024	.1067	1.0000											
S1.4	-.5184**	-.4607*	.0729	1.0000										
S2.1	-.0944	-.1155	-.1243	.0550	1.0000									
S2.2	-.1527	-.2315	.0868	.0642	-.4003*	1.0000								
S3.1	-.0296	.0641	.1728	.4569**	-.1578	.2840	1.0000							
S3.2	-.1714	-.1452	-.0369	.0402	-.2349	.3954*	-.2840	1.0000						
S3.3	-.1281	.2111	-.1319	.3210	.1539	.3154	-.0335	-.1539	1.0000					
S3.4	-.1809	-.1477	-.0653	.0725	-.3529	.0152	.3028	-.0009	.0335	1.0000				
S3.5	-.1872	-.0279	-.1612	.1272	-.1575	.0370	.0696	-.1049	-.0009	.0996	1.0000			
S4.1	-.0844	-.1108	.2805	.1735	.0993	.0388	.0370	.2397	-.2023	-.2023	-.0900	1.0000		
S4.2	-.0794	-.1433	-.0781	.1612	-.1539	.3744*	.1534	-.0900	.2397	-.0617	-.1049	.7330**	1.0000	
S4.3	-.2310	-.1084	-.0826	.7541**	-.3701*	-.0388	.1827	.0338	-.0561	.0696	-.0900	-.1121	-.1121	1.0000
S5.1	-.1789	-.0327	-.0368	.2151	.3529	-.1405	-.2043	.4397*	.1827	-.1827	.2023	.0838	-.2759	-.0796
S5.2	-.1074	-.0704	-.0627	.0585	-.0515	.1913	.2962	-.2759	.1985	.1985	-.1235	.5335**	.3575	-.1062
S5.3	-.2007	-.1977	-.1831	.0627	.1523	-.0456	-.1330	.1985	.0233	-.0867	-.0111	.5470**	.3575	-.0833
S5.4	-.2907	-.0140	-.0628	.1656	.1430	.1958	.4651*	-.0111	.7190**	.3200	.1225	.1158	.2574**	.0338
S6.1	-.2049	-.2777	.1563	.0021	.0963	.0267	-.0267	-.0867	-.1501	-.1225	.2602	-.1391	.5823**	-.1391
S6.2	-.0377	-.2625	-.0070	-.0869	.0673	.1430	-.0528	.3200	.1334	.2350	-.2521	.1540	-.1132	.0338
S6.3	-.1235	-.0479	.0312	.1771	-.0190	.0963	-.2361	-.1501	.0118	.2615	.2067	.0226	-.2726	-.1391
S6.4	-.2176	.0505	-.0265	.0496	.4483*	.0673	-.5601**	-.2602	-.3184	-.3054	.0336	.0336	-.1646	.1073
S7.1	-.3767	.1058	.2403	.3660	.3660	-.0190	.5789**	-.0867	.2282	-.0561	-.1382	-.1828	.0488	.0497
S7.2	-.3067	.0981	.0710	.1447	.2493	.4483*	.5359**	.1421	-.0867	-.1382	.1041	.1073	.1275	.3119
S7.3	-.0170	.5090**	-.4403*	.0059	.2461	.3660	.3123	.2557	.1418	.1852	.0253	.0253	.1073	.1275
S7.4	.4708	.3325	-.0059	.3528	.1312	.2461	.1250	-.2493	-.2282	.1421	.5260*	.5260*	.1320	.0497
S7.5	.0395	-.4278*	.2550	.2980	-.0286	.1250	-.1152	-.3132	.2350	.2557	.0115	.1320	-.0210	.1873
S7.6	.0614	.0626	.2980	-.0840	-.0515	.0484	-.2032	.1989	.3200	-.1989	.2685	.0163	-.0873	-.1072
S7.7	.1099	.2170	.1312	-.1400	-.0140	-.4033	-.2491	-.2522	.2127	.2522	.1319	.1241	.3101	.1072
S8.1	-.1490	-.1120	-.0792	.0161	-.1342	-.2491	.0328	.1319	-.2130	-.3802	-.2021	-.0873	-.2918	.3101
S8.2	-.0858	-.0293	-.1400	.1036	-.1405	.1550	.2113	-.3802	-.0650	-.4465**	-.1549	-.3101	.3988*	-.1028
S8.3	-.0942	-.1371	.0161	.1246	.2497	.2704	-.0545	-.4465**	.3433	.3004	-.1724	.3988*	-.1028	-.0854
S8.4	-.2050	-.0742	-.0048	.1083	.1591	-.1591	-.5030**	.3004	.4610*	-.2918	.0891	.1028	.0925	.0925
S8.5	.0618	-.0759	.1083	.1579	-.1508	.2704	-.0545	-.2918	-.0490	-.0873	-.0517	.0854	-.0298	-.0854
S8.6	-.3141	-.1335	-.1363	.0099	-.1400	.1334	-.0294	-.0873	.1758	.1395	-.1395	.0815	.0815	.1028
S9.1	.7056**	-.0458	.1106	-.0099	-.2103	.3331	-.4216*	-.1549	-.0402	.0271	-.4654*	-.4355**	-.6355**	-.0450
S9.2	.2767	-.1272	-.0099	.1579	-.1649	.0833	.2879	-.2261	.2690	-.0846	-.0846	-.0051	.0915	.0915
S9.3	-.2157	.0291	-.1876	.3263	-.2688	.2955	.2514	-.1322	-.0108	.1217	.8319**	.5212**	.1872	.1028
S9.4	-.2101	.1212	-.0726	.0931	.0674	-.1365	-.0218	.1902	-.1507	.1217	-.2791	-.0441	.1427	-.0925
S9.5	-.1086	-.2625	.2655	.3263	.1848	.3548	.1131	-.0642	.1303	-.0524	-.0524	.0441	.1427	.0317
S9.6	.1413	.0781	-.2196	-.2962	.1660	-.2169	.3534	-.2298	-.0977	.1303	.3403	.5212**	.3076	-.1964
S9.7	-.0154	-.3176	-.1386	.2934	-.1182	-.3259	.2003	-.0229	.0811	-.1158	-.1158	.4999*	.3832*	-.2120

* - SIGNIF. LE .01   ** - SIGNIF. LE .001

PEARSON CORRELATION COEFFICIENTS

	S5.1	S5.2	S5.3	S5.4	S6.1	S6.2	S6.3	S6.4	S7.1	S7.2	S7.3	S7.4	S7.5	S7.6
S1.1	-.2310	-.1789	-.1074	-.2007	-.2907	.2049	.0377	.1235	.2176	-.3767	.0170	.4708		.0395
S1.2	-.1433	-.1977	-.2777	-.2625	-.0479	.0505	.0981		-.3325		.0626	.2170		.1120
S1.3	-.1084	-.1064	-.0140	-.0080	-.1058		.1058		-.4278*	.0905		.2059		-.2752
S1.4	-.0327	-.0822	-.0704	-.0070	.0312	.2403	.0710		.1147	.2550	.0792		-.2059	
S2.1	-.0704	-.1656	-.1563	-.0265	.1771	-.0265	.0253	-.4403*	.3528	.2980	-.0840		.0161	
S2.2	.2151	-.0627	.0021	-.0070	.0496	-.0336	.1828	.5260*	-.0286	-.1342	-.1400			
S3.1	-.0627	-.0628	.2574	-.0869	.1447	.0226	.1073	.1320	.2519	.1312	-.0210		-.1405	
S3.2	-.0515	-.1430	.0338	-.1391	-.0661	.0488	-.3119	.0497	.0816	-.0125	-.0873		.0618	
S3.3	-.1831	.1523	.2726	-.1132	-.0823	-.1646	-.1275	.1873	-.0484	.0515	.3101		.1550	
S3.4	.3781*	.1430	.0833	.1540	-.1797	.3821	-.0488	-.3881	.2461	-.0292	-.2032		-.4033	
S3.5	-.1523	-.0267	-.1062	.2067	.0330	.1444	.1073	.1956	-.0140	-.1152	-.0747		.0328	-.6586**
S4.1	.1430	-.0190	-.1391	-.3054	.1334	.1852	.1828	.1788	.3123	.0484	-.1989		.2127	
S4.2	-.0456	.0673	.2726	-.2521	.1418	-.1421	.1382	.1041	-.3132	-.2032	.2522		.4465*	
S4.3	.1958	-.0963	.0833	.2067	.1540	.1828	.0253	.0115	.3802	-.0163	-.2885		.3004	
S5.1	1.0000	.4651*	.5369**	.3886*	.3184	.5359*	.1250	.2493	.0369	.3123	.0196		-.3988*	
S5.2	.4651*	1.0000	.5877**	.5877**	.5601**	.5789**	.5359*	.2461	.2519	.1584	-.2032		.1028	
S5.3	.5369**	.5877**	1.0000	.5877**	.2577	.3834	.2345	-.3119	.1956	-.0125	.0198		.0743	
S5.4	.3886*	.5877**	.5877**	1.0000	.1609	-.4832*	.3279	.0818	.5082**	.3293	.1410		.1808	
S6.1	.6579**	.5601**	.5877**	.3705*	1.0000	.8496**	.3425	.2363	-.0378	-.0329	.1251		.1610	
S6.2	-.1089	-.0867	.0525	.0525	.8496**	1.0000	.3419	.2133	-.1322	.5082**	.1410		.2020	
S6.3	-.1440	-.0233	-.0114	-.1507	.3425	.3419	1.0000	.2876	.1625	-.0731	.2096		-.0727	
S6.4	.3821	.3200	-.2053	.1609	-.4596*	.2133	.2876	1.0000	.1663	.2413	.1516		.3806	
S7.1	.1444	-.0111	-.3279	-.4832*	.8496**	-.1322	.1625	.1663	1.0000	.1663	.0183		.0123	
S7.2	.0447	.1358	.3293	-.0378	-.1507	-.1625	-.0731	.2413	.1663	1.0000	.1153		.1058	
S7.3	.1956	.7617**	.5082**	.4832*	.1852	.2133	.0183	.4448	.0183	.1153	1.0000		.1722	
S7.4	.0198	.2574	-.0378	-.1322	.2067	.2413	.2876	-.5402**	-.1663	.5402**	.5402**	1.0000	1.0000	
S7.5	-.0541	.5470**	.4832*	.2363	-.3425	.3419	.2876	.1663	.5402**	-.2503	-.3214		1.0000	
S7.6	1.0000	-.1062	-.0378	-.0329	-.1625	.2133	.0183	.3214	-.3239	-.2537	-.0449		.1051	
S7.7	.3576	.0833	-.1775	-.0649	.1516	.2133	-.2226	-.3239	-.0772	.1188	-.1051		.1722	1.0000
S8.1	.3789*	.3789*	.0369	.2020	.3027	-.1259	.1058	-.0512	.0412	.1729	-.0077		.1026	.7965**
S8.2	.3886*	-.5830**	-.1675	-.2653	.1071	-.0609	-.2963	.3143	-.3317	.0052	.3355		.1722	-.1125
S8.3	.6579**	.9171**	.6909**	-.1031	-.0848	-.1067	.3615	-.2748	.1609	.1609	-.0743		1.0000	-.2236
S8.4	-.1089	-.5226**	.3188	.0618	.1822	.1667	-.0555	.2584	.1732	.1453	-.1538		.1722	.3719
S8.5	-.1440	.4498*	.4189*	.1989	-.0543	-.1822	-.0539	-.0690	-.4616*	-.3287	-.3287		-.1051	.2015
S8.6	.3821	.7715**	.3223	.2643	.1493	.1859	-.0628	.1839	-.5968*	-.1993	-.3893		1.0000	.0312
S9.1	.1444	-.4760*	-.4841*	.1549	.2441	.1467	.2312	.1848	.1386	-.0690	.0045		-.5147*	-.3719
S9.2	.0447	-.2987	.3503	-.0270	.2643	-.0635	-.3163	-.3163	-.1609	-.1993	.5147*		.0032	-.2236
S9.3	.1956	-.0122	-.1512	-.1549	-.0891	.1316	.3092	.5444**	-.1732	-.1609	-.0750		.0312	-.1797
S9.4	.0198	.3088	.1766	.1513	-.0891	-.0635	-.4592*	-.4616*	-.1925	-.1925	.0887		-.3437	.0928
S9.5	-.0541	.1871	-.2063	.0136	.1316	-.0165	.0746	-.2664	-.4783	.2183	-.3391		-.3512	-.2951
S9.6	-.3881	.0491	.2969	.7703**	.1220	.1935	.1265	-.1262	.4369*	-.2749	-.2749		-.4783	.1246
S9.7	-.0743	.1609	.2950	.3328	.1690	.2596	.4069	.6299**	.2183	-.2315	-.2315		.1744	-.3429

* - SIGNIF. LE .01   ** - SIGNIF. LE .001

P E A R S O N   C O R R E L A T I O N   C O E F F I C I E N T S

	S7.7	S8.1	S8.2	S8.3	S8.4	S8.5	S8.6	S9.1	S9.2	S9.3	S9.4	S9.5	S9.6	S9.7
S1.1	.0614	.1099	-.1490	-.0858	-.2050	.0618	.3141	.2767	-.2157	-.2101	-.1086	.1413	-.0154	
S1.2	-.0293	-.1371	-.1697	-.1335	-.0458	.1272	.7056**	.6333**	-.2625	.0781	-.0345	-.3176		
S1.3	-.0759	-.1363	-.2077	-.1277	-.1106	.0291	.1212	-.1876	-.0726	.2196	-.1258	-.1386		
S1.4	.1844	.1246	-.1036	-.2548	-.0829	-.0099	-.3267	-.5080*	.3263	.2982	-.0380	-.2934		
S2.1	.2497	.2775	-.1170	.1083	.1579	.2340	-.1644	.0877	.1981	.1514	-.0952	-.1062		
S2.2	-.1591	-.1170	-.3487	.1039	-.1400	.1006	-.2103	.0674	.1848	.1660	-.3621	-.1182		
S2.3	.2704	.0365	.3336	.3424	.1400	-.2103	.2688	-.1365	.3548	.3621				
S2.4	-.2113	.0864	.0172	-.1508	.3331	.0833	-.0386	.2955	.1365	.1848	-.3259			
S3.1	-.0545	-.0172	-.5222**	.3958*	.3098	.1334	-.4988**	-.0164	-.1365	.3548	-.1576			
S3.2	.6937**	.3958*	.4610*	.4610*	-.4988**	-.0386	.2879	.2514	.1507	-.0642	-.1434			
S3.3	-.0294	-.1113	-.2583	-.0490	-.0402	-.0754	-.0386	-.0218	-.1303	.0452	-.2298			
S3.4	-.0650	.2583	.1974	.1974	-.1758	-.4216*	.2690	-.1322	.1303	.3186	-.1449			
S3.5	-.5030**	.1974	.3433	.3433	-.1395	.0271	.0108	-.1507	.0977	-.0524	.1427			
S4.1	-.2918	-.1549	-.2261	-.0919	.2015	-.0108	.0846	.1902	.2791	-.0441	-.0974			
S4.2	.1724	.3419	-.0037	-.0517	-.1395	.1217	-.4654*	.1872	-.8319**	.3403	-.2444			
S4.3	.1925	-.5682**	.5737**	.0891	.1480	-.4355*	.1170	.4352	.5212**	.1427	.1964			
S5.1	-.0854	-.4788**	-.4162*	-.4168*	-.4654*	.0450	.0051	.2458	.0317	.3076	.3832*			
S5.2	-.2739	.0977	-.0298	-.0298	.0925	.0815	-.3388	.0635	.2429	.3275	.2871			
S5.3	-.0610	-.1177	.2219	.4059*	.1225	.0450	-.2987	.0219	.2063	.1871	.0631			
S5.4	-.1675	-.5830**	.5137**	.4498*	.1035	-.4760*	-.1512	.0122	.3088	.0491	.3213			
S5.5	-.0369	-.4832**	-.5226**	.7715**	.2070	-.1363	.1766	.7703**	.2063	-.0682	-.1572			
S6.1	.3027	.2653	.3188	.4189*	.3503	-.1512	-.3198	.1220	.2950	.1871	-.3213			
S6.2	.4563*	.1071	-.1031	.0553	.3223	-.4841*	-.1549	.0136	-.0390	.2950	-.1711			
S6.3	-.3032	-.0848	-.0848	-.1989	-.1549	.0270	.0891	-.0615	.1690	-.1236	-.1310			
S6.4	-.1259	-.0609	.1822	.1493	-.1467	.2643	-.0891	.0225	.1935	-.0390	-.4943**			
S7.1	-.0512	-.1067	-.0543	-.1493	-.0635	-.0891	.1316	-.0225	.1935	.1690	.3141			
S7.2	.0412	-.2963	.4000	.1667	.2312	-.4592*	.3092	.0746	.2596	.0890	-.0422			
S7.3	.1729	-.0317	-.0555	-.0628	.0163	-.0622	.5444**	.5923*	.4069	.0455	.0026			
S7.4	-.0077	.3615	.2584	.1839	.1848	.3163	-.4616*	-.1262	-.0835	-.0982	-.1040			
S7.5	-.1026	-.3355	-.3287	-.1993	-.5147*	.0887	.3437	.1732	.4369*	.1136	.1478			
S7.6	.7965**	-.1173	.3719	.2015	.0312	-.1797	-.0750	-.2664	.1925	.6299**	.1982			
S7.7	1.0000	-.0256	-.1173	.2160	-.1626	.0415	-.1481	.1119	.1061	.1529	.0518	.0732	-.0719	-.0304
S8.1		1.0000	-.2555	.1194	-.0809	.1037	.3546	-.2908	-.2596	-.3449	.0361	-.0987	-.2246	-.0495
S8.2			1.0000	.6535**	.6525**	.2556	-.3727	-.0426	-.0680	.4236**	.3237	.2283	.1733	.2961
S8.3				1.0000	.8981**	.8981**	.3546	-.2908	-.2596	-.3449	.0361	-.0987	-.2246	.2611
S8.4					1.0000	.1951	.2716	-.1542	.1489	-.0141	.2424	.2598	.2424	.1950
S8.5						1.0000	-.0822	-.0713	-.1542	-.0433	-.3152	-.0507	.4880**	.4880**
S8.6							1.0000	.1718	-.1542	-.1032	.4049*	.1673	.4328*	.4328*
S9.1								1.0000	-.1489	-.2811	-.3152	.1332	-.1119	.2961
S9.2									1.0000	-.0433	-.2572	.1004	-.1298	-.0495
S9.3										1.0000	.0998	-.2943	.3045	-.0304
S9.4											1.0000	.0998	-.0719	.4806
S9.5												1.0000	-.1430	-.0639
S9.6													1.0000	.1645
S9.7														1.0000

* - SIGNIF. LE .01   ** - SIGNIF. LE .001

APPENDIX 3

Selected References to Books on Research Method, Statistical Analysis, and Computer Techniques.

We have cited works in Part II which may serve as useful guides to research methods and statistics. In the following we present a further selection of some useful works. Within each section we have ordered the books from the more introductory works to those more advanced and difficult.

A. Research Methods

A. W. Johnson, *Quantification in Cultural Anthropology: An Introduction to Research Design* Stanford: Stanford University Press, 1978; W. P. Shively, *The Craft of Political Research* 2nd edition (Englewood Cliffs: Prentice Hall, 1980); R. Brown, *Explanation in Social Sciences*, (Chicago: Aldine, 1963); W. D. Crano and M. B. Brewer, *Principles of Research in Social Psychology*, (New York: McGraw-Hill, 1973); and D. L. Phillips, *Knowledge from What?: Theories and Methods in Social Research*, (New York: Rand McNally, 1971).

B. Theory Construction

H. M. Blalock, Jr., *Theory Construction*, (New Jersey: Prentice-Hall, 1968); A. L. Stinchcombe, *Constructing Social Theories*, (New York: Harcourt, Brace and World, 1968); H. M. Blalock, Jr., *Causal Inferences in Non-Experimental Research*, (Chapel Hill: University of North Carolina Press, 1964; H. M. Blalock, Jr., *Causal Models in the Social Sciences*, (New York: Aldine Atherton, 1971); S. Rokkan, *Comparative Research Across Cultures and Nations*, (Paris: Mouton, 1968).

C. Measurement and Scaling

G. G. Bechtel, *Multidimensional Preference Scaling* (The Hague: Mouton, 1976); C. L. Taylor, *Aggregate Data Analysis: Political and Social Indicators in Cross-National Research*, (Paris: Mouton, 1968); R. M. Dawes, *Fundamentals of Attitude Measurement*, (New York: John Wiley, 1972); W. Dick and N. Hagerty, *Topics in Measurement: Reliability and Validity*, (Chicago: Rand McNally, 1970); M. E. Shaw and J. M. Wright, *Scales for the Measurement of Attitudes*, (San Francisco: McGraw-Hill, 1967).

D. Statistical and Computer Methods

A. A. Afifi and S. P. Azen, *Statistical Analysis: A Computer Oriented Approach* 2nd edition (New York: Academic Press, 1979); H. M. Blalock, Jr., *Social Statistics*, Revised 2nd edition (New York: McGraw Hill, 1979); D. Freedman, R. Pisani, and R. Purves *Statistics* (New York: Norton, 1978); J. M. Tanur et al., *Statistics: A Guide to Political and Social Issues* San Francisco: Holden-Day, 1977); Paul F. Velleman and David Hoaglin, *Applications, Basics, and Computing of Exploratory Data Analysis* (Boston: Duxbury, 1981); S. R. Wright, *Quantitative Methods and Statistics: A Guide to Social Research* (Beverly Hills: Sage, 1979); P. R. Lohnes and W. H. Cooley, *Introduction to Statistical Procedures with Computer Exercises*, (New York: John Wiley, 1968); R. J. Rummel, *Applied Factor Analysis*, (Evanston: Northwestern University Press, 1970); P. G. Hoel, *Introduction to Mathematical Statistics*, (New York: John Wiley, 1947); P. R. Rao and R. L. Miller, *Applied Econometrics*, (San Francisco: Wadsworth, 1971); H. Theil, *Principles of Econometrics*, (New York: John Wiley, 1971).

E. Empirical Studies and Method

T. R. Gurr, *Politimetrics: An Introduction to Quantitative Macropolitics*, (Englewood Cliffs, N.Y., Prentice-Hall, 1972); J. V. Gillespie and B. A. Nesvold, *Macro-Quantitative Analysis: Conflict, Development and Democratization*, (Los Angeles: Sage, 1971); J. A. Sonquist, *Multivariate Model Building: The Validation of a Search Strategy*, (Ann Arbor, Mich: Institute for Social Research, 1970).

F. Sampling and Experimental Procedures

B. Williams, *A Sampler on Sampling* (New York: Wiley, 1978); S. Sudman and N. M. Bradburn, *Asking Questions: A Practical Guide to Questionnaire Design* (San Francisco: Jossey-Bass, 1982); W. M. O'Barr, D. H. Spain and M. A. Tessler, *Survey Research in Africa: Its Applications and Limits*, (Evanston: Northwestern University Press, 1973); D. T. Campbell and J. C. Stanley, *Experimental and Quasi-Experimental Designs for Research*, (New York: Rand McNally, 1963).

APPENDIX 4

Selected Listing of Journals, Periodicals, and Handbooks on Africa

The number of serials which have information on Africa numbers well over 4,000. For a list of these see Library of Congress, *Sub-Saharan Africa: A Guide to Serials*, (Washington, Library of Congress, 1970) and the Conover and Duignan, *Guide to African Research and Reference Works*, (*op. cit.* Appendix 1). For film and videotape see *Africa in Film and Videotape: A Compendium of Reviews of Films and Videotapes in the United States Concerning Africa 1960—1981* (East Lansing, Mich.: African Studies Center, Michigan State University, 1982). For periodicals published in Africa see Carole Travis and Miriam Alman comps., *Periodicals from Africa*, Boston: G. K. Hall, 1977).

1. General circulation periodicals which cover current events are: AFRICA. B. P. 1826 Dakar, Senegal; economic development of Tropical Africa; (monthly); AFRICA REPORT. 866 United Nations Plaza, New York, N. Y. 10017, U.S.A.; (nine per year); AFRICAN DEVELOPMENT. African Buyer and Trader, Wheatsheaf House, Carmelite St., London, E.C.4, England; f. 1965; (monthly); and WEST AFRICA. Overseas Newspapers (Agencies) Ltd., Cromwell House, Fulwook Place, London, W.C.1; f.1917; (weekly). The newspapers from the various countries are also major sources of information. The most important French language source is JEUNE AFRIQUE (monthly).

2. For additional information on current affairs see publications such as AFRICA DIGEST. Africa Publications Trust, 2 Arundel St., London W.C.2; (six times yearly); AFRICA QUARTERLY. Indian Council for Africa, 5 Balwantray Mehta Lane, New Delhi, India; AFRICA RESEARCH BULLETIN. Africa Research Ltd., 1 Parliament St., Exeter, England; f. 1964; monthly bulletins on (a) political and (b) economic subjects; AFRICA CONFIDENTIAL. Research Publications Services Ltd. Victoria Hall, Fingal Street, East Greenwich, London S.E. 10, England.

3. Research periodicals which are concerned with the analysis of African phenemona include: AFRICA. International African Institute, 38 King Street, London WC2E 8JR England; (quarterly); BULLETIN OF THE SCHOOL OF ORIENTAL AND AFRICAN STUDIES. School of Oriental and African Studies, University of London, London, W.C.1, England; f.1917; (three issues annually); JOURNAL OF AFRICAN HISTORY. School of Oriental and African Studies, University of London, London, W.C.1, England; (four times yearly); EAST AFRICA JOURNAL. East African Institute of Social and Cultural Affairs, P.O.B. 30492, Uniafric Building, Koinange Street, Nairobi; (monthly); EAST AFRICAN STUDIES. East African Institute of Social Research, Makerere University College, Kampala, Uganda; irregular; CAHIERS D'ETUDES AFRICAINES. Ecole Practique des Hautes Etudes, VIe Section, Division des Aires Culturelles, 20 rue de la Baume, 75 Paris 82, France; (quarterly); CANADIAN JOURNAL OF AFRICAN STUDIES. Committee on African Studies in Canada, Loyola College, 7141 Sherbrooke West Street, Montreal, Quebec, Canada; (twice yearly); JOURNAL OF AFRICAN LANGUAGES. African Studies Center, Michigan State University, East Lansing, Mich. 48823, U.S.A.; JOURNAL OF ASIAN AND AFRICAN STUDIES, Department of Sociology, York University, Toronto 12, Canada; JOURNAL OF MODERN AFRICAN STUDIES. Prof. David Kimble, University of Malawi, P. O. Box 278, Zomba, Malawi; political and economic; (quarterly); JOURNAL OF RELIGION IN AFRICA. University of Aberdeen, Scotland; and ODU. A Journal of African Studies, Institude of African Studies, University of Ife, Nigeria; irregular.

4. Useful handbooks and reviews are AFRICA. Africa Magazine, 28 Great Queen St., London, W.C.2, England; (annual); AFRICA CONTEMPORARY RECORD. Holmes and Meier, New York; annual documented survey; AFRICA; SOUTH OF THE SAHARA. Europa Publications, 18 Bedford Sq., London, W.C.1 B 3 JN; (annual); THE CAMBRIDGE ENCYCLOPEDIA OF AFRICA, Cambridge University Press, New York, 1981; ECONOMIC BULLETIN FOR AFRICA. Economic Commission for Africa, Addis Ababa, Ethiopia; (twice yearly); WEST AFRICAN ANNUAL. John West Publications Limited, 212 Broad St., Lagos, Nigeria; (annual).

5. Bibliograhic sources have been treated in Parts III and V of this book. For others see AFRICANA JOURNAL (formerly *Africana Library Journal*). Africana Publishing Company, 101 Fifth Avenue, New York, New York 10003; CURRENT BIBLIOGRAPHY OF AFRICAN AFFAIRS. African Bibliographic Center, P.O.B. 13096, Washington, D.C. 20009, U.S.A.; f. 1962 (monthly); and THE AFRICAN BOOK PUBLISHING

RECORD. P.O.Box 56, Oxford OX13EL, England; (quarterly). The latter covers new and forthcoming publications by African publishers in English, French and the African vernacular languages. Some useful bibliographies are John L. Collier, *Africa, Sub-Sahara: A Selected Functional and Country Bibliography* (Washington, D.C.: Center for Area and Country Studies, Foreign Service Institute, Department of State, December 1982), *Africa: A Bibliographic Survey of Literature* (Washington, D.C.: U.S. Government Printing Office, 1973), *American Doctoral Dissertations on Africa, 1886-1972* (Waltham, Mass.: African Studies Association, 1974) and Peter Duignan and L. H. Gann, *A Bibliographic Guide to Colonialism in Sub-Saharan Africa* (New York: Cambridge University Press, 1973).

BLACK AFRICA
A Comparative Handbook
Second Edition

by Donald George Morrison
with Robert Cameron Mitchell and John Naber Paden

The most comprehensive and authoritative work of its kind, this is the second updated edition of the acclaimed book named one of the outstanding reference works of the year by the American Library Association on its original publication.

This data textbook has long been a necessary aid for Africanists. I welcome the opportunity to have a new and updated edition of this work, secure in the knowledge that it will continue to be of immense help to Africanists and persons interested in specific data on Africa.

Dr. Elliot P. Skinner,
Franz Boas Professor of Anthropology, Columbia University.

Revised and expanded by the original team of authors, BLACK AFRICA is organized in two parts:

COMPARATIVE PROFILES of 41 independent Black African nations, covering:
Demography, Ecology and Pluralism
Economic Development and Social Mobilization
Political Development
International Relations
with comparative data on patterns of property inheritance, educational expenditures, literacy rates, primary school enrollment, number of political parties, economic aid, and hundreds of other variables.

COUNTRY PROFILES of 41 independent Black nations
Ethnic Patterns
Language Patterns
Political Patterns
National Integration and Stability

43 Maps, 600 Figures and Tables plus extensive bibliographic information for each nation.
Hardcover, 8 1/2 x 10 3/4—768 pages—$169.50

Copublished in the U.S. and Canada by

IRVINGTON PUBLISHERS, INC.
740 Broadway, New York, NY 10003

PARAGON HOUSE
90 Fifth Avenue, New York, NY 10011